The Third World and Decision Making in the International Monetary Fund

A publication of the Graduate Institute of
International Studies, Geneva

The Third World and Decision Making in the International Monetary Fund

The Quest for Full and Effective Participation

Tyrone Ferguson

 Pinter Publishers, London and New York

© Pinter Publishers Limited, 1988

First published in Great Britain in 1988 by
Pinter Publishers Limited
25 Floral Street, London WC2E 9DS

British Library Cataloguing in Publication Data
A CIP catalogue for this book is available from the British Library

Library of Congress Cataloging-in-Publication Data
Ferguson, Tyrone.
  The Third World and decision making in the
International Monetary Fund.
  'A publication of the Graduate Institute of
International Studies, Geneva.'
    Bibliography: p.
    Includes index.
    1. International Monetary Fund—Developing countries
2. International Monetary Fund—Management.
3. Decision-making. I. Graduate Institute of
International Studies (Geneva, Switzerland) II. Title.
HG3881.5.I58F47 1988   332.1'52   87-32797
ISBN 0-86187-957-0

Typeset by Joshua Associates Limited, Oxford
Printed by Biddles of Guildford Ltd

Contents

Foreword

These are times of great economic turbulence, of increasing material inter-dependence paradoxically running parallel to a growing resort to selfish unilateral action (or inaction). The resulting feeling of insecurity and vulnerability to environmental conditions and of loss of control over one's economic destiny, particularly among the smaller and weaker members of the international community, explains their strong claim for participation in the taking of decisions on common economic problems that affect them directly and often severely; a claim that they perceive not only as an imperious necessity but also as a requirement of elementary justice.

Indeed, this claim flows directly from the first principle of the Charter of the United Nations, that of 'sovereign equality' (Art. 2, para. 1), which does not only mean that a State is free to act on the international level without having to submit its decisions to another instance: it also means that decisions directly affecting a State cannot be taken without its participation and consent, for this would amount to deciding for it or negating its freedom to decide for itself. Thus viewed, it is an application of self-determination to collective decision-making.

No wonder that the claim for full and effective participation in such decisions is most strongly pressed by the newcomers to the international scene, the Third World countries, who, in spite of their weight, feel excluded or at best marginalized in this context, while, as the weakest members of the community, invariably bearing most of the brunt of decisions taken by the others.

The problem with the process of international decision-making, however, and more particularly when it comes to economic matters, is that it is so diffuse and unstructured that it is almost impossible to seize it and pin it down for purposes of international regulation, except within institutionalized structures.

This is why the author of the present study focuses on the IMF, which has been in this regard the sorest bone of contention. For not only was the initial design of the Fund, with its heavily weighted voting formula, far from perfect in terms of 'full and effective participation' but subsequent developments went even further away from the ideal. First, with the General Agreement to Borrow in the early 1960s the decision-making process passed completely out of the Fund and into the exclusive hands of the Group of 10. A decade later a crucial decision was taken unilaterally by the United States in 1971, when it severed the link between the dollar and gold, thus scrapping the Bretton Woods monetary system of fixed exchange rates and writing off most of the monetary reserves of Third World countries in the process.

Similarly, in the effort to stabilize the actual precarious situation and in the search for a new international monetary order, and in spite of symbolic gestures towards associating Third World countries in the process (such as the creation of the Group of 20, then the Interim Committee of the Board of Governors), the real decision-making power remains exclusively in the same hands, whether they are called the Group of 5, 7 or 10/11, and whether they meet within the Fund or in other venues such as the meetings of the major industrial countries or at the Bank of International Settlements.

Based on exhaustive research and a masterly grasp of a rather nebulous and secretive environment, Tyron Ferguson's analysis expertly guides us through the vicissitudes of the process of decision-making within the Fund in general. He describes clearly and in great detail the origins and evolution of the claim of Third World countries for a more meaningful participation in this process, before examining its actual functioning in a number of issue areas of particular interest to the Third World.

Initially, the IMF articles of agreement fulfilled the double role of an international monetary code of good conduct and the constitution of a short-term credit facility helping member States in difficulty to abide by the rules of the code. The decisions of the Fund's organs dealt either with the management of the system, i.e. the application of the code as it stood, or with the evolution or, more radically, the changing of the system itself.

The study demonstrates in a very convincing manner, that when it came to the mere management or application of the system, the Fund organs gradually tightened their requirements in terms of internal adjustment and surveillance, through what came to be known as 'conditionality', a price which often proved to be socially and politically exorbitant, but which developing member States had to pay in order to obtain the Fund's certification of creditworthiness. Conditionality has been and still is the most contentious issue between the Fund and its developing member States.

The controversy over 'international liquidity' and the introduction of the SDRs provide a very good example of the struggle over the process of decision-making. The Group of 10 wanted to limit the creation of new liquidity to themselves. The developing countries, with the support of the UNCTAD, fought to establish a link between the creation of new liquidity and development financing. In insisting on locating this new function within the Fund, they found a strong ally in the Fund's bureaucracy, but not for their claim for a share of the new liquidity pegged to their needs rather than to their quotas. And it was this last solution that finally prevailed. A measure of recognition of the special position and needs of the developing countries, was achieved, however, through the creation and the gradual evolution of the CFF. Both the SDRs and the CFF were relatively minor or rather normal developments of the system. But when it came to radical decisions or actions entailing the total discarding of the system and its replacement, there was no room for any meaningful participation.

The merits of Tyron Ferguson's excellent study are manifold: the firmness of analysis, the clarity of thought and exposition and the numerous insights it provides into the functioning of the IMF, the most hermetic of contemporary international organizations. But its greatest merit is that through an in-depth and penetrating study of a very (perhaps the most) difficult case, it admirably illustrates the present possibilities, limits and obstacles facing the Third World in its quest for a fairer share not only in the final product of the international economic system but also in the running of the system itself.

Georges Abi-Saab
Professor of International Law
and Organization
Graduate Institute of International Studies
Geneva
November 1987

Acknowledgements

I would like, firstly, to thank the Swiss Federal Commission for providing me with the scholarship that enabled me to successfully complete my doctoral studies. My gratitude also goes out to Prof. Yves Collart of the Graduate Institute of International Studies and Mme S. Bourquin. The Feris Foundation granted me a study fellowship in 1984–85, allowing me to pursue my research on the IMF in Washington, DC. In this regard, I would like to say a special word of thanks to Mr William Carter and all the individuals at the IMF who willingly opened their doors to me.

Prof. Abi-Saab provided the intellectual guidance and stimulation during the preparation of this thesis. While he set high standards of scholarship, at the same time his many kindnesses, constant encouragement and overall confidence in me lessened the burden of my task. I would also like to acknowledge my indebtedness to Mr Victor-Yves Ghebali of the Institute and Mr Richard Eglin of the GATT, whose many criticisms and suggestions were of immense help.

Introduction

The multilateral institutional process that was established after the Second World War is currently facing a deep-rooted crisis.[1] While not all institutions are affected to the same degree by the erosion of confidence in multilateral cooperation among certain major countries and groups of countries, the two principal systems of post-war institutions—the United Nations and the Bretton Woods—have both felt its impact.

On the one hand, the United Nations system has come under increasing attack, since the mid-1970s, by several Western, industrialized countries—a major target of their dissatisfaction being the dominant control, summed up in the charge of tyranny of the majority, now exerted by developing countries. This control has resulted from the observance in the United Nations institutions of the principle of the sovereign equality of states. This factor has allowed the developing nations to use their overwhelming numerical majority to obtain formal endorsements of their preferred policies in areas as diverse as politics, economics, culture, human rights, science and technology, to name just a few. Developed countries, which bear the major financial responsibility for the functioning of these organizations, have thus witnessed, in the case of the United Nations, an overturning of the ideological basis of the post-war institutional structures they were largely instrumental in creating and its take-over by the developing member-countries of these institutions. In the context of their own decision-making powerlessness, when measured purely in terms of voting power, the developed countries had found it largely impossible to withstand this coherent assault of the developing countries.

On the other hand, the Bretton Woods institutions have, at one time or another, been the target of attack from the group of developing or Third World countries. A pivotal explanation for their discontent has to do with the ordering principles of Bretton Woods decision making—the weighted voting process— and the resultant effect of a less central role for these countries in the decision-making process, when compared with their situation in the United Nations system.

In other words, both major sets of post-war institutional processes have been found wanting at various times by either developed or developing countries, and a crucial, common basis for discontent has been the decision-making structures of these international organizations. More profoundly, however, the crisis of multilateralism reflects the collapse of consensus as to how best international relations, in its broadest sense, should be organized. The struggle over institutional processes, therefore, is merely symptomatic of a wider struggle over the substantive bases for a reconstruction of the international political, legal, economic, information and cultural orders, in the wake of the fundamental changes that have taken place in post-war international relationships.

In an effort to better understand the nature and scope of the prevailing multi-lateral crisis, the present study will seek to examine the situation with regard to one such institution, the International Monetary Fund (IMF). This institution, for reasons that will become apparent in the course of the analysis, has historically been the more controversial of the Bretton Woods institutions—a controversy that has deepened substantially during the past decade. The study will therefore focus on the criticisms, demands and achievements of the Third World countries in relation to the operations and functioning of the IMF.

The concept of a group of countries known as Third World clearly creates certain definitional and analytical difficulties.[2] While accepting the crucial importance of such questions, this study starts off from the position that the nomenclature 'Third World' is a useful delimiting category in the context of the practice of international relations generally, and the narrower framework of its study. The fact is that 'Third World' has come to define a sub-group of countries in the international system—the countries that participate in neither the coherent, Western liberal arrangements nor those of the Eastern socialist countries.

Unlike the latter two sets of countries, the Third World countries are not characterized by any definitive, coherent ideology of socio-political or economic organization. Yet, increasingly in the post-Second World War period, they have found it politically advantageous to create organizational mechanisms, at various levels, to seek a concertation of their international behaviour. Moreover, they do have several things in common. They have a similarity of historical experience of colonial domination by various Western industrialized countries and a contemporary condition of relative deprivation and poverty, vis-à-vis the latter. They are generally seen as countries now in the process of nation-building and economic development.

While, at the present time, several of them have succeeded in moving out of pervasive poverty, they still prefer to remain identified—at least in terms of coordinating mechanisms—with the other, less well-off developing countries. Whether it is the newly industrializing countries (NICS) or the OPEC countries, there still remain fundamental disparities in economic well-being, as well as industrial and technological development compared to the developed countries, and a high level of external economic dependence. Particularly with respect to the OPEC countries, by and large, their improved status in the international economy is founded on a very fragile basis. Many of the OPEC countries, on the basis of simple per capita income, outrival the majority of developed nations. But such a comparison hides the fundamental reality of the monocultural basis of this economic achievement, and thus its essential fragility and non-sustaining nature, dependent as it is on high prices for their petroleum products.

This study accepts that there is no such thing as a monolithic Third World. On the contrary, the analysis will point on many occasions to the immense heterogeneity that characterizes this group of countries. However, the fundamental justification for use of the 'Third World' appellation is the subjective identification of these countries with the status of Third World, rather than the objective factors that would result in a differentiation among them. Moreover, its use allows us to examine the flaws and constraints, if any, that go along with an approach that groups these countries together as an undifferentiated whole.

Overall, the socialist countries are excluded from this analysis. This relative omission was not a question of choice, but rather derived from the fact that not many of these countries are members of the Bretton Woods institutions,[3] and the few that are, have only assumed membership in recent years. Where, however, their positions on international monetary issues and the IMF, as manifested outside its institutional process, are apposite, they will be alluded to.

Finally, the International Monetary Fund operates a host of different financing facilities. While many of them are specifically dealt with in the context of the analysis, others have not been, even though passing references to them are made. Appendix 1, therefore, provides a brief outline of some of the important facilities to which reference has been made.

Notes

1. One report refers to it as 'the creeping paralysis that afflicts multilateralism'—See Committee for Development Planning, 'Report on the Twenty-first session and Resumed Twenty-first session' (Geneva, 19–21 November 1984 and New York, 20–23 April 1985), *Official Records*, Economic and Social Council, 1985, Supp. No. 9, New York, United Nations, 1985, p. 4, para. 19.
2. For a discussion, see Leslie Wolf-Phillips, 'Why Third World?', *Third World Quarterly*, 1, No. 1, January 1979, pp. 105–16.
3. Another consideration is that the socialist countries have attributed the blame for the economic under-development of the Third World countries to past colonial and imperialistic domination by major Western countries. In light of this historical responsibility, the latter countries are required to make substantive concessions to the demands of developing countries: for a discussion, see Marian Paszynski, 'The Concept of New International Economic Order and the Socialist Countries', *Development and Peace*, 1, Autumn 1980, pp. 26–41.

Part I
The Setting of the Investigation

Chapter 1

The nature of the inquiry

1. The specification of the problem

A central feature of prevailing international economic relations is what has come to be popularly known as the North–South issue,[1] encompassing a concerted effort on the part of the developing countries to seek fundamental changes in the structures, institutional processes and substantive areas of concern of the post-Second World War international economic order. The North–South issue became globalized at the beginning of the 1970s[2] and remains today a prime contentious area within the international system.

If the North–South division suggests, in however unrefined terms, the geo-political dimensions of the problem, then the concept of the New International Economic Order (NIEO) sums up the substantive aspects of Third World demands and the underlying aim of these countries to effect a re-ordering of international economic relationships to secure greater advantages and benefits for themselves. The starting-point of the research then is the fact of the North–South conflict.

The agenda of change that underpins the NIEO—and the ultimate realization of change—cannot be divorced from the overall institutional setting within which the struggle has been taking place. Institutions are the arena for the recognition and reconciliation of the grievances and competing visions of the membership.[3] But that reconciliation—the process of negotiation of change—is, in the final analysis, dependent on the decision-making structures within institutions.[4] It is this awareness by Third World countries of the pivotal role of the decision-making process[5] that has made the whole question of institutional reform of the post-war international economic organizations one of their core concerns.

The claim for a right to participate in international decision making regarding economic relations has become a recurring theme of the NIEO process. This claim was enshrined in the major instruments pertaining to the NIEO that were adopted by the UN General Assembly in 1974 and 1975. Thus, Article 10 of the Charter of Economic Rights and Duties of States stipulates that:

> All States are juridically equal and, as equal members of the international community, have the right to participate fully and effectively in the inter-national decision-making process in the solution of world economic, financial and monetary problems, *inter alia*, through the appropriate international organizations, in accordance with their existing and evolving rules, and to share equitably in the benefits resulting therefrom.[6]

In an effort to comprehend the nature of the problem that confronts the developing countries with respect to decision making, the study will examine the relationship between these countries and the decision-making process of the post-war institutional economic order. The study will have a single-institution focus—the IMF. The time-span of the study will be the decade and a half dating from 1970, coinciding as this does—admittedly not in a totally neat temporal frame—with the NIEO campaign of the Third World. It will be necessary, however, to treat in brief the earlier years of the Fund's operations to obtain insights and comparative perspectives on the topic.

The choice of the decision-making process as the central preoccupation of the research is neither accidental nor whimsical. From a historical vantage-point, the management of international systems has from time to time—and particularly when consensuses collapse—foundered on the arrangements relating to decision making.[7] Discontent has usually emanated from two sources: new aspirants to power and status, and newly emergent and small states, both demanding a stake in the taking of decisions. It has been fuelled by the fact that particular historical systems have tended to be governed by a privileged elite of states who assume the responsibility for international management on the basis of their pre-eminent situation in the configuration of state-forces internationally. This tendency has been especially marked at the level of the international political system.

The Third World countries in contemporary times have challenged the monopolization of decision making by a limited group of developed countries in the political, legal, cultural and economic domains. They have argued for (i) the right to participate and (ii) full and effective participation in the taking of decisions in international economic organizations.[8] And the point of departure for this claim has been the juridical equality of states.[9]

Historically, controversy over decision making has been—and continues to be—rooted in the glaring contradiction between the fundamental governing principle of international relations, that is the sovereign equality of states, and the fact of the inequalities among states in their material circumstances and capacities for political influence. The critical problem, then, that has beset international regimes seeking to construct decision-making structures mutually acceptable to national sovereignties is the reconciliation of the principle of sovereign equality with the reality of the material facts of life. This problem has been met—if not resolved—at different times by decision-making modalities that, on the one hand, conceded the formal equality of states, while granting recognition, on the other, to the reality of differential state power through such practices as the veto and the weighting of votes.

In so far as developing countries are concerned, the question therefore arises as to whether the intent is in effect to translate the principle of the juridical equality of states, in operational terms, into the strict observance of the rule of an equal voice for every state in decision making, as reflected in the one state/ one vote method. The answer to this question will have to be found in a rigorous analysis of the origins of the claim, its legal foundation and the evolving norms governing the issue in the IMF.

Adherence to formal equality implies, firstly, a right to participate in the taking of decisions.[10] Oppenheim has further posited that the equality of states in international law has several other consequences, including the fact that 'legally . . . the vote of the weakest and smallest state has . . . as much weight as the vote of the largest and most powerful.'[11] Within such a conception, then, insistence on adherence to the sovereign equality of states would signify no differential voting power among the international membership.

It is the thesis of this study that the intent of Third World countries was not to insist on the strict application of any such interpretation of the principle in so far as their participation in the decisional process of the IMF was concerned. Rather, they have been keenly conscious of a third consideration that Oppenheim had alluded to, that is, the crucial distinction between legal equality and political equality: 'the enormous differences between states as regards their strength are the result of a natural inequality which . . . finds its expression in the province of policy. Politically, states are in no manner equals.'[12] These countries, it will be argued, in recognizing the dilemmas created by the principle of equality in a world of material inequalities have sought to give it substantive meaning through the implementation of other standards of participation when it involved intergovernmental economic organizations with action-oriented mandates.

The study will thus endeavour to pinpoint and elucidate these other standards of participation by which developing countries have tried to obtain a satisfactory share in the decision-making process of the IMF. This will involve a two-fold process of measurement. Firstly, by looking at the actual formal and informal dimensions of decision making, an effort will be made to see whether changes have been put into place, with a view to giving developing countries a greater share of decision making. Such an approach will allow us to examine rules and standards of decision making that attempt to give content, from the vantage-point of these countries, to the principle of full and effective participation.

At the second level, the analysis will shift to a consideration of how the procedural aspects of decision making have affected the ways in which substantive concerns have been dealt with and resolved in the IMF. Through an in-depth examination of certain strategic issues for developing countries, an attempt will be made to measure policy and programmatic changes in the light of Third World representation thereon to test the effectiveness or otherwise of their decision-making role in the institution.

This approach to decision making facilitates an exploration of the dilemmas posed by change within international organizations—another objective of the research. Organizations are clearly the result of consensuses among the membership—as to what tasks the organization is to perform, how these tasks are to be pursued and the procedural infrastructure to expedite these tasks. When, however, there occurs a disruption of the consensus, it follows that the organization will serve as the battleground for the redefinition of a new consensus. The major time-period of the IMF's operations with which the study is concerned has been characterized by just such a breakdown in the international economic consensus. The effort to reconstruct a consensus has basically pitted the developed against the developing participants in the international economy. The heart of the agenda of the latter group of countries has been one of thoroughgoing change.

It is contended that a positive disposition to transformations within international organizations is premised on the existence of certain conditions and circumstances, both in the external environment of the organization and within the organization. Internally, the crucial factor has to do with the change-making or change-resisting structures of the organization—the decision-making process.[13] With respect to the external dimensions, the literature on regime transformation has identified three general conditions conducive to change.[14] There is, firstly, the question of manifestly defined lines of cleavage among the membership of an organization in respect of the substantive tasks to be performed and the manner in which these are to be carried forward. Secondly, change is pre-conditioned on shifts in the distribution of power within the international system, with the new claimants to power being the major advocates for change. And, thirdly, organizations are susceptible to change in response to unsettled environmental conditions—at times of crisis and disturbances in the broader international environment within which the organization is located.

A task of the study, therefore, will be to bring these considerations to bear in regard to Third World participation in the decision-making process of the IMF. It will be necessary to search for the existence, or otherwise, of these underlying conditions that must be satisfied to achieve the objective of change in an institution. At the same time, the analysis will attempt to see whether change is an automatic or spontaneous consequence of the existence of these objective circumstances and what is the nature of the forces that will be resistant to, or intolerant of change. Importantly, also, the scope of the analysis will permit an examination of the advocates of change—their mobilization capacities and the assets they exploit in pursuance of their objectives. This will entail some measure of analysis of Third World organizational behaviour, their degree of unity and overall capacity to affect the process of decision making.

In summary, the inquiry has three main objectives. The first will be to elucidate what the developing countries are seeking to achieve in terms of their claims for participation in the decision-making process of the IMF, with a view to defining the substantive content of their demand for full and effective participation, on the basis of equality. The second objective of the analysis will involve, by exploring the dilemmas posed by change in organizations, an assessment of the responsiveness, or not, as the case may be, of the IMF to the claims of the developing countries. Finally, the analysis will attempt to portray and evaluate the bargaining capabilities or constraints that these countries confront within the political process of the Fund—capabilities or constraints that either facilitate or impede the objectives they have set themselves.

2. The framework of analysis

The core concern of the research has to do with decision making in the IMF. Decision making is the most important feature of the operations of international organizations. As Schermers has stated it:

Decision-making is the most important activity of international organizations. In principle all mutual consultations, fact-finding studies and debates in international organs lead to some form of conclusion, summarised in a legal formula which is expressly approved by the organ concerned.[15]

Having said that, the question arises as to what is meant by decision making.

Basically, decision making is about choice—the selection of the optimum option from a limited set of options under consideration by decision makers.[16] Inherent in this conception are two things: the process of choosing and the outcome of the choice process. These two components of decision making are crucial to the presentation of the framework for the analysis.

Studies of decision making in international organizations have tended to highlight one or other of these facets, and invariably the focus has been on the decisional process.[17] But if, from an analytical standpoint, there is a usefulness in studying the process of decision making, such a limited approach cannot present the total picture. Decision-making analyses should be concerned as much with an assessment of who gains what from the choice process—the whole question of outcomes.[18] In a word, the concept of decision making employed in this analysis will stress the dynamic interplay between decision process and decision outcome.

The activities surrounding the taking of decisions comprise essentially a political process. This political process necessarily has a relationship to the formal decision-making structures of an international organization— constrained as it is by the formal edifice which encompasses the rules, the division of authority, legal effects of decision and the provisions for change that are all enshrined within the constitutional framework, as well as the informal practices developed by the organization's membership over time. These are the basic parameters within which decision making is conducted, and it is through the activation of these elements of the decision structure that we can observe the underlying political process at work. For, as Pfeffer has noted, while:

[s]tandard operating procedures, rules, and behaviour repertoires clearly exist and are important in organizations ... it is necessary to be aware that these various rules, norms, and procedures have in themselves implications for the distribution of power and authority in organizations and for how contested decisions should be resolved. The rules and processes themselves become important focal points for the exercise of power ... Sometimes they are part and parcel of the political context that occurs within organizations.[19]

This perspective on the interconnection between the structural aspects of decision making and the political process sheds light on the manner in which institutional actors exploit the decisional structures to achieve desired outcomes. And central to this exploitation is the exercise of an actor's relative power standing in the overall scheme of things within the organization. As Pfeffer has underscored:

Organizational politics involves those activities taken within organizations to acquire, develop, and use power and other resources to obtain one's preferred outcomes in a situation in which there is uncertainty or dissensus about choices.[20]

Outcomes, then, are contingent on the disposition of power among the participants within an organization.

The study of decision making in international organizations is a relatively undeveloped area of organizational research. In fact, no definitive theoretical perspectives on decision-making analysis have as yet been evolved; the state of the literature is basically at the pre-theory stage. The limited work done so far has witnessed a groping to find the analytical tools that, when linked together, may eventually stand as a coherent theory on the subject. These shortcomings having been noted, the present study will utilize selected aspects of existing approaches to see what can usefully be said in regard to IMF decision making.

A survey of the literature reveals that approaches have tended to concentrate on one or the other of three orientations: (i) the actors within an organization; (ii) structures and function; and (iii) the relationship of an organization to its environment.[21] To a large degree, these analytical approaches are derivatives of the more substantive theoretical developments in the study of organizations in general.[22]

A more careful scrutiny of these three approaches indicates that each can be embraced within one or other of the two broad schools of organizational research.[23] The first such school has been identified as the 'closed system' school,[24] where the organization is conceived as a closed entity, separate from its environment and comprised of a set of stable and easily identifiable participants.[25] The structures of organizations, the participants, functional mandates, constitutional features and other elements internal to the organization, have been some of the central concerns of studies of the closed-system adherents. Thus, the orientations specified at (i) and (ii) above can be seen to fit into this school of organizational research.

When applied to the issue of decision making in international organizations, it has been aimed essentially at coming to terms with the exercise of control and influence in an organization or at descriptively presenting the structural attributes of the decision-making process therein. The work of Cox and Jacobson, entitled *The Anatomy of Influence: Decision Making in International Organization*,[26] exemplifies the former approach to the study of organizational decision making[27] and represents the most developed model of its kind. Their objective was clearly specified as entailing the presentation of an explanatory framework of how influence was exercised in international organizations. However, this early work of Cox and Jacobson does have some important deficiencies in terms of a practical application.[28]

In an organization such as the IMF, the internal operations of which are virtually closed to the outside observer, the undeniably sophisticated model that they have elaborated has a limited utility in generating authoritative insights into the political influence process therein. Unless the analyst has been a participant-observer, he faces insurmountable problems in arriving at a full and analytically defensible portrayal of what goes on in the IMF.[29] Moreover, Cox and Jacobson have themselves pointed up an important shortcoming in their model—the fact that its applicability is geared essentially to moments of relative stability in the international system.[30] What this implies is that, at historical junctures of fundamental systemic crisis—as is the case with the main time-focus of this inquiry—their analytical framework becomes veritably inappropriate. This leads to the third, and for the purposes of the present study, the most basic flaw in the model—that is, its inapplicability to highlight and account for change in international organizations.[31]

And, finally, the Cox-Jacobson framework emphasizes the political influence process without an adequate consideration of the correspondence between process and outcome. As Finkelstein has argued:

> . . . an approach which seeks to isolate process from substance involves some severe limitations . . . [and] while it may be possible to perform some kind of analysis of what the political processes are without reference to the substance with which they deal, it is not possible to *evaluate* or *appraise* the processes on that basis.[32]

Since the present study is concerned as much with substance as with process, then this deficiency is another important obstacle to the utilization of this model. It should also be noted that the level of analysis they used focused on the internal functioning of organizations. It was not that they were unaware of a relationship between an organization and its environment. But, in this original formulation of organizational decision making, the role of the environment was not seen as a prominent explanatory variable; where environmental factors were brought into play, there was, in fact, an almost mechanistic quality to the connection between environment and organization.

For the purposes of the present study, the second school of organization research has useful insights into the analysis of the performance of organizations. The starting-point of the 'open-system' school is the contention that 'organizations are not closed systems, sealed off from their environment, but are open to and dependent on flows of personnel and resources from outside their own system.'[33] In this conception, an organization is defined as 'a coalition of shifting interest groups that develop goals by negotiations; the structures of the coalition, its activities and its outcomes are strongly influenced by environmental factors'[34]—a definition that points to the interplay between the internal dynamics of the organization and events and circumstances external to it.

Because the environments of organizations never remain stable for any protracted period of time, it is incumbent on organizations to establish the decision mechanisms to facilitate internal change consistent with external flux. External change signifies a corresponding process of change in the demands and concerns of the constituencies of organizations. The survival of organizations, then, is dependent on their capacity to satisfy the shifting demands of their memberships. As Stogdill observes:

> The survival of an organization is rooted in the relationships that it maintains with its physical-social environment. It must be capable of coping with environmental change. In other words, an organization should provide itself with the functions, arrangements, and mechanisms necessary to assess its

internal condition, as well as those needed to assess the presence and trend of environmental change.[35]

The environment, thus, becomes a critical variable in accounting for changes, or the absence thereof, in an international organization. A clear interconnection is hereby drawn between what goes on inside the organization and what is occurring outside.

This novel way of looking at organizations was influential in inducing Cox and Jacobson to undertake a thoroughgoing modification of their earlier analytical presentation.[36] Noting that the decade of the 1970s was characterized by profound and persuasive change in the international environment, they argued that '[a] somewhat different approach to the study of decision-making in international organization is required than the approach we adopted in the later 1960s.'[37] This new approach has sought to provide a macro-perspective or systems-based outlook to the analysis of organizational decision making.

It starts off by locating international organizations within a 'world system of power relations. International institutions have to be seen as functioning within that larger system. The starting-point would be a structural picture of power relations which are always the starting-point of the decision process.'[38] The aim here is to present the environment in terms of differential power capabilities among actors or groups of actors. The second phase of the analysis—an accounting for how change takes place in an international organization—is built upon the foundations of this preliminary task. In the words of Cox and Jacobson:

> The issue of change in institutions is . . . secondary to the question of change in hegemony. A change in hegemony can come about through the emergence of a counter-hegemonic force . . . [T]he counter-hegemonic force will result from a combination of (a) an increase in the material resources available to a subordinate group and (b) a coherent and persistent articulation of the subordinate group's demands that challenges the legitimacy of the prevailing consensus.[39]

The argument here is that change is premised on a deliberate challenge from new claimants to power. The concern, then, is to draw the identifiable lines of cleavage—including the actors who are on either side of this challenge—within the international system that spills over in the focal organization of the study.

The image of the disposition of international power and the presentation of the patterns of international conflict will then be applied to test how they impact on the structures and substance of decision in the studied organization. What is implied here is that internal processes form a continuum with the dynamics of environmental change, readjusting in parallel with observable transformations externally. This proposition of environmental-intraorganizational symbiosis is, however, meaningless, if left like that; it signifies an essentially deterministic relationship between these two elements. What the analyst has to do is to focus on the instrumental means by which the conditions in the environment are brought to bear in an organization to affect its internal operations. As Pfeffer and Salancik stated it:

A perspective which merely posits some relationship between the environment and the organization does not provide theoretical understandings. There is an important distinction between a theory and the empirical predictions derived from the theory ... A focus on the 'how' of change leads one to consider who brings change about and who resists it ... If change is a consequence of decisions, who is empowered to take actions which alter the organization becomes critical. One is inevitably led to consider who controls the organization and how such power and influence distributions arise.[40]

The focus of analytical attention is not restricted to the external dimensions of an organization's functioning; rather, the analyst has to provide equally a vantage-point from within the organization.

These elements of the modified Cox-Jacobson framework will be the basis for the conduct of the inquiry. Relating the systems approach to the study of decision making in international organization, we can hypothesize that the correspondence between environmental factors and intraorganizational evolution will be reflected at two levels: firstly, the structures and practices of decision making, and secondly, in the distribution of benefits. If the analyst can posit easily definable shifts in the environment of an organization, then it should follow that a parallel process of change will emerge in the infrastructure of decision making, including the political influence process, and in the outcomes of organizations.

The utilization of this analytical framework necessitates the fulfilment of three initial tasks. There has to be a precise specification of the concept of the environment. Then, since there has to be a sketch of the power relations manifest in the international system, it is necessary to provide an operational definition of the concept of power. Finally, in order to measure the correspondence between environmental flux and institutional responsiveness, the precise features of organizational decision making in which we may expect to witness correlational change will have to be delineated.

(a) The environment

As Scott has noted, there is not a great deal of consensus in the organization literature on how environments are to be defined, described or measured.[41] Scott has indicated that two basic approaches are evident in the literature: on the one part, the conception of the environment as a source of information, where the preoccupation is the uncertainty that confronts organizations, and on the other, the conception of the environment as a stock of resources, where the concern is the degree of dependence by the organization on others for vital resources.[42] The first conception is clearly not helpful in delimiting the contours of the environment for the present task.

The latter conception, however, does have a certain minimum amount of usefulness in our definitional objective. Organizations are here seen as entities that are essentially not internally self-sufficient; they require resources from the environment. This implies a level of resource dependency whereby 'organizational behaviour becomes externally influenced because the focal organization must attend to the demands of those in its environment that provide the resources necessary and important for its continued survival.'[43] In the context of scarce resources, organizations will seek to attract the resources needed for their functioning by adapting structurally to satisfy the concerns of those who provide these resources.

As Pfeffer and Salancik have observed, where an organization faces incompatible demands from its membership, then its 'attempts to satisfy the demands of a given group are a function of its dependence on that group relative to other groups and the extent to which the demands of one group conflict with the demands of another.'[44] Pfeffer and Salancik have identified three criteria of measurement of the criticality of resource dependence by the organization: (i) the importance of the resource to the continued survival of the organization; (ii) the level of discretion by the actor or group of actors on whom the organization is dependent over the allocation and use of the resources; and (iii) whether alternate sources are available for the vital resource.[45] Already, two component features of the environment of organizations are apparent: the membership and, more precisely, a differential presentation of the quantum of resources provided by the membership.[46]

A clearer delimitation of the contours of the environment may also be had from looking at the nature of the organization under scrutiny. Thus, the IMF is an economic organization, dealing with certain specialized functions in monetary relations. By extension, at a general level, the broad features and trends in the international economic system should have some impact on the IMF's operations. Included here are other organizations whose tasks have a measurable bearing on those of the Fund—the idea of organizations-in-contact.[47] Moreover, at the narrower level of monetary affairs, those occurrences external to the Fund that affect its capacity to pursue its mandate in the monetary sphere are also crucial in any conception of the environment.

The environment, then, will be drawn at two levels: the general economic environment and the more focused environment—what some analysts have called the task environment.[48] What will be pinpointed in terms of delineating the general economic environment are (i) the composition of membership;[49] (ii) the configuration of economic power; (iii) the patterns of conflict among the membership; and (iv) institutional developments in the international economy with a potential bearing on the focal organization. Regarding the task environment of the IMF, the study will have to present particular economic developments, at clearly defined historical moments, that should elicit responses within the area of monetary competence of the Fund. These developments cannot be routine occurrences, but rather phenomena that have the potential to destabilize the proper functioning of the monetary regime and that should be recognized as such. In this regard, a word of caution should be introduced here. A degree of selectiveness will be necessary in the absence of any hard-and-fast criteria as to what constitute non-routine phenomena.

(b) Power

The concept of power has been central in the literature of organizational decision making.[50] Power connotes the ability of a particular actor—or group of actors—to prevail in a context of disagreement as to the best way to proceed in any given situation.[51] To this end, the analysis has to be concerned with what accounts for one actor's capacity to exert power in relation to other actors and the specific manifestation of the power outcome. The former task involves a determination of the sources of power, while the latter requires an examination of the consequences of power in an organizational setting. Pfeffer has added a third criterion of measurement of the power standing of actors, that is, the symbolic and representational dimensions of power and argues that:

> [t]he most reasonable approach in diagnosing power then is to look for a convergence of power indicators within social systems. There should be a correlation between the ranking of the determinants of power, the consequences of power, the symbols of power, and the reputational and representational indicators of power.[52]

In regard to the sources of economic power, what one has to focus on is the relative contributions of the membership to the critical resource(s) on which the particular organization is dependent for the proper execution of its mandate: 'These might be money, expertise and skills, information, materials, or any other relevant resources which an interest-unit has at its disposal.'[53]

In the case of the Fund, it is money, the currency contributions of the members. These currency contributions are equal to the quotas that countries are allocated in the Fund, which are in turn a function of the relative importance of the member-countries in the international economy.

The task is somewhat simplified for us by the practice of the IMF itself. From its inception, the Fund has defined a set of economic variables that it has consistently used, with appropriate modifications, to construct a picture of the comparative economic importance of member-countries at periodic historical intervals. If this economic weight-in-the-world approach is not neatly synonymous with an actual power ranking of countries, it nevertheless provides a preliminary image of their relative economic strengths.

The key economic variables employed by the Fund are national income, trade shares (exports and imports) and international reserves.[54] Calculated quotas for all members are obtained by using a variety of formulae that grant differential weights to each of these variables, and these calcualted quotas then serve as the basis for negotiations on the actual quota allocations to the membership. These quotas have several important functions in the Fund, but in respect of our present purpose, they represent the extent of the members contributions, individually and collectively, to the financial resources of the Fund.[55]

In an *a priori* manner, then, by examining certain basic economic indicators—GNP, trade and international reserves—we can get a more or less reliable impression of the structure of power in the international economy. Extending the analysis further, by looking at resource contributions of the membership, we can get a preliminary picture of the disposition of potential power within the IMF.

But the approach so far is no more than a static view of power in an organization. Two other factors are important. Firstly, organizational power can also be measured at other levels that provide a more dynamic appreciation of the standing of actors. In particular, in this regard, is the capacity of individual actors to coordinate their positions to increase their bargaining capacities *vis-à-vis* other participants or groups of participants. This is the process of political coalition-formation in an organization. Coalition or group politics is clearly a function of the extent to which a particular set of participants recognizes commonalities among themselves—as to conditions, values and outlooks, and preferred outcomes—and organize themselves to promote a coherent and consistent position on the issues. As Pfeffer notes:

> Consensus on preferences or definitions of the situation means that the subunit and its members will be more likely to speak with one voice and to pursue a consistent course of action in a number of different forums. This consensus, in an otherwise uncertain world, provides the subunit with additional power.[56]

Thus, the analyst has to be concerned with group politics and the level of group cohesiveness in terms of increasing the group's bargaining power. Moreover, group concertation has traditionally been of especial attraction to participants whose objective power position is one of weakness.[57]

The other important consideration is that the capacity to exercise power is not the same thing as the actual activation of this power capacity.[58] The exercise of power has to be a conscious, tangible act on the part of the actor. Activation, thus, has to go hand-in-hand with the ultimate objective of the exercise of power.

For the purposes of the analysis, two ways of testing whether power has been activated will be used. Participants concerned with asserting power will seek to have it mirrored in the rules and practices of decision making, and, to ensure this, will attempt to attain membership of the key decision-making organs. Secondly, embodied in the final decisions are the preferred outcomes of actors, and those actors who have consciously used their power capabilities in the choice process will have these reflected in the decisions of organizations.[59] This approach will represent the *a posteriori* evaluation of the initial image of power that the analyst must construct.

(c) Organizational decision making

Finally, what needs to be precisely stated are those aspects of decision making that will be scrutinized in an effort to measure the correlation between environmental change and internal readjustments. This scrutiny will take in the two levels at which Fund decision making evolves: the level of informal practices and the level of the formal rules and structures.

At the latter level, four aspects of Fund decision making will be looked at. These are the formal rules of weighted voting, majority decision making, the practice of consensus and standards of representation on decision organs. In respect of informal practices, the central preoccupation will be the internal coalition-formation process or group politics in the IMF, and the external coalition-forming process—the organizations-in-contact phenomenon. In so far as the environment of decision is characterized by fundamental changes, then we can hypothesize that the organization will feel the imperative need to refashion structures and practices to accommodate the transformations in the environment. The proof will have to be found in changes in rules, structures and practices that can be shown to be attributable to these environmental occurrences.

3. Other methodological concerns

Within this larger framework that will underlie the analysis, there is the more specific methodological concern of the choice of the activities of the Fund that should be given special attention. The pioneering works on decision making in international organization—and much of the accompanying sophisticated methodology—have been concerned with the voting behaviour of participants as a reliable guide to patterns of decision-making participation. The analysis of voting behaviour is not a very useful approach to the study of decision making in the IMF. This is for the simple reason that, notwithstanding the provision for voting written into its constitution, voting in effect rarely occurs in the Fund. Decision making is the result of a consensus-building process.[60] A methodology transcending the study of voting behaviour is therefore necessary.

Two techniques of analysis have been brought into play. The first one involved the content analysis of the main documentary sources of the IMF. The principal such sources have been the *Summary Proceedings of—Annual Meeting*, the *Annual Reports of the Executive Directors*, *IMF Survey*, *Selected Decisions of the International Monetary Fund*, *Documents of the Committee of Twenty* and the Communiqués of committees and groups in the Fund. Together, these primary sources provide the raw material of the positions of countries, groups of countries and the Managing Director on the multitude of issues dealt with in the Fund in its various decision organs. They have been supplemented by the insights presented in the authoritative histories of the IMF[61] and in those publications—the *Pamphlet Series*, *Finance and Developmnent* and *Staff Papers*— where staff views are outlined. In addition, interviews—on a non-attribution basis—were very helpful.[62]

The final methodological problem related to the selection of issues for the analysis of outcomes in the Fund. Clearly, not all issues carry the same degree of salience to the various participants in a decision process. Moreover, it is well-nigh impracticable and unmanageable to deal in the present study with all the monetary and related matters that have appeared on the Fund's agenda over the history of its existence. A measure of selectivity was therefore called for. Since the study focuses on the interests of Third World countries in decision making, the approach entailed the isolation of a few issues of evident strategic interest to them.

The selection of these strategic issues was a major preoccupation of the initial stage of the study. This was done by a thorough analysis of the positions and statements of developing countries in the Fund. The main criteria of selection used were (1) the prime emphasis given to certain topics by these countries over a continuous period of time; (ii) the counterpart emphasis granted such issues by contending actors in the Fund, as well as management officials and extra-institutional parties; (iii) the degree of controversy such issues generated within the decision process and (iv) a manifest search for solutions to these problems by the institution.

This approach has resulted in the choice of the following four issues for concentrated attention

  (i) the SDR and related link question;
 (ii) the exchange rate mechanism;
(iii) the Compensatory Financing Facility and
(iv) the conditionality problem.

These issues, it will be shown in Part III, are areas of strategic concern for developing countries and have occupied their attention in respect of obtaining outcomes favourable to their interests.

4. Structure of the research

Part I of the study comprises two chapters. The first chapter involves a presentation of the problem and the analytical approach for the research. The second provides an overview of the international economic system. In this latter chapter, main stress is given to drawing the environmental features with which the analysis will be concerned.

Part II, also comprising two chapters, will concentrate on decision making in the IMF—the procedural dimension. This Part will begin with a description of how decisions are taken in the IMF—the formal and informal aspects—and the practical consequences that flow therefrom. Attention will then shift to the emergence of Third World discontent with their role in the process, the articulation of their demands for change, the nature and content of the demands, how they have gone about seeking change and the institutional response, if any, to these demands, as well as sources of resistance.

As part of the practical study of the consequences for the Third World of the peculiar decision-making structure in the Fund, Part III will focus on outcomes, through a detailed analysis of the four strategic issues earlier alluded to. The intent will be to permit a more focused examination of the decision-making process and whether and how these countries have been able to use this process to highlight their grievances and the success or failure of these efforts to redress the situation.

Notes

1. The North–South issue has become a shorthand reference in the international relations literature for the observable axis, characterized by conflict, between the developed countries of North America, West Europe, Oceania and Japan, on the one hand, and the developing countries of Latin America, Africa and Asia on the other. For a discussion, see Roger D. Hansen, *Beyond the North–South Stalemate*, New York, McGraw-Hill Book Co., 1979, pp. 3–4.

2. As we shall see in later chapters, the North–South'issue actually began in the 1960s— some would date it even earlier—with UNCTAD I being the major turning-point. But, in terms of its political globalization, it was the beginning of the 1970s that was the critical historical juncture—the breakdown of the Bretton Woods system, the movement of the economic issue to the highest concern of the non-alighest countries, the convening of Special Sessions of the UN General Assembly in 1974 and 1975 and of the Conference on International Economic Cooperation (CIEC), all attest to this assessment.

3. See Robert W. Cox, 'The crisis of world order and the problem of international organization in the 1980s', *International Journal*, 35, No. 2, Spring 1980, p. 374.

4. Ibid., p. 373.

5. As Weintraub has put it: 'At the heart of the [North–South] dialogue is the issue of power. How can the South gain more "say" in making decisions on international economic matters?' See Sidney Weintraub, 'What life is left in the North–South Dialogue?' *The World Economy*, 2, No. 4, February 1980, p. 453. See also, C. Fred Bergsten, Robert O. Keohane & Joseph S. Nye, 'International economics and international politics: a framework for analysis', *International Organization*, 29, No. 1, Winter 1975, p. 6.

6. General Assembly Res. 3281 (XXIX), adopted on 12 December 1974. See also Res. 3201 (S-VI), para. 4 and 3202 (S-VI), para. 2, 'Declaration and Programme of Action on the Establishment of a New International Economic Order' of 1 May 1974 and Res. 3362 (S-VII), entitled 'Development and International Economic Cooperation', of 16 September 1975, para. 16.

7. See C. Fred Bergsten *et al.*, *The Reform of International Institutions* (A Report of the Trilateral Task Force on International Institutions), The Trilateral Commission, 1976, p. 9.

8. See Article 10 of the 'Charter of Economic Rights and Duties of States', quoted above.

9. Ibid.

10. See Fouad Abdel-Moneim Riad, 'Formal Equality and Substantive Equality' in Gray Dorsey, ed., *Equality and Freedom: International and Comparative Jurisprudence*, Vol. 3, New York, Oceana Publications, 1977, p. 1041. See also L. Oppenheim (H. Lauter-pacht, ed.), *International Law: A Treatise*, Vol. 1, 8th edn, London, Longman, Green & Co., 1955, p. 263.

11. Oppenheim, op. cit., p. 263.

12. Ibid., p. 275. See also Frederick K. Lister, *Decision-Making Strategies for International Organizations: The IMF Model*, Monograph Series in World Affairs, University of Denver, Vol. 20, No. 4, 1984, pp. 8–10.

13. For a discussion, see Evan Luard, 'The Process of Change in International Organizations', in Evan Luard, ed., *The Evolution of International Organizations*, London, 1966, pp. 9–24.

14. Oran R. Young, 'Regime dynamics: the rise and fall of international regimes', *International Organization*, 36, No. 2, Spring 1982, pp. 277–97; see also Stephen D.

Krasner, 'Transforming International Regimes: What the Third World Wants and Why', *International Studies Quarterly*, **25**, No. 1, March 1981, pp. 119–48.

15. Henry G. Schermers, *International Institutional Law*, Vol. 2, Leiden, A. W. Sijthoff, 1972, p. 305.

16. Clearly involved in decision making is the option not to act at all. Bachrach and Baratz have drawn a clear distinction between a decision not to act and a non-decision-making process. The latter conception will not be dealt with in this analysis; what we are more concerned with is either the selection among alternatives or a decision not to act at all. For a discussion of the issues involved in the non-decision-making process, see Peter Bachrach and Morton S. Baratz, 'Decisions and Non-decisions: an Analytical Framework', *The American Political Science Review*, **57**, 1963, pp. 611–12.

17. See Ernst B. Haas, *Beyond the Nation-State*, Stanford, California, Stanford University Press, 1964, p. 105.

18. Ibid.

19. Jeffrey Pfeffer, *Power in Organizations*, Marshfield, Mass., Pitman Publishing Inc., 1981, pp. 30–2. See also Runo Axelsson *et al.*, 'Organization Power in Organizational Decision-Making' in Malcolm Warner, ed., *Organizational choice and constraint: Approaches to the sociology of enterprise behaviour*, London, Saxon House, 1977, p. 157.

20. Pfeffer, op. cit., p. 7. See also Haas, op. cit., p. 23.

21. See Leon Gordenker and Paul R. Saunders, 'Organisation Theory and International Organisation' in Paul Taylor and A. J. R. Groom, eds, *International Organisation: A Conceptual Approach*, New York, Nichols Publishing Co., 1978, p. 86.

22. See W. Richard Scott, *Organizations: Rational, Natural and Open Systems*, Englewood-Cliffs, New Jersey, Prentice-Hall Inc., 1981, pp. 10–11.

23. For a discussion, see James D. Thompson, *Organizations in action*, New York, McGraw-Hill Book Co., 1967, p. 4.

24. Ibid., pp. 4–5.

25. See Scott, op. cit., p. 22.

26. Robert Cox & Harold K. Jacobson, *The Anatomy of Influence: Decision Making in International Organization*, New Haven, Yale University Press, 1974.

27. Examples of the latter genre, relevant to decision making in the IMF are: Joseph Gold, *Voting and Decisions in the International Monetary Fund*, Washington DC, IMF, 1972, and Lister, op. cit.

28. For a good critique, see Lawrence S. Finkelstein, 'International Organizations and Change', *International Studies Quarterly*, **18**, No. 4, December 1974, pp. 485–520.

29. As an example, the author undertook a series of interviews with senior officials in the main Fund decision-making organ—the Executive Board. Many of the insights gleaned during this exercise could not have been had by a mere exegesis of documentary sources; more importantly, many of the truly insightful discoveries were provided in confidence, with the understanding that they could not be used. In short, analysis of the influence process loses a lot in the face of these crucial constraints.

30. See Robert W. Cox & Harold K. Jacobson, 'The decision-making approach to the study of international organization' in Georges Abi-Saab, ed., *The concept of international organization*, Paris, UNESCO, 1981, p. 80.

31. Finkelstein, 'International Organizations and Change', op. cit., p. 491.

32. Ibid., p. 492.

33. Scott, op. cit., p. 22.

34. Ibid., p. 22.

35. Ralph M. Stogdill, 'Dimensions of Organization Theory' in James D. Thompson, ed., *Approaches to Organizational Design*, University of Pittsburg Press, 1966, p. 45. See also

Gordenker and Saunders, 'Organisation Theory and International Organization', op. cit., p. 88. Haas contends that an adaptive organization must satisfy four conditions: (i) it must be sensitive to its environment; (ii) it should possess the instruments of conflict resolution that enable it to redefine objectives; (iii) it must be capable of developing its own dynamic programme to ensure the support of the membership; and (iv) the task fulfilment must be satisfying to members—see Hass, op. cit., p. 96.

36. See Robert W. Cox & Harold K. Jacobson, 'The decision-making approach to the study of international organization', op cit., pp. 79–104.

37. Ibid., p. 86.

38. Ibid.

39. Ibid., p. 94.

40. Jeffrey Pfeffer & Gerald R. Salancik, *The External Control of Organizations*, New York, Harper & Row, 1975, p. 227.

41. Scott, op. cit., p. 165.

42. Ibid., p. 168.

43. Pfeffer, op. cit., p. 193.

44. Pfeffer & Salancik, op. cit., p. 45.

45. Ibid.

46. For an application of the resource dependency thesis to the study of an international organization, see Michael Ernest Akins, *United States Control over World Bank Group Decision-Making*, Ann Arbor, Michigan, University Microfilms International, 1981. Akins finds that financial dependency is seriously limited as an explanatory factor for control—in so far as the United States is concerned—over Bank decision making. Without seeking to challenge this conclusion as it applies to the particular organization studied, it can be said that there are manifold important differences between the IMF and the World Bank that caution against a generalizing of these findings. For instance, World Bank membership resources are a combination of paid-up and callable resources, with callable the preponderant portion. IMF membership resources are paid up in full. Secondly, the major part of the Bank's loanable resources are obtained on the international credit markets, while quotas are the main source of Fund credit—and when the Fund has borrowed resources, these have come from official, governmental loans. These differences in the quality of financial dependency need to be taken into account in assessing the merits of the resource dependency proposition.

47. See Axelsson, et al., 'Organization Power in Organizational Decision-Making', op. cit., pp. 146–7.

48. Thompson, *Organizations in Action*, p. 27. In their earlier work, Cox & Jacobson had also dichotomized the organizational environment in a somewhat analogous manner—into a general and specific environment: see Cox & Jacobson, *The Anatomy of Influence*, pp. 26–36.

49. It is evident that the composition of membership and the patterns of conflict among the membership are at once elements of the general economic environment and of any given organization at any particular moment.

50. See Pfeffer, op. cit., p. 1.

51. See Bachrach and Baratz, 'Decisions and Nondecisions: An Analytical Framework', op. cit., pp. 632–5.

52. Pfeffer, op. cit., p. 59.

53. Axelsson *et al.*, 'Organization Power in Organizational Decision-Making', op. cit., p. 150.

54. Other economic variables have also been included, for example, export variability. But these have been marginal in terms of obtaining an overall position of the economic standing of countries. For an in-depth discussion of this whole question,

see Lister, op. cit., Ch. 3, pp. 43–78. See also UNDP/UNCTAD, *Studies on International Monetary and Financial Issues for the Developing Countries: Determination of Quotas and the Relative Position of Developing Countries in the International Monetary Fund* (Report to the Group of Twenty-Four), UNCTAD/MFD/TA/14, of 15 May 1981.

55. The other important functions of quotas are the determination of (i) voting strength; (ii) the limits of foreign exchange borrowing for each member, and (iii) the allocation of Special Drawing Rights (SDRs).

56. Pfeffer, op. cit., p. 123. See also Philip Allott, 'Power Sharing in the Law of the Sea', *American Journal of International Law*, 77, No. 1, June 1983, p. 6.

57. Pfeffer, op. cit., pp. 160–1.

58. Axelsson *et al.*, 'Organization Power in Organizational Decision-Making', op. cit., pp. 150–1.

59. Pfeffer, op. cit., p. 49.

60. Discussed in detail in Chapter 3 herein.

61. At the time of writing, these histories have covered the first three decades of the Fund's existence and thus will provide only a partial representation of events in regard to the main time-scope of the study.

62. A programme of interviews of Fund officials was carried out over the five-month period, January–May 1985 (see Appendix 2 for a brief description of the interviewing process). Twenty-one (21) interviews were held, involving officials at the government-representational and management–staff level. On average, these interviews lasted one hour and ranged frankly over the issues examined in this analysis. The composition of the officials interviewed is as follows: at the governmental-representational level, a total of nine. They included two ex-Ministers of Finance/ex-Governors of the IMF from developing countries; four Alternate Executive Directors, three from developed countries, and one from a developing country and two Advisers to Executive Directors. At the staff level, two heads of department (one current, one former) were interviewed, as were one deputy head, two other officials of comparable rank and six economists. Finally, three officials of the UNCTAD Secretariat were interviewed in late 1985.

Chapter 2

Post-war international economic relations in perspective: from Bretton Woods to the new international economic order.[1]

1. Introduction

A new international economic order[2] came into existence at the end of the Second World War. The establishment of this new order was consciously undertaken largely under the leadership of the United States and the United Kingdom.[3] These two countries actually initiated the planning of post-war economic relations while hostilities were still in progress and a major concern was to avoid a recurrence of the anarchical economic conditions, both nationally and internationally, that had existed in the interwar period and that were blamed in no small measure for the outbreak of the Second World War.[4]

The plans formulated by the respective government officials in the United States and the United Kingdom pertained to arrangements in the monetary, financial and trade spheres.[5] The formal negotiations regarding the monetary and financial aspects were held in July 1944 at Bretton Woods, New Hampshire in the United States, and resulted in the creation of two institutions, the IMF and the International Bank for Reconstruction and Development (IBRD). Formal negotiations on international trade took place in Havana, Cuba three years later when the Charter for the International Trade Organization (ITO) was drawn up. In the end, however, the ITO did not materialize since the ratification process for its operationalization was never completed.[6] Taking its place as the multilateral framework for the conduct of international trade was the General Agreement on Tariffs and Trade (GATT), agreed to in 1947 and initially conceived as an interim arrangement pending the coming into effect of the ITO.

This triadic structure—GATT, IMF, IBRD—encompassing trade, monetary and financial relations, was the institutional framework that became operative in the post-war years as the basis of a clearly defined system of international economic interaction. And, while the trade dimension was negotiated apart from the monetary and financial issues, in a real sense the agreements in these areas represented a coherent, interrelated set of arrangements to govern international economic relations.[7] It is from this perspective that many analysts of the post-war international economy speak of the Bretton Woods system,[8] implying thereby certain easily distinguishable features—a specific ideological orientation, a legalistic approach, common membership and the institutional constructs.

Negotiation and operationalization of the post-war international economic order

(a) A summary view of the negotiations

Forty-four (44) countries were invited by the United States government in 1944 to participate in 'a United Nations conference for the purpose of formulating proposals of a definite character for an international monetary fund and possibly a bank for reconstruction and development'.[9] Developing countries were a numerical majority at Bretton Woods, totalling twenty-seven of the forty-four countries in attendance.[10] The other significant note regarding participating countries was the presence of the Soviet Union.[11]

What is clear from the records is that developing countries did not affect to any great degree the negotiations or the outcome.[12] The fact is that the terms of the debate had already been set in the bilateral exchanges between the United States and the United Kingdom, thus in large measure pre-determining the outcome. What is more, there was no perception among the developing countries present of an identity of interests or circumstances that would have led to a concertation of positions, and thereby, the probability of a more serious consideration of their views. At the same time, it must be underscored that these countries were not, on the whole, passive observers of the Bretton Woods proceedings. Several developing countries, both at Bretton Woods and during the pre-Conference consultations, did seek to articulate, and have debated the issues they perceived as individually beneficial.[13]

Of the two institutions that emerged out of the negotiations, the IMF was seen as the more important. The records of the Conference reveal that the IBRD was more in the nature of a side-issue during the negotiations.[14] Its Articles of Agreement were a virtual mirror image of those of the IMF and were actually formulated in the wake of agreement on the Fund. Importantly, also, membership of the IBRD was mandatorily premised on a prior accession to membership of the IMF.[15]

The IBRD was designed to provide financing resources for (i) the economic reconstruction of countries that had suffered war-time destruction and (ii) the economic development of the less developed countries. It was evident from both its designation and the expressed intent of the initiators of the post-war economic order that the priority concern of the IBRD would be its reconstruction mandate.[16] It was just as clearly envisaged, though, that the reconstruction phase would be both temporary and of relatively short duration. Thereafter, the Bank's focus would shift to the second prong of its mandate—development financing.[17]

The IMF was conceived as having a tripartite division of functions in terms of regulatory, financial and consultative responsibilities.[18] As a regulatory agency, the IMF specified the rules and norms of monetary behaviour for its membership. The major features of this code of conduct related to the exchange rate regime and currency practices that members were required to observe.[19] Members were further required to adhere to the Fund's convertibility standard outlined in Article VIII of the Agreement.[20]

In respect of its financial task, a clear division of labour *vis-à-vis* the IBRD was delineated—in contrast to the developmental, and thus long-term, nature of the Bank's financing, the IMF was created to cater for the balance-of-payments, and thus short-term, financing needs of members in difficult external payments situations. Members provided the Fund, to the quantitative extent of the quotas they had each been allocated, with the monetary resources—partly in gold, partly in the domestic currency—that were to serve as the main source of its lending activities.[21] By standing ready to lend foreign exchange to countries in serious payments deficit, the Fund sought to avert the imposition of exchange restrictions and other deflationary measures inimical to the attainment of an open trading system and international monetary stability.[22]

Finally, the IMF was to serve as the forum for consultation and negotiation of cooperative solutions to international monetary problems. And, in the constitutional requirement for annual consultations between the Fund and those members availing themselves of the transitional provisions of Article XIV,[23] the Fund included a mechanism whereby it could review the economic behaviour of member-countries.

What was achieved at Bretton Woods in regard to international monetary relations was simply an underwriting of the dominance of the United States in the international economy.[24] In terms of its economic manifestations, the pre-eminence of the United States could at once be seen in such indicators as the overwhelming bulk of the international gold reserves that the United States had in 1946—some 60 per cent of the non-Communist world total—and its importance in world trade, providing 30 per cent of total export trade in 1947.[25] It was evidenced in the amount of the contribution that the United States was designated to provide to the IMF under its quota in 1945—over 30 per cent of the total initial Fund resources—and its status as the only member-state that indicated its intention to freely exchange gold for its currency under Article IV, Section 4(b) of the Articles of Agreement—an undertaking characterized by Gold as 'the primary norm of the par value system'[26] of the Fund.

Finally, one area of concern raised by several developing countries at Bretton Woods related to trade in primary commodities. The specificity of primary commodity trade to the economic fortunes of these countries was addressed and proposals submitted for the convening of a conference thereon.[27] A resolution on trade relations that anticipated the Havana meeting and that incorporated a precise concern for commodity trade problems was adopted.[28]

As with the monetary and financing arrangements, the formative plans pertaining to international trade originated in the United States and the United Kingdom.[29] During the Havana negotiations, developing countries *en masse* criticized the British–American proposals[30] and undertook an activist campaign to have their interests included in the ITO Charter. There was a measure of substantive achievement: a section on development was written into the Charter; they achieved provisions relating to commodity trade, and interestingly, they argued for, and attained, a decision-making process for the proposed ITO based on the principle of one-nation/one-vote.[31]

These achievements of the developing countries at Havana were ultimately made meaningless by the demise of the ITO; and, as a substitute, GATT proved a disappointment. Formulated as an interim arrangement, GATT did not include many of the concessions they had obtained at Havana.[32] In fact, not many developing countries acceded to the agreement at the beginning—out of an original GATT membership of twenty-three, only nine countries could be classified in the developing category.[33]

GATT specified at one level the principles to govern international trade relations, stressing in particular the principles of non-discrimination—and its corollary, the most-favoured-nation standard—and reciprocity of treatment. The GATT framework also outlined the negotiating mechanism—tariff bargaining between countries—to achieve the gradual reduction of the barriers to the flow of international trade.

Finally, the institutional constructs represented by the IMF, IBRD and GATT embodied a definitive philosophical outlook on international economic relations. It signified a broad consensus of the participant international community as to the ideological basis for international economic organization. The key organizing principle around which the economic interactions among nations were to be pursued was that of liberalism.[34] This liberal outlook on the international plane was a simple transposition of the consensual ideological frame of reference for the organization of national economies of the creators of the post-war economic order.

(b) The operationalization of the Bretton Woods System

What the American and British planners could not have foreseen was the nature of the world that actually emerged out of the ruins of the war. The definitive characteristic of that world was the immediate collapse—once the war had ended—of the collaboration between the Western countries and the Soviet Union, and the resultant period of East–West tension that it ushered in. This fundamental political reality was to have an important shaping effect on the evolution of post-war international economic relations. Firstly, it ensured the voluntary opting out from participation in the Bretton Woods arrangements of the Soviet Union and the socialist countries of Eastern Europe.[35] Membership of the international economic system therefore included the developed economies of West Europe, North America, Oceania and Japan, on the one hand, and the developing economies of Latin America, Asia and Africa, on the other. Secondly, in the context of an intense ideological and geo-strategic rivalry with the Soviet Union, the United States assumed the leadership role in the international economy. Thirdly, economic relations were subordinated to the larger dimensions of the East–West political competition.

Two other developments were also to have significant consequences for the actual functioning of post-war international economic relations. These were the economic reconstruction in Western Europe and the decolonization process that began in the immediate aftermath of the achievement of peace.

It became apparent soon after the war had ended that the massive reconstruction needs of Western Europe could not be met by the Bretton Woods institutions.[36] Taken together with the strategy of containment adopted by the Truman administration in the United States in 1947 to confront what was perceived as the Soviet threat, the urgency of economic reconstruction dictated, in the thinking of the American political leadership, an approach outside the framework of the prevailing international economic arrangements. This was the rationale for the European Recovery Programme (ERP) of 1947.[37]

An immediate consequence of this American aid programme was to make temporarily irrelevant the carefully crafted Bretton Woods institutions.[38] This is evident from the marginal use of IMF and IBRD resources by the European countries once ERP assistance had started to flow in 1949: whereas in 1947–48, these countries used US $558m and $508m of Fund and IBRD credit respectively, in 1949–50, they borrowed only $71m from the IBRD and nothing from the Fund. Minimal use was made of IMF resources by the membership overall in the early years of the 1950s, the 1950–54 years witnessing a total use amounting to $411.7m, compared to $777.2m in 1947–49.[39]

The other important event that was manifestly not factored into the planning process for post-war international economic relations was decolonization that led to independence for a host of small, and economically poor, countries. Upon attainment of independence, the ex-colonies by and large opted for participation in the Bretton Woods system.[40]

Notwithstanding a priority concern of the United States with the problems of the countries in West Europe, the fact of an intense East–West strategic rivalry globally forced the United States to offer certain economic inducements to the ex-colonies. These economic inducements initially took the form of technical assistance.[41] In specific terms, there was, firstly, the Point Four Program announced by the United States in 1949,[42] followed shortly thereafter by the US-supported Expanded Program of Technical Assistance (EPTA) under United Nations auspices.[43] Technical assistance, later to be combined into a broader conception of development aid, signified the definitive feature of the relations between the developed and developing countries in this first phase of post-war economic interaction.

While the task of economic reconstruction in West Europe—and Japan, it must be added—was being effectively pursued with large-scale American financial support, the developing countries themselves began to articulate their own economic grievances. The first such manifestation was essentially conformist. It conformed to the perspective defined by the developed countries, that focused in a uni-dimensional manner on the provision of aid to fill the investment resources gap that was diagnosed as the critical variable impeding the development process.[44]

Developing countries undertook a compaign at the start of the 1950s to obtain financial assistance from the international community on behalf of development.[45] The principal diplomatic energies of these countries were directed towards the creation of a development financing agency—the Special United Nations Fund for Economic Development (SUNFED)[46]—under the aegis of the United Nations. This move reflected their stated discontent at the manner in which the existing development finance institution, the World Bank, was functioning.[47] The proposal for SUNFED encountered the firm opposition of the Western developed countries and did not come to fruition.[48]

Table 2.1 Evolution of Third World membership of the UN and selected international economic organizations ( ) = total membership

Year	UN		IMF		GATT	
1945/47	(51)	31	(32)	19	(23)	9
1961	(104)	60	(67)	49	(42)	19
1971	(132)	98	(120)	96	(80)	52
1980	(151)	115	(138)	112	(87)	58

Note: Year 1947 for GATT.
Sources: Various UN, GATT and IMF publications.

This quest for aid by the developing countries obtained a global consensus in 1960 with the adoption by the General Assembly of the United Nations of a resolution pointing to an international aid target of 1 per cent of the GNP of the industrialized countries.[49] Thus, the early stirrings of discontent by developing countries did not go wholly unheeded by the international community. There was a level of modest achievement, both within the United Nations and in a process of institutional grafting by the World Bank.

Quite clearly, the institutional question was central to these early manifestations of divergences between developed and developing countries. It was no accident, then, that the developed countries were the main advocates of evolutionary action within the IBRD; it was an institution that they controlled in terms of decision making. At the same time, the attempt of the developing countries to locate international aid measures within the United Nations system was deflected because they had come to form, by the beginning of the 1960s, a solid majority in that institution and, when voting together, as they were to do increasingly on economic issues, they represented the overwhelming decision-making force in the United Nations—see Table 2.1. Another consideration was that the socialist countries were members of the United Nations—unlike the situation in the IBRD and IMF—and tended for their own reasons to side with the developing countries on these issues.

3. The emergence of the Third World—the decade of the 1960s

The international economic context of the 1960s witnessed two general developments: firstly, by the early 1960s, the new economic strength of the West European countries had become incontestable, and secondly, the virtual completion of the decolonization process was in sight. Regarding the first of these developments, the measurable indices of the performance of countries comprising the EEC were instructive. From a 14 per cent share of world exports in 1953, they had attained 25 per cent by 1960; from an 11 per cent share of international reserves in 1953, in 1960 they possessed 26 per cent—see

Table 2.2 Shares of selected countries and groups of countries in world exports and international reserves (% shares)

	Exports					Inter. reserves				
	1953	1960	1970	1975	1980	1953	1960	1970	1975	1980
World	100	100	100	100	100	100	100	100	100	100
Developed countries	70	71	77	70	66	78	82	76	59	60
of which US	20	17	15	13	12	45	32	15	–	–
of which EEC	14	25	31	37	35	11	26	31	30	35
Developing countries	26	24	19	26	29	18	15	19	38	37
of which OPEC	5	6	5	14	16	3	3	5	25	20
Others	5	5	4	5	4	33	2	4	3	3

Note: Until 1970, EEC shares computed for 6 original member-countries and thereafter for 9 members, including Ireland, Denmark and UK which joined the EEC in 1973.
Where figures do not add up to 100, it is because of rounding.
Source: IMF, *International Financial Statistics* (various issues).

Table 2.2; in 1960 the EEC countries were producing 17 per cent of the world's GDP, compared to 14 per cent in 1950—see Table 2.3—and apart from Japan, had the highest average growth rates in the 1950s—5.6 per cent annually. The significance of this performance by the EEC countries is evident when it is contrasted with that of the United States—see the relevant Tables—indicating that, as a group, their position was comparable to that of the United States.

In respect of the second development, decolonization, the high point in the process was reached in the early 1960s, when a host of new states, predominantly from Africa, gained their independence—of the thirty-six new members joining the Fund between 1960 and 1965, twenty-eight were from Africa and thirty-four were developing countries overall. Decolonization led to a changed international political landscape and to new global concerns. Economically, the reconstruction focus of the late 1940s/early 1950s gave way in the 1960s to a concern with the development problems of the developing

Table 2.3 Shares of world GDP of selected countries and groups of countries (% shares)

	1950	1960	1970	1975
World	100	100	100	100
Developed countries	85	84	85	83
of which US	–	46	42	35
of which EEC	14	17	21	26
Developing countries	15	16	15	17

Source: Computed from UN, *Statistical Yearbook* (various issues).

nations. This was most prominently seen in the decision taken within the United Nations to designate the 1960s the Development Decade.[50]

The changed international political landscape that was a consequence of decolonization had its visible impact in the early 1960s, not in terms of economic importance or performance of these countries individually, but in regard to the political implications, on the one hand, of this development and, on the other, the conscious politicizing by developing countries of international economic relations. Their overwhelming numerical preponderance aside, their role in the international economy was one of lessening, rather than increasing importance. Here again, the economic indicators are helpful. Whereas in 1953, developing countries accounted for 26 per cent of world exports, this share had declined to 24 per cent in 1960 and to 19 per cent by 1970—see Table 2.2. Their aggregate international reserves were 15 per cent of the world's total in 1960, compared with 18 per cent in 1953—see Table 2.2. Their share of the world's GDP was virtually unchanged between 1950 and 1960—15.1 per cent and 15.6 per cent, respectively (Table 2.3).

The economic relations between the developed and the developing countries were also entering a difficult period at the beginning of the 1960s. This was evident in the pattern of retrenchment that became discernible in the aid performance of the OECD countries; between 1960 and 1970, the trend had been declining aid levels, when these are measured as a proportion of GNP— see Table 2.4. It is to be remembered that, in the conception of the developed countries, aid was the crucial touchstone of the development prospects of the poor countries, so that this weakening aid performance was bound to lead to a deterioration in the economic relations between these two groups of countries.

Table 2.4 ODA performance for OECD and OPEC countries (as groups): selected years, 1960–1980 (as % of GNP)

	1960	1965	1970	1975	1980
OECD	0.52	0.49	0.34	0.36	0.38
OPEC	–	–	–	2.92	1.74

Source: IBRD, World Development Reports, 1980 and 1982.

In the absence of economic leverage, either individually or collectively, developing countries at the start of the 1960s undertook a series of basically political initiatives in an effort to influence the evolution of international economic relations. At one level, another perspective on the problematic of development was gaining currency among developing-country spokesmen. The work of the Secretariat of the Economic Commission for Latin America (ECLA) under the leadership of Raul Prebisch was seminal to this indigenous theoretical presentation on development.[51] Prebisch's formulation postulated several obstacles, both nationally and internationally, to the prevailing development process, laying particular stress on a long-term tendency for the terms of trade of the primary commodity exports of developing countries to deteriorate relative to the manufactured goods of the developed countries.[52] The latter, because of their economic structures and their status as manufactured-goods producers, were seen as benefiting disproportionately from international trade.[53]

This unequal international division of labour was neatly summed up in the centre–periphery dichotomization of countries, corresponding to the industrialized and primary-producing developing countries, respectively. In a word, Prebisch's presentation marked the public statement of the division of the international economy into two coherent groups of countries. Implicit in the presentation, moreover, were the disparities in the bargaining power between these two sets of countries—their differential capacities to affect the workings of the international economic system.

Prebisch's diagnosis of the structural constraints impeding development led to prescriptions for action along several lines, at the national and international levels.[55] It also served as the starting-point for a new campaign by developing nations on behalf of structural reforms of the international trading system. Trade became the point of convergence around which they publicly advertised their discontent with the functioning of international economic relations.

The existing institutional framework for the conduct of international trade was brought into question. GATT was perceived as inconsistent with the developmental objectives of developing countries.[56] The conclusion was reached that 'there was no available forum that the developing countries considered capable of taking an over-all view and devoting its entire attention to their trade and development problems'.[57] Beginning in 1961, developing countries were to utilize the United Nations as the pressure point for an initiative, the ultimate intent of which was the convening of an international trade conference.[58]

The United Nations Conference on Trade and Development (UNCTAD) convened for the first time in 1964 and was seen as filling the institutional gap for their trade problems. But UNCTAD was to become more than this. Since its nomenclature also pinpointed an interest in problems of development, then its span of interest was essentially limitless in regard to economic issues. Hereafter, UNCTAD was to encroach, at least in respect of its deliberations and pronouncements, on the specific mandates of the other specialized institutions. It was to serve as the principal locus of Third World efforts to obtain changes in the trade and other economic relationships between developed and developing countries.[59] At the management level, moreover, UNCTAD did not mask its partiality towards the developing countries; the Secretariat saw itself as advancing solutions favourable to the economic development of the poor countries.[60]

UNCTAD, thus, was the main institutional construct of the 1960s—as a result of the deliberate activism of developing countries. With its wide-ranging responsibilities in economic matters, it inevitably had to come into contact with, or at least be taken into account by, the other institutions of the international economic system,[61] the more so since its majority membership—the developing nations—were also members of these other institutions. In fact, the

Bretton Woods institutions and the GATT did not remain aloof from or unaffected by these currents in the international economic environment; the early 1960s saw a reviewing process of their own policies as regards the developing countries.[62]

The other important outgrowth of UNCTAD—a development that basically formalized the North–South division and that changed the tactics of Third World bargaining relations with developed countries—was the establishment of a developing-country caucusing group, the Group of 77 (G77), on economic matters.[63] The significance of the G77 was that it

> became an integral part of UNCTAD, was one of the most important agents for the socialization of the developed countries in matters relating to international political economy, and established itself firmly in all major relevant parts of the United Nations system as the Third World's principal organ for the articulation and aggregation of its collective economic interest and for its representation in the negotiations with the developed countries.[64]

It stood to some extent as the counterpart to the OECD framework.

These attainments notwithstanding, up to the end of the 1960s, the developing countries as a collectivity remained the junior partners in international economic relations. Their numerical majority in the international system and political activism did not translate to augment their collective economic impact in the functioning of the international economic system. In a summary assessment of economic conditions at their Second Ministerial Meeting in 1971, the G77 enumerated a host of economic indicators relating to per capita income, trade, external debt and ODA that added up to a picture of economic decline for these countries.[65] Their conclusion was that '[t]he gap in the standard of living between the developed and developing countries had widened as a result of all these unfavourable trends; since their meeting in Algiers in 1967, the poor countries have become relatively poorer and the rich countries richer'.[66] In a word, the economic power structure had not changed in so far as the developing countries were concerned.

4. The breakdown of the Bretton Woods monetary arrangements and the NIEO campaign—the 1970s into the 1980s

Four broad developments were to characterize the international economic system during the course of the 1970s and into the 1980s. These were the collapse of certain important aspects of the Bretton Woods arrangements—though these were rectified to some extent during the 1970s—the emergence of radical shifts in the relations of power that, for the first time, extended outside the circle of the industrialized countries to take in certain developing countries, the NIEO campaign of the Third World and, finally, the worsening economic environment that became generalized by the end of the 1970s. These general features of international economic relations were to be paralleled by related economic evolutions that were to have direct consequences in the monetary sphere. The important events in this regard were the changes in the global balance-of-payments situation in the 1970s, the role of the commercial banks as a key financial intermediary from the mid-1970s, the increasing importance of the commodity question at that historical juncture and the debt problem of the early 1980s.

(a) The collapse of the Bretton Woods system

On 15 August 1971, the United States government announced a series of economic measures to deal with what had developed into a crisis situation in its balance of payments.[67] The American action was to have substantial lasting effects on the Bretton Woods monetary arrangements. American behaviour, however, was only one manifestation of the instabilities that had begun to beset international monetary relations during the 1960s.

That decade had, in fact, opened to a debate on the question of the liquidity requirements of the international monetary system. The deficiences in the liquidity-creation mechanisms of the existing arrangements—basically gold production and the running of deficits in the major reserve centres, especially the United States—were formally conceded in negotiations that extended throughout most of the 1960s and that culminated in the 1969 amendment of the IMF's Articles of Agreement, establishing the SDR scheme.[68] This act signified more than a recognition of flaws in the reserve-creation functions of the system; it also underscored the problems of the American dollar—the lack of confidence by the international community in the central role that this currency had come to play in the system.

By the mid-1960s, the American payments deficits had become a matter of international concern, and by the end of the decade had attained crisis proportions. These were the background circumstances to the measures adopted by the United States in August 1971. The suspension of convertibility by the United States hit at one of the key elements of the post-war monetary arrangements:

> The action taken by the United States on the external front removed one of the foundation stones of the international monetary system as it had operated since World War II under the Bretton Woods Agreement.[69]

The floodgates were thereafter opened to repudiation of other fundamental features of the Bretton Woods monetary order, in particular the regime of fixed exchange rates.[70] A period of disorder thus ensued in international monetary relations at the beginning of the 1970s.

These substantive threats to the monetary regime were paralleled by the tensions that began to affect its procedural and institutional framework. Initially, it was a question of the challenges by West European nations to continuing American dominance of management arrangements.[71] A process of accommodation to the demands of these countries for integration into international economic management thus became necessary. In the 1970s, the challenge, as we shall see, has come from the developing countries.[72] Ultimately, however, this historical moment—the start of the 1970s—in the words of the Fund's historian, 'marked the end of an era, a great divide in economic history. The "old world economic order" had crumbled'.[73] This was clearly the climacteric to those discernible trends of the 1960s that have just been briefly described.

(b) Changes in underlying economic power relations—the emergence of OPEC

The breakdown of the Bretton Woods monetary order was swiftly followed by an important shift in international economic power relations. The early 1970s witnessed the emergence of a sub-group of developing countries—the oil-producing countries—as a significant factor for influence in the international economy. Less observable at the time, but increasingly evident as the 1970s progressed were the significant changes in the international division of labour involving another set of developing countries—in current terminology, the newly industrializing countries (NICs).[74]

The context of OPEC's action had to do with both political and economic events. Politically, there was firstly the fact of *détente* at the beginning of the 1970s.[75] Secondly, the process of political decolonization had virtually run its course.[76] Since the decolonization struggle had been the priority item on the Third World agenda of international action, its successful pursuit thus cleared the way for the assumption by these countries of another priority task, in fact, the corollary of political independence, that is, economic decolonization.[77]

It was therefore no accident that the start of the 1970s coincided with a widescale nationalistic posture on economic issues by developing countries. Domestically, this economic nationalism took the form of an onslaught on foreign private investment activities in individual economies, and on the prominent institutional representation thereof—the transnational corporations (TNCs). Internationally, economic nationalism was expressed in a new activism on international economic relations and the demand for a NIEO.

The focal attention on foreign investment operations and the TNCs was an outgrowth of the reality of external control over the vital natural resources of these countries—a residual aspect of the colonial experience. In the nationalistic context of the early 1970s, therefore, developing countries began to reassert control over their natural resources, using a variety of methods.[78]

This was the background to the series of actions taken by the oil-producing developing nations, beginning in 1971, under the auspices of their producers' association—OPEC—to redefine their economic relationships with both the oil companies and consuming developed countries. OPEC challenged the oligopolistic position of the TNCs in the petroleum market by taking over price-setting and production functions.[79]

OPEC's actions underscored a new influence of the oil-producing developing countries in the international economic system. The measurable impact of OPEC on international economic relations was evident in a number of important indicators. Their combined international reserves grew from approximately 5 per cent of the world's total in 1970 to 25 per cent in 1975, while their export trade share rose from 5 per cent in 1970 to 14 per cent in 1975—see Table 2.3; their new role as significant donor countries in the international development assistance efforts—when compared to the OECD aid performance and as measured by GNP proportions, they had become important disbursers of aid to developing countries (Table 2.4). The OPEC countries were also to become the major lenders to the IMF from the mid-1970s, especially in regard to the financing of the Fund's 1974 and 1975 oil facilities and its supplementary financing facility of the late 1970s—see Table 2.5. Another important index of OPEC's new economic importance was the larger use of their currencies in respect of transactions involving the Fund and its membership—from a position of virtually no use up to the end of the 1960s, their currencies began to be used from the mid-1970s (see Table 2.6).

Table 2.5 Source of financing for IMF oil (OF) and supplementary financing facility (SFF) (million SDRs)

	OF (1974)	OF (1975)	SFF
Total	3,046.9	3,855.5	7,784
OECD countries	396.9	1,500.0	4,550
OPEC and other oil producing developing countries	2,650.0	2,355.5	3,234

Source: IMF, *Finance and Development*, 13, No. 2, June 1976 and *IMF Survey*, 23 March 1981.

Table 2.6 Currencies used in drawings in the IMF for selected years (million SDRs)

	1954	1968	1976	1979	1947–79
World	63	3,517	7,010	1,843	50,210
US dollar	63	790	2,720	108	13,997
Deutsche Mark	—	836	324	—	8,087
Japanese yen	—	102	600	42	3,166
Oil-exporting countries' currencies	—	10	1,176	284	5,333

Source: *IMF Survey*, 24 November 1980.

Apart from the impact on individual economic fortunes among the OPEC membership, the new price relations inaugurated by OPEC were to have larger international economic implications, in terms both of the task environment of the IMF and broader international economic relations. The most readily visible effect in the first category had to do with the global balance-of-payments situation. As the Fund's Managing Director noted in his presentation of the thirty-first Annual Report of the IMF:

> The traditional pattern of current account balances that prevailed until 1973 has changed substantially. Particularly striking is the huge increase in the surplus of the major oil exporting countries and the roughly similar increase in the deficit of other primary producing countries.[80]

The magnitude of the shifts in the current account balances of the OPEC countries, relative to those of the developed and other developing countries, is readily seen from the data in Table 2.7. For the non-oil producing developing countries, the current account deficits had grown not only in terms of magnitude, but proportionate to GNP—from 1.1 per cent of GNP in 1973 to 5.1 per cent in 1975.[81] External payments deficits, the more so in regard to the latter group of countries, were hereafter to be an area of dominant worry in the international economy.

Table 2.7 Summary of balance of payments on current account: selected group of countries, 1973–1982 (billion US dollars)

	1973	1974	1975	1978	1980	1981	1982
Developed countries	20.3	−10.8	19.8	32.7	−40.2	−0.3	−3.6
Developing countries							
oil exporting countries	6.7	68.3	35.4	2.2	114.3	65.0	−2.2
non-oil developing	−11.3	−37.0	−46.3	−41.3	−89.0	−107.7	−86.8

Note: IMF classifications of countries are somewhat different from the classifications used in this analysis; nevertheless, the differences are not so great as to disturb the significance of the order of magnitudes presented above.
Source: IMF, *Annual Report*, 1983.

A second fundamental effect of OPEC's action related to the fact that many of these countries did not have the domestic absorptive capacity to utilize, in an immediate and meaningful way, their immense oil revenues. This fact, coupled with the tremendous balance-of-payments impact on the international economy, argued for recycling mechanisms to lessen the destabilizing consequences for all international economic actors. A wide array of recycling processes was used, including loans to international financial institutions, ODA and, most prominently, the private commercial banking system came to assume a pivotal financial intermediation role in the mid-1970s. An IMF study of the disposition of the current account surpluses of the oil-exporting developing countries, estimated at US $357 billion over the years 1974–80, shows that $328 billion (85 per cent of the total) were invested in the industrial countries and in the Eurocurrency markets. Some $154 billion of this went into the commercial banking system.[82] This was the catalyst to the pivotal role played by private commercial bank lending from the mid-1970s onwards in financing the deficits of many developing countries.[83]

Commercial bank lending in the 1970s was concentrated, however, in a limited number of well-endowed developing countries, predominantly the NICs.[84] Bank lending is a function of the assessment by the private bankers of a country's creditworthiness, the major criteria of which revolve around the capacity of the country to generate the export earnings to service the ensuing debt, as well as its growth performance and development prospects. Thus, the NICs, with their diversified export structures, increasing exports of manufactures and outstanding growth rates, were well-placed to tap the international private banking system for their financing requirements throughout the 1970s.

These countries were increasingly perceived as the success story of the 1970s in the area of manufactured export trade. Their share of world exports of manufactures increased substantially from 2.59 per cent in 1963 to 7.12 per cent in 1976.[85] Nearly three-quarters (73 per cent) of total developing country manufactured exports had their origin in seven Asian and Latin American countries in 1979: Taiwan, South Korea, Singapore, Hong Kong, Brazil, Mexico and Argentina.[86] Put another way, the adoption of an export-oriented development strategy by several developing countries, located mainly in East Asia and Latin America, had paid dividends in terms of their trade roles internationally. These were the developing countries that the World Bank had identified as being relatively successful in dealing with the negative occurrences in the international economy during the 1970s. They were the developing countries that were the main borrowers in the international credit markets, especially in terms of borrowing magnitudes throughout the 1970s.[87]

This expansion in commercial bank lending was to have a dramatic impact on the indebtedness of the relevant developing countries. The debt problem, or rather the international focus thereon, of the early 1980s—as we shall later see—would be highly skewed to dealing with the difficulties of a few NICs. The other consequence of bank lending was the displacement of the IMF from its central role in balance-of-payments financing.[88]

The environmental impact of oil and OPEC's success could also be gauged by the effect they had on the whole context of the international discourse on the commodity problem. Immediately, the commodity question was elevated to the highest level of North–South relations in the mid-1970s. Speaking before the Sixth Special Session of the UN General Assembly in 1974, President Boumedienne of Algeria—at whose instance the Special Session was convened—urged the developing countries to see in OPEC's initiative:

the first illustration, and at the same time the most concrete and the most spectacular illustration of the importance of raw-material prices for our countries, the vital need for the producing countries to control the levers of price control, and lastly, the great possibilities of a union of the raw-materials-producing countries.[89]

The immediate reaction of the developed nations to OPEC's action did not to any degree invalidate this assessment. A period of public disagreement among the developed countries ensued—serving to confirm perceptions of their vulnerability and dependence on certain Third World strategic raw materials.[90]

The commodity question became a central element of North–South relations at this moment because many developing countries saw a chance to duplicate the success of OPEC in their dealings with the developed countries.[91] The exploitation of this 'commodity power' was perceived as the crucial bargaining asset in seeking to redress the prevailing imbalances in the economic relationships between these two groups of countries.[92]

(c) The NIEO demands of the Third World

OPEC's action was also to have a significant impact on the context of North-South negotiations in the mid-1970s. It was to have a catalyzing effect on these negotiations.[93] Despite their new-found financial wealth, the OPEC countries for a variety of reasons continued to operate within the negotiating framework of the developing countries—the G77[94]—and opted to utilize their economic influence *vis-à-vis* the developed countries to press the NIEO demands of the Third World as a whole.[95] OPEC's common stand with these countries, therefore, served to change somewhat the negotiating equation between North and South, thereby seeming to create a more positive climate for the achievement of results by the developing countries. The perception of a unified Third World group[96] versus a disorganized developed-country approach was a key element in the international economic environment of the mid-1970s. Third World bargaining capacity received an additional boost from the assumption by the non-aligned movement of a priority concern with the economic agenda in the early 1970s.[97]

When allied with the G77 demands, the non-aligned focus on the economic issues conduced to strengthen and intensify the negotiating position of the developing nations in the existing circumstances. For the G77 was by no means quiescent in the face of the crises in development and broader international economic relations. It was at UNCTAD III that the G77 took its most decisive action anticipative of the NIEO. President Echeverria of Mexico, in his address before UNCTAD, proposed the elaboration of a Charter for Economic Rights and Duties of States[98]—a proposal that led to two years of negotiations under the aegis of UNCTAD and culminated in the adoption of the Charter under the terms of General Assembly resolution 3281(XXIX) of 12 December 1974.[99]

This activism of the developing countries had the intellectual guidance of a growing indigenous Third World analysis of the problematic of development.[100] This was the process of evolving what Mahbub ul Haq has termed 'intellectual self-reliance [to] give some form and substance to our aimless search for appropriate development strategies at home and to our disorganized efforts to coordinate our negotiating positions abroad'.[101] In short, by the early 1970s, the building of a Third World negotiating infrastructure, encompassing the caucussing groups—the G77, the Group of 24 and the non-aligned movement—the intellectual analyses and new elements of practical influence in OPEC, were in place. It was against this background that the NIEO negotiations were to begin.

What the NIEO campaign has signified above all else is that there was a breakdown in the consensus that had undergirded post-war international economic relations for a quarter of a century. What the developing countries were presenting was competing vision for the organization of the international economy.[102] This competing vision embodied extreme differences in the substantive treatment of issues, in the philosophical and juridical foundations of international economic relations and the institutional structuring of these interactions.

Philosophically, the NIEO has meant, in contrast to the liberal orientation of the post-war order, a more interventionist approach to international economic relations.[103] This economic interventionism has implied a juxtaposition on the international plane of the pattern of economic behaviour in some developed countries that has come to be known as 'affirmative action' and that aims at providing a certain minimum amount of social compensation and special privileges to disadvantaged groups in these societies.[104] Paralleling this challenge to the philosophical ordering principle has been Third World criticism of the juridical bases of the Bretton Woods system.[105] And, finally, the inauguration of the NIEO was predicated on transformations at the institutional level of economic relations, involving a refashioning of the old institutions and the creation of new ones, as required.

The NIEO negotiations can be divided into two distinct phases: (i) the years of the mid- to late 1970s and (ii) the post-1979 years. The mid-1970s represented the high point of Third World activism and initiative on international economic relations—reflected in the numerous negotiating conferences convened to discuss these issues. Contrastingly, the post-1979 years have marked the demise of the NIEO.

A variety of institutional settings were employed during the mid-1970s for the conduct of the NIEO negotiations. These included the Sixth and Seventh Special Sessions of the UN General Assembly, held in 1974 and 1975 respectively, CIEC over the 1975–77 years and the Fourth Session of UNCTAD in 1976.[106] In the final analysis, however, up to the end of CIEC in 1977, the record of the negotiations was devoid of practical achievements, and certainly of any immediate prospects for the implementation of the NIEO. Opening the G77 Ministerial Meeting in Arusha in 1979, President Nyerere of Tanzania noted:

> ... it is also true that the kind of dialogue we have been conducting—at UNCTAD, Paris, Geneva, New York and everywhere else—has brought no fundamental changes in the world economic order ... [T]he problem remains: we have not succeeded in changing the structure of power. The world still works against the interests of the poor.[107]

This perception of negotiating deadlock, after several years of intensive discussions between developed and developing countries, in a multiplicity of institutional contexts, was the impetus for the next stage of the NIEO dialogue.

(d) The global negotiations initiative in an environment of economic crisis

Beginning in 1979, the developing countries moved to have inaugurated a process of global negotiations on international economic relations. The proposal for global negotiations was nothing more than a variant of the NIEO. It had to do as much with the sense of disappointment at the absence of practical achievements on the NIEO, as with developments in international economic—and political[108]—relations that have to a large extent disrupted the North–South discussions.

Economically, the development performance of developing countries was substantially affected by several events. These events emanated from actions taken and existing economic circumstances in two sets of countries: the OPEC and the major industrialized countries. OPEC in 1979 once again raised the price of oil significantly—prices more than doubled between end 1978 and early 1980.[109] The immediate impact was on the external payments situation of the non-oil developing countries, as reflected in their current account deficits, which widened from $41.3 billion in 1978 to $89 billion and $107.7 billion in 1980 and 1981 respectively—see Table 2.7.

Balance-of-payments problems, therefore, continued to be a dominant worry for developing countries at the beginning of the 1980s. Simultaneously, they encountered the negative effects of the economic deterioration that was then afflicting the developed economies. High levels of inflation and unemployment and an overall recessionary environment characterized these economies: compared with 3.4 per cent in 1973, the unemployment average in 1981 was 6.5 per cent and inflation rates were 8.8 per cent and 8.6 per cent in 1980 and 1981 respectively. Average growth rates of 5 per cent in 1976 had deteriorated to 1 per cent in 1981.[110] The world situation was summed up thus in the IMF's *World Economic Outlook* for 1980:

> The world economic picture is grim. The estimates and projections contained in this report depict a severe worldwide problem of inflation; a general pattern of slow growth of output, with a threat of recessionary tendencies in the industrial world; a sharp slump in the growth of volume of world trade; and a sudden and major worsening of the distribution of balances on external account among the major groups of countries.[111]

It was in this environment that policy-makers in the developed countries took the decision at the end of the 1970s to make the curbing of inflation their priority economic concern.[112] In the battle against inflation, various fiscal and monetary measures—including tighter credit, higher interest rates, cuts in government expenditure—with a deflationary impact on economic activity were implemented. This policy emphasis on curbing inflation had a concomitant external dimension in terms of restricted credit availabilities, decreased ODA and curtailment of international liquidity via SDR allocations.

The cumulative impact of the economic retrenchment in the developed countries and the oil price increase on the non-oil developing countries was manifold: a compounding of external deficits; increased costs of manufactured and other imports as a result of inflation; declining commodity export prices and earnings as a counterpart of the recession, and increased protectionism against their manufactured products. For the developing-country borrowers in the international credit markets, what the Fund's Managing Director termed 'a radical change in the financial environment'[113] proved an additional burden economically. This changed financial environment, characterized by an appreciating dollar—in which a major part of their debt was denominated—and high real interest rates, served to increase the debt-servicing requirements of the developing countries.

The debt problem of the developing countries suddenly emerged as a major potential destabilizing force in the international economy in late 1982.[114] Its origins were in the immense financing role assumed by the commercial banking system after the oil price increase of 1973, to which reference has previously been made.

The debt-carrying capacity of the developing countries depended crucially on international economic conditions of expanded growth and trade. It also depended on the existence of manageable interest payments. Such has not been the case since the start of the 1980s, which have been characterized by 'extraordinarily high interest rates'[115] in the private credit markets and, as the IMF's 1983 *Annual Report* has underlined:

> The high interest rates of the 1981–82 period generated large and unexpected additions to debt service costs, not only for new borrowing but also—under the floating interest rate arrangements applicable to most international commercial bank loans in recent years—on a considerable proportion of the debt already outstanding.[116]

The combination, therefore, at the beginning of the 1980s, of the recession and protectionism in the developed countries, increased oil prices, deteriorating commodity prices and a changing international financial context, brought into question the debt-servicing capacity of developing-country borrowers:

> In fact, the mounting concerns of creditors in 1980 and 1981 had already caused them to lend increasingly on short term. By early 1982 creditors became very much exercised about the growing size of the total debt outstanding, the increasing proportion of short term debt—which made many debtors highly vulnerable to any decline in credit—and the persistence of high interest rates.[117]

Not only did the commercial banks begin to question the prudence of continued exposure in developing countries, but a decision was taken to cut back severely on lending to these countries.[118] This marked the start of the debt problem that has been preoccupying the attention of the international financial community since. As one Fund official has written, 'External debt appears to have replaced oil prices as the prime international economic preoccupation'.[119]

It was against this unfavourable background internationally that Third World countries sought to move the NIEO negotiations into their contemporary phase. The origin of the proposal for global negotiations was instructive for what it said about Third World cohesion. The initiative had come from the OPEC countries. The aim was basically to deflect an emerging dissatisfaction of the developing non-oil producing nations with the oil price increase of 1979—and to a certain extent with the aid performance of OPEC.[120]

At UNCTAD V in Manila and the non-aligned summit in Havana in 1979, as well as various meetings of the Group of 77 in 1979–80, growing criticisms of

OPEC were uttered by other developing countries.[121] This was the context of OPEC's proposal for global negotiations and, as one analyst has noted, '[t]hey wanted to use the negotiations as a ploy to head off oil-price pressures mounted against them by oil-importing countries, both developed and developing'.[122]

The fact is, the public negotiating consensus of the developing countries apart, their unity was founded on rather fragile bases. A disaggregation of these countries indicates a marked differentiation of economic circumstances and performances from a historical vantage-point—even without taking into account the diversity of prevailing ideologies, political structures, resource endowments and the like.

The *World Development Report* for 1981 provides a summary presentation of the uneven performance of certain discrete groups of developing countries. Thus, while per capita GNP was more than doubling between 1950 and 1980 for middle-income developing countries—as designated by the World Bank— from $640 to $1,590 (in 1980 dollars), the increment for the low-income countries was not even of the order of 50 per cent—from $170 to $250. Average annual GDP growth, in percentage terms, while relatively high for developing countries as a whole over the 1970s—some 5 per cent—masked the low average rates of 1.5 per cent for low-income Africa. Whereas the share in world production of developing oil exporters and middle-income countries increased from 4 to 9 per cent to 5 and 11 per cent, respectively, between 1970 and 1980, low-income countries had made no headway, remaining at 2 per cent of the world's total. Regarding export trade, oil-producing countries increased their share of the world's total from 5 per cent to 8 per cent between 1970 and 1980, while middle-income countries in both years had a 13 per cent share. The low-income countries, in contrast, witnessed a halving of their share from 2 per cent in 1970 to 1 per cent in 1980.

When the OPEC nations proposed global negotiations in 1979 it was merely a papering over of a fundamental split among developing nations. In contrast to the mid-1970s, therefore, when it was the developed countries that were disunited at first in reaction to the OPEC action and the NIEO demands of the Third World, it was now the latter that were advocating global negotiations from a position of weakness. The conception these countries had of global negotiations, moreover, merely served to harden the resistance of the developed countries to their demands. The global negotiations proposal had two major emphases. Its substantive emphasis envisaged a process of negotiations that took in certain defined areas of concern—raw materials, energy, trade, development, money and finance. In regard to a negotiating framework, the developing nations argued for an institutional arrangement that gave the United Nations system central control over the negotiation process.

It was on the insistence of a central role for the United Nations that the global negotiations proposal foundered. The developed countries were uncompromising in their determination to safeguard the authority and autonomy of the specialized agencies—IMF, IBRD, GATT. One analyst has posited that:

the changes called for under money and finance seemed most threatening to the developed nations. While there were familiar calls for a link between the allocation of SDRs and development finance and improved balance of payments financing, it was other subitems which received most of the attention. These were subitems on 'Effective and equitable participation of the developing countries in the decision-making process' of the international monetary system and 'Amending, as required, the Articles of Agreement of the International Monetary Fund ... in accordance with the needs of the developing countries'. These subitems attracted attention precisely because they struck at the very root of Western economic power.[123]

This procedural impasse has effectively doomed the global negotiations proposal, ushering in a period of hiatus in North–South negotiations.

Conclusions

The distinctive feature of the general environment of the first decade and a half of post-war international economic relations was the dominant leadership role of the United States. It was a period, moreover, when the aid relationship dominated the economic interaction between the developed and the developing nations. With regard to the specific monetary tasks of the IMF, for most of this period there was a clear marginalization of the institution. In the second period, covering basically the 1960s, important changes occurred in the international economic power structure, the signal event was the re-emergence of the West European countries as a new factor for influence. In the North–South relations, the intensity of the political decolonization process reshaped the membership configuration of the international system and pointed to a new concern with the problems of the developing countries. These developments were instrumental in the creation of novel institutional structures—UNCTAD and the G77—and in the thematic stress on trade relations between developed and developing countries.

The central period of interest in this study, the years 1970–85, initially saw a comprehensive challenge to the post-war international economic order by the Third World. At a broad level, this challenge signified a breakdown of the consensus that had underpinned that order since the time of Bretton Woods and its most visible manifestation was the NIEO campaign. This systemic challenge, for a time, was supported by the transformation of the international economic power structure that embraced a sub-group of developing countries and the political unity displayed by these countries in the mid-1970s. In terms of the specific monetary environment, three developments were particularly notable. These were the balance-of-payments problems that affected the entire international economic system, the related issues of the new role of the commercial banks in the intermediation process of the financial surpluses of the OPEC nations and the commodity debate.

By the end of the period, the NIEO challenge had virtually run its course. In the context of general economic recession in the early 1980s, new economic experiments in several important developed countries—the United States and the United Kingdom, especially—and the new administration that took office in the United States in early 1981, with its lack of interest in the multilateral economic process, the developing countries found themselves on the defensive in the North–South framework. In the narrower context of monetary relations, the two dominant themes were the continuing balance-of-payments problems of developing countries and the debt problem. In so far as the infrastructure of political influence within the international economic system was concerned, there was the sense of a Third World that was less than unified—the weakening of their bargaining influence of the 1970s. Contrastingly, while developed countries on the whole did not display any relative greater unity, an important sub-group—the United States, the United Kingdom, West Germany and Japan—was sufficiently unified in their outlook on the operation of the international economic system to pose a counter-threat to the demands of the developing countries.

The relationship of these general and specific environmental factors to Fund decision making can be represented in the following propositions. Firstly, it is not expected that Fund decision making will be a major concern to international actors during this first period. This is for two reasons: the leadership role of the United States—acquiesced in by the other participants—and the peripheral status of the IMF. Secondly, in so far as decision-making processes are influenced by power structures, then in the second period, it is the West European countries that should be the main beneficiaries of any observable changes. However, with the emergence of the G77 and UNCTAD as institutional processes identified with Third World economic concerns, then the contention is that IMF behaviour and policies will come under increasing pressure from these extra-institutional sources of Third World influence.

Thirdly, the systemic challenges represented by the NIEO phase of Third World activism, in encompassing in explicit terms decision making in the IMF, should evidence correlational evolutions in respect of both process and outcome. The main test of responsiveness at the level of process would have to be in regard to an integration of OPEC nations into management structures, on the basis of their new economic influence. This increased decision-making role of OPEC would naturally spill over into an increased decision-making role for the Third World, in so far as the former have continued to operate within the ambit of the G77. At the level of substantive policies, the test of Fund responsiveness would have to be seen in how it dealt with specific environmental developments as they affected developing countries and in the context of the bargaining strengths these countries brought to bear in the negotiation of outcomes. Finally, the post-1980 period, it is contended, should evidence at best, for the developing countries, a standstill in achievements—in regard to both decision-making influence and substance—and at worst, a reversal of the gains of the 1970s.

Notes

1. This chapter is based to some extent on the lecture series on the NIEO conducted by Prof. Georges Abi-Saab over the course of the 1983–84 academic year at the Graduate Institute of International Studies in Geneva.

2. For the purposes of the analysis, the geographical boundaries of the international economic order will take in the developed countries of the OECD, the developing countries of the G77 and China. Strictly speaking, in the absence of the socialist economies, we should more properly speak of two parallel international economic systems, or as Miriam Camps notes, two and one-half systems—see Miriam Camps, *The Management of Interdependence: A Preliminary View*, New York, Council on Foreign Relations, 1974, p. 42.

3. For the historical details, see Richard N. Gardner, *Sterling-Dollar Diplomacy in Current Perspective (The Origins and the Prospects of our International Economic Order)*, new expanded edn, New York, Columbia University Press, 1980.

4. See the opening remarks of the Chairman of the Bretton Woods Conference, *Proceedings and Documents of the United Nations Monetary and Financial Conference*, hereafter referred to as *Proceedings and Documents*, Vol. 1, Bretton Woods, New Hampshire, US Government Printing Office, Washington DC, 1948, p. 81.

5. Apart from Gardner's work, above-cited, historical accounts relating to each of the specific international economic areas of trade, money and investment can be found in the following works: Clair Wilcox, *A Charter for World Trade*, New York, The Macmillan Co., 1949 for the trade issue and J. Keith Horsefield, *The International Monetary Fund, 1945-65: Twenty Years of International Monetary Cooperation*, Vol. 1, Washington DC, IMF, 1969, pp. 3-118 and Armand van Dormael, *Bretton Woods: Birth of a Monetary System*, London, Macmillan Press, 1978 for the monetary arrangements and in regard to the financial proposals, Edward S. Mason and Robert E. Asher, *The World Bank since Bretton Woods*, Washington DC, The Brookings Institution, 1973, pp. 1-35.

6. See Gardner, op. cit., pp. 369-78.

7. For a discussion of this conception, see Eric Roll, *The World after Keynes: An Examination of the Economic Order*, London, Pall Mall Press, 1968, pp. 91-2.

8. Ibid. See also Joan Edelman Spero, *The Politics of International Economic Relations*, New York, St Martin's Press, 1977, pp. 21-5.

9. *Proceedings and Documents*, Vol. 1, p. 4.

10. These countries were: from Africa—Egypt, Ethiopia and Libya; from Asia—India, Iran, Iraq and the Philippines; from Latin America—Bolivia, Brazil, Chile, Columbia, Costa Rica, Cuba, Dominican Republic, Ecuador, El Salvador, Guatemala, Haiti, Honduras, Mexico, Nicaragua, Panama, Paraguay, Peru, Uruguay, Venezuela; and from Europe, Yugoslavia.

11. Both the British and American proposals, in their original formulation, sought to address the role of the Soviet Union in the IMF—see 'Preliminary Draft Proposals for a United Nations Stabilization Fund ...' and 'Proposals for an International Clearing (or Currency) Union' in Horsefield, op. cit., Vol. III, pp. 72-3 and p. 15, para. 55, respectively.

12. An indication of the role of these countries is glimpsed in this report: 'During the discussion of the part the smaller nations have played in the negotiations the Secretary [US Treasury Secretary Morgenthau] exhibited a somewhat cavalier attitude. Some of the smaller nations had objected to minor points but that didn't alter the fact that the recommendations as published constituted a consensus of their views ... Morgenthau was also somewhat off-hand in the part which the smaller nations would take in fixing the gold parities of their post-war currency. "We'll ask their advice and then fix it for them", he remarked amid laughter'— quoted in van Dormael, op. cit., p. 140.

13. For details, see Horsefield, op. cit., Vol. I, pp. 93-108. India, for instance, had tried to broaden the Fund's purposes to include the development issue. The later line of cleavage between developed and developing countries was foreshadowed in the

Indian proposal. For a discussion, see Joseph Gold, '... "To Contribute thereby to ... Development": Aspects of the Relations of the International Monetary Fund with its Developing Members', *Columbia Journal of Transnational Law*, Vol. 10, Fall 1971, pp. 267–302.

14. See W. M. Scammell, *The International Economy since 1945*, New York, St Martin's Press, 1980, p. 18.

15. See Art. 2, Sec. 1(a) and (b) of the 'Articles of Agreement', IBRD, as amended effective 17 December 1965.

16. See opening remarks of Lord Keynes—in his capacity as Chairman—to the first meeting of the Second Commission on the IBRD at Bretton Woods in *Proceedings and Documents*, Vol. 1, p. 84 and US Treasury Department, *The Bretton Woods Proposals: Questions and Answers on the Fund and Bank*, Washington DC, US Government Printing Office, 15 March 1945, pp. 15–16.

17. *Proceedings and Documents*, Vol. 1, p. 85.

18. Another important function—that of the creation of international liquidity—was added as a result of the first amendment of the Fund's Articles of Agreement, which became effective in July 1969—see Ch. 5 of this study for further details.

19. Basically, a system of fixed exchange rates was defined, though these rates were not unalterable since provision was made for changes in the exchange rate of a member experiencing an external situation of 'fundamental disequilibrium'—Art. IV, Sec. 5(a). (Unless otherwise indicated, reference in this chapter to the Fund's Articles is to the original Articles.) Countries were prohibited from engaging in currency restrictions against current transactions—though a transition period was provided for those economies that needed it, during which time existing exchange restrictions could be kept—Art. XIV.

20. For those members that did not immediately adhere to the convertibility standard, it was envisaged that the end of the transitional period would coincide with the implementation of currency convertibility.

21. Art. III, Sec. 3(b) and (c).

22. See, for example, 'US Commentary—Questions and Answers on the International Monetary Fund' in Horsefield, op. cit., Vol. III, p. 139.

23. After the second amendment of the Articles of Agreement came into force in April 1978, the Fund's consultation powers were derived from the new Article IV.

24. As Gardner has noted: 'The United States, of course, was the dominant element. For better or worse, only the US had the resources to make these institutions work. Moreover ... the war was still on ... There was complete dependence on the United States militarily, politically and economically. No wonder, then, that the US role at Bretton Woods was decisive'—see Richard N. Gardner, 'The Political Setting' in A. L. Keith Acheson *et al.*, *Bretton Woods Revisited*, The Macmillan Press, 1972, pp. 20–1.

25. Shares computed from statistics provided in IMF, *International Financial Statistics*, July–December 1950.

26. Joseph Gold, *Legal and Institutional Aspects of the International Monetary System: Selected Essays*, Vol. II, Washington DC, IMF, 1984, p. 85.

27. See proposals by delegations of Brazil, Cuba and Chile in *Proceedings and Documents*, Vol. 1, pp. 482–4.

28. See Resolution VII on 'International Economic Problems, relating to trade', ibid., p. 941.

29. Anglo–American understandings on the outlines of an international trading system were also followed by a process of consultations with other countries prior to the convening of the formal conference in Havana in 1947. In these pre-Havana consultations, the Anglo-American proposals came under intense criticism from

developing countries, especially as regards the absence of any link between trade and development—see Wilcox, op. cit., p. 31.

30. Ibid., p. 47.

31. For a discussion, see Jock A. Finlayson and Mark W. Zacher, 'International trade institutions and the North–South dialogue', *International Journal*, 36, No. 4, Autumn 1981, pp. 733–6.

32. See Branislav Gosovic, *UNCTAD: Conflict and Compromise (The Third World's Quest for an Equitable World Economic Order through the United Nations)*, Leiden, A. W. Sijthoff, 1972, p. 11.

33. They were Burma, Sri Lanka, India, Lebanon, Pakistan, Syria from Asia and Brazil, Chile and Cuba from Latin America.

34. As Behrman puts it: 'The post-World War II system of *laissez-faire* called for non-intervention in international trade and capital movements . . . Governments agreed to a set of rules, constraining their power to interfere in international markets, as reflected in the Fund, the Bank, the GATT . . . Economic and commercial decisions were supposed to be made in a self-regulating market system, which was assumed to provide not only the most efficient use of the world's resources but also a just and equitable distribution of the benefits of economic growth'—see Jack N. Behrman, 'Toward a New International Economic Order', *The Atlantic Paper*, No. 3, 1974, p. 17.

35. The Soviet Union, though participating in the Bretton Woods negotiations, did not join the IMF and IBRD. Two of the current socialist economies of Eastern Europe, Poland and Czechoslovakia, were founder-members, but they both withdrew from membership of these institutions in 1950 and 1954 respectively. Within recent years, a new interest, on the part of the socialist countries, has been evinced in membership in the IMF and IBRD. Already, Hungary and Poland are in the IMF.

36. See Spero, op. cit., p. 35.

37. The ERP or Marshall Plan aid was carried out in the coordinative framework of the new European institution, the Organization of European Economic Cooperation (OEEC). The OEEC also served as the precursor to the integrative aspirations of the European countries, evident in the creation of the European Economic Community (EEC) in the late 1950s. The OEEC was to become in 1960 the Organization of Economic Cooperation and Development (OECD), expanding to include developed countries outside the European continent and serving as the coordinating forum among these countries on economic matters.

38. Scammell, op. cit., p. 31.

39. Source: Horsefield, op. cit., Vol. II and IBRD, *The International Bank for Reconstruction and Development*, 1946–53, The John's Hopkins Press, Baltimore, 1954.

40. Virtually all these countries have become members of the IMF and IBRD, the only current exception being Angola.

41. The Cold War origins of the American technical assistance programme was explicitly stated in Secretary of State Acheson's testimony to the Senate Committee on Foreign Relations in 1950—see 'Aid to Underdeveloped Areas as Measure of National Security: Statement by Secretary Acheson' (before the Senate Committee on Foreign Relations on the Point 4 legislation, 30 March 1950), *Department of State Bulletin*, Vol. XXII, No. 562, 10 April 1950, p. 552.

42. The Point Four Program took its name from the fourth point, stressed in President Truman's inaugural address of 1949, as contributing to the attainment of international peace and freedom—see 'Inaugural Address of the President, 20 January, 1949', *Department of State Bulletin*, Vol. XX, No. 500, 30 January 1949, p. 125.

43. See General Assembly Resolution 304(iv) of 16 November 1949.

44. For a discussion, see Paul Streeten, *Development Perspectives*, New York, St Martin's Press, 1981, pp. 104–5.

45. Robert E. Asher *et al.*, *The United Nations and Economic and Social Cooperation*, Washington DC, The Brookings Institution, 1957, p. 474.

46. For a historical account, see John G. Hadwen and Johan Kaufman, *How United Nations Decisions are Made*, 2nd edn, Leyden, A. W. Sijthoff, 1961, pp. 85–111.

47. Asher *et al.*, op. cit., p. 446.

48. Several things were done, however, in compensation: firstly, the International Finance Corporation (IFC) was established in 1956 as an affiliate of the IBRD to facilitate private capital transfers to developing countries; secondly, in 1957, the UN Special Fund was created and, finally, another World Bank affiliate came into being in 1960—the International Development Association (IDA)—as the soft loan arm of the Bank to cater for the development financing needs of the low-income developing nations.

49. See General Assembly Res. 1522(XV) of 15 December 1960.

50. See General Assembly Res. 1710(XVI) of 25 September 1961.

51. For a presentation of Prebisch's perspectives, see *Towards a Dynamic Development Policy for Latin America*, New York, UN, 1963.

52. Ibid., pp. 78–85. It should be noted that the terms of trade argument has come under increasing attack in respect of its technical credibility. The point, however, is that developing countries coalesced around the analysis and used it as the basis for their ideological attack on the existing structure of international trade.

53. Several arguments were adduced in support of this thesis: the dominance of manufactured goods in their production and export structures; the high income elasticity of demand for these goods, compared to the low demand elasticities associated with primary exports; the organization of labour in the developed countries and their bargaining capacity to gain increasing increments of the productivity gains.

54. For a discussion, see Craig N. Murphy, 'What the Third World Wants: An Interpretation of the Development and Meaning of the New International Economic Ideology', *International Studies Quarterly*, 27, No. 1, March 1983, p. 65.

55. Domestically, a structural shift from raw materials production to manufactures was advocated as the main area of action. Internationally, Prebisch argued for a new framework for international trade that would orient policy in a number of directions, including increased resource flows from developed countries, commodity agreements and compensatory finance to deal with the commodity trade problem and importantly, a less protectionist, more preferential environment for the manufactured exports of developing countries.

56. See 'Commodity and trade problems of developing countries: institutional arrangements' (report of the Group of Experts appointed under Economic and Social Council Resolution 919 (xxxiv)), *Official Records, ECOSOC*, 36th Session, Geneva, 1963, para. 200, p. 32.

57. Gosovic, op. cit., p. 9.

58. For a historical account, see ibid.

59. As a former UNCTAD Secretary-General has stated it: 'UNCTAD came to be seen as being primarily a forum in which the developing countries gave expression to their problems and their demands, a forum in which they sought to apply a degree of pressure on the international community to gain recognition of these problems and the need for solutions' —see Gamani Corea, *Need for Change: Towards the New International Economic Order* (Selection from Major Speeches and Reports), Oxford, Pergamon Press, 1980, p. 2.

60. Ibid.

61. For a discussion of the relationship between the IMF and UNCTAD, see Edgar Jones, 'The Fund and UNCTAD', *Finance and Development*, 8, No. 3, September 1971, pp. 28–33.
62. Reference was previously made to the two new funding windows—IFC and IDA—established by the World Bank. The GATT reaction was the incorporation into its legal framework of a new Part IV to cater to some of the specific trading problems of the developing countries.
63. For the historical details, see Karl P. Sauvant, *The Group of 77: Evolution, Structure, Organization*, New York, Oceana Publications, 1981, p. 3. Already a process of Third World institutionalization—in the political sphere—had emerged with the creation of the non-aligned movement in the mid-1950s. Another significant institution created to increase bargaining capabilities among a particular group of developing countries was OPEC in 1960. In short, the 1960s were to signify the era of Third World concertation, through institution-building, to strengthen negotiating capacity *vis-à-vis* the developed countries.
64. Ibid., p. 3.
65. See 'The Declaration and Principles of the Action Programme of Lima', 7 November 1971 in Peter Mutharika, comp. and ed., *The International Law of Development: Basic Documents*, Vol. 4, New York, Oceana Publications, 1979, p. 2433.
66. Ibid.
67. In terms of external economic impact, the important measures were the suspension of convertibility of foreign-held dollars into gold and other reserve assets in the monetary field, and the imposition of a 10 per cent import surcharge in the commercial area.
68. See Chapter 5 herein for further details.
69. IMF, *Annual Report*, 1972, pp. 1–2.
70. Floating, rather than fixed, exchange rates became the norm among the currencies of the major industrialized countries during the 1970s.
71. For a discussion, see Spero, op. cit., p. 48.
72. See Chapter 4 for details.
73. Margaret Garritsen de Vries, 'Economic Shocks of the 1970s Viewed as Signs of Profound Change in World Relationships', *IMF Survey*, 7 January 1980, p. 5.
74. See OECD, *The Impact of the Newly Industrializing Countries on Production and Trade in Manufactures* (Report by the Secretary-General), Paris, 1979.
75. As Bergsten put it, *détente* defined a downgrading of the East–West conflict as the dominant global issue-area and '[a]s a result, dependence on the United States by its allies has greatly diminished and the salience of the security issue has been greatly reduced. Economic differences would thus rise toward the surface even if they had not themselves increased in magnitude.'—see C. Fred Bergsten, *Managing International Economic Interdependence: Selected Papers of C. Fred Bergsten, 1975–76*, Lexington, Mass., Lexington Books, 1977, p. 6.
76. That is, decolonization in the sense of formal political independence. Apart from the remnants of colonialism in Southern Africa, that were to remain problematic for the other extant colonies, political independence was merely a matter of time.
77. As Bedjaoui stated it: 'The second phase, which is that of "supplementary" but completely decisive revolution, consists in the gradual erosion of the privileges of the dominating foreign power. This is economic decolonization. It has to include a series of changes which are more profound and more gradual ... [and] carry through to their conclusion the incomplete or uncertain achievements of the first revolution, the acquisition of political independence'—see Mohammed Bedjaoui, *Towards a new international economic order*, Paris, UNESCO, 1979, p. 88.
78. These included renegotiation of concession agreements, new tax and royalty

arrangements, majority ownership and participation and the decisive act—the nationalization of foreign-owned investments.

79. See Jahangir Amuzegar, *Oil Exporters' Economic Development in an Interdependent World*, Occasional Paper No. 18, IMF, Washington DC, April 1983, p. 3.

80. IMF, *Summary Proceedings of the 31st Annual Meeting of the Board of Governors* (hereinafter *Summary Proceedings*), Washington DC, 1976, p. 15.

81. Source: IBRD, *World Development Report*, 1980, p. 10.

82. See IMF, *World Economic Outlook*, June 1981, pp. 45–6.

83. See IBRD, *World Development Report*, 1981, pp. 49–53. As one analyst has written: 'The role of the private banks in international monetary relations has been greatly enhanced as a result of repeated increases in oil prices since 1973, which have generated enormous financing problems for many oil-importing countries . . . The recycling of the surplus earnings of OPEC countries . . . has . . . fallen primarily to private credit markets'—see Benjamin J. Cohen, 'Balance-of-payments financing: evolution of a regime', *International Organization*, 36, No. 2, Spring 1982, p. 457.

84. For a discussion, see IBRD, *World Development Report*, 1981, p. 52. See also UNCTAD VI, *International financial and monetary issues* (Report by the UNCTAD Secretariat), TD/275, 26 January 1983, p. 48, para. 201.

85. Source: OECD, *The Impact of the Newly Industrializing Countries in Production and Trade of Manufactures*, p. 19.

86. Source: Albert Fishlow *et al.*, *Trade in Manufactured Products with Developing Countries: Reinforcing North–South Partnership*, New York, The Trilateral Commission, 1981, p. 23.

87. See IMF, *World Economic Outlook*, 1984, pp. 60–1.

88. For a discussion, see Jacques J. Polak, 'The Role of the Fund' in *The International Monetary System: Forty Years after Bretton Woods* (Proceedings of a Conference held at Bretton Woods, New Hampshire, May 1984), pp. 245–71.

89. *General Assembly Official Records*, A/PV 2208 (Sixth Special Session), 10 April 1974, p. 4.

90. As Hansen wrote: 'the Northern response to the challenge to the present international political and economic order raised by the Arab oil embargo and the quadrupling of oil prices by OPEC was one that caused considerable dissension within the North itself . . . [I]t led to a short period of intense competition for special bilateral relationships which further threatened Northern cohesion in the face of OPEC's actions'—Roger D. Hansen, *Beyond the North–South Stalemate*, New York, McGraw-Hill, 1979, p. 22. See also C. Fred Bergsten, 'The Threat from the Third World', *Foreign Policy*, No. 11, Summer 1973, pp. 102–24.

91. As Bhagwati noted: 'reliance on commodity exports, which had always been thought of as a sign of dependence and the necessity for industrialization, was now considered a source of strength! The economic concept of "commodity power" was born'—see Jagdish N. Bhagwati and John Gerard Ruggie, eds, *Power, Passion and Purpose: Prospects for North–South Negotiations*, Cambridge, Mass., The MIT Press, 1984, p. 23.

92. See Corea, op. cit., pp. 6–9.

93. Jagdish N. Bhagwati, 'Why there is no mileage left in Global Negotiations', *The World Economy*, 6, No. 2, June 1983, p. 137.

94. As Amuzegar has stressed, when all is said and done, these countries remain developing countries, as evidenced from economic structures, basic monocultural production and export activities, shortage of skilled labour, low literacy and life expectancy rates and early-stage industrialization—see Amuzegar, *Oil Exporters' Economic Development in an Interdependent World*, pp. 9–11. What is more, OPEC had two basic worries—the reaction of the other developing countries to the price

increases and that of the developed countries. They were also hearing threats of military action from developed-country spokesmen. Unity with the developing countries was therefore an important safeguard in both cases.

95. See 'Declaration of the OPEC Summit Conference, 1975', Algiers, 6 March 1975, in Alfred George Moss & Harry Winston, comp., *A New International Economic Order; Selected Documents*, 1945–75, Vol. 1, New York, UNITAR, pp. 621–8.

96. Thus it is that a State Department spokesman, in Congressional testimony, recorded official surprise at the unity of the Third World in the aftermath of the oil price increase in 1973. Replying to a question as to whether the increase should lead to pressure on the Arab world, he remarked: 'We believe that it should, and, in fact, I think we have been a little surprised at the developing countries, that the developing countries have not spoken out more strongly about the disastrous effects that these new high prices can have on them'—see *Hearings before the Sub-committee on Europe and the Near East and South Asia of the Committee on Foreign Affairs*, 93rd Congress, 1st and 2nd Sessions, 1 November 1973 and 19 February 1974, US Government Printing Office, Washington DC, 1974, p. 53.

97. As Bedjaoui put it: '*il n'est pas exagéré d'affirmer que dans l'histoire du non-alignment, la conférence de Bandeong de 1955 et celle de Belgrade de 1961 ont été à la lutte de libération politique ce que la conférence d'Alger de 1973 à été au combat d'émancipation économique des pays du Tier-Monde*'—Mohammed Bedjaoui, '*Non-Alignment et Droit International*', *Recueil des Cours*, III, 1976, p. 428.

98. See *Proceedings of the United Nations Conference on Trade and Development*, Vol. 1a, Part 1, Third Session, Santiago de Chile, 1973, p. 186.

99. For a discussion of the Charter negotiations, see Robert F. Meagher, *An International Redistribution of Wealth and Power: a Study of the Charter of Economic Rights and Duties of States*, New York, Pergamon Press, 1979.

100. By no means were these analyses reflective of a monolithic diagnosis of the problem: they ranged in fact from conformist perspectives to dependency and Marxist theoretical outlooks. A review of the literature on the NIEO, including Western writings, can be found in Robert W. Cox 'Ideologies and the New International Economic Order: Reflections on Some Recent Literature', *International Organization*, Vol. 33, No. 2, Spring 1979, pp. 257–302.

101. Mahbub ul Haq, *The Poverty Curtain: Choices for the Third World*, New York, Columbia University Press, 1976. p. 84.

102. This is what Cox has called 'a counter-hegemonic challenge' to the Bretton Woods consensus or hegemony—Cox, 'The crisis of world order and the problems of international organization in the 1980s', op. cit., pp. 385–94.

103. For a discussion, see ul Haq, op. cit., pp. 153–62. Proposals for international regulation of markets in primary commodities, preferential treatment and the negation of reciprocity in trade relations between developed and developing countries are symptomatic of this tendency. Producers' associations, control of the activities of TNCs, the right to permanent sovereignty over natural resources and its corollary, the right to nationalization, are all regulative processes tending at once to weaken the market-oriented approach to international economic relations and to validate international and national intervention in economic arrangements.

104. The concept of affirmative action is to some extent apprehended in Polanyi's 'principle of social protection'—see Karl Polanyi, *The Great Transformation*, Beacon Hill, Boston, Beacon Press, 1957, p. 132.

105. For a discussion, see Bedjaoui, *Towards a new international economic order*, op. cit., Ch. 1.

106. For a discussion, see Branislav Gosovic & John Gerard Ruggie, 'On the creation of a new international economic order; issue linkage and the Seventh Special Session

of the UN General Assembly', *International Organization*, **30**, No. 2, Spring 1976, pp. 309–45. A critical assessment of CIEC may be found in Jahangir Amuzegar, 'A Requiem for the North–South Conference', *Foreign Affairs*, October 1977, pp. 136–59.

107. 'Address by President Nyerere to the Fourth Ministerial Meeting of the Group of 77', 12 February 1979, in UNCTAD, *Arusha Programme for Collective Self-reliance and Framework for Negotiations*, Manila, May 1979, Doc. TD/236, Annex II, p. 5.

108. What should not be overlooked was the transformed political outlook in the United States towards developing countries after 1979 in the aftermath of the Marxist takeover in Nicaragua and Grenada; the collapse of the reliable American ally in Iran and the climaxing event of the Soviet intervention in Afghanistan. In the American view, these events marked the unravelling of *détente* and a resultant re-emergence of the East–West axis in international relations and ensured for that country a downgrading of the North–South economic agenda.

109. See IBRD, *World Development Report*, 1980, p. 14.

110. Source: IBRD, *World Development Report*, 1983, p. 1.

111. IMF, *World Economic Outlook*, May 1980, p. 3.

112. See 'Communiqué of the Interim Committee of the Board of Governors, IMF, 13th Meeting, 1 October 1979, as carried in IMF, *Annual Report*, 1980, p. 152.

113. See 'Excerpts from remarks on "The IMF and the Developing Countries"' by the Managing Director: University of Neuchâtel, Switzerland, 3 March 1983, *IMF Survey*, 7 March 1983, p. 73.

114. For a background discussion, see 'Fund Historian traces origins and development of Fund involvement in the world debt problem', *IMF Survey*, 17 January 1985, pp. 1–4.

115. IMF, *Annual Report*, 1983, p. 29.

116. Ibid.

117. 'Fund Historian traces origins . . . debt problem', op. cit., p. 3.

118. See Alden W. Clausen, 'Third World Debt and Global Recovery', *Aussenwirtschaft*, September 1983, p. 249. See also IMF, *Annual Report*, 1983, p. 18.

119. Bahram Nowzad, 'The Extent of IMF Involvement in Economic Policy-Making', *The AMEX Bank Review Special Papers*, No. 7, 1983, p. 16.

120. This clearly portended a split within the Third World. Apart from the effects of the oil price increase on their economies, the non-oil developing countries were displeased not so much with OPEC's quantitative aid as with the geographical distribution of this aid. In fact, OPEC aid when measured in terms of GNP was superior to that of the OECD. Distributionally, however, the bulk of this aid was geographically concentrated among a few Arab and Muslim African states—for a study of OPEC aid, see Paul Hallwood and Stuart Sinclair, *Oil, Debt and Development: OPEC in the Third World*, London, George Allen & Unwin, 1981, Ch. 6.

121. See John P. Renniger & James Zech, *The 11th Special Session and the Future of Global Negotiations*, New York, UNITAR, September 1981, pp. 5–6.

122. Muchkund Dubey, 'A Third World Perspective' in Bhagwati and Ruggie, eds, op. cit., p. 77.

123. Renniger and Zech, op. cit., p. 6.

Part II

The Decision-Making Process in the IMF:
The Challenge of the Third World

Chapter 3
The formal and informal aspects

1. Introduction

The history of the institutional organization of international society has manifested consistently a crucial tension as regards the structuring of processes of decision making. As Jenks has stated it:

> There is no more difficult problem confronting international organisations today than that of evolving modes of taking important decisions which will command general respect and give such decisions the weight necessary to make them effective in practice. The problem has been a continuing one throughout the history of international organisation and we are still far from having achieved any satisfactory solution of it.[1]

The crux of the dilemma posed by decision making in international organizations revolves around the adherence in international relations to the principle of the sovereign equality of states[2] in juridical terms, and the reality of the material inequalities that distinguish states—in respect of population, territorial size, economic capabilities and military strength. The problem, then, has been to reconcile these tensions, in a practical way, through appropriate methods of decision making.

More precisely, the tension has been between advocates of absolutist versions of equality, on the one side, and of relative equality, on the other.[3] The practical manifestations of the absolutist version—rationalized as flowing from a strict observance of the sovereign equality of states—have been in the rules and standards of equality in voting and representation. These have typically been the one nation/one vote rule, equal representation, and unanimity in the taking of decisions.[4] Contrastingly, relative equality has been mirrored in rules and procedures for decision making that define inequalities in voting strength and representation: the granting of veto power and permanent representation on limited membership organs to powerful states and the majority basis for decisions.[5]

The problem, therefore, has been:

> to find an arrangement which would show a measurable and acceptable relation between authority and responsibility, which would exclude no participant arbitrarily from a share in authority, while bringing the share into relation not to sheer power but to the weight of responsibility carried by the several members.[6]

Attempts to devise workable structures of decision making that stand a chance of promoting the mandates of international organizations have shown a tendency to take account of three factors. These are the dimensions of the material inequalities that actually exist among states, the nature of the functional tasks of the particular organization and the legal effects that flow from its decisions. Where material inequalities are significant—as regards, for instance, a nation's capacity to contribute to the resources of the institution—and where the sweep of authority of the institution is likely to have a substantial impact on a nation's interests[7] and decisions carry with them the consequence of an obligatory implementation, then the trend has been towards a diminution of the appeal of absolutist perspectives of equality and the elevation of relative equality in designing systems of decision making.

2. The decision-making process of the IMF—a retrospective vantage-point

In the immediate post-Second World War years, two separate trends in the organization of international society became evident. The first trend is associated with the San Francisco Conference of 1945 that resulted in the United Nations family of organizations, while the second trend is associated with the Bretton Woods Conference. At San Francisco, the basic political framework for the conduct of international relations was constructed. The juridical core of the United Nations Charter is the sovereign equality of states and, in respect of decision making, it is operationalized in the one-state/one-vote rule in the several decision-making organs of the institution. Yet, there are two features of this process that have served to moderate the full effect of this apparent egalitarianism.

These two features emerge if we look at the two principal United Nations organs: the General Assembly and the Security Council. Decisions of the General Assembly are couched in the form of recommendations—that is, except for those decisions that bear on the internal functioning of the Assembly itself, which have an obligatory force for the addressees. Recommendations do not carry for the membership the same legal consequences as do binding decisions of an international organization, depending as they ultimately do on the sovereign will of the various states as to whether they shall be implemented or not. To a large extent, moreover, the recommendatory essence of the General Assembly resolution flows from the nature of the task mandate that was conferred on this body—the fact that its competence, though sweeping in respect of subject matter, is essentially one of deliberation. In contrast, not only does the Security Council's mandate grant it the power to take enforcement action againt delinquent member-states under Chapter 7 of the Charter, but its decisions are also binding on the membership as a whole in consequence of Article 25. These considerations were behind the veto power that was given to the five permanent members of the Security Council—another clear derogation from the equality principle.[8]

Turning to the Bretton Woods Conference, it is not evident from the historical records—both of the pre-Conference informal consultations and the Conference proceedings themselves—that the proposal for a system of weighted voting in the IMF aroused any degree of controversy.[9] Already, in the nineteenth century a measure of practical experience with weighted voting arrangements, specifically in the functional organizations, had been built up.[10] Thus, as regards decision making in the IMF, even though there were several criticisms and counter-proposals, these had to do with the question of the criteria to be used in the allocation of voting power, rather than the principle of weighted voting *per se*. Moreover, as will shortly be seen, these criticisms emanated from a variety of countries, rather than a particular group of countries.

The earliest drafts that served as the basis for Anglo–American discussion of the Fund did underscore a concern that the decision-making structure to be agreed on should ensure that the responsibilities and authority of the major powers were safeguarded. Keynes' 1942 draft of the Clearing Union proposal would, in fact, have secured a special decision-making role for the United States and the United Kingdom through a designation of 'founder-States'[11] status to these two countries. The implication of founder-States status was clearly outlined in the proposal:

> ... it would be an advantage if the proposed Union could be brought into existence by the United States and the United Kingdom as joint founder-States ... *The management and the effective voting powers might inhere permanently in the founder-States* [emphasis added].[12]

In the event that this proposal for permanent decision-making control by the United States and the United Kingdom failed to win acceptance, the Keynes plan presented the option of a temporary period of Anglo–American dominance.[13] This proposal of permanent Anglo–American management control or at the least a temporary period of such control, was to go farther than anything the Americans were to propose.

Interestingly, the earliest American version of the Fund[14] posed in definitive terms the problem of voting power in an institutional setting comprising small and large states:

> ... the real problem is how to distribute the voting power. If each member of the board were to be given an equal vote, then the small country that invested one million dollars would have as much power in making decisions as a country that has subscribed a hundred or a thousand times that amount. With the possibility that the number of small countries participating will be much greater than the large countries, a one-vote-one-member arrangement is palpably unwise.[15]

If this American statement of the issue showed a sharp perception of the essential dilemma raised by the presence of small and large states—and the resultant potential for unequal contributions to the resources of the institution— for decision making, then the American response to the other side of the issue, as formulated by the British in its elitist conception of decision-making, just as sharply perceived the untenability of any such arrangement:

> On the other hand, to accord voting power strictly proportionate to the value of subscription would give the one or two powers control over the Fund. To

do that would destroy the truly international character of the Fund, and seriously jeopardize its success. Indeed, it is very doubtful if many countries would be willing to participate in an international organization with wide powers if one or two countries were to be able to control its policies.[16]

American coolness to the idea of a special founder-States status for the United Kingdom and the United States alone was paralleled, in the early informal consultations, by the criticism of several other countries with which the United Kingdom was in consultation.[17] Against this background, the United States ostensibly sought to design a decision-making arrangement that would avoid the two extremes of strict equalitarianism or permanent elitism.

There was a definite evolution in British thinking on decision making for the IMF by the time of its second version of the Clearing Union proposal of April 1943. The presentation of the issue was then framed in terms similar to that of the United States: 'The management of the Institution must be genuinely international without preponderant power of veto or enforcement to any country or group; and the rights and privileges of the smaller countries must be safeguarded'.[18] One can only speculate that this fundamental change in British outlook was largely influenced by the coolness of the United States and the criticisms of other countries of their earlier extremist formulation.

In the event, Anglo–American negotiations culminated in a consensus on the question of voting arrangements and other structural aspects of decision making for the IMF. Agreement was reached on the principle of weighted voting, on the creation of a governing board and an executive committee as the main management organs and on the principle of majority decision making.[19] As envisaged in the 'Joint Statement', the board was conceived as the plenary forum, with each member-country having the right of representation thereon, while the executive committee was seen as a limited-membership organ.[20]

There is no record that the principle of weighted voting was disputed at Bretton Woods: rather, its endorsement was clearly stated. This emerged during the deliberations of the Committee on Organization and Management and it was indicated that:

> the Committee realized that the management of the Fund has to be pre-
> pared to deal with possible or potential conflicts of interest which ultimately
> may have to be voted upon. There was no doubt that in the management of
> the Fund large countries should have stronger representation—and certain
> privileges.[21]

There were criticisms, however, of certain aspects of the voting proposals. Dissatisfaction hinged basically on the vital question of the criteria to be used for the allocation of quotas—and, hence, of votes in the Fund[22]—and on the dominant voting power and effective veto that would accrue to the United States under the system of weighted voting.[23]

Determination of a country's contribution to the resources of the institution, it was proposed, should be based on a formula taking account of seven factors indicative of the country's economic strength and, to a minor degree, of its international trade.[24] Despite attempts by several countries to have included criteria, other than purely economic ones,[25] the ultimate decision was an allocative system based entirely on economic criteria. Allocation of votes, then, was to be reflective of the relative economic importance of the member-states in the international economy.

At the same time, it was agreed at Bretton Woods to moderate somewhat the effects of a weighted voting arrangement that depended solely on the economic strength of countries. A system of allocation of a certain uniform number of votes—basic votes—to every member was introduced. Sponsored by the United States, the principle of basic votes mirrored that country's concern, earlier alluded to, to give smaller countries a sense of participation in the institution and to simultaneously dilute the preponderant control that would flow to the large nations under a procedure of voting allocations determined exclusively by economic criteria.[26]

Another feature of decision making adopted at the Bretton Woods Conference was that of majority voting. In the preliminary Anglo–American discussions, there was one respect in which there was a fundamental divergence of views, notwithstanding acceptance of the principle of majority decision making. This disagreement related to the American proposal that, though decision making in general should be governed by a simple majority vote, certain decisions should require higher majorities for approval.[27] The special majority advanced by the Americans for these important decisions was set at 80 per cent. The British objected to the proposal on the ground of the veto power such a requirement would grant the United States over many of the Fund's decisions.[28] Once again, this Anglo–American divergence was resolved during their bilateral exchanges with an understanding that the 80 per cent majority requirement would be preserved, but for a far more limited number of decisions.[29] Other countries made known their discontent with this question of voting majorities, especially the practical effect of the 80 per cent majority that granted the United States alone a veto power.[30] In the end, however, the United States view prevailed and the original Fund Articles of Agreement subscribed to simple majority voting for the majority of Fund decisions, and high special majorities for a few important decisions.

Finally, the tripartite structural division of the Fund into (i) a plenary; (ii) an Executive Board and (iii) a Secretariat, headed by a managing director, did not cause any particular controversy. This structural division was based on the original proposal in the 'White Plan'.[31] There was a measure of disagreement, though, as regards the proposals pertaining to the Executive Directors—specifically their functional status and membership composition, with several of the smaller countries tabling proposals that would have favourably increased their presence on the Executive Board. None of the proposals, however, would have fundamentally disturbed the objective of having five of the Directors represent, as a right, the countries with the five largest quotas in the Fund.

In short, the divergences that emerged at Bretton Woods in respect of decision making had to do with the operational details, rather than the general principles, proposed for the taking of decisions. Concern with details reflected the interest of individual countries in striking the best possible deal in terms of voting influence. In so far as the developing countries were concerned, whatever individual proposals were made were guided by similar considerations. As Marquez has observed:

> As for the developing countries, it seems that, generally speaking, they were not so much concerned about their absolute as about their relative importance ... But even this tendency was not very consistent, since for example Mexico, which was offered a quota similar to that allotted to Brazil, did not mind transferring $10 million of it to two other Latin American countries.[32]

None of the decision-making proposals, either at the level of principles or operational details, generated any major controversy from the side of developing countries at Bretton Woods.

3. Decision making in the IMF: the formal apparatus

Any description of the formal apparatus of decision making in the IMF would necessarily have to proceed on three levels. On the first, it would entail an outline of the rules and norms that govern the taking of decisions and the structural division of authority in the institution. Secondly, it would have to analytically relate these decisional features to the functional scope of the IMF and the legal effects of its decisions. Finally, formal decision making cannot be separated from the constitutional provisions for amendment. This is for the simple reason that dissatisfaction with the extant decision-making process by any country or group of countries can lead to a movement for change, depending on the ease—or conversely the difficulty—with which change can be effected through the constitutional amending process.

(a) The rules of decision making—weighted and majority voting

There are two essential rules governing Fund decision making. These are the rules of weighted and majority voting. Weighted voting can be defined as:

> a system which assigns to members of international organizations votes proportioned on the basis of predetermined relevant criteria; it can mean something as simple as so many votes per so many millions of population, or something as complex as a mathematical formula based upon multiple factors which have been assigned varying weights.[33]

As already indicated, in the Fund votes are weighted overwhelmingly on the basis of the quotas allotted to each member, modified slightly by the allocation to each member of a uniform number of votes; the formula is the aggregate of 250 basic votes plus one vote for each SDR 100,000 contributed to Fund resources.[34] The criteria that determine quotas stress the importance of the particular country in the world economy, and thus its capacity to contribute the convertible financial resources required by the Fund in its operations.[35] The distribution of quotas, therefore, is intended to closely reflect the relative economic importance of member-countries.

The granting of basic votes has not to any significant extent diminished this outcome of a procedure that relates voting rights to economic strength.[36] This is explainable by several factors. Basic votes represent a small proportion of the global quantum of votes granted most members at any particular moment.[37] Then there is the fact that the Fund's constitution makes no provision for increases in the number of basic votes on a periodic basis to keep in step with increases in quotas. The basic votes have thus remained unchanged over the life of the Fund at 250 votes. Finally, over the years, quotas have in fact increased substantially, with a consequential diminution of the relative share of basic votes in terms of total votes. As shown in Table 3.1, the share of basic votes has declined from a high of 11.3 per cent in 1946 to a mere 5.6 per cent in 1982.

Table 3.1 Basic votes as a proportion of
total votes (selected years)

Year	%
1946	11.3
1960	10.3
1970	10.3
1975	9.9
1980	5.1
1982	5.6

Source: Lister, op. cit., p. 40.

What this has meant is that the major countries, economically, have been assured of an overwhelming dominance when voting shares are taken into account. Contrastingly, the smaller countries—mainly, though not exclusively developing countries—have, individually and collectively, represented a minority shareholding in the decision-making process. Significantly, also, despite the expressed concern of the United States during the formative stages of discussion on the Fund to avoid giving to any country preponderant or veto power, the reality is that the system of weighted voting did result in the United States having a preponderance of the voting rights and an effective veto over substantive decisions of the Fund. The distribution of votes is provided in Table 3.2—and, as is evident, among the original membership, the United States alone carried 33.5 per cent of the total votes in 1946, the developed countries as a whole 74.4 per cent and the developing countries 25.6 per cent. Over the years there has been a gradual reduction of the shares of both the United States and the developed countries, and a correlative increase in that of the developing countries, as a group, but this change has not been radical enough to upset the balance of power in the IMF, as manifested in terms of raw voting power.[38]

Table 3.2 Distribution of votes in IMF—selected years, 1946–1985

	1946	1960	1965	1971	1978	1985
Developed countries	74.4	73.0	67.3	70.2	63.7	63.2
of which, US	33.5	26.1	22.5	21.9	19.9	19.2
of which, EEC	12.8	17.3	16.2	18.3	25.5	26.5
Developing countries	25.6	27.0	32.7	29.9	36.6	35.6
of which, OPEC	—	—	4.2	5.0	9.8	11.0
Others	—	—	—	—	0.5	1.1

Source: For years 1946 through 1971, UNCTAD, *The International Monetary Situation; Report by the Secretariat of UNCTAD* (TD/140/Rev. 1), 1982, Annex 1. For years thereafter, *IMF Survey*, 18 September 1978 and IMF, *Directory*, 18 March 1985.

The second fundamental rule of Fund decision making is that of majority voting. Most decisions of the Fund require a simple majority vote,[39] but higher majorities are necessary for certain identified categories of decisions[40] and '[t]he tendency has been to confine the smaller majority to operational decisions that are not routine but are nevertheless not of the same importance as the decisions for which the larger majority is required.'[41]

The wider array of high special majorities, specified under the original Articles of Agreement, covered only a limited number of decisions—in fact, nine decisions. As a result, however, of the first and second amendments of the Agreement, there has been an expansion in the number of decisions that require special majorities—to 18 after the first amendment, and to 39 after the second.[42] There was a parallel simplification, through reduction, of the number of special majorities after the second amendment to two—70 per cent and 85 per cent majorities.

In seeking to comprehend the voting arrangements in the IMF, one has to draw the clear interconnection between differential voting power and the majority principle, in particular the requirement of high majorities for the crucial decisions of the Fund. High majorities have served two basic purposes: they have given important members or groups of members, acting together, a veto over the most important decisions of the organization, and when allied with weighted voting, have had the effect of elevating the search for consensus in the taking of decisions:

> Qualified majorities make it easier for countries to resist developments they do not like, but they also make it more difficult to get action on proposals which they favor ... Where there is a conflict in the wishes of important groups of countries, a system of qualified majorities will obviously force a delay in action until an acceptable compromise is reached.[43]

Where enough countries or groups of countries have the requisite voting strength to block important decisions because of the requirement of high majorities, then the efficacious functioning of the institution can only proceed on the basis of compromise and the search for common ground.

Contemporaneously, only the United States, acting alone, has veto power over decisions that require 85 per cent of the voting power. Over the history of the Fund, no other country has had this broad veto right. However, groups of countries—the EEC and the developing countries—now have enough votes to block decisions demanding an 85 per cent majority, while the latter group and the Group of Ten countries[44] both dispose of the necessary voting strength to veto decisions requiring the 70 per cent majority. In a word, in respect of their practical effects, the combined rules of weighted voting and majority decision making have served as a system of checks and balances to protect the interests of specific members or groups of members, on the one hand, and have facilitated another Fund decision-making practice—the consensus mode.

(b) The practice of consensus in Fund decision making

In reality, voting has been a rare occurrence in the taking of decisions in the IMF.[45] The actual practice observed in the Fund is decision making by way of consensus.[46] This practice is employed in the two formal decision-making organs—the Board of Governors and the Executive Board—and in *ad hoc* and other committees established by the competent organs of the Fund.

The consensus procedure has been underwritten in the supplemental sources of law in the IMF—the *By-Laws and Rules and Regulations*.[47] It is specified in the 'Rules and Regulations', under the provision regarding voting in the Executive Board, that: 'The Chairman shall ordinarily ascertain the sense of the meeting in lieu of a formal vote. Any Executive Director may require a formal vote to be taken.'[48] A similar stipulation is provided in the 'By-Laws' in respect of voting in the Board of Governors.[49] The consensus procedure is the sole method for taking decisions in any special committees set up by the Fund.[50]

The definition of 'the sense of the meeting', adopted by the Executive Directors in 1947, however, underscored that the voting strength of members remains a crucial consideration with regard to the evaluation of consensus on any matter: 'These words [the sense of the meeting] were explicitly defined by the Directors in 1947 to be a position supported by those Directors having sufficient votes to carry the question if a veto were to be taken'.[51] Not only is consensus integrally linked to the fact of the relative voting power of the membership, but always hovering in the background is the constitutional right of members to demand a formal vote at any time.

In the practice of international organizations, as well as in the literature on organizational decision making, in contemporary times, there has been a noticeable trend towards the embracing of consensus decision making. As Jenks has observed, the consensus mode is nothing 'new in international organisation though it is only recently that it has begun to attract attention as a principle and to secure general recognition'.[52] Consensus is both a procedure for the taking of decisions and the ultimate outcome of that procedure—the substantive content of the decision.[53] In this way, a mitigation of conflict, where positions at the beginning diverge immensely, is achieved.

In the Fund, the consensus decision has the same legal effect as a decision by vote; it is not merely recommendatory, but binding for the membership as a whole.[54] The pragmatism of the consensus method has been explained thus by a former Managing Director of the IMF:

> The political reality is that on a major issue you cannot outvote any given group of members, the United States being a group in itself. You cannot outvote the United States, or the Common Market, or the developing countries as a whole. So the major role of the Managing Director is to achieve a consensus; and this allows decisions to be taken with the minimum of fuss.[55]

In the context of the IMF, moreover, the consensus approach has a distinct appeal to all identifiable groups, and the more so with the minority membership, in terms of voting power. The fact is that a mutual veto over all the Fund's important decisions—those requiring the 70 per cent and 85 per cent majorities—is held by both the majority and minority membership, acting together. This mutual veto ensures that a continual ignoring of the minority opposition can never be politically prudent since the latter may, by simply activating its veto power, frustrate the will of the majority. Additionally, no member or group of members, in the absence of an overwhelming convergence of views, can attain the maximal objectives that it espouses.

The attraction for the minority membership, therefore, of consensus decision making is, to begin with, the avoidance of a perennial voting down of their proposals—and, conversely, the automatic adoption of the proposals of the majority. Secondly, the consensus mode provides the minority participants with an opportunity to participate in decision making.[56] Finally, since the consensus procedure entails consultation, negotiation and compromise, it conduces to the achievement of an integration of some of the interests of the minority membership.

(c) The structure of decision making

Constitutionally, the Fund has a tripartite structural division: a Board of Governors, an Executive board and a Secretariat, headed by a Managing Director.[57] Each of these structures was granted clearly defined functions under the Articles of Agreement. The Board of Governors, statutorily, is the principal organ of the Fund. All powers not directly conferred on either the Executive Board or the Managing Director, are vested in the Board of Governors. However, with the exception of certain important powers that are expressly reserved to it, the Board of Governors has the authority to delegate its residual functions to the Executive Board and the maximum such delegation has been made.[58] Since 1974, there has been operating in the Fund an Interim Committee, which was appointed by the Board of Governors in an advisory capacity. Though not a part of the formal decision-making structure, the Interim Committee, because of its significance in the policy-formation process, will also be briefly looked at.

The Board of Governors

This is the plenary organ of the Fund, each member-country being entitled to appoint a Governor and an Alternate Governor thereto.[59] Each Governor may cast the number of votes allocated to the country he/she represents. In essence, then, the Board of Governors combines an element of the egalitarian tradition in decision making by virtue of the provision granting the right of representation in its deliberations to all members, and of the inegalitarian orientation in the weighting of votes that the members may cast. The Board meets annually, and the annual meeting has served as 'an occasion on which a few decisions are taken, but on which the more important activity is the statement by Governors of their views on the policies of the Fund and on the direction it should take'.[60] Herein lies the main importance of the annual meeting to the analyst.

The reserved powers of the Board of Governors include such significant ones, *inter alia*, as the admission of new members, approval of allocations of both quotas and SDRs, and whether to increase or decrease the number of Executive Directors. Nevertheless, the Board of Governors, is, in practice, not the central decision-making organ in the Fund.[61] Even those decisions that it does take are based on the deliberations and recommendations of the Interim Committee or on the preparatory work of the Executive Board.

The Executive Board

The next tier of decision making in the IMF is the Executive Board. The Directors are required to carry out the substantive work of the Fund, in terms of the taking of decisions, and to this end 'shall function in continuous session at the principal office of the Fund and shall meet as often as the business of the Fund may require'.[62] Because of the maximum delegation of its authority by the Board of Governors to the Executive Directors, in conjunction with the substantial decision-making powers directly conferred on it by the Articles of Agreement in regard to the day-to-day operations of the Fund, the Executive Board is the pivotal decision-making organ of the institution: 'The powers exercised by the Executive Board relate to all activities of the Fund, including its regulatory, supervisory and financial activities. The breadth of these powers, the links with members, and continuous session give the Executive Board the central role in the Fund'.[63]

To fully appreciate the significance of the sweep of authority that inheres in the Executive Board, one has to relate it to the composition of the Board's membership. The Executive Board is the limited-membership organ of the Fund.[64] There are two categories of representation on this body: appointed and elected representation. The original Articles of Agreement required at least twelve Directors, five of whom were to be appointed by the members with the five largest quotas, with the rest elected by the remaining membership.[65] Over time, the number of Executive Directors has been augmented to take account of the growing membership[66]—see Table 3.3. Under the prevailing Agreement, provision is made for a minimum of twenty Directors, five appointed and fifteen elected. Moreover, by a decision of the Board of Governors, it is possible for the

Table 3.3 Number and distribution of Executive Directors among groups of countries: selected years—1946–1982

	1946	1950	1956	1960	1964	1978	1982
Total Directors	12	14	16	18	20	21	22
Developed countries	6	8	11	11	11	11	11
Developing countries	4	5	4	6	8	9	11*
Others†	2	1	1	1	1	–	–
Appointed Directors	5	5	5	5	5	6	6
Developed countries	3	3	3	4	4	5	5
Developing countries	1	1	1	1	1	1	1
Others	1	1	1	–	–	–	–

* Including the People's Republic of China.
† For 1946, Czechoslovakia and the Republic of China and thereafter the latter.
Source: Various IMF publications.

two members—not entitled to appoint Directors because of their quota contributions—whose currencies have been much in use by the Fund in the two years preceding an election, to also appoint Directors.[67]

The five appointed Directors have historically come predominantly from the developed countries. The exceptions until Saudi Arabia in 1978, were India and the Republic of China, both of whom were entitled to appoint Directors from the inception of the Fund. India's entitlement was the accidental outcome of the Soviet Union's decision not to join the IMF, thus permitting its place as one of the envisaged five largest contributors to the institution's financial resources to fall to India. The Republic of China and India ceased appointing Directors in 1960 and 1970, respectively, when they were no longer counted among the five largest contributors. Thus, three developed countries—the United States, the United Kingdom and France—have uninterruptedly appointed Directors over the history of the Fund. West Germany, from 1960, and Japan, since 1970, have been elevated to virtual permanent membership of the Executive Board.

Elections are held biennially to elect the remaining Directors. Countries form themselves into groups, whose voting power aggregate the requisite minimum under the rules of elections,[68] to elect the Director to represent them. If, at the beginning, geography was not a prime determining consideration in the formation of groups, current practice has shown a movement towards this factor. The fact is that, over time, there has evolved a set of consistent groups for the purpose of electing Directors. The Latin American states have always been sub-divided into coherent regional constituencies,[69] and the Asian and African states have also moved in this direction, whereby their elected Directors represent a cluster of geographically-defined countries.[70] Nevertheless, there are still a few developing countries that are represented by Executive Directors from developed countries.[71]

With regard to numerical representation, up to the early 1970s, Directors from developed countries have dominated the Executive Board—see Table 3.3.

Developing nations have, however, substantially improved their presence on the Board over the years. These countries held four of the twelve directorships in 1946 and four of an expanded Board of sixteen in 1956; by the beginning of the 1980s, they shared an equal number of directorships with the developed countries—eleven of a total Board of twenty-two Directors.[72] The argument has been heard that their representation is even more favourable than these pure numbers suggest since those developed-country Directors with developing members in their constituencies have to reflect to some extent during the Board's deliberations, the views of these countries on different issues.[73]

Two other tendencies need to be underlined in regard to the composition of the Executive Board. Apart from the fact that developed countries have dominated at the level of appointed Directors, several other developed countries have been able, because of their large quotas, to repeatedly attract the required votes to ensure election for long periods of time. Thus, Canada, Belgium and The Netherlands have uninterruptedly had their nationals elected to directorships from the inception of the Fund, as have Australia and Italy, dating from their respective membership. The second tendency has been that a few large developing nations, also because of their large voting power relative to the smaller countries, have had their nationals continuously elected to the Board.[74]

The importance of long, uninterrupted periods of service on a central decision-making organ cannot be overstated. Continuous service facilitates the building of a supportive tradition of representation, comprising familiarity with the issues, a keener historical perspective, knowledge of the niceties of procedure and the like—even if personalities change periodically. It facilitates the exercise of influence over an institution's programmes and policies, both at formative and implementative stages of the process.[75] The practice of those constituencies which change country-origin of elected Directors biennially, contrastingly, lessens their overall capacity for influence.[76] New Directors take time to learn about the institution, the issues and the procedures, and in a two-year tenure can never fully master the substance and the processes of the decision environment.[77] And, since this deficiency affects in the main some of the constituencies of developing countries, they have it within their power to elaborate improved mechanisms of representation.

The Interim Committee

This Committee was created in 1974 to take the place of the Committee of Twenty[78] and to bridge the hiatus between the disbandment of the latter and the activation of the proposed Council.[79] It had increasingly been recognized that the periodicity of Board of Governors meetings and the unwieldiness of this forum signified the absence of a body in the Fund with the political authority to take needed decisions on important policy issues. As one Fund Executive Director has written:

As to decision making, the experience of recent years has shown that the Fund lacks an organ at the political level that can substantively decide major questions. By default, these questions have been taken outside the Fund to the ministers and governors of the Group of Ten, to the exclusion of the representatives of other members, the vast majority of which are LDCs. The full Board of Governors of the Fund, where members are represented by ministers and central-bank governors, is obviously too large for effective decision making.[80]

This perception of a decision-making deficiency was the impetus for the proposal of the Council and the actual establishment of the Interim Committee.[81]

The terms of reference of the Interim Committee were to advise the Board of Governors regarding the broad functions of supervising the management and adaptation of the international monetary system and dealing with sudden disturbances potentially threatening to the system. The resolution of the Board of Governors setting up the Interim Committee specified that members should have the status of governors of the Fund, ministers or officials of comparable rank. The Committee is not a part of the formal decision-making structure of the Fund. Nor does it have any binding decision-making powers. Congruent with its position as an advisory body to the Board of Governors, its conclusions have merely recommendatory force.

This Committee is another restricted-membership forum in the Fund and is basically the steering committee of the Board of Governors. Its importance in the decision-making process derives from the fact of the high standing of the members—invariably Ministers of Finance—and the wide sweep of its advisory functions in policy matters.

A major consideration in the holding of one of the Committee's two annual meetings just prior to the Fund's Annual Meeting—the other is normally held in the spring—is to ensure an impact on the decisions that have to be taken by the Board of Governors. And, as the Fund's historian observes, 'the work of the Interim Committee greatly facilitates and expedites the day-to-day work of the Executive Board and of the Fund's management and staff by providing regular guidance on the issues being considered in the Executive Board'.[82] It is from this perspective that the deliberations and conclusions of the Interim Committee touch each of the formal decision-making structures in the Fund. The political force of the Committee's conclusions over the years has made it 'an integral and key part of the Fund's policy-making machinery'.[83]

(d) Legal effects of decisions and the mandate of the IMF

This delineation of the basic features of formal decision making in the Fund is ultimately meaningless, unless placed in relation to the scope of the substantive mandate of the institution[84] and the legal effects of its decisions. With respect to the latter, as Zamora has noted: 'Decisions made by international organizations are not all of the same force or effect'.[85] The main distinction in this regard is between the recommendatory or obligatory effect of a decision.

As far as the IMF is concerned, its decisions have a binding force on member-states. The Articles of Agreement stipulate that accession to membership entails a series of obligations in international and national monetary affairs. The language of the various provisions speaks definitively in terms of obligations and the Fund member is enjoined to take 'all necessary steps to enable it to carry out all its obligations under this Agreement'[86] in accordance with national law.

The binding effect of Fund decisions relates to areas of fundamental national, economic interests for member-states.[87] As already indicated, the substantive mandate of the IMF embraces regulatory, financial and consultative responsibilities. The regulatory function originally extended to critical questions relating to a country's exchange rate policy and general foreign exchange practices:

> The power to approve or disapprove par values was conceptually the most important provision in the Articles: this was the first time that states had agreed to such an invasion of sovereignty. The Second Amendment of the Articles terminated this power unless at some future time a system of par values is reinstated by nearly unanimous agreement. But the 'surveillance' mandate in the new Article IV does give the Fund substantial authority to evaluate the adequacy of exchange rates.[88]

Regarding its financial task, not only was the Fund required to manage the large currency resources contributed by the membership, but its lending mandate allowed the Fund, through the conditionality requirements, to delve even deeper into areas of national policy-making. Finally, members have an obligation to provide a broad range of information on their economic performance, 'even if the member regarded it as sensitive and was not publishing it'.[89] In a word, the Fund's mandate embraces vital areas of a country's economic organization and performance.

Countries do not give up to international organizations sovereign control over vital national interests such as these without the assurance of certain checks and balances to the broad sweep of the institution's authority. As a former Managing Director has stated it:

> ... I do not think that it is realistic to expect countries to sacrifice the freedom to make decisions unilaterally unless they get in return what they consider to be appropriate participation in multilateral decisions. In an international organization charged with making decisions bearing on the economic interests of member countries, power has to be exercised according to three criteria. Firstly, it has to reflect realistically the importance of various members in the world economy; secondly, it has to recognize the special interests of members, especially the smaller or poorer countries, in decisions which touch their vital interests; thirdly, it must be sufficient to overcome the capricious objections of individual members to the clearly expressed and soundly-based will of the majority.[90]

There is, thus, an interconnection between the nature of an organization's responsibilities and the arrangements for the taking of decisions. The combination of the binding force of decisions and a substantive mandate is the basis for the rules of weighted voting and majority decision making. These rules, theoretically, represent the protective superstructure of checks to the misuse of power. Conversely, in the pragmatic practice of consensus, one of the balancing mechanisms of the process, the decision-making structure seeks to guarantee workability and the carrying-out of decisions. Finally, these factors of the obligatory effects of decisions and a substantive mandate are the foundation for another decision-making facet, that is the formal requirements for change embodied in the amendment process of the IMF.

(e) The Amendment Process

The significance of the amendment procedure of an international organization relates to the fact that organizations represent the consensual will of the participants. The constitution is the juridical embodiment of this will. A decision to change aspects of the organization's operations that are constitutionally-bound requires, logically, the consensus agreement of the membership.

It is for this reason that amendments to the Fund's Articles of Agreement are difficult to achieve. Amendments entail a double majority for approval—three-fifths of the members, on the one hand, and 85 per cent of the total voting power, on the other.[91] Gold has elucidated further the rationale for this double majority:

> A requirement of acceptance in terms of proportions of both membership and voting power is common in the charters of financial organizations because of the weighted voting power of members. The purpose of the double requirement is to ensure that amendments will not be effected by a large number of members with a small proportion of the voting power or by a small number of members even though they have a large proportion of the total voting power.[92]

The practical consequence of this amending procedure in the Fund is that, as things presently stand, the United States, the EEC countries, the developed and developing countries, when acting together, all have a veto power over constitutional amendments. Fundamental change in the IMF is thus potentially constrained by the difficulty inherent in the amending process.

4. The informal practices of decision making

Organizations have shown a tendency to evolve a set of informal practices—outside the ambit of formal decision-making arrangements—that at once have a dynamic of their own and that have an important relationship to the formal process. Understanding these informal practices is a crucial aspect of coming to terms with decision making in an organization:

> It is impossible to understand the nature of a formal organization without investigating the networks of informal relations and the unofficial norms as well as the formal hierarchy of authority and the official body of rules, since

the formally instituted and the informally emerging patterns are inextricably intertwined.[93]

Decision making in the Fund has evidenced over the years the observance of such a pattern of informal practices. For the purposes of the analysis, two categories of practice have been isolated for treatment: (a) the group process and (b) the phenomenon of organization-in-contact.[94]

(a) Groups in the Fund

One practice that has come to substantially affect decision making in the IMF is that of group politics. Groups have developed into integral parts of the political process in international organizations. In the Fund, groups do not have any constitutional or formal status in terms of decision making. Yet, they have attained an informal recognition and a practical efficacy in the functioning of the institution.[95]

The group process had its origins in the formation of the Group of Ten (G10) in 1962, as a direct offshoot of the negotiations among these countries for the General Arrangements to Borrow (GAB).[96] The establishment of the G10 basically signified an informal opening-up of the management structure for international monetary relations to include the European countries. This was a clear informal recognition of the new economic influence of a revitalized Europe in the international economy. Hereafter, the G10[97] was to assume a major decision-making role in the Fund, by virtue firstly of their initiating action—outside the framework of the institution—on the principal international monetary issues and, secondly, the evolution of a consensus on the solutions to the issues. Because of their overwhelming voting strength, prior agreement among the G10 had meant that the IMF served merely to endorse their decisions:

> There can be no doubt that the Group of 10 countries, meeting in their various forums, have usurped an important part of the decision-making responsibility that the founding fathers of the Fund had intended to vest in the Fund's Executive Board. The Board, therefore, may on occasions be reduced to rubber stamping propositions put to it by the nine Executive Directors who come from the Group of 10 countries, which control slightly over 50 per cent of the Board vote.[98]

The decision-making influence of the G10 was further strengthened by the fact that its membership coincided with that of the OECD's Working Party 3—the review forum of the industrialized countries in international monetary matters.[99] The G10 countries thus brought to bear overwhelming voting power, the capacity to veto all decisions of the Fund—in the time-period of the 1960s— and, importantly, a coordinated, well-defined position on the monetary issues. Their decision-making influence was further buttressed by the absence for over a decade of a counter-challenge from any other group of countries in the Fund. These factors made for the exercise of a dominance in Fund decision making by the G10.[100]

The year 1972 witnessed the establishment of a competing group representing the developing countries—the Group of Twenty-Four (G24).[101] The G24 represents the minority shareholders, in terms of voting power, but also the preponderant numerical membership, in the IMF. The overriding task of the G24 has been to evolve and defend a common position for the Third World members of the Fund on the international monetary issues.[102] The G24 and the G10 not only have separate identities and represent different constituencies, but they generally articulate contending approaches on monetary problems:

> Not only did these various groups exist, and not only were they increasingly active, but they also began to take somewhat conflicting positions. In fact, by 1971 the crystallization of the membership into groups holding somewhat diverse positions on major international monetary questions had become a trend . . . In addition, there had emerged an increasing consciousness of the differing interests as between developed and developing countries.[103]

There are other, less prominent groups in the IMF. At the level of the Executive Board, for instance, developing countries have tried as much as possible since the mid-1960s to coordinate positions. Interestingly, this informal consultation process among Third World Executive Directors predates the institutionalization of the G24—beginning as it did in 1966.[104] The other significant level of group functioning in the IMF relates to the practice of regional group caucusing within the broader compass of the G24. Four regional groups of developing countries have become evident over the years: the Latin American, the Commonwealth Caribbean, the African and Arab groups.[105]

This multi-level process of Third World concertation in the Fund, which has intensified since 1972, has served to redress somewhat the negotiating imbalance relative to the developed countries. When juxtaposed with the politics of the G10, it has signified—paralleling the North–South divide on global economic relations—the basic political alignments that characterize the IMF. Ironically, in an institution that prides itself on a one-world ethos, transcending the constitutional differentiation among members,[106] it was the main founding-nations that introduced the concept of separateness among groups of countries. In fact, when one looks at the long time interval between the appearance of the G10 in 1962 and the G24 in 1972, one is struck by the slow reaction of the developing countries to this forced informal dichotomization of the Fund membership.[107]

(b) Organizations-in-contact

The other dimension of informal decision making isolated for analytical treatment has to do with the impact of external organizations—with mandates impinging on that of the Fund—on the policies and behaviour of the IMF. For the purposes of the study, UNCTAD has been selected as the key institution around which the analysis will revolve. As part of the United Nations system, it represents one of the universal-membership forums of the international system. It has a broad mandate in international economic matters—preoccupied as it is with trade and development issues. Against the background of the activist initiative of the developing countries for its establishment and the predominant membership of these countries, UNCTAD, as earlier noted, has come to distil an imperative concern with the development problem and the solutions thereto, particularly at the international level. It has not been reticent or hesitant in pronouncing on the international monetary issues of the day, especially as they affect the developing nations.

The nature of the relationship between the IMF and the United Nations system was formally defined in a legal instrument, the 'Agreement Between the United Nations and the International Monetary Fund', entered into on 15 November 1947. Though the IMF was therein designated a specialized agency of the United Nations in terms of Article 63 of the UN Charter, the organization was simultaneously given an independent status, in so far as its operational mandate was concerned: 'By reason of the nature of its international responsibilities and the terms of its Articles of Agreement, the Fund is, and is required to function as, an independent international organization'.[108] There is a requirement of consultation,[109] but the Fund is not bound to accede to the recommendations emanating from the United Nations system.[110] As a subsidiary organ of the UN General Assembly, UNCTAD is governed by this legally defined relationship.

Consultation has been an important part of the relations between the IMF and the pertinent organs of the United Nations system. The fact of consultation has permitted UNCTAD to impress its views, and ultimately the Third World perspective, on international monetary issues. The formal independence of the IMF notwithstanding, UNCTAD has repeatedly expressed positions, in the form of resolutions,[111] on international monetary relations, many of which:

> have been of a key nature, calling for studies of problems which the Fund can best carry out or for modifications or changes in Fund policies ... Those reaching the Fund have received close attention, sometimes because the Fund was already confronted by the same problems, but also because the problems of developing countries are constantly brought to the attention of the Fund through its consultations with member countries and by its Executive Directors and Governors.[112]

There are, however, fundamental constraints to the influence that the organs of the United Nations system may have on the policy-formation process of the IMF.[113] The main constraint resides in the practical, action-oriented mandate that the IMF has for international monetary matters—in contrast to the deliberative competence of UNCTAD. The second obstacle relates to the obligatory force of Fund decisions and the recommendatory nature of those of an organization such as UNCTAD. Finally, there is the crucial question of how UNCTAD is perceived within the IMF—its standing in the eyes of the main decision-making participants in the Fund.[114]

In the end, though, UNCTAD does have a viewpoint on international monetary issues and this viewpoint has been consistently conveyed in resolutions and in the process of consultations with the IMF. The practical consequence of this organizations-in-contact process on Fund policies and behaviour can only be finally resolved by analysing specific decisions taken by the Fund in the context of the content of the UNCTAD viewpoint, to see what ways, if any, this viewpoint has been integrated into the appropriate decisions of the Fund.

Conclusions

The Fund's decision-making process proceeds on the basis of two rules: that of weighted voting and majority decisions. The other main facet of decision making is the structural division of authority that is formally stipulated in the Fund's constitution. Each of the three main organs—the Board of Governors, the Executive Board and the Managing Directorate—has its own decision-making competence and, since 1974, the advisory Interim Committee has come to play an important part in influencing, at the policy-making level, the decisions that these organs are required to take. In essence, decision making is characterized by fluctuations in the locus of authority, depending on the nature of the issue to be decided on.

While weighted voting remains the overarching dimension of Fund decision making, the rule of majority voting has emerged as a significant check to dominant voting power. The balancing effect of these two rules has facilitated the actual practice, on a day-to-day basis, of consensus decision making. The pragmatism of consensus has to be seen in the context of the substantial task mandate of the institution, the fact of the binding force of decisions and the difficulty of generating fundamental change by way of amendments to the Fund's Articles of Agreement.

Informal decision making in the Fund is primarily exerted at the level of group politics. In this regard, the two major groupings of countries define the essential political cleavages within the institution, paralleling the situation in the broader international economic system. The influence process, as determined by formal decision structures, is thus counterpointed at this level of informal behaviour.

These various elements of the Fund's decision-making process can be divided into two conceptions: positive decision making and negative decision making. The former relates, firstly, to the voting power that a country disposes of, or that groups of countries can amass, to achieve their desired outcomes; secondly, the favourable standards of representation on the limited-membership organs of the IMF and, thirdly, at the informal level, to the depth of the group political process. Negative influence is embodied in the veto power that individual countries or groups of countries hold over decisions of the Fund and amendments to its Articles of Agreement.

From this perspective, a concern with formal decision-making influence has two facets. Countries or groups of countries have to be concerned with relative voting strength and numerical representation on restricted-membership organs, as a means of exerting positive influence in the IMF. Informally, they have to evidence a capacity to coordinate positions, mirrored in the group political process. Simultaneously, they also have to be interested in veto power, as a means of negative influence—to block undesirable lines of action.

Notes

1. C. Wilfred Jenks, 'Unanimity, the Veto, Weighted Voting, Special and Simple Majorities and Consensus as Modes of Decision in International Organisations' in R. Y. Jennings, ed., *Cambridge Essays in Honour of Lord McNair*, 1965, p. 48. See also Inis L. Claude, jun. *Swords into Plowshares: The Problems and Progress of International Organization* (3rd edn), New York, Random House, 1964, p. 111.
2. For a discussion of the equality principle in relation to international relations, see Herbert Weinschel, 'The Doctrine of the Equality of States and its Recent Modifications', *American Journal of International Law*, 45, No. 3, July 1951, pp. 417–42. See also David Mitrany, *A Working Peace System*, Chicago, Quadrangle Books, 1966, pp. 64–5.
3. See Fouad Abdel-Moneim Riad, 'Formal Equality and Substantive Equality' in Gray Dorsey, ed., *Equality and Freedom: International and Comparative Jurisprudence*, Vol. 3, Dobbs Ferry, New York, Oceana Publications, 1971, pp. 1041–3.
4. Claude, op. cit., p. 112. See also Djura Nincic, *The Problem of Sovereignty in the Charter and in the Practice of the United Nations*, The Hague, Martinus Nijthoff, 1970, pp. 100–1.
5. Riad, 'Formal Equality . . .', op. cit., p. 1042.
6. Mitrany, op. cit., p. 64.
7. See Nincic, op. cit., p. 107.
8. What is clear is that there is a reluctance within the international society of nations to underwrite an unqualified egalitarianism. Moreover, where the scope of an institution's mandate carries with it an obligatory implementation, the major powers have been concerned to safeguard a right of veto over decisions of the institution.
9. See Joseph Gold, 'The origins of weighted voting power in the Fund', *Finance and Development*, 18, No. 1, March 1981, pp. 25–8.
10. See Elizabeth McIntyre, 'Weighted Voting in International Organizations', *International Organization*, 3, No. 4, 1954.
11. See 'Proposals for an International Currency (or Clearing) Union', 11 February 1942 in Horsefield, op. cit., 3, para. 3, p. 3.
12. Ibid., para. 55, p. 15.
13. Ibid., para. 57, p. 16.
14. Entitled 'Preliminary Draft Proposal for a United Nations Stabilization Fund . . .', April 1942—see Horsefield, op. cit. Vol. 3, pp. 37–82.
15. Ibid., p. 76.
16. Ibid., pp. 76–7.
17. See van Dormael, op. cit., p. 66.
18. Horsefield, op. cit., Vol. 3, p. 20.
19. See 'The Joint Statement' in Horsefield, op. cit., Vol. 3, p. 134.
20. Ibid.
21. *Proceedings and Documents*, Vol. 1, p. 137.
22. As the Fund's history notes, Australia, Belgium, Bolivia, Brazil, Chile, Czechoslovakia, France, The Netherlands, Norway and Poland all 'suggested changes in the formula, mostly designed to include elements favorable to the country making the suggestion'—Horsefield, op. cit., Vol. 1, p. 33.
23. Australia, Belgium and Norway 'objected to the provisions giving the United States an effective veto'—ibid., p. 34—while Australia, Belgium and Mexico 'sought to impose a limit of 20 per cent of total votes for any one member'—ibid., p. 81.
24. Ibid., p. 29 and p. 96.

25. For instance, Brazil suggested that a member's votes should be related to its population or trade—ibid., p. 74.
26. See Joseph Gold, 'Weighted Voting Power: Some Limits and Some Problems', *American Journal of International Law* 68, No. 4, October 1974, p. 688.
27. See 'The White Plan' in Horsefield, op. cit., Vol. 3, p. 45.
28. Gold has noted that 'the United States was proposing a special majority of 80 per cent, which would give it a *liberum veto* over all important decisions if, as was possible, it had 25 per cent of the total voting power. He [Keynes] pointed out that a minority of little more than 20 per cent would be able to prevent a change supported by a large majority, including the United States'—see Joseph Gold, 'The origins of weighted voting power in the Fund', op. cit., p. 28.
29. Ibid.
30. See note 23 *supra.*
31. See 'The White Plan' in Horsefield, op. cit., Vol. 3, p. 45.
32. Javier Marquez, 'Developing Countries and the International Monetary System: the Distribution of Power and its Effects' in *Money in a Village World* (Papers from a Colloquium on the Interests of the Developing Countries and International Monetary Reform), Geneva, Committee on Society, Development and Peace, 1970, p. 41.
33. McIntyre, 'Weighted Voting in International Organizations', op. cit., p. 484.
34. Art. XII, Sec. 5(a)—unless otherwise indicated, references hereafter to the Articles of Agreement are to the amended version of April 1978. It is to be noted that under the original American proposal, basic votes were set at 100 votes—see 'The White Plan' in Horsefield, op. cit., Vol. 3, v(3), p. 45.
35. For an extended treatment of how quotas are arrived at, see *IMF Survey*, 5 June 1978, pp. 166-8. See also Lister, op. cit., Ch. 3.
36. See Allan G. B. Fisher, 'Relative Voting Strength in the International Monetary Fund', *The Banker*, April 1968, p. 335.
37. At the same time, the importance of basic votes to many developing countries should not be understated. As Mohammed notes: 'The importance of the basic votes is indicated by the fact that these votes comprise at least half of the voting power of 24 members. All members in this category are developing countries'—see Azizali F. Mohammed, 'The Decision-Making Process in the International Monetary Fund' (unpublished paper presented at 'Fifth International Seminar of Economic Journalists'), New Delhi, 11–13 February 1985, p. 2.
38. This issue will be discussed further in Chapter 4.
39. Art. XII, Sec. 5(c).
40. Under the original Articles of Agreement, these higher majorities were a majority of the total voting power, two-thirds, three-fourths and four-fifths, as well as a unanimous vote. Under the amended Agreement (1978), the special majorities have been reduced to two—70 per cent and 85 per cent. For an extended discussion, see Joseph Gold, *Voting Majorities in the Fund*, Pamphlet Series No. 20, Washington DC, IMF, 1977.
41. *Proposed Second Amendment to the Articles of Agreement: A Report by the Executive Directors to the Board of Governors*, Washington DC, IMF, March 1976, pp. 61-2.
42. See Gold, *Voting Majorities in the Fund*, pp. 6-7.
43. 'Excerpts from an address on "National Sovereignty and International Monetary Cooperation"', by Managing Director of the Fund to the American Philosophical Society, Philadelphia, Pennsylvania, 19 April 1973, *IMF Survey*, 23 April 1973, p. 114.
44. For details of the Group of Ten, see section 4(a).
45. Horsefield, op. cit., Vol. 2, p. 8.

46. Managing Director, 'The Role of the Fund in the International Monetary System', *IMF Survey*, 23 October 1972, p. 89.
47. Both these instruments have a legal status, defining other obligations binding on the Fund's membership. This legal status is stated, in both instances, in their prefatory sections: e.g. 'These By-Laws are adopted under the authority of, and are intended to be complementary to the Articles of Agreement...'—see *By-Laws, Rules and Regulations*, IMF, 39th Issue, 1 July 1982, p. 1.
48. 'Rules and Regulations', Rule C-10, ibid., p. 25.
49. 'By-Laws', Section 11, ibid., p. 12.
50. 'Rules and Regulations, Rule C-11, ibid., p. 25.
51. Horsefield, op. cit., Vol. 2, p. 9.
52. Jenks, 'Unanimity, the Veto ... as Modes of Decision in International Organisation', op. cit., p. 56. It is the method currently applied in a broad variety of institutional settings, including the World Bank, the non-aligned and the G77 groups of countries. It was the decision procedure employed during the Law of the Sea and CIEC negotiations.
53. See Ebere Osieke, 'Majority Voting Systems in the ILO and the IMF', *International and Comparative Law Quarterly*, **33**, pt. 2, April 1984, p. 405.
54. As Besteliu has put it: 'Whatever the attitude expressed when a decision is put to a vote or agreed by consensus, once legally adopted it becomes binding for all member-states, without distinction'—see Raluca Miga Besteliu, 'The Procedure of Consensus in the Adoption of Decisions by the International Monetary Fund and the International Bank for Reconstruction and Development', *Revue Roumaine d'études internationales*, 4 (38), 1977, p. 525.
55. Pierre-Paul Schweitzer, 'Political Aspects of Managing the International Monetary System', *International Affairs*, **52**, No. 2, April 1976, p. 212. A former Alternate Executive Director has stated it thus: 'it has been an unwritten rule that great efforts will be made to avoid outvoting either the United States, the European countries or the developing countries, if they hold strong views and if the latter two groups are relatively united among themselves'—see 'Remarks on International Monetary Relations and a New International Economic Order—Dr T. de Vries', *Netherlands International Law Review*, **24**, xxiv, 1977/3, p. 539.
56. Besteliu notes that 'during the lengthy negotiations involved in the consensus procedure ... there is a growing tendency of attaching more importance to arguments used in support of a certain position than to the possible voting power of the member supporting it. All through such negotiations, every member has equal possibilities to assert and maintain its own position ... From this point of view, at least, members having a smaller voting power actually take part in the decision-making process'—see Besteliu, 'The Procedure of Consensus ...', op. cit., p. 526.
57. The role of the Managing Director in decision making does not form a part of the analysis. The analysis accepts that he does have a key decision-making role—something that was repeatedly stressed during interviews—but for reasons essentially of manageability, an in-depth examination of his role is excluded. Where, however, the behaviour of the Managing Director is crucial to a particular decision, it will be indicated and treated in the study.
58. See Joseph Gold, 'The Structure of the Fund', *Finance and Development*, **16**, No. 2, June 1979, p. 13.
59. Governors have traditionally held the rank of Ministers (normally of Finance) or Central Bank Governors in the national-governmental context.
60. Gold, 'The Structure of the Fund', op. cit., p. 12.
61. See Frank A. Southard, jun., *The Evolution of the International Monetary Fund*, Essays in International Finance, No. 135, December 1979, p. 3.

62. Art. XII, Sec. 3(g). The Board normally meets twice weekly—on Mondays and Wednesdays—but may also meet at other times, as required by the exigency of developments.
63. Gold, 'The Structure of the Fund', op. cit., p. 13. This view of the Board was confirmed repeatedly during the course of interviews. At the same time, it was stressed that the Fund was characterized by a number of focal points regarding decision making. No organ has a monopoly of recommendatory or decision-making power. An extended discussion of the role of the Executive Board in decision making can be found in E. Hexner, 'The Executive Board of the International Monetary Fund: A Decision-Making Instrument', *International Organization*, **18**, No. 1, Winter 1964, pp. 76–9.
64. Jacobson has written thus about the significance of limited-membership bodies: '[T]hey are a recognition that smaller groups tend to be more efficient decision-making bodies than larger ones. They also contravene the doctrine of sovereign equality by giving those states or constituent units that are members greater opportunity for influence than those that are represented only in the assemblies'— see Harold K. Jacobson. *Networks of Interdependence: International Organizations and the Global Political System*, New York, Alfred A. Knopf, 1979, p. 96.
65. Each Director is empowered to appoint an Alternate Executive Director—see Art. XII, Sec. 3(e). These Alternates have the full powers of a Director in the absence of the latter and may also attend meetings of the Board. Directors elected by developing nations have evolved the practice of appointing Alternates from among the other members of their constituencies, thereby allowing a wider range of developing-country views to be presented before the Board. This factor cannot be overstated in regard to the sense of participation it gives to developing countries.
66. Under the terms of the Articles of Agreement, the Board of Governors, by an 85 per cent majority, may increase—or for that matter decrease—the number of elected Directors: see Art. XII, Sec. 3(b).
67. Art. XII, Sec. 3(c).
68. The voting power of individual countries thus becomes important in regard to these elections. As Gold notes: 'the relationship of voting power within the group may be important for some members because it may determine whether they will be able to take a leading part in the choice of the executive director whom they elect and what voice they will have in the formation of opinion within the group'—see Gold, *Voting and Decisions in the International Monetary Fund*, op. cit., p. 28.
69. What is more, under the original Agreement, two of the seven elective positions were expressly set aside, constitutionally, for the Latin American countries. This provision no longer operates under the amended Agreement.
70. As we shall see later, one of the demands of the Third World in the early 1970s was for the restructuring of the Executive Board to permit, *inter alia*, a geographical rationalization of the directorships.
71. For instance, in the 1982 elections, the Director from Canada was elected to represent nine English-speaking developing countries from the Caribbean, the Director from Australia seven Asian/Pacific countries, the Director from The Netherlands three European developing nations and the Director from Italy one European developing country.
72. This is counting the People's Republic of China. China not only considers itself a developing country—in fact, several representatives interviewed stated that China sees itself as the leader of these countries—but operates within the framework of the caucusing group of Directors from developing countries.
73. This was a recurring observation during the interviews. It was pointed out that

these Directors could not totally ignore the views of the developing countries since dissatisfaction might impel a search for more congenial groups with which to align, thereby denying to these Directors in future elections the votes required to be elected.

74. The major examples of this tendency are Brazil, India, Indonesia, Iran, Argentina and Mexico. Brazil has served on the Board from the beginning of the Fund, as has India. Indonesia has been on the Board for most of the period of its membership in the Fund, while Iran, Argentina and Mexico have been regularly elected. It is only among the African members that this pattern of the election of the large countries is not apparent; in effect, there is a more balanced distribution between the larger and the smaller African nations.

75. See Rolf M. Jeker, 'Voting Rights of Less Developed Countries in the IMF', *Journal of World Trade Law*, **12**, No. 3, May/June 1978, p. 218.

76. This is particularly the case with the African and two of the Latin American constituency groups of the IMF—though in the case of the latter, the fact of the historical association with the Fund from its inception has mitigated, in the thinking of Latin American representatives, the full effect of this limitation. Moreover, the Latin American countries have operated as a coherent sub-grouping of countries since the early 1960s, thereby giving a greater coherence to their representation in the Fund.

77. During interviews, several African representatives pointed out that they have tried to moderate this deficiency by a practice whereby appointees are typically afforded a six-year cycle of service on the Board: consecutive two-year periods as Adviser, Alternate and Director respectively. Another compensating factor is that, for the most part, Directors usually come from the most senior levels of the governmental-financing bureaucracy, bringing with them a technical expertise and broad experience in the areas of competence of the Fund.

78. The 'ad hoc Committee on Reform of the International Monetary System and Related Issues' set up in 1972 to attempt a reconstruction of the monetary regime—see resolution No. 27-10, adopted by the Board of Governors on 26 July 1972.

79. One of the proposals of the Committee of Twenty was for the creation of a new organ in the Fund—the Council: see *International Monetary Reform: Documents of the Committee of Twenty*, Washington DC, IMF, 1974, p. 18. The fate of the suggested Council is instructive for what it says about the influence of developing countries in the Fund. The Council has not materialized because several developing nations were firmly opposed to its immediate creation and insisted on an 85 per cent majority in the Board of Governors for a decision regarding its activation—see Gold, *Legal and Institutional Aspects of the International Monetary System*, Vol. I, pp. 279–82. As intimated to the analyst, African countries in particular and some Latin American countries felt that the Council represented a threat to the Executive Board—it is to be remembered that the Council would have wide decision-making powers and would have a status higher than that of the Executive Board. These countries felt, moreover, that Board representatives are better placed than Ministers to handle the complex monetary problems requiring the taking of decisions.

80. Alexandre Kafka, *The IMF: The Second Coming?*, Essays in International Finance, No. 94, Princeton, July 1972, p. 35.

81. Ibid.

82. 'Historian Reviews Origins and Achievements of Interim Committee of the Board of Governors', *IMF Survey*, 1 April 1985, p. 98.

83. Ibid., p. 101.

84. It is evident that structures are important to the decision-making process. The mandates of organizations are just as important in this respect. As Jacobson has put

it: 'The mandate and structure of organizations provides a framework within which decisions must be taken, and they inevitably shape the process of decision making'— Jacobson, *Networks of Interdependence*, p. 83.

85. Zamora, 'Voting in International Economic Organizations', op. cit., p. 569.

86. Art. XXXI, Sec. 2(a).

87. See 'The White Plan' in Horsefield, op. cit., Vol. 3, p. 40.

88. Southard, op. cit., p. 2.

89. Ibid.

90. Managing Director, 'Excerpts from an address on "National Sovereignty and International Monetary Cooperation"', op. cit., p. 115.

91. Art. XXVIII(a).

92. Gold, *Legal and Institutional Aspects of the International Monetary System*, op. cit., Vol. 1, p. 322.

93. Peter M. Blau & Richard W. Scott, *Formal Organizations: A Comparative Approach*, San Francisco, Chandler Publishing Co., 1962, p. 6.

94. These two practices do not exhaust the informal practices that are apparent in the IMF. They were selected because of their central role in defining the political influence process in the institution.

95. See de Vries, *The International Monetary Fund, 1966–71*, op. cit., Vol. 1, pp. 618–20.

96. The members of the G10 are Belgium, Canada, France, Italy, Japan, Netherlands, Sweden, United Kingdom, United States and West Germany. For further details on the GAB, see Chapter. 4.

97. Though the G10 is the focal group of developed countries in this analysis, it should be indicated that an even narrower group—the Group of Five (G5), comprising the United States, United Kingdom, France, West Germany and Japan—also operates informally in the Fund. The G5 membership coincides with the developed countries that appoint Directors. For a discussion of the G5, see Gold, *Legal and Institutional Aspects of the International Monetary System*, op. cit., Vol. 1, pp. 17–18.

98. Brian Tew, 'The Position and Prospects of the International Monetary System in Historical Perspective' in Tony Killick, ed., *Adjustment and Financing in the Developing World: The Role of the International Monetary Fund*, Washington DC, IMF (in association with the Overseas Development Institute), 1982, p. 172.

99. For a discussion, see Solomon, op. cit., p. 42.

100. See Robert W. Russell, 'Transgovernmental Interaction in the International Monetary System, 1960–72', *International Organization*, **27**, No. 4, Autumn 1973, pp. 431–64.

101. Discussed in more detail in Chapter 4.

102. See de Vries, *The International Monetary Fund, 1966–71*, op. cit., Vol. 1, p. 619.

103. Ibid., p. 620.

104. It is known as the 'Group of Nine' (G9), the current membership of which numbers eleven Directors, including the Director from the People's Republic of China. Sauvant has written thus about the importance of the G9: 'Since the Executive Directors of the developing countries have access to the resources of the Fund, they make an important input into meetings of the G24 and provide a part of the background material required for its deliberations'—Sauvant, *The Group of 77*, op. cit., p. 93.

105. Regional caucuses among the developing nations—apart from the Latin American— are relatively recent developments in the Fund. The African and Commonwealth Caribbean caucuses began in the mid-1970s and the Arab in the late 1970s. Latin America, in contrast, had started to coordinate their positions in the Fund in the 1960s.

106. One can compare the situation in the other Bretton Woods institution, the World

Bank, where an explicit differentiation among the membership is written into the constitution.

107. One can only speculate as to the reasons for this. There seems to have been an optimism among developing countries that UNCTAD would be a panacea for all their economic problems, at the international level. Even though the principal focus of their complaints in the mid-1960s was on the working of the international trade regime, there was no hesitation, firstly, in setting up under the aegis of UNCTAD expert groups to study the international monetary situation, and secondly, in passing resolutions directed at the IMF.

108. 'Agreement Between the United Nations and the International Monetary Fund', Art. 1(2)—as reproduced in Horsefield, op. cit., Vol. 3, p. 215.

109. Ibid., Art. IV(1).

110. See Edgar Jones, 'The Fund and UNCTAD', *Finance and Development*, September 1979, p. 29.

111. As Jones noted: 'The main impact of UNCTAD comes from its recommendations which emanate mainly from developing countries and which, in general, crystallize issues they wish to have resolved so as to promote their economic and social advancement'—ibid.

112. Ibid.

113. While pointing out these constraints at this stage of the analysis, the actual extended examination of their significance will be done in conjunction with the treatment of the substantive issues in Part III.

114. In this regard, UNCTAD's positions stand a better chance of being heeded in the IMF, depending on the seriousness with which it is perceived as an organization by the institutional actors in the Fund. This was a position that was repeatedly stressed in interviews with Fund officials.

Chapter 4

The Third World and the frontal challenge to decision making in the IMF

1. Introduction

Not surprisingly, a perusal of the main documentary sources of the Fund's activities during the first decade and a half of its existence does not indicate any expressed criticism of Fund decision making on the part of developing countries. This was the period largely of presumptive US leadership of the international economy. It was the period, as has previously been pointed out, of a generalized dependence of the other international economic actors, developed and developing alike, on the economic strength of the United States for the rebuilding of economies after the war and for the overall revitalization of economic relations. This was not the context suitable to challenges of prevailing international management structures. It was a period, moreover, characterized in the main by an IMF that was peripheral to the broad operationalization of international economic relations.

Developing countries, anyhow, had a more concentrated concern for most of this period—the campaign for increased development assistance. And, in so far as there was a problem with institutional process, it had basically to do with the functioning of the other Bretton Woods organization, the World Bank, which was concerned with the development assistance task. The specific manifestation of this problem was the effort by these countries to relocate the aid mandate within the UN system.

2. The emergence of Third World discontent with Fund decision making: the early phase

It was in the early 1960s that there emerged an observable critical outlook by developing nations on international decision making pertaining to monetary affairs. The immediate cause of the first such criticisms was the creation in 1962 of the General Arrangements to Borrow (GAB) by ten industrialized nations.[1] The GAB was conceived essentially as a mutual-security credit arrangement restricted to the participant countries of the Group of Ten (G10). It envisaged that any deficiency in the Fund's credit capacity that potentially could limit access of these countries to needed resources was to be met by borrowing from the pool of resources on call from these countries. The G10 group had originally initiated consideration of the GAB during 1961 outside the framework of the IMF and it was only by virtue of the insistence of the Fund's Managing Director that the institution became eventually associated in the discussions of the proposal at a late stage in its evolution.

The Managing Director's criticism of the procedural approach to the establishment of the GAB underscored a sharp awareness of the implications of what was then being proposed and discussed by the G10 countries. As he stated it: 'Attention has been concentrated on making arrangements with the governments of the main industrial countries. This is, of course, a question of profound interest to all members of the Fund'.[2] Undoubtedly, the Managing Director was simply articulating the bureaucratic imperative—that of safe-guarding the centrality of the institution in international monetary affairs. From this perspective, any acquiescence in extra-institutional action by a self-selected group of countries could have conceivably ended in shifting the institutional locus of authority to this group, in the process marginalizing the IMF.

This interpretation was manifestly the import of the Managing Director's counter-proposals as regards the envisaged GAB. He argued that:

(1) Any borrowing arrangements to which the Fund could agree must be fitted into the framework of the Fund according to the Articles.
(2) The authority of the Fund must not be impaired.
(3) The draft must provide for the decision whether to borrow to be made by the Fund.[3]

The institution, in effect, was profoundly conscious of its own best interests *qua* institution.

During a meeting of the Executive Board in late 1961, Executive Directors of several developing countries expressed their apprehension regarding this development. The Indian Director opined that 'the Board might find itself obliged to concur in decisions taken elsewhere',[4] while the Director from Brazil expressed the fear that the GAB 'would result in the organization of a group of rich countries playing a large role within the Fund structure. He wondered why the Fund was concerned in the arrangements, since the participants were to decide how much to lend, and for what purpose'.[5]

These criticisms were continued at the 1962 Annual Meeting of the Fund.[6] Yet, it must be stressed at this point that developing-country reaction to the GAB was neither generalized nor consistent. Few of the Governors from these countries referred to the matter during their presentation at the Meeting, and there were, in fact, favourable comments on the GAB by several.[7] The important thing, however, was the beginning of a perception by developing nations of the role of the international decision-making process in the monetary sphere.

Another initiative by the G10 countries—this time in 1963, involving the inauguration of a process of study and discussion of the question of the adequacy of international liquidity outside the Fund setting—demonstrated that the GAB was no isolated, aberrant act of this new, narrowly-restricted group of countries.[8] Developing countries, as a whole, could not ignore the implications of this new development, against the background of the negotiating modality for the GAB, as well as its outcome—that is, the exclusivist nature of both the process and the beneficiaries of the arrangement. The year 1963, therefore, was to mark the start of a more activist and coherent campaign by the developing countries against the decision-making trends in international monetary matters that were then unavoidably apparent.

Third World Governors at the 1963 Annual Meeting made repeated critical references to the pattern of consultations that the G10 had put in train on the liquidity question and the threat posed thereby to the authority of the IMF. As the Indian Governor put it:

> An increase in world liquidity will call for special effort and cooperation on the part of the highly industrialized countries. But it is a problem that concerns all countries, including the less developed ones . . . The appropriate focal point for further action to safeguard and strengthen the international payments system has, clearly, to be the International Monetary Fund.[9]

This was to become a recurring theme of Third World presentation over the next several years at Annual Meetings of the Fund.

From a tactical, political point of view, mutual support was extended to each other by these countries and the Managing Director since they both had an interest in having the issues considered in the Fund. The Managing Director located himself in the centre of the debate, and on the side of the developing nations, by arguing the imperative of a process of negotiations within the Fund and a liquidity-creating mechanism that catered to the needs of all members of the institution.[10]

Hereafter, decision making on international monetary issues was to become a central area of contention for the developing countries in general. An examination of the positions of these countries shows that what was at issue at this early stage were two things. The first was that they were being effectively locked out of the discussion of important international monetary issues because of the evolving practice of prior closed negotiations carried out by the G10. And secondly, there was the tendency of the latter nations to seek to bypass the international monetary institution in the negotiating phase, but then to present the Fund membership with a *fait accompli*.[11] What needs to be remembered is that at this moment of the Fund's history, any agreement among these ten nations carried with it the weight of overwhelming voting power in the Fund— disposing as they collectively did of over two-thirds of the total votes.

Developing countries were not content to press their demand for decision-making participation on this matter only within the institutional confines of the IMF. In fact, one can say that the extra-institutional campaign was even more intensive, because it was pursued under the auspices of the newly-formed Group of 77 and with the strong technical and political support of the also newly-created UNCTAD.

The Ministerial Meeting of the Group of 77 in 1967 declared in its Charter of Algiers that: 'Developing countries should participate from the outset in all discussions on international monetary reform and in the operation of new arrangements for Special Drawing Rights in the IMF.'[12] UNCTAD had appointed a Group of Experts in 1965 to present views on the subject and their report argued extensively the developing-country perspective on the liquidity question.[13] The matter was also debated in the 1966 Session of the General Assembly, which adopted a resolution on international monetary reform on the initiative of developing countries. Resolution 2208(XXI) argued the participatory right of all countries in discussions and decisions on international monetary reform.[14]

It is important to underline that Third World discontent with international monetary relations at this particular moment—the early to late 1960s—revolved around the efforts at usurpation of the Fund's decision-making authority by the G10, rather than the internal Fund decision-making arrangements. On both the GAB and initial SDR discussions, the G10 practice of closed informal negotiations demonstrated that non-representation of developing countries could only guarantee an outcome that ignored consideration, much less incorporation of their specific interests in the final formal decision. Developing nations therefore became vociferous advocates of the centrality and institutional authority of the IMF in the international monetary system. The fact that the Managing Director was supportive of their complaints and his frontal aggressive role in articulating the Fund's fundamental concern with the monetary problems affecting the developing countries[15] were no doubt influential in creating this favourable Third World disposition towards the institution at that time. As Marquez has written:

> No doubt, the increasingly liberal Fund policies, as well as its proof of concern for the LDCs—e.g. with the establishment of the compensatory financing scheme—also helped. The developing countries saw in the IMF a friendly agency, at least a much friendlier one than the Ten, taken as a group. So, instead of a new machinery over which the developed countries would have had a still larger control, the developing countries stood by the Fund as the agency empowered to create SDRs.[16]

By the end of the 1960s, a new dimension to Third World dissatisfaction with international monetary decision making had become evident. In this regard, certain structural aspects of Fund decision making began to attract growing critical comment. Specifically at issue was the composition of the Executive Board, and to this end, the developing members in 1970 raised the question of an increase in the number of Executive Directors—from the existing twenty to twenty-one.

As explained by the Governor of Malaysia at the 1970 Annual Meeting, this proposal to augment the size of the Executive Board was based on the consideration 'that it would facilitate regroupings on regional lines, because as a result of the fact that many of us came in at different times, we had sometimes no choice but to join groups of countries in regions halfway across the world and such countries had problems rather different from our own.'[17] Particularly among the African membership, there was the perception that the two directorships they then held were not procedurally guaranteed by the rules of the election.[18] These criticisms spurred a decision by the Executive Directors to undertake a study regarding the size and structure of the Executive Board. In welcoming this study, several Third World representatives outlined the principal factors that should operate in the search for agreement on any modifications to this organ. The changes sought were intended in the main to ensure an equitable regional distribution of the directorships, and to strengthen the trend towards regionally defined constituencies of countries for the election of Directors.[19]

It is important to point out that this movement for change was also justified on the basis of the changed membership of the international system—the numerical increase in Third World membership.[20] Opposition to this attempt at an increase in the number of Executive Directors was expressed by several developed countries on the grounds that a larger Board would detract from its efficient functioning.[21]

In the end, though, this struggle for structural modifications of the Executive Board was no more than a symptom of an emerging, more fundamental campaign by the developing countries to change various aspects of the Fund's decision-making process. This was the clear implication of the statement by the Indian Governor during the 1970 Annual Meeting that:

> In our judgment, the whole question of the structure of management, distribution of quotas, as well as of voting rights, needs to be examined afresh and thoroughly . :. Whatever else this reform might encompass, it must clearly reduce the weightage of economic power and reflect instead the aspirations of the vast majority of the people in the world . . .[22]

This incipient movement for general structural change in Fund decision making was given added impetus by the international monetary disruptions of 1971, and the reversion to unilateral and exclusivist decision making that characterized these developments.

There was, to begin with, the unilateral decision by the US government of 15 August 1971 regarding the convertibility of its currency. This US action was followed by the Smithsonian Agreement of 18 December 1971 among the G10 nations, whereby a new pattern of exchange rates was to prevail among their respective currencies in an attempt to reconstruct the par value system. The significance of these decisions resided not merely in the procedural approach which centred the adoption of decisions, in one instance, on a unilateral basis, and in the other, in a limited-group context and without reference to the views of developing countries.[23] Equally as important were the negative economic consequences these decisions carried for the economies of the latter group of countries.[24] Hereafter, the terms of the debate on international monetary decision making was to shift radically to incorporate both the role and practices of the G10 and the suitability of certain features of the Fund's decision making process *per se*.

3. Demands for change in decision making: the contemporary phase

The contemporary phase of the Third World campaign for changes in Fund decision making dates from the start of the 1970s and was soon to become an integral part of the NIEO efforts of these countries. Moreover, no longer was the campaign solely reactive responses to specific acts of the G10; rather, it assumed that dimensions of a systemic challenge. It has been a campaign prosecuted within and without the IMF.

In fact, the most immediate outgrowth of the international monetary events of 1971 was the formation of the Group of Twenty-Four (G24)—the Third World caucusing group in the IMF. The decision to establish the G24 was taken at the Second Ministerial Meeting of the G77 in November 1971, when the Ministers determined that:

It is entirely unacceptable that vital decisions about the future of the international monetary system which are of concern to the entire world community are sought to be taken by a limited group of countries outside the framework of the International Monetary Fund.[25]

The Ministers then decided, 'with a view to ensuring full participation of the developing countries in searching for a solution to the present international monetary crisis and to safeguard the interests of the developing countries, [to] invite the President of the Second Ministerial Meeting of the Group of 77 to consult with the Governments of the Group of 77 to consider the establishment of an intergovernmental group . . .'[26] The formal arrangements were subsequently agreed to at a G77 meeting in Geneva—in January 1972—leading to the creation of the G24.[27]

Where previously, the G10 was the sole coherent grouping of countries in the IMF, since 1972 the G24 has served as a competing group presence. The developing countries no longer had to depend primarily on external pressure to challenge Fund policies. Nor, for that matter, was the G10 going to be able, by the mere force of coordinated positions—backed by overwhelming voting power—to automatically have its writ legitimized in the Fund. The G10 now had to negotiate monetary matters with another coherent grouping of countries who, as a former Managing Director has written, 'became very active and took their job very, very seriously.'[28]

In the years following the establishment of the G24, the practice developed of convening meetings of the Group immediately before Annual Meetings of the Fund, and, after the creation of the Interim Committee in 1974, prior to the sessions of this Committee. This practice permits the distillation and presentation of a common developing-country perspective before the main policy-framing convocations of the Fund. Regional caucuses of the Latin American, African, Arab and Caribbean sub-groups in the IMF, as well as the contributions of their Executive Directors are crucial inputs into the shaping of Third World positions.

What, in short, the creation of the G24 signified for the international monetary system was, firstly, the formalization to some extent of the North-South divide in the IMF. It also meant the beginning of a group political process on the part of developing countries and, finally, an attempt by these countries to evolve a countervailing force to the monopoly position of the G10 in Fund decision making.

The Communiqués that follow meetings of the G24 reflect their consensus agreement on the international monetary system. They are the authoritative documentary sources for apprehending the Third World positions, and in the evolution of their perspectives on decision making since 1972, one can virtually connect the specific environmental circumstances of the moment to the substantive emphases of the G24 positions.

Thus it is that at its very first meeting in April 1972, the Group 'expressed its dissatisfaction that important decisions affecting the International Monetary System have been taken by a small number of developed countries to the exclusion and neglect of the interest of the rest of the international community, and that these decisions have adversely affected the economies of developing countries.'[29] This statement sets out clearly the contextual circumstances of the G24 deliberations and in its further elaboration that 'the most important task facing it [G24] at this moment is to provide for fundamental improvements in the decision-making process regarding international monetary issues',[30] it underlines the perceived critical importance to these countries of participation in decision making. More pointedly, the G24 reiterated support for the IMF as the central institution for international monetary decision making, and defined in precise terms its position on the proposal to establish a committee to study the question of international monetary reform:[31]

> The committee should be composed of 20 Governors, each selected from a constituency that appoints or elects an Executive Director, in a manner to be determined by each constituency. The representation of developing countries in this Committee should not be less than in the present Board of Executive Directors. Such a Committee would represent a satisfactory compromise between the participation of the entire membership of the Fund in decision-making, and the need to limit members to levels that would promote effective consultation and negotiation.[32]

Finally, the G24 stated its discontent with the system for the determination of quotas.[33]

What is patent at this time is Third World concern with three elements regarding decision making: the reassertion of Fund authority, standards of representation on limited-membership bodies in the Fund, and voting power, as reflected in the distribution of quotas. As we have just seen, in so far as the first two elements are concerned, the G24 positions had a definitive content. On the question of quota determination, their position was nothing more than a statement of general principle, lacking specific criteria or guidelines for the rectification of this unfair—from their perspective—situation.

Two years later, in 1974, a marked evolution in the thinking of the G24 had become apparent. The environmental circumstances are once again important to understand the new directions articulated by these countries. OPEC had already acted on the oil prices and their new financial strength was incontestable. Secondly, there was the generalized deterioration in the balance-of-payments situation of the non-oil developing countries. These background circumstances were the manifest impetus to a more precise definition of the G24 stance on Fund quotas and voting power:

> Present quotas and voting power in the Fund do not reflect adequately the needs or the importance of the developing countries in the world economy in terms of population, capacity for development, and supply of raw materials.

Nor do the quotas adequately reflect either the ability of developing countries to contribute, or their need for access, to balance of payments finance. In line with principles of efficiency, equity, and democracy, all developing countries should have a substantially higher share of both quotas and voting power in the Fund than those that they presently command.[34]

This is more than a statement of general principle; it advocates increased quotas and voting power for each developing country. It posits specific criteria that should be considered in the allocation of quotas and voting strength—criteria of population, development capacity, raw materials, and the new potential creditors and debtors in the IMF. These are criteria—were they to be implemented—more favourable to Third World countries.

More than anything else, however, what was intended by this G24 position was an effort at a greater recognition of the oil-producing developing nations in Fund decision making. As the Governor for Iran argued at the 1974 Annual Meeting:

there is need to re-examine ineffective institutional structures not only for the purpose of removing present inequalities but also to allow and encourage greater participation on the part of those capable of greater contributions . . . [We] welcome the initiative and the constructive attitude shown by some of the distinguished governors today in proposing a more effective role for the oil producing countries in the management and the direction of . . . the Fund.[35]

The oil-producing developing countries had two main objectives: a more prominent representation on limited-membership bodies and larger quotas in the Fund.[36]

This more sweeping articulation of demands for participation has also to be placed in the context of the simultaneous prosecution of the NIEO claims of the mid-1970s. In the NIEO negotiations, the Third World role in international decision making was a principal recurring theme. Thus, throughout the decade of the 1970s and into the 1980s, this issue has continued to be a priority concern for these countries. In the Fund itself, by the end of the 1970s, they were arguing for a specific quantitative limit to the quantum of quotas they should be allotted, as a group. They pressed for 45 per cent of Fund quotas.[37] Moreover, they have repeatedly stressed that any readjustment of votes to increase their global voting power should not entail a decrease in the voting strength of any individual developing country.[38] In this view, changes in voting strength to benefit developing countries could only be at the expense of the industrialized members as a whole, by decreasing their overall share.

One modality through which the developing nations have attempted to increase their share in Fund voting power was by advocating an augmentation of the number of basic votes to be granted each member. It is to be remembered that basic votes have remained unchanged at 250 votes over the life of the Fund.[39] In its Communiqué of 9 February 1983, the G24 expressed 'the view that the basic votes, which have remained unaltered since the inception of the Fund, should be appropriately raised'.[40] And since basic votes have essentially been to the benefit of the small members, then the result of any increase in the number of basic votes would be to increase the global voting strength of these countries, the moreso since they represent an overwhelming numerical presence in the IMF.[41]

A final component of Third World proposals to enlarge their influence in decision making had to do with representation on the staff, and more pointedly in the senior management echelons of the Fund. In 1980, they had begun to argue 'the need for early recruitment by the Fund of a larger number of middle- and senior-level officials.'[42] from developing countries. The rationale for this particular claim was provided by the Governor for Saudi Arabia at the 1980 Annual Meeting thus:

> While the number of staff from developing countries has increased over time, the association and participation of individuals from developing countries in the process of policy formulation have not been sufficiently promoted. It would be imperative to increase the number of appointments from developing countries at middle and upper levels, to bring in staff with several years of work experience in developing countries, and to widen representation of differing educational backgrounds.[43]

The Brandt Commission study has noted that, though there has been an increase in the representation of Third World nationals on the IMF's staff over the years, this increase has basically been at a junior level, while 'most of the key positions in middle and higher levels continued to be held by people from developed countries, mainly USA and UK.'[44] But, as is evident in the above-quoted statement of the Saudi Arabian Governor, the issue is more than one of mere numerical representation; it has fundamentally to do as well with the educational and socialization process of the staff at the professional level.[45]

There was a parallel process of extra-institutional support of Third World demands for participation in decision making. The focus here will be mainly on the UN system, specifically UNCTAD and the General Assembly.[46] This extra-institutional articulation was expressed, for instance, in resolution 84(XI), adopted in 1971 by UNCTAD's Trade and Development Board.[47] Among the terms of this resolution was a request to the UNCTAD Secretary-General to undertake urgent consultations with the Fund's Managing Director to ensure that the interests of the developing countries were taken into consideration during international monetary discussions. In his subsequent report to the Trade and Development Board on these consultations, the Secretary-General reported that the Managing Director 'said that he was conscious of the need for all members of the International Monetary Fund, including the developing countries, to participate fully in negotiations and decisions relating to any further evolution of the international monetary system'.[48] The Managing Director further assured that these countries 'would continue to be fully consulted ... and receive every opportunity to express their views and participate in the decision making.'[49] An examination of resolution 84(III), adopted at UNCTAD III, shows that its basic theme was to argue the case for Third World participation in international monetary decision making. The UN Expert Group set up to study the structure of the UN system also advocated in

1975 that 'the distribution of voting rights under the weighted voting system in the World Bank and the International Monetary Fund (IMF) needs to be revised to reflect the new balance of economic power and the legitimate interests of developing countries in a greater voice in the operation of these institutions.'[50]

The single, most definitive expression of the Third World position can be found in Article 10 of the Charter of Economic Rights and Duties of States, to which reference has previously been made. The significance of this Charter provision inheres in the fact that the elaboration of the Charter was itself a Third World initiative that sought to provide a new orientation to the juridical basis of international economic relations in the changed circumstances of the 1970s. It has already been indicated that the main elements of the claim are (i) the right to participate, devolving from the fundamental juridical principal of equality; (ii) full and effective participation; and (iii) participation in accordance with existing and evolving rules.

In terms of assessing the meaning of these principles of participation, what can immediately be said is that the intent has not been to subscribe to a voting arrangement of one-nation/one-vote, in so far as the IMF is concerned.[51] Even the most radical of Third World perspectives on international monetary matters, the 'Arusha Initiative',[52] concedes that Fund decision making realistically cannot be egalitarian.[53] Verweay has observed that:

> When they speak of 'equal' participation, what they mean in fact is 'equitable' participation; which, in practice, comes to a claim to legal inequality in the sense that they demand a share in the decision-making power unrelated to the criteria applicable to the developed countries, which are allocated their share in accordance with the manifestation of economic or financial power . . .[54]

Apart from the fact that, strictly speaking, these countries have not advocated equal participation, as Verway states, the point is that Article 10 speaks of participation in accordance with existing and evolving rules. The existing rule in the IMF is one of weighted voting—clearly inconsistent with the equality rule.

And, as we have seen, none of the practical demands of these countries within the ambit of the Fund has shown any inclination towards the implementation of a pattern of decision making that would grant to each member-state an equality of voting rights. As we shall shortly see, these countries have been seeking to define, in operational terms, a new conception of participation, on the basis of equality, in regard to international economic relations.

The meaning of the other main element of the claim—full and effective participation—becomes evident when account is taken of the definitions provided in the companion General Assembly resolutions that have served as the conceptual foundation of the NIEO—resolutions 3202 (S-VI) and 3362 (S-VII). In the former resolution, it is specified as an objective of the developing countries:

> Full and effective participation of developing countries in all phases of decision-making for the formulation of an equitable and durable monetary

system and adequate participation of developing countries in all bodies entrusted with this reform . . .[55]

Resolution 3362 (S-VII) stipulates that:

The process of decision-making should be fair and responsive to change and should be most specially responsive to the emergence of a new economic influence on the part of developing countries.[56]

An exegesis of these two provisions points to elements of participation that are concrete and definitive, on the one hand, and those that are less tangible and more abstract, on the other.

In the former category are three specific concrete demands: (i) participation 'in all phases' and 'in all bodies'; (ii) participation 'in the formulation'; and (iii) the requirement of responsiveness. These are standards of participation that are clearly measurable and, as Bedjaoui has noted, the decision-making process can easily be given substance in these respects:

The aim of this demand is the involvement of all interested states at every one of the different steps in the process of elaborating decisions. This implies, first of all, participation in the examination of questions and . . . participation in the definition of the problems to be discussed, i.e. in what might be called the establishment of the 'agenda' of world affairs. In the second place, this presumes participation in the adoption of the decision itself, following a variety of procedures . . . Finally, this means participation in monitoring the application of the decision, for the decision is only as good as its application.[57]

Moreover, the reference to the necessity for responsiveness to the emergence of a new economic influence on the part of developing countries signifies that the concretization should take into account developments in the international economy that have served to increase the influence of developing countries and accordingly to grant them voting strength commensurate with these changes.

The references to 'adequate' participation and the fairness or equity of the decision-making process are less helpful as guidelines to the establishment of participatory standards. In fact, the allusion to adequate participation negates any claim to the one-nation/one-vote rule, and sets a more elusive standard.

The effectiveness of participation in decision making would appear to relate to the practical effects or consequences of the decisions taken by the IMF, as they impinge on developing countries. The implication is that the monopolization of decision making by an exclusive group of countries is neither theoretically nor practically conducive to the consideration of the interests of countries excluded from the process nor does it result in decisions that cater to their concerns. 'Full' participation along a procedural continuum—in all phases, in all bodies and in the adoption of decisions—leads inexorably to the consideration of Third World interests and 'effective' participation connotes the culmination of this process in substantive policies and programmes aimed at the resolution of the particular problems of these countries.

Finally, an interesting proposal that has been repeatedly raised under the auspices of UNCTAD—a proposal with evident significance for decision making—was the possibility of membership of the socialist countries in the IMF.[58] This issue was raised frontally in the early 1970s, but has recently been referred to more indirectly by arguing the principle of universality of membership in the Bretton Woods institutions.

In a tactical sense, the UNCTAD proposal aims to strengthen Third World bargaining capacity in the IMF *vis-à-vis* the developed countries by duplicating the patterns of alignment in UNCTAD, whereby there is the perception of support from the socialist countries of the positions of the developing countries. The difficulty, however, with this proposal is that the initiative for membership of the IMF has to come from the socialist countries themselves, rather than from UNCTAD.[59]

4. The institutional response to Third World claims

Neither the international community nor the IMF itself has remained impervious to the clamour for change in Fund decision making by the developing countries. The response has taken many forms, but more particularly concrete action, to satisfy some of their complaints.

Firstly, the initial demand in the mid-1960s for the right to participate in the decisional process and for the reassertion of the central authority of the Fund met with a certain degree of success. Since what was at issue was the G10 monopolization of the negotiation process, as well as their practice of closed decision making that for the most part bypassed the IMF, then the measure of success of Third World advocacy could be seen, at one level, in the reaction of the G10 nations and their willingness to open up the process. At the 1965 Annual Meeting of the Board of Governors, one of the leading G10 members, the United Kingdom, gave the assurance that:

> at the next stage [of the discussion of international liquidity], countries which are not included in the earlier discussions will be brought fully into the picture before there is any final enactment of such new arrangements as may be agreed. This stage is necessary in order to ensure that the basic interests of all members of the fund are adequately represented and appropriately considered, for all countries have a vital interest in such arrangements.[60]

The G10 position that accepted the prudence of a Third World role in the decision making on the SDR question was in contrast to the original inclination of many of the G10 membership to have an SDR arrangement and the decisions leading thereto restricted to a small group of developed countries.

The Managing Director provided the proposal that permitted an integration of the entire membership in the ultimate decision on the SDR facility. Since the G10 studies and discussion of the issue had already reached an advanced stage, the Managing Director opined that 'it would be very useful to seek ways by which the efforts of the Executive Directors and those of the Deputies of the Group of Ten can be directed toward a consensus as to desirable lines of action.'[61] This modality gained the approval of the G10 countries,[62] and, commencing in November 1966, a process of joint meetings between Executive Directors and Deputies of the G10 was set in train until agreement was reached on the SDR arrangement. This process therefore allowed a role for the developing countries, through their Executive Directors, in the shaping of the SDR scheme. But, it must be emphasized that this was not a wholly satisfactory role for the simple reason that in terms of participation at these joint sessions, the developing-country representatives were clearly outnumbered. Apart from the headstart that they had through their preliminary work on the liquidity question, the G10 countries had the added advantage of a double representation—through their Executive Directors and Deputies—in these negotiations.[63]

In the end, however, the developing countries achieved a measure of recognition of their participatory importance in international monetary negotiations. Moreover, their involvement in the SDR decision-making process—unsatisfactory though it might have been—could only have helped to weaken the incipient trend towards exclusivist, closed negotiations among the G10 countries, while strengthening the IMF's institutional authority in international monetary relations.

As already discussed, this small achievement of the developing nations was threatened by the events at the beginning of the 1970s. The reversion to the practice of closed decision taking spurred a more coherent and activist campaign by the Third World on behalf of their right to participate, on the one hand, and to strengthen their own position in the Fund decision process, on the other. Once again, the G10 had to address the complaint of non-representation made by developing countries and to recognize, as the US Governor put it at the 1973 Annual Meeting, that 'The day has long passed—and rightly so—when discussions of trade and monetary issues could take place primarily in a relatively closed circle of industrialized countries.'[64] In essence, since the early 1970s, there has been a growing recognition by the developed countries of the inescapable necessity of Third World participation in the management structures governing international economic relations.

This recognition was explicitly signalled at the time of the Seventh Special Session of the General Assembly in September 1975 by the US spokesman who, in arguing for a new cooperative approach to international economic relations, posited the need for a consensus which should include 'the broadest possible participation in international decisions. The developing countries must have a role and a voice in the international system, especially in decisions that affect them'.[65] With specific reference to the IMF, the decision by the Board of Governors in 1972 to establish the Committee of Twenty was to mark the most important Third World triumph to date. This institutional mechanism permitted these countries to participate, for the first time, in monetary reform negotiations from the outset of the process. It signified, as one observer has written, 'the end of the monopoly control of the Group of Ten countries, and the beginning of a new era in the process of negotiating reform to the system. Power effectively passed to a new and larger body composed of ministerial and other officials who had political responsibilities in their own countries.'[66] Finally, this arrangement represented the full reassertion of Fund authority in international monetary relations.

What was evidently appreciated by the Third World nations was that formal integration in decision making was ultimately meaningless without an institutional decision-making infrastructure that facilitates effective involvement. It is to this end that the efforts since the early 1970s have been geared to achieve basic structural changes to benefit and ameliorate their capability to affect the formulation of policy in the IMF. Here again, institutionally, there have been modifications in the crucial areas of standards of representation, voting power and majority voting.

Since the principal decisions of the Fund take place essentially in the limited-membership context of the Executive Board, while overall policy formation is now determined in the Interim Committee, then the struggle of the developing countries was to ensure for themselves a favourable standard of representation. The 1970 effort to increase the Executive Board by the addition of one Director was unsuccessful. Yet, something else significant happened. The Executive Board changed the Fund's administrative rules to allow the appointment of an adviser 'to assist each executive director who has been elected by more than ten members.'[67] This decision has been to the overwhelming benefit of the developing countries because many of their constituencies are the ones with more than ten members.[68]

Under the second amendment of the Articles, the provision relating to elective Executive Directors was changed to permit the election of a minimum of fifteen Directors. This was nothing more than the formalization of the prevailing situation at the time of the second amendment. It was moreover earlier indicated that there has been a gradual, but steady accretion in the number of developing-country Directors, to the point where, after the 1982 elections, they held eleven of the twenty-two directorships. Developing countries have thus attained parity with their industrialized counterparts in one of the *de facto* primary decision-making organs of the Fund. The full appreciation of this achievement can only be had if account is taken of their global voting share. With approximately one-third of total voting power in 1982, these countries yet had half of the directorships.

The principle has been accepted in the Fund that any *ad hoc* limited-membership committees, dealing with strategic policy issues, should be patterned in regard to composition along the lines of the Executive Board.[69] This was the standard that governed the first such body—the Committee of Twenty—and that, thereafter, has been used for its successor the Interim Committee, and been suggested for the Council. This has meant that those members that appoint, and those that form constituencies to elect, Executive Directors have the right to representation to these organs. In the present scheme of things, then, developing countries have an equal number of seats on the twenty-two member Interim Committee to that of the developed countries.

The composition of these committees has been favourable to the developing countries in another respect—in the right of committee members to appoint a pre-determined number of associates. Making reference to the origins of the Committee of Twenty, Gold has written:

The constituencies consisting of numerous countries exerted heavy pressure in favor of associates because their nations would then be able to be present during the deliberations of the Committee even though they were not members of the Committee.[70]

The import of associates for the developing countries was, firstly, that it allowed them to expand country-representation in the negotiating process. And, as Gold has further observed 'The number of representatives at the table can compensate for relative weakness or can provide additional strength.'[71]

Multiple-country representation permitted a larger variety of views to be aired during the negotiating process, the more so since these associates—from the developing countries—invariably had a similar rank as that of the main Committee representative, that of a Finance Minister or Governor of Central Banks.[72]

When the time came to establish the successor Interim Committee in 1974, the precedent of the Committee of Twenty was the basic model employed, except that there was no provision for the appointment of Deputies. For several reasons, the developing countries advocated as large a supportive membership as was feasible in the context of the opposition of the industrialized nations:

> Countries wished to have their own national representatives attend the meetings of the Interim Committee mainly in order to be involved directly in its activities, but they also wished to make it apparent for domestic reasons that they were among the captains of their fate. The absence of homogenous interests among the countries of some constituencies was yet another reason. Some developing countries thought that the presence of substantial numbers of their representatives would make the rejection of their proposals by the representatives of developed countries more difficult . . .[73]

Members of the Interim Committee were entitled to appoint a maximum of seven associates, thus broadening the scope for Third World participation in the Committee. Additionally, Executive Directors were granted the right of attendance and participation in the Committee's work.

On another key demand of the developing nations—that of the practical recognition of the recently acquired financial importance of the oil-producing countries—two things were done. Firstly, in the area of voting power, the oil-producing countries as a group have benefited significantly since 1974 from the readjustment of Fund quotas and voting allocations. It was agreed in 1975 by the Interim Committee in respect of the Sixth General Review of Quotas that 'the quotas of the major oil exporters should be substantially increased by doubling their share as a group in the enlarged Fund, and that the collective share of all other developing countries should not be allowed to fall below its present level'.[74] This doubling of the quotas of the developing oil-producers took them from a share of 5.05 per cent prior to the quota review to 9.89 per cent in 1975 of the Fund's total voting power (see Table 3.2).

The second concrete manifestation of the Fund's responsiveness to the new economic influence of the developing, oil-producing countries was seen in its decisions on Saudi Arabia. As was emphasized earlier, the IMF has over the past decade borrowed substantially from several OPEC countries to strengthen its liquidity position against the backdrop of the widespread payments deficits facing many of the membership, the resultant tremendous calls on its resources and the Fund's own liquidity constraints in terms of quota-based resources. Saudi Arabia was a major official lender to the Fund over this period.[75]

What Saudi Arabia obtained in return was, firstly, the entitlement to appoint an Executive Director in November 1978, under the terms of Article XII, Sec. 3(c) of the Articles of Agreement—an action that resulted, at the time, in an increase in the number of Directors from twenty to twenty-one.[76] Secondly, there was a Fund decision in 1981 sanctioning a selective increase in Saudi Arabia's quota—more than doubling the quota, from SDR 1,040.1 million to SDR 2,100 million and thereby doubling its voting power, from 1.74 per cent to approximately 3.5 per cent.[77] The 1981 decision meant that Saudi Arabia had attained the status of sixth largest contributor to quota resources and the *de facto* right to appoint an Executive Director.[78]

It is in the area of global Third World voting power that not much headway has been recorded. This is not to say that these countries have made no gains. Already in the mid-1950s, the Fund had introduced a small-quota policy for the benefit essentially of developing countries.[79] In the 1960s, the formulae for calculating quotas were slightly modified to grant a greater weight to the export variability component—also to the advantage of developing countries.[80] Then, in the mid-1970s, under the Sixth General Review of Quotas, a decision was taken whereby the envisaged increase in the quotas of the oil-producing nations was not to result in a reduction of the aggregate quotas of the non-oil developing countries.[81] This increase, therefore, had to be at the expense of the developed countries and implied larger global voting rights for the Third World.

There are three ways, theoretically, to effect adjustments in voting power in the IMF. The first way is by changing the quantum of basic votes granted each member—an approach that necessitates an amendment of the Articles. The second way is to obtain changes in the criteria that are used for the allocation of quotas—this has been the favoured approach of the developing countries. And, finally, an improvement in the relative economic performance of countries has traditionally been rewarded by increased quotas in the Fund.

It is only in recent years, as we have seen, that developing nations have begun, consistently, to try the first approach.[82] The problem with this approach is that, under the best of circumstances, constitutional amendment is a difficult process.[83] It is even more difficult to garner the requisite support—at a purely procedural level—to begin the consideration of a single-issue amendment. It is surprising, moreover, that the developing countries did not raise this question of desirability for a change in basic votes at the time of the negotiations in the mid-1970s of the second amendment of the Articles—especially since these negotiations coincided with the Sixth General Review of Quotas when developing countries were concerned to achieve higher quotas.[84] In the event, an increase in the number of basic votes has been strongly opposed by several developed countries, in particular the United States.[85]

The two other means of achieving changes in quotas, and hence in voting power, do not depend on constitutional amendment. The criteria used for the allocation of quotas are not written into the Fund's Articles. Thus, agreement to

change the extant criteria will have to be a political decision of the membership. And the developed countries have shown no inclination to move in this
direction. That leaves the third option: a prior amelioration of the economic
performance of developing countries, which may then be underwritten in their
relative quota shares in the IMF. Prospects in this regard for many of these
countries are not immediately optimistic.[86]

Finally, in so far as majority decision making is concerned, developing
countries have also benefited as a result of the changes under the second
amendment. It was earlier pointed out that the 70 per cent and 85 per cent
majorities extend to a broad range of important decisions in the Fund. The
developing countries were strong supporters of this approach. Speaking of the
special majorities agreed to under the second amendment, Lister has observed
that they were 'affected by the growing role played by developing-country
members in the bargaining over which powers should be so limited and by how
much.'[87] Developing countries stand in the same relation to veto power as the
United States and EEC for decisions requiring an 85 per cent majority, and as
the developed countries for decisions necessitating the 70 per cent majority.

The point is, however, that the ability to veto major decisions of the Fund—
while important in itself—is only one side of the coin of decision-making
influence. It is essentially a negative influence. This capacity to block major
decisions suggests a reactive posture in decision making. The flip-side of the
coin is obviously positive decision-making influence—a perspective repeatedly
stressed in interviews with Third World representatives at the Fund. What they
are interested in, from this vantage-point, is the capacity to initiate in the
confidence that the decisional mechanisms will permit a favourable consideration of their initiatives on the basis of the technical merits of the presentation.

5. The Third World campaign for change in Fund decision making: an analytical perspective

This presentation of Third World efforts to change international monetary
decision making has demonstrated that the desirability of change has not been
seriously contested by the main participants in the system. What has proved
problematic, however, has been the feasibility of change—the translation of the
necessity for change into practical and mutually acceptable structures of participation. At the same time, the reality of economic conditions has served as a
determining factor to moderate and, in effect, to give a pragmatic content to the
demands of the developing countries.

This is patently the case regarding the interpretation they have bestowed on
the guiding principle of the juridical equality of states, on which the claims for
participatory rights have been founded. Allegiance to formal equality has not
meant, in substantive operational terms, a one-state/one-vote standard of
application. No such interpretation has emerged from an analysis of the content
of the claims, as they pertain to the Bretton Woods institutions.

The difficulty in itself of achieving a restructuring of voting power in the
Fund, on any other grounds but that of contributions to, and responsibility for,
the operations of the system has been underscored thus by Mahbub ul Haq:

on the voting structure I am more pessimistic, because there is a fatal flaw in the conception of the Bretton Woods institutions. They are called international institutions, but they are not. They are really an uneasy coalition of bilateral interests. They are a shareholders' company, and if the borrowers wish to have majority control, the lenders will take their money and go away. I have not seen a single bank or a single lending institution, national or international, where the borrowers are in majority control. So the only way the voting structure can change in favor of borrowing countries is if they—the developing countries—become lenders to the institutions, because votes are in relation to the capital they subscribe.[88]

This is the fundamental dilemma facing developing countries in respect of their participation in multilateral financial organizations—their preponderant membership majority, but simultaneously an incapability, because of their underdeveloped economic status in the main, to contribute in a major way to the financial resources of these organizations.

And, even were they able to contribute at greater levels of magnitude to the needed operating resources of the IMF, they come up against another vitally important constraint—non-usability for the most part of their currency resources. Speaking on the occasion of the 1983 agreement to increase Fund quotas under the Eighth General Review of Quotas, the Managing Director observed in respect of the credit basis of the quotas that: 'What counts is the usability of the resources'.[89] He further went on to note that any level of Fund quotas 'yields, as a rule of thumb, 50 percent in usable resources'.[90] In essence, usable currency resources are derived from the contributions of the industrialized, and a few developing, countries.

The real problem, therefore, is the consequence of increases in the quota shares of developing countries for the financial integrity of the institution—on which its most important function, from the point of view of these countries, is dependent:

> There was a danger, therefore, that redistribution of voting power from the industrial to the developing countries, and thus from countries that supplied the Fund with most of its usable resources to countries that needed to borrow these resources, might reduce the total volume of resources available to the Fund.[91]

An augmentation of non-usable currency resources that would follow any agreed increase in the quotas of the Third World as a whole entails a diminution in the lending capacity of the institution. This has to be a major consideration confronting these nations in the search for suitable modalities to increase their voting strength in the IMF.[92]

Moreover, even were an acceptable solution to be found to this central question of new criteria to govern the distribution of quotas, another problem immediately crops up. From a retrospective viewpoint, the ratification of the status of new centres of power in international systems—whatever the prevailing mode of ratification at any historical moment—has always followed, rather than preceded, the actual manifestation of the newly-obtained power standing for the particular actor(s). It follows, as Zamora has argued, that 'to reform the world economic system, the developing countries must alter economic realities, and then see to it that international organizations reflect those new realities.'[93] The examples of the EEC and OPEC countries attest to the responsiveness of the IMF to this dynamic of international life. The newly-acquired economic importance of these two groups of countries was validated through the process of an elevation in their status within the management structure of the Fund.

Developing countries, on the whole, have displayed a realistic appreciation of the implications of this twin dilemma. They have sought to deal with them by giving a novel meaning to the principle of equality in so far as decision making is concerned—moving towards standards of representation based on the concept of group, rather than of nation. The important thing in this perspective is the attainment of a position of equality, as a group, vis-à-vis the developed countries, also as a group, in the decision-making process. Group shares and group results are the measures of acceptable operational standards of equality: 'Rather than insistence on equality of voting between nations ... the real emphasis of the developing countries seems to be on relative equality among groups or blocs of nations.'[94] This practical interpretation of the fundamental legal principle of the equality of states signifies a compromise with the reality of the widely disparate material circumstances of states—and thereby, their capacity to affect—and their responsibility for the functioning of the inter-national economic system.

The gradual accession of the concept of group equality as an acceptable standard—to the developing nations—for the operationalization of the principle of equality has already been indicated in the analysis of the substantive content of their demands. The aspiration towards parity of voting strength, and the achievement of equality of representation on limited-membership organs, are the major indicators of this tendency. No less so is the veto power these countries hold in common with other discrete groups of countries over the important decisions of the Fund. But, there is another reliable test of intentions: that of Third World practice regarding decision-making processes within their own regional financial institutions and what they have agreed to in recently established international financial institutions for the negotiations of which they have played an important role.

There is a plethora of such institutions that the analyst can examine. They are all institutions with an important financial function and can be divided into those of exclusively developing-country membership—the AfDB, the AMF and the OPEC Special Fund—and the remainder where participants come from both the developed and the developing nations. In the first category are to be found the regional development banks and funds.[95] The International Fund for Agricultural Development (IFAD) and the Common Fund are examples of the second type of institution.

The practice in the regional development banks and funds shows con-clusively that developing countries have followed the traditional pattern of international financial organizations in designing decision-making systems, eschewing any strict application of a one-nation/one-vote formula. Decision-making structures have generally been modelled after those in the Bretton Woods institutions.[96] Decision making is governed by the rules of weighted and majority voting. In the allocation of votes, provision is made for a number of basic votes to be distributed equally to all members,[97] but the bulk of the voting power is shared out in relation to the participants' contributions to the financial resources of the institution. Simple and special majorities are required for specified categories of decisions. However, in the IDB and ADB, as Krasner points out, the distribution of votes in proportion to contributions is a modified version of the Bretton Woods system since 'votes are allocated on the basis of callable as well as paid-in capital, and contributions to special funds are not included. These practices give LDC members far more votes than they would receive under a system based on their contributions to the Bank's usable resources.'[98] This notwithstanding, the point is that voting power is largely determined by contributions and the requirement of special majorities in these institutions enshrines for the developed and developing categories of country-participants an overall veto over principal decisions.

The structural differences of the AfDB are more significant for what they achieved than anything else. Under its Articles of Agreement, non-African membership is excluded, with the result that developed countries are constitutionally barred from participation. In terms of voting distribution, there was a more marked modification of the weighted voting system compared with the IDB and the ADB:

> Votes were allocated exclusively to African states according to a formula that tended to equalize influence: basic votes, allocated equally to each member, accounted for 50 per cent of the total. The maximum ratio between the country with the largest number of votes and the one with the smallest was 5 to 1, while the maximum ratio of subscription was 3 to 1.[99]

This structural divergence—constitutional exclusion of non-African member-ship and a stronger divorce of voting power from contributions—from the practice of the other regional, as well as international, financial organizations has ultimately constrained the Bank's capacity to attract the development resources necessary to perform its funding tasks credibly.[100] In the end, the African nations sought to redress this critical limitation through the establishment in 1973 of the ADF, that was open to developed-country membership. They have, however, attempted to safeguard African control of the institution by devising a system that granted a distribution of votes and representation on the basis of equal group shares, the pertinent groups being the African and the non-African members.[101]

Finally, the OPEC Special Fund ostensibly sought to have a decision-making system that, on the surface, appeared egalitarian. Whereas there was a large differential in the contributions of the various OPEC states to the Fund's resources—for example, of the twelve original contributors, Saudi Arabia and Iran each contributed 25 per cent and Venezuela 12 per cent of the initial resources—the Governing Committee comprised one representative from each contributing member. Each representative had one vote. Decisions basically required a two-thirds majority, but this majority had to represent countries contributing 70 per cent of the resources. The real effect of this requirement was analogous to that of the weighted voting arrangement.[102]

It is at the level of recently-negotiated international financial organizations that a more precise view of the Third World outlook on group equality can be had. The earliest such organization is the IFAD. IFAD's constitution was formalized in 1976. Its decision-making system represents an important departure from both the weighted voting and the one-nation/one-vote systems of the Bretton Woods and the UN-related institutions, respectively. Constitutionally, IFAD categorizes its member-states into three explicit groups: Category I (developed countries); Category II (OPEC countries); and Category III (developing countries).[103] A total of 1,800 votes is divided equally among these three groups of members—each group disposing of 600 votes. In the limited-membership Executive Board, comprising eighteen seats, each category of countries is allotted an equal number of seats. It is in this sense—that of group—that the equality principle prevails in IFAD.

Another unique feature of the voting structure is that there is not a uniform methodology for the allocation of voting power within each individual category. In Categories I and II, voting power is distributed under a formula whereby contribution is the main criterion. At the same time, a stated percentage of the votes are allocated on an equal basis to all category members—17.5 per cent of the total in Category I and 25 per cent in Category II. Contrastingly, the 600 votes allotted to the bloc of countries in Category III are distributed on the strictest egalitarian basis—each member is granted an equal number of votes. It is to be noted that, in terms of the IFAD arrangement, Categories I and II were conceived as the main donor countries—developed and developing—to the Fund's resources and Category III countries were envisaged as the potential recipients.[104] Contributing countries were thus more interested in safeguarding the link between resource contributions and voting power.

The decision-making arrangements for IFAD is patently another indicator of a transcending group interpretation of the equality principle. The group is the essential frame of reference. The mechanics of group arrangements relating to distribution of votes and representational rights are an intra-group prerogative.

At a first glance, it would appear that developing nations, in the sense used throughout this analysis, had achieved fundamental control over decision making in IFAD by virtue of their combined two-thirds majority of both votes and representational rights, especially in the context of the simple majority requirement for decisions in the Governing Council and the three-fifths majority in the Executive Board. In reality, however, several built-in safeguards in the decision-making process served to dilute this appearance of a Third World dominance. These safeguards included the requirement of special majorities—two-thirds, three-quarters and four-fifths—for important decisions of the organization. Moreover, the quorum requirement for meetings of both the Governing Council and the Executive Board was so constructed that, in theory, the developed countries could actually block the holding of meetings.[105]

No less interesting is the decision-making structure agreed for the Common Fund in 1980. In essence, the Common Fund operates under a system of weighted and majority voting, but what is different is that the allocation of voting weights to individual participants followed an *a priori* agreement among the negotiating countries—interestingly, including the socialist countries—concerning the distribution of a certain proportion of the total financial contributions to discrete groups of countries.[106] Group votes are then distributed according to the weighted vote formula outlined in Schedule D of the 'Agreement Establishing the Common Fund for Commodities'.[107] Each country-participant is granted 150 basic votes, and additional votes in proportion to contributions. The developing nations have, once again, by stressing the group concept, achieved a favourable decision-making position when it is placed in the context of their envisaged contributions to the financial resources of the Common Fund.

The majority voting principle, though, serves as the crucial safeguard for the interests of the major contributors. Three categories of majorities are specified: simple, qualified and highly qualified, which are defined in the Agreement as 'more than half of all votes cast', 'at least two-thirds of all votes cast' and 'at least three-fourths of all votes cast'[108] respectively. The latter two majorities are necessary for important decisions, on the one hand, and those decisions having significant financial consequences, on the other. The principal decisions of the Common Fund, therefore, can be vetoed by either of the two main groups of countries.

This analysis has attempted to delineate the movement towards the concept of group as the operational standard for the principle of equality in so far as financial organizations are concerned. Significantly, this movement has for the first time attained a *de jure* status under the provision of the IFAD constitution. As Zamora has stated: 'It is interesting to note that the participants have begun to resolve the voting issue by reference to blocs, with more emphasis on the voting power of blocs than on that of individual countries'.[109] This trend represents the strongest practical indication of Third World recognition of the untenability in financial institutions of decision-making processes that operate according to the one-nation/one-vote principle of participation: 'Although developing countries have been the ones to espouse the one-country, one-vote principle, equal voting is in fact resisted by the more powerful developing countries, and therefore the LDCs have placed greater emphasis on equality among groups of nations—or bloc voting'.[110]

In a sense, moreover, the stress on group participatory rights is a logical outgrowth of the pattern of Third World functioning within international organizations since the mid-1960s, where a firm group ethos has been the defining parameter. UNCTAD, it should be recalled, saw the first institutionalization of the group approach. Since then, the countervailing power of the developing countries, from their standpoint, to the dominant control by the developed countries of international economic relations has been explicitly stated in group terms.[111] The Third World group process has been the focal point for action on behalf of a host of bargaining objectives and North–South negotiations have basically proceeded on the basis of groups of countries.

Yet, an approach to the structuring of decision making on equal participatory rights for discrete groups of countries leaves unresolved a host of important problems in trying to transpose it to the Bretton Woods institutions.

Specifically with reference to the IMF, there is the fundamental constraint, constitutionally, 'that the IMF Articles of Agreement do not permit making a *legal* distinction between categories of Member States: formally, all Members whether developed or developing, should enjoy the same facilities'.[112] As one study has indicated, in discussing the problems relating to a mutually satisfactory distribution of Fund quotas:

> Rigidly applying a weight-in-the-world formula would be simplest, but would not satisfy the developing countries. Another relatively simple approach would be to split the total among groups of countries—55% industrial, 15% oil producers, 30% developing might be acceptable—and let them decide who gets what within each group. That is probably a non-starter as well, since it formalises a split that the IMF has strived to avoid.[113]

At the same time, it must be stressed that the hesitance of the Fund to integrate in an unambiguous juridical sense this vital distinction between groups of members notwithstanding, the practice has been an apparently irreversible movement to a *de facto* recognition of differences among countries.[114] This practice is manifested as much in the many policies of the Fund that cater—both explicitly and implicitly—to the concerns of developing countries, as in a more constant reference in Fund decisions and policies to its developing members.[115]

Actually, though, the central dilemma regarding Third World participation in Fund decision making has to do with the reluctance of international systems, historically, to underwrite *a priori* the influence of countries incapable of assuming a commensurate responsibility for the operations of the system. This, in the final analysis, is the fundamental stumbling-block to the attainment by the developing countries of the desired 45 per cent for Fund voting power.

Several other problems suggest themselves when the group approach to decision making is looked at more critically. Groups are not, when all is said and done, monolithic entities. It is true that group action presupposes certain overriding common objectives that impel centripetal tendencies. But groups also comprise individuals with their own particularistic priorities and interests.[116] The intensity of the presence of these individual interests can just as well serve to undermine the efficacy of group action.

It is now an accepted part of the Third World reality to point to the pervasive heterogeneity of the group. This heterogeneity has, within recent years, led to a growing awareness of the centrifugal potentialities of the group. This was the unmistakable message of the address of Tanzania's President Nyerere before the G77 Ministerial Meeting in 1979:

> the pressures towards disunity are strong. The more advantageously placed among the Group of 77 are being flattered and wooed and offered concessions in this or that matter which is of immediate interest to them. And there are forces within every subgroup—from OPEC to the Least Privileged—which are inclined to take offers of special treatment, or special representation, and then—instead of using these as a base for further Third World advance—to lose interest in the wider struggle.[117]

One practical manifestation of this tension has been the suspicious attitude of many Third World countries towards limited-membership forums. Non-participants have not been fully convinced that their own specific concerns will be pressed with the same degree of resolution that participants will bring to their own concerns.

The group approach to decision making, moreover, implies that group voting is what is important. The decision-making influence of the group can only ultimately be expressed if all group members are willing to act in political unison when the time comes to take decisions. The realities of international life have indicated, on the contrary, that if a political consensus can be achieved at levels of general principle, it becomes more difficult to sustain such a consensus when the moment arrives to translate general principles into operational measures that impinge substantively on the diversity of interests inherent in a group as large as the Third World.

Conclusions

There have been two phases in the Third World campaign for changes in international monetary decision making. The first phase lasted for much of the 1960s. The overriding concern was not the Fund's decision-making process itself; rather, the reaction was to the G10 effort to marginalize the Fund in international monetary relations and to the practice of elitist decision making by these countries. In the second, contemporary phase, the preoccupation has shifted to the structure of Fund decision making. This on-going phase began in the early 1970s. The Third World nations have been seeking a restructuring of the main elements of decision making, in particular weighted and majority voting and standards of representation in limited-membership organs.

Above all else, what the analysis has shown is an attempt by these countries to define new standards of operationalization for the equality principle. They have been moving towards the elevation of a concept of equality where group shares and group results are the central operational criteria. The group approach has been the transcending mode of behaviour in Third World negotiations with the developed countries, and the group ethos has increasingly been transposed as the pivotal referent in measuring negotiating outcomes.

Both phases of the Third World campaign for changes in international monetary decision making have had moderate success. Congruent with the proposition that consensus decision making facilities compromise and at the same time set limits to how much can be attained in bargaining situations, these countries have had a significant improvement in their decision-making role in the Fund. The early struggle, in which a tactical political alliance was formed with the Managing Directorate, resulted in deflecting the G10 effort at usurping Fund authority. A grudging though not full integration of developing countries into the decisional process was also achieved.

It was in the 1970s that the most prominent gains were made. Full integration was signalled with the establishment of the Committee of Twenty in 1972 and the successor Interim Committee in 1974. These Committees, though without formal decision-making authority, permitted these countries a participation that extended over all phases of decision making. As regards the issues of standards of representation and the majority rule, developing countries have had important successes. They stand in a position of parity with the industrialized countries—an equal number of representatives on the limited-membership bodies of the Fund and a parallel veto power over the Fund's important decisions. It is in the crucial area of voting power, however, that they have remained at a disadvantage. The aspiration for an equality of voting power with the developed countries has not been met. At the same time, the sub-group of oil-producing countries have increased significantly their voting power and influence in the Fund since the mid-1970s. The prospects, moreover, for modifications in the voting arrangements to benefit developing countries, do not appear bright in the near future—unless, that is, there is a dramatic positive change in underlying economic circumstances. As we have seen, the Fund has historically recognized such changes by granting increased management responsibilities to the appropriate actors.

Notes

1. See Decision No. 1280-(62/I) of 5 January 1962 in IMF, *Selected Decisions of the International Monetary Fund and Selected Documents* (hereinafter *Selected Decisions*), 10th issue, 30 April 1983.
2. IMF, *Summary Proceedings of the Sixteenth Annual Meeting of the Board of Governors* (hereinafter *Summary Proceedings*, 19--), Washington DC, 1961, p. 158.
3. Horsefield, op. cit., Vol. 1, p. 511.
4. Ibid., p. 514.
5. Ibid.
6. See, for instance, the statements by Governors from Tunisia and Yugoslavia, *Summary Proceedings*, 1962, p. 86.
7. See, for example, the statement by the Governor from Pakistan, *Summary Proceedings*, 1962, p. 86.
8. The liquidity question is discussed in greater detail in Chapter 5 herein.
9. *Summary Proceedings*, 1963, pp. 76–7. The overwhelming majority of Governors from developing countries that addressed the 1963 Annual Meeting—and subsequent Annual Meetings during the 1960s—presented their criticisms in similar terms.
10. See, for instance, 'Concluding Remarks by the Managing Director' to the 18th Annual Meeting, *Summary Proceedings*, 1964, p. 183.
11. It needs to be stressed that the G10 membership is not coterminous with the developed-country membership in the Fund. In fact, several developed countries joined in criticizing the evolving tendency towards a closed decision-making practice: see, for example, the statement of the Australian Governor in *Summary Proceedings*, 1965, p. 79.
12. See 'The Charter of Algiers', adopted at the Ministerial Meeting of the G77 on 24 October 1967, as reproduced in Peter A. Mutharika, comp. and ed., op. cit., Vol. 4, p. 2421.
13. See UNCTAD, *International Monetary Issues and the Developing Countries*, Report by the Group of Experts, New York, United Nations, 1965.

14. See General Assembly resolution 2208(XXI), adopted on 17 December 1966: in operative paragraph I, the General Assembly 'endorses the need for those developed and developing countries which so desire to be fully represented in the discussions leading to any new international monetary reform arrangements, including those relating to the problems of international liquidity, and to participate fully in the operation of such arrangements as may be made.'

15. As the Fund's historian has written: 'Almost immediately upon taking office, Mr Schweitzer became known as the first Managing Director of the Fund to be particularly concerned about the developing countries, and as one who was eager to see that solutions to the world's monetary problems were truly international, reflecting the interests of the developing, as well as of the industrialized nations', see Margaret Garritsen de Vries, *The International Monetary Fund, 1966–71: The System under Stress*, Vol. I, Washington DC, IMF, 1976, p. 633.

16. Javier Marquez, 'Developing Countries and the International Monetary System: Selected Issues' in Hans W. J. Bosman and Frans A. M. Alting von Geusau, eds, *The Future of the International Monetary System*, Leyden, A. J. Sijthoff, 1970, p. 122. See also V. K. R. V. Rao, 'Monetary Reform and the Developing Countries', *Euromoney*, August 1972, p. 8.

17. *Summary Proceedings*, 1970, p. 65.

18. See de Vries, *The International Monetary Fund, 1966–71*, Vol. I, p. 631. See also statement by Governor from Upper Volta before the 1970 Annual Meeting, *Summary Proceedings*, 1970, p. 169.

19. See, for example, statements by Governors from Trinidad and Tobago and Upper Volta in *Summary Proceedings*, 1970, pp. 145 and 169, respectively.

20. De Vries, *The International Monetary Fund, 1966–71*, Vol. I, p. 631.

21. *Summary Proceedings*, 1970, p. 65.

22. *Summary Proceedings*, 1970, p. 64.

23. See Joseph Gold, *Legal and Institutional Aspects of the International Monetary System: Selected Essays*, Vol. I, Washington DC, IMF, 1979, p. 230. For an extended treatment, see Chapter 6 herein.

24. For a discussion of these effects, see *Reform of the International Monetary System: A Report by the Executive Directors to the Board of Governors*, Washington DC, IMF, 1972, p. 48 and UNCTAD, *The International Monetary Situation: Report by the Secretariat of UNCTAD*, Doc. TD/140/Rev.1, 1972, pp. 1–2.

25. 'The Declaration and Principles of the Action Programme of Lima', op. cit., p. 2435.

26. Ibid., p. 2436.

27. The G24 comprises twenty-four members, with the geographical regions—Africa, Asia and Latin America—each appointing eight members. In the manner of the G10, the G24 was structured to function at two levels: a Ministerial level and a level of Deputies, who were designed to be the technical arm of the group and who normally meet prior to G24 Ministerial meetings to undertake the preparatory work. For a detailed background account, see Sauvant, op. cit., pp. 60–9.

28. Schweitzer, 'Political Aspects of Managing the International Monetary System', op. cit., p. 216.

29. 'Communiqué: Intergovernmental Group of Twenty-Four on International Monetary Affairs' (hereafter 'Communiqué: G24), First Ministerial Meeting, Caracas, 6–7 April 1972, in Karl P. Sauvant, comp., *The Collected Documents of the Group of 77*, New York, Oceana Publications, 1981, p. 298. Unless otherwise indicated, references to G24 Communiqués are taken from Sauvant's compilation.

30. Ibid.

31. The Committee on Reform of the International Monetary System and Related Issues (Committee of Twenty), was established by resolution No. 27-10 of 26 July

1972, adopted by the Board of Governors, with the task of advising and reporting on all aspects of reform of the international monetary system.

32. 'Communiqué: G24', 1st Ministerial Meeting, pp. 298–9.

33. The G24 position on quotas was that 'the present system of determining Fund quotas . . . does not reflect the relative economic position of Fund members', ibid., p. 299.

34. 'Communiqué: G24', 7th Ministerial Meeting, 9–10 June 1974, pp. 307–8.

35. *Summary Proceedings*, 1974, p. 159.

36. Ibid., pp. 159–60.

37. 'Communiqué: G24', 20th Ministerial Meeting, 24 April 1980, p. 353. It is interesting to note that, in a report of a Group of Experts set up by the Chairperson of the Non-aligned movement, it was proposed that the voting share of developing countries should be raised to 50 per cent—see *Directions for Reform: The Future of the International Monetary and Financial System* (Report by a Group of Experts), India, Vikas Publishing House, 1984, p. 67. This proposal is not inconsistent with the G24 position of 45 per cent of quotas, since the latter translates into roughly 50 per cent of voting power when account is taken of basic votes.

38. 'Communiqué: G24', 19th Ministerial Meeting, 28 September 1979, p. 348.

39. Since the quantum of basic votes is precisely specified in the Articles of Agreement, any change will necessitate an amendment of the Articles.

40. 'Communiqué: G24', 26th Ministerial Meeting, 9 February 1983, *IMF Survey*, 21 February 1983, p. 53.

41. This Third World proposal to increase basic votes was undoubtedly influenced by the UNDP/UNCTAD joint study, commissioned by the G24 in 1981, on Fund quotas. That study contained a series of simulations of various new formulae, including higher levels of basic votes, that would, if applied, increase dramatically the quotas and hence the voting power of developing countries: see UNDP/UNCTAD, op. cit., pp. 15–16.

42. 'Communiqué: G24', 21st Ministerial Meeting, 27 September 1980, p. 355. This is not really a new argument by developing countries. As early as 1962, India was speaking in a similar vein: see *Summary Proceedings*, 1962, p. 83. What was different was the generalized statement of the claim, in contrast to episodic references in the earlier years.

43. *Summary Proceedings*, 1980, p. 149.

44. *The Brandt Commission Papers* (Selected Background Papers prepared for the Independent Commission on International Development Issues, 1978–79), Geneva–The Hague, IBIDI, 1981, p. 161.

45. As the Brandt Commission Papers put it: 'Some of the developing country staff members holding senior positions were educated in USA or UK and had inadequate experience of managing men and affairs in their own countries. Their approach to problems was occasionally seen to be based on the experience and outlook of developed countries rather than those of developing countries' (*The Brandt Commission Papers*, p. 161). This problem of staffing, while important, does not form a part of the present study. There are clear methodological difficulties involved in trying to measure such qualitative concepts as educational and socialization processes. Where, however, the quantitative indicators may prove helpful they will be adverted to in passing.

46. Pressure exerted by other extra-institutional actors can be seen, for instance, in *Towards a New International Economic Order: A Final Report by a Commonwealth Expert's Group*, London, Commonwealth Secretariat, 1977, pp. 96–7.

47. See also Resolution 84(III) entitled 'The international monetary situation', adopted at the Third Session of UNCTAD, on 21 May 1972.

48. Trade and Development Board, *International Monetary Issues—Note on consultation between the Managing Director of the IMF and the Secretary General of UNCTAD*, Doc. TD/B/C.3/98/Add.I, 8 December 1971, p. 1, para. 2.

49. Ibid., p. 1, para. 2.

50. See *A New United Nations Structure for Global Economic Cooperation* (Report of the Group of Experts on the Structure of the UN System), New York, United Nations, 1975, p. 5.

51. This assessment is borne out by an exegesis of the *travaux preparatoires* of the Charter, as found in *UNCTAD: Trade and Development Board, 1973–74*, Doc. TD/B/AC.12/1-4.

52. The 'Arusha Initiative' was the outcome of a conference involving representatives, both governmental and academic, from developed and developing countries that met in June/July 1980 in Arusha, Tanzania, to discuss international monetary relations. It is considered the radical Third World perspective, because of the intellectual orientation of the participants and some of the extremist views propounded at the conference. Reference to these views will be made later in this study. For the text of the 'Arusha Initiative', see *The Arusha Initiative: A Call for a United Nations Conference on International Money and Finance*, General Assembly Doc. A/S-II/AC.1/2, of 28 August 1980.

53. Ibid., p. 8, para. 19(a).

54. Wil D. Verway, 'The New International Economic Order and the Realization of the Right to Development and Welfare—a Legal Survey', *Indian Journal of International Law*, Vol. 21, No. 1, January–March 1981, p. 38.

55. General Assembly resolution 3202 (S-VII) of 1 May 1974, Sec. II(d).

56. General Assembly resolution 3362 (S-VII) of 16 September 1975, Sec. II(16).

57. Bedjaoui, *Towards a New International Economic Order*, p. 196.

58. See Trade and Development Board, *International Decision Making*, Doc. TD/B/C.3/98, of 8 December 1971, p. 42, para. 130. See also Trade and Development Board, *Report of the Ad Hoc Intergovernmental High-Level Group of Experts on the Evolution of the International Monetary System*, Doc. TD/B/AC.32/L.4, of 4 August 1980, p. 10, para. 41. It is interesting to note, however, that this proposal has never formed a part of Third World presentation within the ambit of the Fund.

59. The accession of several socialist countries, including Romania, China, Hungary and Poland, shows that these countries do not find the structures and policies of the Fund as representing fundamental constraints to participation. The Fund, however, has had an ambivalent attitude to the question of membership by socialist countries, as attested by this opinion of an ex-Managing Director: 'The second fact that helps the Fund (and I hesitate to say it in public, but it is relevant) is that its membership does not include the Soviet Union. I think it is perhaps regrettable, because it damages the Fund's claim to universality. But it does simplify life! ... This simplifies life because there are no major ideological confrontations' (see Schweitzer, 'Political Aspects of Managing the International Monetary System', op. cit., p. 210).

60. *Summary Proceedings*, 1965, p. 89. For the expression of similar sentiments, see statement by the US Governor (ibid., p. 107).

61. Ibid., p. 30.

62. Ibid., p. 107.

63. See Y. S. Park, *The Link between Special Drawing Rights and Development Finance*, Princeton Essays in International Finance, No. 100, Princeton, 1973, p. 6.

64. *Summary Proceedings*, 1973, p. 57.

65. *GAOR* (7th Special Session), A/PV 2327, 1 September 1975, p. 5, para. 47.

66. George C. Abbott, 'Effects of Recent Changes in the International Monetary System

on the Developing Countries', *Aussenwirtschaft*, March 1979, p. 64. See also Graham Bird, *The International Monetary System and the Less Developed Countries*, London, Macmillan, 1978, p. 22. There were occasions subsequently when the G10 and the G5 have negotiated among themselves—especially during the negotiations for the second amendment—and presented the remaining membership with their agreed outcomes. But this has been a declining feature of Fund decision making.

67. De Vries, *The International Monetary System, 1966–71*, Vol. 1, p. 632. Advisers basically have the same terms and conditions of service as Executive Directors and their Alternates. They attend meetings of the Executive Board and, in the absence of an Alternate, the practice is for the Adviser to act in that capacity.

68. There was another advantage to the developing countries of the appointment of Advisers. It allowed Executive Directors to have a broader spectrum of member-country perspectives since many of these Advisers come from countries other than those of the Directors and Alternates.

69. Gold, 'The Structure of the Fund', op. cit., p. 15.

70. Gold, *Legal and Institutional Aspects of the International Monetary System: Selected Essays*, Vol. I, p. 267.

71. Ibid., p. 18.

72. Thus, at a typical meeting of the Committee of Twenty, the nine developing-country constituencies were represented by twenty-seven Ministerial-level personalities, and two of the other constituencies with developing-country members had Ministerial-level representatives from these countries as Associates.

73. Gold, *Legal and Institutional Aspects of the International Monetary System: Selected Essays*, Vol. I, pp. 268–9.

74. IMF, *Annual Report*, 1975, p. 98.

75. Saudi Arabia loaned US$3.2 billion of the total $6.8 billion borrowed by the Fund for the financing of its 1974 and 1975 oil facilities, $2 billion of $7.7 billion for the supplementary financing facility of 1979 and $8 billion of the medium-term borrowing—and a substantial portion of the $6 billion of short-term loans—for the financing of $15.3 billion for enlarged access credit. Further, Saudi Arabia entered into an associate agreement in 1983 under the GAB to provide $1.5 billion to that borrowing arrangement.

76. It should be pointed out that, when an appointment under Art. XII, Sec. 3(c) is activated, the Board of Governors is empowered to decrease the number of elective Executive Directors—see Art. XII, Sec. 3(b). The Governors left unchanged the number of elective Directors at fifteen, notwithstanding Saudi Arabia's appointment of a Director—a decision to the benefit of the developing countries, since any reduction in the number of elective Directors could only have been at their expense.

77. Suzanne Wittebort, 'Saudi Arabia's new clout at the IMF', *Institutional Investor*, (international edn), September 1981, p. 146.

78. See Press Conference on the Managing Director on the Saudi loan to the Fund in *IMF Survey*, 6 April 1981, p. 99.

79. See *IMF Survey*, 17 April 1978, p. 123. See also Lister, op. cit., p. 55.

80. Ibid., p. 58. It is generally accepted that developing countries, because of their structures of production and export—predominantly of raw materials—are vulnerable to sudden fluctuations in export prices and earnings of these products. The export variability component of the quota formula basically benefits these countries.

81. See reference note 74.

82. The question of an increase in the number of basic votes was first raised by developing countries during Executive Board discussion of the size and structure of the Board at the beginning of the 1970s. No consensus was reached on this issue so

that the proposal was not approved by the Executive Board: see Gold, *Voting Majorities in the Fund*, p. 6.

83. This is as a result of the double majority required for effecting amendments—three-fifths of the members and 85 per cent of the total voting power.

84. As Gold notes, only one developing-country Governor raised the issue of basic votes in the context of the second amendment exercise and he speculates that it might not have been raised then because of the experience during Executive Board discussion earlier in the 1970s (see Gold, *Voting Majorities in the Fund*, pp. 5–6). This consideration notwithstanding, one would think that the negotiations for both the second amendment and the Sixth General Review of Quotas would have been a most propitious time for reconsideration of the issue. There was no guarantee that it would have been accepted then, but the bargaining position of developing countries was at its optimum in the framework of a broad-based amendment negotiation and the new economic influence of the oil-producing nations.

85. This was intimated to the researcher by several representatives during the course of interviews.

86. As several developed-country Board representatives indicated during interviews, non-oil developing countries have been very fortunate in having their voting power unaffected in the Sixth and Seventh Reviews of Quotas. They pointed out that many of these countries are not improving economically, and quite a few are in fact retrogressing. This should have meant reduced quotas for the appropriate countries. This perspective might have been a main consideration during the Eighth Review of Quotas that led to a small reduction in the overall quotas of the non-oil developing countries.

87. Lister, op. cit., pp. 94–5.

88. Roger D. Hansen, ed., *The 'Global Negotiations' and Beyond: Toward North–South Accommodation in the 1980s*, Austin, Texas, University of Texas, 1981, pp. 115–16.

89. *IMF Survey*, 21 February 1983, p. 55.

90. Ibid.

91. Leo van Houtven, 'The Framework for Policy Making in the Fund' in A. W. Hooke, ed., *The Fund and China in the International Monetary System*, Washington DC, IMF, 1983, p. 54.

92. Several developing-country representatives intimated that it was awareness of this dilemma that has led to increasing emphasis on changes in basic votes. The allocation of basic votes, it should be recalled, is divorced from quota contributions to the Fund and does not impact in any way on the Fund's financial integrity. What was further stressed was the fact that they were interested in practical ways to increase their influence in decision making—a building upon the negative influence of the veto power to the positive influence that automatically goes along with voting strength.

93. Zamora, 'Voting in International Economic Organizations', op. cit., p. 603.

94. Ibid., p. 600. See also Catherine Gwin, 'Strengthening the Framework of Global Economic Organizations' in Bhagwati and Ruggie, eds., op. cit., p. 165.

95. Included here are the Inter-American Development Bank (IDB), the Asian Development Bank (ADB), the African Development Bank (AfDB), the African Development Fund (ADF), the Arab Monetary Fund (AMF) and the OPEC Special Fund.

96. For a discussion, see John Syz, *International Development Banks*, Dobbs Ferry, NY, Oceana Publications Inc., 1974, p. 34. See also Zamora, 'Voting in International Economic Organizations', op. cit., pp. 593–4.

97. There is one aspect of the practice of the ADB regarding the allocation of basic votes that, were it to be operative in the IMF, would have averted the observed

diminution in the proportion of the share of basic votes in overall voting power. The ADB allots 20 per cent of all votes as basic votes: this means that increases in quota contributions have no effect on the relative share of basic votes in total votes in the Bank.

98. Stephen D. Krasner, 'Power Structures and Regional Development Banks', *International Organization*, Vol. 35, No. 2, Spring 1981, pp. 317–18.

99. Ibid., p. 322.

100. As Krasner notes: 'The independence of the Bank could only be purchased at the expense of limited financial resources. The African Development Bank illustrates the global structural limits within which Third World countries must function. Industrialized states, even hegemonic ones, have not been willing to transfer substantial funds to institutions that deny any formal power to donors and reject the prevailing norms and principles of the international economic regime.' Ibid.

101. Ibid.

102. Zamora, 'Voting in International Economic Organizations', op. cit., p. 588.

103. See Art. 3, Sec. 3(a) and Schedule I of the 'Agreement Establishing the International Fund for Agricultural Development' (as adopted by the UN Conference on the Establishment of an International Fund for Agricultural Development, at its 5th meeting, 13 June 1976), as reproduced in A. Peter Mutharika, op. cit., Vol. 3. There are two sets of anomalies to be pointed out. Ecuador, a member of OPEC, is designated a Category III country. Four countries not normally identified among the G77 membership—Greece, Israel, Portugal and Turkey—are also located within Category III.

104. See General Assembly resolution 3503(XXX) on 'Establishing of the IFAD' of 6 February 1976, preambular para. 7.

105. A quorum for meetings of the Governing Council 'shall be constituted by Governors exercising two-thirds of the total votes of all its members, provided that Governors exercising one half of the total votes of the Members in each of categories I, II and III are present' (see Art. 6, Sec. 2(g) of the 'Agreement Establishing the International Fund for Agricultural Development'). See also Art. 6, Sec. 5(f) for a similar provision on the quorum requirement for the Executive Board.

106. The envisaged proportional financial obligations are as follows: developed countries, 51.4 per cent; developing countries, 32.1 per cent; the socialist countries, 9.8 per cent; China, 3.4 per cent; others, 3.3 per cent. See Ken Laidlaw and Roy Laishley, *Fund for the Future—UNCTAD: Common Fund for Commodities*, London, Development Press Services, 1980, p. 25.

107. See UNCTAD, 'Agreement Establishing the Common Fund for Commodities', Doc. TD/IPC/CF/CONF/24 of 29 July 1980, pp. 53–4. The specified voting distributions were as follows: developed nations, 40.2 per cent; G77, 45.0 per cent; socialist countries, 7.7 per cent; China, 2.9 per cent; others, 4.2 per cent. This result of the voting formula would give to the two major groups of countries in the Common Fund an approximate equal share of voting strength.

108. Ibid., p. 3.

109. Zamora, 'Voting in International Economic Organizations', op. cit., p. 584.

110. Gwin, 'Strengthening the Framework of Global Economic Organizations', op. cit., p. 165. See also *The North–South Dialogue: Making it Work* (Report by a Commonwealth Group of Experts), London, Commonwealth Secretariat, 1980, p. 66.

111. See 'Address by President Nyerere of Tanzania to the Fourth Ministerial Meeting of the Group of 77', op. cit.

112. Verweay, 'The New International Economic Order and the Realization of the Right to Development and Welfare—A Legal Survey', op. cit., p. 41.

113. 'Ministry without Portfolio: IMF—A Survey', *The Economist*, 26 September–2 October 1981, p. 15.

114. For a discussion, see Gold, 'Professor Verwey, the International Monetary Fund, and the Developing Countries', op. cit., pp. 500–4.

115. Until the second amendment, the Fund's Articles had scrupulously eschewed any explicit differentiation among the members. The Articles, under the second amendment, make a specific reference to developing countries. Thus, in the provision anticipative of the Council, it is specified that one of the tasks of this organ would be a review of developments in the transfer of real resources to developing countries (see Schedule D, 2(a) of the 'Articles of Agreement').

116. As Olson has noted: 'Just as those who belong to an organization or a group can be presumed to have a common interest, so they obviously also have purely individual interests, different from those of the others in the organization or group' (Mancur Olson, *The Logic of Collective Action*, New York, Schocken Books, 1968, p. 8).

117. 'Address by President Nyerere of Tanzania to the Fourth Ministerial Meeting of the Group of 77', op. cit., p. 4.

Part III

The Third World as Actors in the IMF: From Formal to Substantive Right to Participate

Chapter 5

The SDR and related questions: the origins of the quest for participation in decision making

1. Introduction

The Fund's Articles of Agreement were amended for the first time, effective 28 July 1969, to create Special Drawing Rights (SDRs)[1]—a new reserve asset for the international monetary system. The amended Articles of Agreement were the outcome of a process of study, discussion and, eventually, negotiations carried out both within and outside the Fund for the better part of the decade of the 1960s. The objective of the SDR arrangement was to fill the partial vacuum in the original Articles regarding deliberate international creation and control of liquidity within the system.

But, aside from this technical objective, the SDR scheme was also significant for the political circumstances surrounding its establishment. For one thing, controversy was stirred by the initial modality by which the issue was examined. At the heart of the controversy was the issue of decision making on international monetary matters. This question of decision making has been characterized in the Fund's history as the 'most difficult and sensitive question in the entire debate'.[2]

A basic challenge to the one-world view that permeated the Fund's constitution was posed by a small group of developed countries, impelling the firm reaction of the developing countries and the Managing Director of the Fund. While the Managing Director sought to reassert Fund authority in international monetary affairs, the developing nations were preoccupied, at the procedural level, with achieving a participatory role in the decisions on international liquidity and, in the substantive sense, with the derivation of direct benefits from any international agreement on the issue.

2. The origins of the SDR—a summary presentation

One of the component features of any international monetary system has to do with the manner in which the liquidity requirements are satisfied within the system.[3] Reserves have both a national and an international significance. Countries needed reserves, in the type of monetary arrangement prevailing in the 1960s—that is, the fixed exchange regime—to defend exchange parities and as a shield in times of balance-of-payments difficulties. An adequate level of reserves—however defined from the technical standpoint—enables a country to moderate the severity of the adjustment measures required to address an external payments deficit. From the international perspective, a properly functioning reserve-creation mechanism would 'provide enough liquidity to permit avoidance of undesirable adjustment policies, but not so much liquidity that inflation and unacceptable international resource transfers are promoted for any lengthy periods of time.'[4]

Under the Bretton Woods monetary system, gold was envisaged as the principal reserve asset, with national currencies playing a subsidiary role. As it evolved in practice, however, the US dollar assumed a large role in meeting the reserve needs of the international economy. The implication of this gold-exchange standard was that international reserves were dependent on the level of gold production internationally and on the balance-of-payments deficits of the United States.[5]

But, inherent in that very arrangement, was a potential instability for the system.[6] It was, in fact, this emerging instability that served as the catalyst for an international examination of the reserve-creation mechanism—or, rather, the absence thereof—of the Bretton Woods monetary regime.[7]

Other economic factors were at work making for international unease on this question. The assumption of Article VIII status in the Fund—that is, the full obligations of external convertibility—by the West European countries at the beginning of the 1960s led to increasing private capital movements and speculative tendencies in the international monetary system, with destabilizing effects on the balance of payments of developed countries. The growing surge in international trade flows from the late 1950s, into the 1960s, required a corresponding growth in international liquidity. The reality, however, was that reserve growth was out of step with the expansion in world trade. As the UNCTAD Group of Experts' Report of 1965 observed, the ratio of reserves to world imports had declined from just over 80 per cent in 1948 to just under 50 per cent in 1964.[8] This was the background to the emergence of the liquidity discussions in and outside the Fund in the early 1960s.

3. The negotiation process for the SDR

In its 1966 report on international liquidity, the G10 noted that the issue of participation in any agreed scheme encompassed three facets—two of which are particularly relevant to the current analysis. These two facets of participation are 'participation in drawing up the scheme and in subsequent decision-making [and] participation in distribution of reserve assets'.[9] These two elements are clearly coincident with the procedural dimensions and substantive outcome, respectively, of the process of decision making.

The initial focus of the liquidity problem revolved around procedural matters. The concern with modality arose out of the G10 decision at the Fund's 1963 Annual Meeting to start a process of study of the reserve needs of the international community.[10] Coming so soon after the experience with the GAB—its exclusivist essence, both as regards procedure and outcome—this G10 initiative elicited an immediate and strong reaction from the Managing Director. His obvious concern was to reassert the institutional authority of the Fund, evidenced in his position that 'in so far as it is found necessary from time to time to expand the level of world liquidity by international action, the Fund will be found to be the instrument through which the bulk of the required expansion can most suitably be carried out'[11] and in his proposal that the study of international liquidity be conducted within the Fund. Tactically, moreover, the Managing Director invited the support of the developing countries by emphasizing that the IMF 'has a unique responsibility to serve all members, both developed and less developed',[12] and by assuring the latter group of countries that, during the proposed Fund studies, 'we will give full consideration to the difficulties and the needs of the developing countries'.[13]

Developing countries, contrastingly, were slow to react to the G10 initiative. Of the twenty-four (24) Governors from developing countries that addressed the 1963 Annual Meeting, only seven (7) adverted to the liquidity question.[14] One can speculate that the central preoccupation of these countries at the Annual Meeting with the newly-established Compensatory Financing Facility[15] and the fact that their own institutional disorganization compared with the G10 were primary reasons for the absence of immediate, generalized reaction. Nevertheless, the response of those Governors from developing countries who addressed the issue was disapproving of G10 intentions and supportive of the Managing Director's approach that sought to have the matter discussed within the IMF.[16] An incipient alliance between developing countries and management, both concerned to protect their own particular interests, was the signal development at this early stage.

This tactical alliance was to mark its first gain immediately in the reaction of the G10 at the conclusion of the 1963 Annual Meeting when the Group instructed its Deputies 'in carrying out [the liquidity] studies to maintain close working relations with the International Monetary Fund and with other international bodies concerned with monetary matters'.[17] A measure of G10/ IMF collaboration was thereby conceded quite early in the process by the G10 countries.[18]

The thinking of the Fund management was defined in further detail by the Managing Director during the course of 1964.[19] The main elements of his presentation continued to be favourable to the developing countries in that he argued:

(i)   that decisions regarding the creation of additional international liquidity directly affected the whole world, and the implications flowing therefrom that all should have a say in the decision-making process;

(ii) that substantial benefits accrued to participants in the liquidity-creating process and '[i]t would seem equitable that all countries should have an opportunity to participate in the benefits, and it would seem particularly regrettable if the poorer countries were those excluded';[20] and

(iii) that the intended G10 approach implied the creation of a division among the Fund membership.[21]

The Managing Director's position—as we shall shortly see—was in reaction to the clear intent of the position of the G10 membership that envisaged an international liquidity scheme where the benefits would be shared out among a small group of developed countries.

Admittedly, there was no monolithic G10 view on the liquidity problem, in both its procedural and substantive manifestations, in the early phase of the discussions.[22] Division within the G10 centred around proponents of an arrangement, on the one hand, restricted to a limited group of industrialized countries and, conversely, one of universal application—in terms of the Fund membership.[23] This division basically pitted the EEC members of the G10 against the United States and the United Kingdom, with the EEC countries representing the limited-group approach.[24] Moreover, as we shall see later, these two contending approaches within the G10 corresponded with the advocacy of a liquidity-creation scheme outside the ambit of the Fund and one in association with the Fund, respectively. Essentially, this intra-G10 divergence signified an attempt by the countries of the EEC to obtain a formal recognition of their new influential position in the international economy—a recognition that had already been informally conceded in the GAB arrangement and the creation of the G10.[25]

It is important to underscore the disunity of the G10 on the international reserves issue at this stage of its consideration. Their disunity was undoubtedly a crucial political factor that determined the evolution of the debate on the issue and that buttressed, in a political sense, the case of the developing countries. Isolated within the G10, the United States and the United Kingdom were to prove more amenable to accepting certain of the positions advocated by the developing countries.

The combination of exclusion of developing countries from the consideration of the question and the realization that non-participation at this procedural level could result in non-participation in the benefits had the effect of prompting developing countries to take an active stand on the issue. A more concerted campaign became evident in the years after 1964, no doubt strengthened by the presence of UNCTAD and the G77 and the work that the UNCTAD Secretariat was to initiate on international liquidity during the 1960s.

In an immediate sense, the issue of decision-making participation assumed a position of prominence in the advocacy of developing countries. Intensified criticisms of the exclusive approach were presented at the Fund's Annual Meetings between 1964 and 1966. These countries uniformly stated their support for the 'multilateral institutional approach'[26] for decisions dealing with international liquidity. At the same time, a mutually supportive stance was evident in the statements of these countries and the Fund's management. Apart from the stated views of the Managing Director, the Fund's staff had completed a study in 1966 on international reserves and in it had convincingly presented the technical arguments for the participation of developing countries in the envisaged reserve-creation scheme. The report noted that the cyclical payments problems of developing countries—a result of their production and export structures that specialized in the main in raw materials—implied periodic replenishment of their reserve stocks to strengthen their capacity to withstand short-run export price and earnings fluctuations. What is more, the Fund staff pointed out that, in the post-war years, developing countries on the whole had been as responsible as developed countries in the management of their reserves and concluded that: 'In light of such considerations as these, it is generally accepted that, if and when it is decided to proceed in the deliberate creation of reserves, all members of the Fund should have an opportunity to participate in their distribution'.[27]

Simultaneously in forums outside the IMF,[28] developing countries began to mobilize an international public consensus favourable to the universalist approach to liquidity-creating arrangements. Reflective of this tendency was the 1965 report of the UNCTAD Group of Experts—set up in pursuance of the decision taken at the first session of UNCTAD to consider international monetary issues as they related particularly to developing countries.[29] This report was devoted overwhelmingly to the liquidity problem and provided essentially a Third World perspective on the matter. There were also the study sponsored by the Inter-American Committee on the Alliance for Progress (CIAP) in 1966[30] and the UN General Assembly debate of 1966 that culminated in the adoption of resolution 2208(XXI).[31]

The combination of these multiple pressure-points—both inside and without the IMF—the support of the Fund's management and disunity among the G10 countries had the desired effect of shifting the G10 towards acceptance of a universalist basis for new liquidity arrangements.[32] This outlook was clearly stated in the G10 Communiqué of July 1966:

> All countries have a legitimate interest in the adequacy of international reserves. Consequently, there is agreement that deliberately created reserve assets, as and when needed, should be distributed to all members of the Fund on the basis of IMF quotas or similar objective criteria.[33]

Up to this point, developing countries were not directly involved in the negotiating process. Discussions and studies until then had been carried out on two parallel, but separate tracks—in the G10 and by the Fund staff. Once G10 agreement to the principle of universal participation in the benefits of reserve creation had been signalled, then, the next objective for developing countries became their actual integration into the negotiating process. It was the Managing Director who once again played a crucial role in providing an answer to the search for a participatory procedure that would integrate developing countries. At the 1965 Annual Meeting, he had suggested the procedure of collaboration between the Executive Directors and the Deputies of the Group of Ten.[34] This proposal was endorsed by the G10 in 1966[35] and a decision on joint meetings was taken at the time of the 1966 Annual Meeting of the Fund. Since developing countries then held nine (9) of the twenty (20) directorships on the Executive Board, this procedure opened the way for the presentation of their views.[36] Four series of joint meetings were thereafter to be held between 1966 and 1967, before agreement was reached on the SDR facility.

So far, developing nations had attained two apparent victories: the acceptance of (i) the principle of participation in any liquidity-creating scheme within the Fund and (ii) association in the negotiations of the elements of any such arrangement. It has already been pointed out, however, that the latter was basically a paper victory, since not only were the studies and discussions initiated by the G10 far advanced at this stage—thus in large measure circumscribing the parameters of the negotiations—but the developing countries were greatly outnumbered in the setting for the negotiations. These considerations notwithstanding, in the context of the tendency for the G10 to monopolize international monetary decision making and their practice of prior negotiations outside the Fund, acceptance of the principle of a participatory role for developing countries should not be understated.

4. Substantive participation—the link proposal of the developing countries

Participation in the negotiation process having been won, the developing countries, in shifting their attention to the substantive aspects of the liquidity negotiations, were concerned to maximize the benefits that would accrue to them in the operations of the liquidity-creating arrangements. The specific contribution that these countries made to the substance of the discussions in this respect was their advocacy of a link between the creation of international liquidity and development finance. The link has been defined 'as an arrangement whereby newly created reserve assets are injected into the international economy according to a distribution formula designed to promote the flow of development finance'.[37] The link proposal was not itself an innovative idea at the time it was raised by the developing nations in the mid-1960s;[38] what was new was the fact that, for the first time, they had publicly coalesced around the idea as a major area of international monetary interest. Thereafter, as Park has noted, 'the link has become a major point of confrontation between the wealthy industrial countries and the poor developing countries'.[39]

There have been two main phases of negotiations within the Fund of the link proposal: firstly, during the negotiations for the first amendment of the Articles of Agreement and, secondly, during the deliberations of the Committee of Twenty in the early 1970s, leading up to the second amendment. Importantly, the link proposal of the developing countries was clearly influenced by the two major developments—as they affected these countries—in the international economic environment of the early to mid-1960s: the marked declining levels of development assistance and the establishment of UNCTAD.

In an international economic context characterized by the curtailment in aid flows from the developed countries—and in the context of the perceived importance of aid to the development process—the developing countries raised the link issue during the liquidity negotiations. The explicit connection between the declining aid levels and the link proposal was stated in the 1965 UNCTAD Group of Experts' Report, which considered as major contributory causes to the negative aid levels the balance-of-payments and reserve constraints of the developed countries.[40] Since any international liquidity-creation scheme would have as one of its consequences an easing of balance-of-payments and reserve constraints, the Group of Experts saw in the link a modality by which developed countries might 'be able to increase the scale of their aid to developing countries and to liberalize its terms'.[41]

Up to the time of the appearance of this Report in 1965, the link idea did not form a part of the substantive advocacy of the developing countries in the IMF.

This is easily gauged by the absence of any references to the link in the statements by Governors from these countries at the 1963 and 1964 Annual Meetings—in 1963, seven (7) Third World Governors referred to the liquidity problem, while in 1964, nineteen (19) of them did so, but none framed the substantive presentation in terms of the link. The UNCTAD Report was undeniably influential in focusing their attention to the proposal and it is no accident that, at the 1965 Annual Meeting, the first public advocacy of the link within the institution was made by the developing countries.[42] In the years thereafter, and into the 1980s, it was to become the single most prominent issue for these countries in regard to SDR negotiations.

Once the developing nations were integrated into the negotiating process in 1966 via the joint Executive Board/G10 Deputies modality, the issue was immediately placed on the negotiating agenda of this forum.[43] The proposal did not advance very far in the negotiations because developed countries raised a series of technical arguments against consideration of any link between reserve creation and increased financing for development. The primary arguments in this regard were, firstly, that reserve creation and long-term development financing were separate problems; secondly, the inflationary implications of distributing a larger quantum of reserves to countries which were going to spend, rather than hold them; and, thirdly, the inadvisability of appending another objective to the untried scheme.[44]

Several considerations evidently went into the easy acceptance by developing countries of the basic non-negotiability of the issue. To begin with, the developed countries were more united in their resistance to the link than they had earlier been on the question of Third World participation in the negotiations. The major G10 proponent of the participation of developing countries, the United States, joined the European members of the Group in stating its opposition and a definitive G10 position was delineated in 1966 when the Group determined that 'deliberate reserve creation is not intended to effect permanent transfers of real resources from some countries to others'.[45] This united opposition, in the context of the original efforts by the majority G10 membership to exclude the developing countries altogether from participation in the arrangement, effectively limited the negotiating scope of these countries.

Another important factor was the Managing Director's position on the issue. He had recorded his non-support of any connection between reserve creation and development finance even before the joint meetings were convened in November 1966. He had noted, in an address he gave in April 1966, that: 'Vital as the securing of adequate resources for development is, I agree that the provision of long-term resources should not be a purpose of a scheme for reserve creation'.[46] Thus, another crucial pivot of intra-mural support for the earlier issue of Third World participation in the process of liquidity negotiations was unavailable for this question of a link.

Additionally, developing countries were influenced by the argument that the new SDR scheme needed to be given time to work.[47] The extra-institutional support of UNCTAD, CIAP and the UN General Assembly for the link had no effect on the outcome of the Fund's deliberations and early in the process of joint Executive Board/G10 Deputies negotiations, a consensus was reached that the link proposal would not be entertained under the original conception of the SDR facility.[48]

What is to be remembered is that the SDR arrangement entailed an amendment of the Fund's Articles of Agreement. This meant that developing countries, at the time of deciding on the SDR, held a veto over the actual coming into effect of the arrangement—a veto they could conceivably have exercised if they had felt strongly about the issue then. It would appear that these countries calculated that they were going to benefit significantly from the new scheme, even in the absence of the link. What was decided in 1969 under the first amendment was that, whenever an international consensus was obtained—a consensus measured in terms of the 85 per cent majority of the total voting power of participants in the SDR scheme[49]—for an allocation of SDRs, the distribution formula specified that distribution would be in proportion to membership quotas in the Fund. As Triffin noted, this distribution formula, in the absence of the link, was more advantageous to these countries compared to other options.[50]

In an immediate sense, this formula had its attractions for the developing countries. At the time of agreement on the SDR, their quota share in the IMF was approximately 25 per cent; thus, they were guaranteed 25 per cent of any SDRs allocated. Other feasible allocation formulas—whether in relation to import trade or reserve shares in the international economy—would have been distinctly unfavourable to them (see Table 5.1). Moreover, as we shall shortly see, any SDRs allocated to them represented a significant, virtually cost-free addition to their international reserves—a consideration they could not ignore.

There were several features of the original SDR scheme that were clearly attractive to developing countries. The SDR decision of the late 1960s, as embodied in the amended Articles, specified the range of technical features surrounding the operationalization of the facility. Apart from the distribution formula that was outlined above, the main features, for the purposes of this

Table 5.1 Share of SDRs in proportion to reserve and import shares for selected groups of countries in 1970 and 1979* (%)

	SDR shares		Reserve shares		Import shares	
	1970	1979	1970	1979	1970	1979
All countries	100	100	100	100	100	100
Developed countries	73.7	66.8	76.0	60.0	78.0	75.5
Developing countries	25.8	32.6	19.0	38.0†	20.0	23.0
Others	0.5	0.6	4.0	2.0	2.0	1.5

* The years 1970 and 1979 coincide with the start of the two allocation periods, so far, for SDRs.
† The favourable reserve share of the developing countries in 1979 is misleading in that the gains between 1970 and 1979 accrued almost totally to the oil-producing countries.
Source: de Vries, *The International Monetary Fund, 1966–71*, Vol. 1, pp. 248–50: *IMF Survey*, 8 January 1979 and IMF, *International Financial Statistics* (various issues).

discussion, relate to (i) the reconstitution or repayment provision; (ii) interest charges for use of and interest remuneration for holding SDRs; (iii) the quasi-automaticity of SDR use; and (iv) the methodology for exchanging SDRs into foreign exchange—either by designation or agreement.[51]

Under the reconstitution provision for use of SDRs, participants could individually use 70 per cent of cumulative allocation over the allocation period without incurring any repayment obligations.[52] Users of SDRs were required to pay interest charges, while holders of SDRs received remuneration in the form of interest payments. The interest rate was set at the nominal figure of $1\frac{1}{2}$ per cent annually—basically not below prevailing market rates, but also a concessional rate. Thus, neither the reconstitution nor interest rate provision was onerous to these countries. SDRs could be used virtually automatically, the only stipulation being the existence of balance-of-payments need; the conditionality that normally attaches to use of Fund resources in the credit tranches was absent. Moreover, SDR use was not tied to procurement of real goods in any specified country or for any specified project. SDRs, in short, were conceptually owned reserves. Finally, SDRs can be exchanged for foreign currency essentially through the process of designation—'the core mechanism of the SDR system'.[53] Under this procedure, the Fund designates a list of members who are required to receive SDRs in specified quantities from other members, whenever the latter indicate an interest in obtaining foreign currencies. Designated countries are, by and large, those in strong balance-of-payments and reserve positions.

These features of the SDR scheme represented practical considerations that undoubtedly influenced the Third World decision to lend support to the new facility and to acquiesce in the decision to omit the link. These countries also calculated that immediate benefits would flow to them once a favourable decision on allocation was taken. It was always envisaged that developing countries would be the ones, in the main, to use rather than to hold these reserves. In fact, this has been the case, as is evident from the data presented in Table 5.2. The non-oil developing countries, at end December 1981, held 51.6 per cent of their SDR allocations as against 83.3 per cent for the developed countries and 118.4 per cent for the oil-exporting developing countries. A Fund study on SDR use for the period 1977–81 shows that seven industrial countries, one oil-exporting country and sixty-one non-oil developing countries used SDRs to obtain foreign exchange under the rules of designation or by agreement, while non-oil developing countries have basically been the only users of SDRs under the designation rule.[54] As Helleiner has noted: 'the less developed countries, although not provided with a large share of *drawing rights*, have, in fact, actually *used* them in much larger proportions than have the developed countries. In terms of real resource flows generated by the SDR system, the less developed countries have been faring relatively well'.[55] In summary, then, developing countries in the IMF had once again demonstrated an acute and pragmatic awareness of the limits of the achievable in the context of the times.

The second major phase of Fund consideration of the link proposal occurred at the time of the international monetary reform negotiations that began in 1972 under the aegis of the Committee of Twenty. In the intervening years

Table 5.2 Allocation, use and holdings of SDRs for selected groups of countries—at end December 1981 (million SDRs)

	Net cumulative allocation	Net use or receipt	Holdings	Holdings as % allocations
All countries	21,433.4	−5,022.0	16,411.2	76.6
Developed countries*	14,927.9	−2,871.9	12,056.0	83.3
Developing countries				
oil exporting	1,493.0	274.4	1,767.5	118.4
non-oil exporting	5,006.0	−2,424.6	2,581.4	51.6
Africa	876.3	−722.1	154.2	17.6
Asia	1,804.7	−706.9	1,097.7	60.8
Latin America	1,734.4	−543.9	1,190.6	68.6
Middle East	228.7	−174.3	54.4	26.3

* Using IMF categorization of countries.
Source: IMF, *International Financial Statistics*, Supp. No. 3, pp. 8–9.

between the coming into effect of the first amendment in 1969 and the start of the Committee's work, Third World advocacy of the link had publicly grown in strength. It was the issue most referred to in the substantive demands of these countries at Annual Meetings of the Fund in the years 1969–72. Intra-mural advocacy was paralleled by increasing extra-institutional support. These included a second UNCTAD Group of Experts Report in 1969 that strongly recommended the link,[56] the UN General Assembly resolution in 1970, ushering in the Second Development Decade[57] and UNCTAD's resolution on the international monetary situation, adopted at the third Conference in 1972.[58] The Pearson Commission had also endorsed it in 1972—in the form of a relinquishment to the IDA by developed countries of a part of their SDR allocations.[59] The link idea was discussed in the United States Congress, where a Congressional Sub-Committee recommended to the full Congress that approval should be given to a draft resolution to be introduced at the 1969 Annual Meeting of the Fund to the effect:

> that the Executive Directors of the International Monetary Fund ... promptly consider an amendment to the IMF Articles of Agreement, supplementing the Special Drawing Rights amendment ... whereby those 18 IMF members who have previously contributed to the International Development Association would direct that 25 per cent of their Special Drawing Rights allocations be retained by the IMF to finance expanded IDA development assistance.[60]

Importantly, also, these years saw the emergence of a split among the G10 membership on the link issue. Several of the G10 countries—in particular Italy—had become strong supporters of the idea.[61] There were just as firm opponents of the link within the Group, including significantly the United States, with its all-important veto over a decision on the matter. Outside the G10 countries,

Australia was the most prominent opponent among the other developed countries.[62]

In essence, the environment of decision making at the start of the Committee of Twenty deliberations was fairly favourable to the developing countries. Their own apparent unity, the contrasting division within the G10 and broad-based extra-institutional support were auspicious indicators of this favourable standing. Another positive element was their position of relative parity in the Committee of Twenty forum, compared with their minority representation in the earlier SDR negotiations. From the vantage-point of negative decision-making influence, their situation was no less favourable. In so far as monetary reform pointed to an eventual amendment of the Articles of Agreement, developing countries held a veto over the implementation of change—a vital bargaining tool to obtain concessions to their advantage.

Thus, when the Committee of Twenty began negotiations in 1972, aimed at a reform of the international monetary system, developing countries placed the SDR/aid link issue on the negotiating agenda. Their overriding preoccupation with the link during the negotiations was explicitly stated by the G24 at its Fifth Ministerial Meeting, when it was noted that:

> developing countries have an interest in all aspects of reform: however, they take the view that, while considerable progress has been made in the discussion of the issues in the monetary field ... there has been no corresponding progress in the general area of transferring real resources to developing countries as an integral part of the economic reform exercise ... [T]he developing countries urge the Committee of Twenty to examine all aspects of the problem of transferring real resources to developing countries.[63]

In their preparatory work, the G24 Deputies had concentrated preponderantly on the link issue and were able to agree to the specific form of link desirable for developing countries—the direct allocation of increased shares to them by the IMF,[64] as against a modality that entailed intermediation by development finance institutions.

This issue of a link formula cannot be overstated in terms of what it meant for the disposition of the developing nations towards the whole idea. It has been very influential in determining the degree of unity displayed by these countries in negotiating with the developed countries. The point is that the link is essentially a portmanteau word, embracing a variety of alternative modalities for the implementation of large amounts of resource transfers for the benefit of developing countries on the occasion of SDR allocations. While there has been a broad measure of agreement among developing countries on the principle of greater levels of resource transfers via the link they have been profoundly divided as to the optimum link mechanism to benefit all developing countries.

Many varieties of the link have been canvassed by various groups and individuals[65] but, for the purposes of discussion, two tendencies might be identified. Under the first, the link would be operationalized in such a way as to channel increased SDRs directly to all developing members of the IMF. The second tendency has envisaged a process of intermediation by the multilateral development finance institutions. In the early discussion of the link during the 1960s, advocacy was overwhelmingly in the form of the latter modality, with a large convergence around intermediation through the World Bank group and, more particularly, the IDA.[66] Proposals for a link mechanism involving IDA intermediation created substantial difficulties for many middle-income developing countries because of the operational philosophy of this institution.

The IDA was essentially conceived to provide concessional assistance to the neediest of the developing nations. In practice, in the time-frame over which the link idea was being first advocated and negotiated—the mid-1960s/early 1970s—IDA loans were disproportionately skewed in favour of two countries, India and Pakistan, which together accounted for 60 per cent of IDA commitments up to 1971.[67] Contrastingly, IDA credits to Latin America represented a mere 3 per cent of total credits between 1966 and 1970. As Asher and Mason have observed, the marginal significance of IDA to Latin America 'has been a source of unending complaint from spokesmen for Latin American members'.[68] In this perspective, then, an intermediation role for IDA in any SDR/aid link scheme was evidently an unattractive proposition for the better-off developing countries. The agreement, therefore, within the G24 Deputies forum on the preferred link mechanism implied that a potential source of division among developing countries as regards the beneficiaries of the link seemed to have been effectively settled since all developing countries, in this conception, stood to share in the benefits of a link agreement.[69]

The seriousness with which the link proposal was negotiated was evidenced in the decision by the Committee of Twenty to set up a Technical Group '[t]o examine arguments for and against, and analyse the technical aspects of, proposals for the establishment of a link between the allocation of SDRs and development finance'.[70] This Technical Group was composed along the lines of the Committee of Twenty, with the constituencies that appoint or elect Executive Directors having the right to representation on the Group. Developing countries therefore had representatives on a virtually equal basis with the developed countries.[71]

The disposition of the United States and the EEC countries was crucial to an outcome of the link negotiations since these were the countries that held a veto over any decision to implement the link. The EEC was divided on the matter, with several countries, notably Italy and France, firmly supportive of the Third World position. At the other extreme was West Germany—the most consistent European opponent of the link—with the other countries arrayed somewhere in between. In short, the division within the EEC signified that they did not represent a major stumbling-block to agreement on the issue.[72] The American position therefore became determinative of the ultimate outcome, and its position was one of opposition, though many observers have indicated that, in the circumstances of the time,[73] the American position was by no means one of unalterable opposition.[74]

What this means is that the negotiating posture of developing countries and the sense of conviction and unity they took to the negotiations became critical inputs into the achievement of a favourable outcome. But agreement among developing nations on the principle of direct SDR allocations still left unanswered the question of the basis for distribution among themselves:

> The appropriate formula for distribution among beneficiaries under Scheme B (direct allocation of link SDRs) has not been discussed in detail among the developing countries themselves, however, and participants from developing countries suggested that further discussion on this issue should be deferred until the developing countries had discussed it further.[75]

Moreover, their public negotiating unity notwithstanding, there appeared to have been serious misgivings among several important developing countries about the entire link proposal. In other words, their public negotiating stance did not fully reflect reality. One recorded indication of this lukewarmness can be gauged from the view of the Brazilian Executive Director—a key actor during these negotiations in his role as Vice-Chairman of the Deputies of the Committee of Twenty and participant in the Technical Group:

> The effectiveness of the link as a means of providing additional development finance cannot be taken for granted. If no SDR issues take place, the whole mechanism will be useless. And even if SDRs are created, it is at least conceivable that the effect of the link will be offset by a reduction in other types of official development assistance.[76]

The developed countries opposing the link were quite aware of such misgivings among influential developing countries and this played an important part in strengthening their opposition.[77] As Dell has noted:

> a case could be made that what defeated the link thus far is not so much the resistance of the major developed countries—even the two countries that provided the strongest opposition to the link made it known informally at a certain stage of the discussions that the link was negotiable within a total package of reform. The link was defeated partly ... by division among the developing countries, some of which seem to have been persuaded by the argument put to them that link aid would not be additional, and that their share of such aid ... would be smaller than their share of existing aid flows.[78]

In the end, the monetary reform negotiations of 1972–74 were never completed. Official explanation for the non-completion of these negotiations places the blame on a series of intervening economic occurrences, including the irretrievable breakdown of the fixed exchange regime in 1973 and the resultant adoption of the floating exchange standard by many of the major countries and the oil price increases of late 1973, with their impact on the balance-of-payments and reserve situations in the international economic system. The Committee of Twenty decided that the uncertainties injected into the system by these developments were not propitious for the elaboration of a comprehensive monetary reform.[79] The implication of this decision for developing countries was that they were never able to test the efficacy of their bargaining chip of a veto over monetary reform to obtain concessions on their main substantive concern during the negotiations—the link issue. Yet, in a sense, the decision—on the recommendation of the Committee of Twenty—to establish the joint IMF/IBRD Ministerial Committee on the Transfer of Real Resources to Developing Countries (the Development Committee) pointed to the concern of the industrialized countries to placate the developing countries.[80]

With the completion of the work of the Committee of Twenty, monetary reform negotiations shifted to the negotiations leading to the second amendment of the Fund's Articles. The link proposal remained a key element of Third World advocacy in this context, but continuing opposition by the United States and West Germany, in particular, served to block an international consensus on the issue. Yet, the international sensitivity to the new activism of developing countries in the economic milieu of the mid-1970s was mirrored in the decision taken during the amendment exercise that the proposed Council would have within its task purview to 'review developments in the transfer of real resources to developing countries'.[81] More tangibly, however, on the recommendation of the new Development Committee in January 1975, the Fund took the decision to set up the Trust Fund.[82] As Triffin has written, '[t]his undoubtedly helped rally LDC agreement to the Press Communiqué [of the Interim Committee] of 8 January 1976 in spite of the absence of any reference to the famous "link" proposal ... A bird in the hand was deemed better than two—or even worse—birds in the bush or the air'.[83]

The Trust Fund was conceptually a balance-of-payments assistance programme, extending basically concessional loans to a limited group of eligible developing countries for the period 1 July 1976 to 30 June 1980.[84] Eligibility for Trust Fund loans was decided on the basis of low per capita income.[85] The concessional terms were embodied in the conditions surrounding Trust Fund loans. These included a repayment period of ten years, with a grace period of five years, and a nominal interest payment of 0.5 per cent annually.[86] As a substitute for the link, it clearly had several deficiencies, prominently the fact that it was a temporary agreement—as against the permanency of the envisaged link—and the restricted scope, even among the developing countries, of the beneficiaries. This latter provision, in fact, aroused the displeasure of several Latin American countries, as expressed by the Governor of Bolivia, speaking on behalf of regional members, in 1975:

> It is a matter of concern to the Latin American countries that the proposal for the establishment of a Trust Fund with concessional terms to relieve the critical balance of payments situation of the most seriously affected countries imposes ceilings that eliminate most of them from consideration.[87]

This Latin American reaction merely records the sensitivity of developing countries to arrangements that benefit one sub-group of countries, rather than the group as a whole.

Since the completion of the deliberations of the Committee of Twenty and negotiations on the second amendment, discussion of the link has, in effect, remained in abeyance. Developing countries and their supporters have continued within the framework of the IMF—as well as outside—to press the claim for the link into the early 1980s,[88] but it is not an issue that has received concentrated negotiation between developed and developing countries since the mid-1970s.

There are several reasons for this state of decisional suspension of the link. Firstly, the environment for decision making on SDR allocations has been clearly unfavourable. The context of the early to mid-1970s was one of high levels of inflation[89] and a sufficiency of international liquidity in the aftermath of the huge surpluses generated by the OPEC countries. In this environment, decisions on SDR allocations were, from a technical standpoint, impracticable. Secondly, decisions on allocations *per se* have been difficult to achieve; after the first allocation for the three-year period, 1970–72, there was a long interval of six years before another allocation was decided in 1978, with distribution commencing on 1 January 1979 for another three-year period. Since the last distribution of SDRs on 1 January 1981, developing countries have been trying unsuccessfully—with the strong support of the overwhelming majority of developed countries—to obtain an international consensus for another decision on allocations. The point is that the link is ultimately meaningless in the absence of decisions to allocate SDRs. It is the latter objective that developing countries have been trying primarily to achieve in the early 1980s. As one Third World Executive Board member put it in the course of an interview: 'The most important thing now is to get a decision on the largest feasible allocation of SDRs. In a tactical sense, then, there is no question of an insistence on the link'. Thirdly, in the United States, the major decision-making participant in the Fund, the environment, in a political sense, for development assistance is extremely negative and the attack on the aid agencies by the new Reagan administration since 1981 was merely mirroring a popular mood in the country.[90]

There were, in addition, certain technical developments relating to the SDR that have served to make the link somewhat less attractive to developing countries. The interest rate on the SDR, since 1 May 1981, has been a market-linked rate, reflecting the full market interest rates[91]—in contrast to the earlier concessional rates—and the interest rates in the international credit markets of the early 1980s have been historically high rates. Since it is the users—in the main, the developing countries, as we have seen—which face the onerous burden of interest charges on SDR use, then higher levels of SDR allocations via the link will not necessarily represent a net benefit to these countries.[92] In a more positive direction, there is no longer a reconstitution provision regarding SDR use—countries can theoretically use the full cumulative amounts of SDRs allocated to them in an allocation period.[93] The combination of these two technical innovations and the political difficulty of arriving at decisions to allocate SDRs have lessened the prominence of the link as a negotiating issue for developing countries. Their realistic position is that the link is a dead issue for the foreseeable future.[94]

It is interesting, finally, to place the debate on the link in the context of contemporary developments on the SDR question, in so far as they elucidate the issue of decision making. The Third World nations have been pressing the issue of a new allocation of SDRs since the early 1980s.[95] These countries have provided a strong case in arguing the need for increased reserves. As the Fund's 1983 *Annual Report* points out—using the various measures to calculate the need for reserves—the reserve/import ratio for all countries fell from 19 per cent in

1973–74 to 17 per cent in 1981–82, but the decline was more marked for the non-oil developing countries: from 21 to 15 per cent, compared to the stable ratio of 15 per cent for the developed nations. Using the measure of reserves/ current account deficits, for all countries, the decline was from 2.7 in 1973–74 to 2.4 in 1981, but for the non-oil developing countries, the decline was from 2.1 to 0.9.[96] Another important measure—access to private international credit— has also been highly unfavourable to the developing countries in that the post-1982 years have witnessed a serious curtailment of new lending.[97]

The developing nations have been strongly supported by an overwhelming majority of developed countries in the Fund, including six members of the G10.[98] And, while publicly the Fund's staff has no position on the matter, work in the Research Department supports the claim for a moderate allocation of SDRs.[99] In fact, the Fund's *Annual Report* of 1981 barely hides the staff's conviction of the need for a new SDR allocation—as it is quite subtly put:

> The difficulties presently being encountered by many countries in expeditiously replenishing their reserve holdings point in the direction of either or both of the following: some lack of global adequacy in the availability of international liquidity or the existence of important impediments, such as those affecting access to international goods and capital markets, to the achievement of a more appropriate distribution of reserves ... In the present difficult environment, official sources of liquidity are likely to play an increasingly important role in supporting countries' efforts to find solutions to external financial problems'.[100]

Essentially, the main opponents of an SDR issue are the United States, West Germany, Japan, and, with much less conviction, the United Kingdom.[101] The view of this group of countries can be summed up in the position that there is no global shortage of reserves currently; that, in the context of the large American external deficits and the major reserve-currency role of the dollar, there is no lack of dollars in the Eurocurrency market and that a new allocation would only encourage developing countries to delay needed adjustment. Moreover, opponents have argued that an injection of SDRs into the system would be sending the wrong signal at a time when the inflation battle was being won and thus could re-ignite inflationary tendencies.

These developed countries opposed to a new SDR allocation have remained unconvinced by the advocacy of either developing countries or academic economists[102] or other important groups[103] who have provided arguments in terms of the maldistribution of the liquidity in the system to the disadvantage of developing countries, the severe debt problem confronting many of them, the curtailment of private international lending to developing countries since the early 1980s and the reserve shortage and balance-of-payments difficulties of the poorest—all necessitating the harshest domestic adjustment possible.

In respect of decision making, what this presentation for the contemporary period has shown once again is that the Fund is not necessarily synonymous with the membership. The overwhelming membership, numerically, supports an SDR allocation for the current basic period. Together, these countries dispose of more than 60 per cent of the total voting power. The Fund staff, privately, is convinced of the need for a new SDR allocation, but the Managing Director, because of his sensitive role in the decision-making process for SDR allocations, cannot take a public stance on the issue. It is a minority of four developed members that is the obstacle to a positive outcome on this question—the United States being clearly the most important of the four.

5. The SDR issue—equality of treatment versus a differential standard

What the SDR and related link negotiations have indicated is the fundamental dilemma that confronts the developing countries in their quest for a participatory role, on the basis of equality. On the one hand, the claim for participation in the liquidity negotiations was prosecuted on the basis of equal, non-discriminatory treatment.[104] Contrastingly, the substantive claim for a link between SDRs and development finance is predicated on Fund acquiescence in an inequality of treatment to the benefit of developing countries. As Gold has noted: 'Proposals to establish a link cannot be supported with the principle that made such an appeal when the cause of developing members was participation in the creation and distribution of new reserve assets. In pressing for a link, developing members and their supporters go beyond uniformity'.[105]

The essence of the agreement reached during the initial liquidity negotiations—in respect of both the procedural and substantive issues—signified the triumph of the equality principle in the face of the challenge posed to this fundamental Fund principle by the discriminatory intent of the proposals of the majority G10 membership. Had these proposals been adopted, then the informal tendency towards discriminatory treatment and the division of the membership that had first emerged at the time of the GAB would have been formally endorsed. A special category of members, for both the procedural purpose of taking decisions and the substantive purpose of the distribution of benefits, would *de jure* have been underwritten in the Fund. In short, what was asserted at this historical juncture of the Fund's operations was the formal allegiance to an equality of participatory rights in decision making and benefits of the Fund membership.

This assessment is even more evident when account is taken of the non-acceptance of the link proposal advocated by developing nations. The link issue is as much a philosophical problem as a technical, operational one. What developing countries have been after is the achievement of a distribution formula that would grant them, relative to the developed countries, a disproportionate share of any international liquidity to be created under Fund auspices. The link proposal, in effect, envisaged an element of discrimination in favour of developing countries.

The philosophical basis of this claim was one of equity or equitable treatment;[106] of using another international instrumentality to seek to redress the economic disadvantages and imbalances inherent in the status of an underdeveloped economy. It was akin to the simultaneous campaign waged by these countries in the trade sphere to attain a formal endorsement, internationally, of preferential and non-reciprocal benefits in manufactured trade.[107]

This perspective leads immediately to the philosophical divergences that have separated the competing visions of the international economic order of the developed and developing countries. It is a perspective 'based on the insight that the effort to narrow and ultimately to eliminate the welfare gap presupposes, to a certain extent, a reorientation of traditional *laissez-faire* international economic law through the replacement of economic domination by economic solidarity, the constraint of free competition by the principle of protection of the weaker members of society, the substitution of legal equality by legal inequality'.[108] This philosophical vantage-point, suffused by a pervasive equitable and preferential standard to the benefit of developing countries, has clashed repeatedly with the efficiency arguments of the developed countries and their rhetorical concern not to interfere with market mechanisms in the functioning of the global economic system.

It has clashed just as fundamentally with the principle of equal or uniform treatment that underpins the Fund's constitution.[109] Adherence to equality of treatment implies that formal distinction among the membership is not encouraged[110] and, until recently, the Fund has been at pains to resist any such tendency.

Resistance, in fact, had begun at the Bretton Woods negotiations when India's attempt to have development of the underdeveloped economies incorporated as a primary purpose of the Fund was defeated. Contemporary efforts at the insertion of a special status of the developing countries have been cast in a campaign to have formal constitutional recognition of it—in the words of the Egyptian Governor before the 1974 Annual Meeting:

> . . . the application of uniform rules to all Fund members is not equitable to developing countries and runs counter to their interests. For this reason we suggest the insertion of a new section in the Articles, dealing with the special status of developing countries so that the application of the rules and practices of the Fund would not strain them with further burdens.[111]

The position of the Managing Director on this issue was clearly spelled out at the Third Session of UNCTAD in 1972 thus:

> He disagreed with the view that the rules of conduct in currency and payments relations that were suitable for developed countries were not appropriate for developing ones, since he believed that the interests of both groups coincided in most matters concerning economic growth and stability. Each group had problems peculiar to its economic situation, but that only meant that the code of conduct governing the system should be capable of flexible application . . . He strongly believed that a universal code applying to all countries and taking full account of their special circumstances should be preserved.[112]

This resistance reveals that, from the legal point of view, significant obstacles stand in the way of the achievement by developing countries of a preferential standard of treatment. This is not to say that Fund practice is strictly in step with this legal constraint; in fact, it was previously pointed out that practice has moved substantially in the direction of the recognition of a special category of members in the Fund—developing countries—necessitating special treatment. It is a practice, moreover, that has begun to be validated, as earlier noted, in formal references within the Fund instruments to this category of members. The point, however, is that in the instance of the link, the principle of equality has served to frustrate Third World efforts at preferential treatment.

6. Conclusions

Decision making was a central problem during the international liquidity negotiations of the 1960s. At one level, it involved the original initiators of the discussion of international liquidity—the G10 countries—and reflected the interplay of critical political imperatives that pitted the EEC members of the Group against the United States and the United Kingdom.[113] The EEC countries were concerned with attaining a formal recognition of their new economic power through an integration into international monetary management. This was the ultimate significance of their insistence on—and achievement of—the 85 per cent majority for decisions pertaining to international liquidity. In the mid-1960s, these countries held 16.2 per cent of total Fund votes (see Table 3.2). Economic power was formalized, in a legal sense, in the veto power granted to these countries in the decision-making process, thereby placing them in a position of equality—in terms of ability to block action—with the United States in the Fund's political process.

Isolated and outnumbered in the G10 framework, the United States and the United Kingdom sought a solution that was favourable to their interests by the adoption of two basic positions: a positive disposition to an institutional role for the IMF in liquidity negotiations and a participatory role for the other Fund members. The G10 was not a formally organized forum and the United States did not carry the decision-making authority in it as it did in the IMF. In the G10, the members met as equals in so far as decision making was concerned.[114] A Fund role shifted, by contrast, the political negotiations dynamics in favour of the US–UK position, because of their combined voting power and the numerical and voting strength that the other Fund members—whose position on the issue was closer to that of the US–UK—brought to the negotiations.

The three major sets of actors in this political alliance—the United States and the United Kingdom, the Managing Director and the developing countries—each needed the other for their own specific ends and it was, eventually, a mutually beneficial alliance since they all achieved their primary objective. For the Managing Director, it was a question of the reassertion of the central authority of the institution in international monetary matters.[115] In so far as developing countries were concerned, the two primary objectives achieved were a participatory role in the negotiations—however inadequate ultimately—and in the sharing of benefits. For the United States and the United Kingdom, it was a liquidity scheme the substantive details of which were nearer to their conception.

What was also interesting at that time was the coherent Third World stance unequivocally supportive of the central position of the Fund in international monetary relations. There was no sense of inadequate participation in Fund decision making *per se*. In fact, the CIAP report, in justifying a central role for the IMF, went as far as to affirm that: 'This institution has long experience in international monetary affairs, and its management is subject to a system of voting which enables all member countries, small as well as large, to have a say'.[116]

It is not wholly accurate, as some analysts have contended, that it was the unity of the developing countries and the political pressures they generated, both inside and outside the organization, that led to their integration into the liquidity negotiations.[117] This was just a partial explanatory factor. Nor is it accurate, as other analysts have argued, that it was '[t]he IMF view [that] won the day'.[118] Reality was, in fact, more complex than either of these partial explanations. It cannot be disputed that these factors contributed significantly to the acceptance of a participatory role for the developing countries. But, analysis has tended either to gloss over or ignore completely the important fact of intra-G10 divisions that forced the isolated minority members to seek alliances outside the Group.

The fact is that on the other issues of fundamental importance to developing countries—the link proposal—they brought to bear as much political pressure, with the support of both UNCTAD and the UN General Assembly, and yet failed to obtain it. What was different in this instance were, on the one hand, a unified G10 position hostile to the link and, on the other, the lack of support of the Managing Director. Therefore, while conceding the political unity of developing countries and the extra-institutional support of the United Nations system and, in particular, UNCTAD, it is also necessary to stress the crucial political significance of the divisions within the G10 and the unambiguous, activist support of the Managing Director as influential explanatory factors in the participation of the developing countries in decision making on international liquidity.

Apart from these considerations, there has been an evident disagreement among official and academic economists regarding the technical merits of the proposed link mechanism. In the context of disagreement at this level, a decision on the link could only have been made on the basis of political acceptability and feasibility, as measured, in the final analysis, by the political power disposition of the negotiating participants. The single, most influential developed country, the United States—with its formal veto power over SDR decisions—has had a history of consistent opposition to the link and it is here that the decision-making requirement assumes a critical importance. One country has the power to block continuously a broad-based international consensus bridging developed and developing countries, representing an overriding numerical majority and a significant voting majority in the Fund.

If the United States has held a veto over the link, the position of developing countries themselves has contributed in its own way to this impasse. As previously stressed, the link is basically a 'portmanteau' concept, embracing a variety of possible schemes for actual operationalization. If developing countries have coalesced around the proposal at the level of general principle, there has been fundamental divergence among these countries when it came to agreeing to the specific variant to be implemented. This divergence has obviously to do with the calculation of benefits to individual countries from the various link schemes.

This sense of intra-Third World disagreement, and the associated lack of conviction among important Third World countries regarding the merits of the proposal *per se*, are well-known to developed countries and has served to buttress the inflexibility of the main link opponents.[119] It also reveals the basic flaw in the group negotiations—the fact that, while it is relatively easy to reach agreements on general principles, it is quite difficult to agree to operational modalities. At this stage, the play of national, rather than group interests becomes the determining factor. The question of who is to benefit and who is to benefit most serves to dissipate group unity as members seek to maximize benefits on an individual basis.

The failure of the developing countries to achieve Fund approval of the link, both at the time of the Committee of Twenty deliberations and the subsequent negotiations for the second amendment, has marked the effective demise of this proposal. The years between 1972 and 1976 were, politically and economically, the most opportune period to obtain its endorsement, since these were the years of greatest Third World leverage in the IMF. This leverage related to the disarray in the international monetary system, the new organizational strength of these countries symbolized by the G24, the environment of Third World assertiveness manifested in the OPEC action and the NIEO campaign and the important fact of the monetary reform negotiations. In respect of these negotiations, developing countries had maximum leverage in terms of their blocking power over a monetary agreement. Failure at that moment and the contemporary international economic environment—particularly the negative popular outlook on the aid question in the principal donor country—have combined to force a Third World retreat on the link proposal.

Finally, to speak of a G10 position in the Fund is an oversimplification of reality, and to speak of a Fund position—in the absence of a specific decision of the institution—is to be analytically imprecise. The G10 is not a monolithic entity, appearances to the contrary notwithstanding. As the Indian Executive Director remarked during the first joint meeting of the Executive Board and the G10 Deputies in 1967, 'one of the discoveries, at least for those countries not in the Group of Ten, had been that the countries of the Group of Ten were not, by any means, a solid phalanx'.[120] There have been—and continue to be—significant intra-Group divisions, no less so when it comes to issues of direct relevance to developing countries. It is not the purpose here to dissect and account for these divisions, but in so far as divisions can be a tactical disadvantage in negotiating contexts, then developing countries have to be as much sensitive as responsive to this reality of G10 functioning, rather than indulging in blanket condemnation of the Group, when it might be at most two or three of these countries that are steadfastly opposed to specific areas of concern to them.

Similarly, there is an imperative need to be more analytically discriminating when ascribing perspectives and positions to the IMF. The institution is made up of over 140 members and though there have evolved over time two relatively coherent groupings of countries, the absence of consensus among the membership on an issue does not automatically mean that the Fund *qua* institution is opposed to the issue. It was seen that the Managing Director and staff had been firm defenders of positions favoured by developing countries. This factor needs to be recognized as well, for it has fundamental implications for the approach to negotiations by countries.

Notes

1. Unlike gold or foreign exchange, SDRs are not tangible monetary assets. Rather, on the occasion of decisions to allocate SDRs to the membership, the Fund merely enters into its accounts the amount of SDRs allocated to each member. These SDRs may then be used, on the request of a member, to purchase foreign exchange within the Fund in the event of a balance-of-payments need. The rules and other conditions surrounding the SDR will be outlined later in this Chapter.
2. De Vries, *The International Monetary Fund, 1966–71*, Vol. 1, p. 121.
3. For the purposes of this analysis, the concept of international liquidity relates to the unconditional monetary assets available to national monetary authorities for the settlement of international transactions. Conceptually, this contrasts with liquidity in the form of conditional credit within the international monetary system. The one is freely usable by national authorities, while defined conditions attach to use of the other—see John Williamson, *The failure of world monetary reform: 1972–74*, New York, New York University Press, 1977, p. 1.
4. C. Fred Bergsten, *The Dilemma of the Dollar: the Economics and Politics of United States International Monetary Policy*, New York, New York University Press, 1975, p. 16.
5. The IMF itself in this period had a small part to play in the liquidity availabilities for its membership. As has previously been stressed, the Fund has a lending mandate. The Fund, though, provides in the main conditional liquidity to borrowing countries and, as such, was not seen under the original dispensation as having a prime function in regard to the provision of reserves to meet the requirements of expanding international transactions. Not all Fund lending, however, was of the conditional variety. Use of the original gold tranche—currently known as the reserve tranche—was unconditional, thereby approximating, in a qualitative sense, reserves owned by a country.
6. This instability was pointed out by Triffin in the late 1950s—see, in particular, Robert Triffin, *Gold and the Dollar Crisis*, New Haven, Yale University Press, 1960. Specifically as regards the US dollar, Triffin pointed out that, were the United States to take steps to resolve its deficits, a shortage of international reserves would ensue. On the other hand, paradoxically, were the deficits to be allowed to continue, and countries took steps to convert their dollar holdings into gold, then the inexorable depletion of the United States gold reserves—a mainstay of the prevailing arrangement—would bring into question the continuing ability of the US to keep to its convertibility commitments—the whole confidence question.
7. Gold, *Legal and Institutional Aspects of the International Monetary System*, op. cit., Vol. 1, p. 90.
8. UNCTAD, *International Monetary Issues and the Developing Countries* (Report of the Group of Experts), UN, New York, 1965, p. 4, para. 15. See also IMF, *Annual Report*, 1966, p. 12.
9. Group of Ten, *Communiqué of Ministers and Governors and Report of Deputies*, July 1966, p. 12, para. 56.

10. See *Summary Proceedings*, 1963, p. 286.
11. Ibid., p. 29.
12. Ibid., p. 183.
13. Ibid. This is simply one of many occasions when there was a marked public divergence of position between the Managing Director and the G10 countries, in particular. This should caution analysts against speaking indiscriminately about a Fund attitude, in the sense that there is a monolithic entity known as the Fund, encompassing members and management and characterized by overall agreement on all issues. This matter will be discussed in greater detail later.
14. These were the Governors from El Salvador, Ethiopia, India, Yugoslavia, United Arab Republic, Brazil and Sudan.
15. See Chapter 7 herein.
16. See, for instance, the statement by the Governor from India in *Summary Proceedings*, 1963, p. 77.
17. Ibid., p. 286.
18. Developing nations could only have benefited from such an arrangement. The fact of G10 collaboration with the IMF meant that the initial tendency to neglect the institution was no longer feasible. The Managing Director's strong advocacy of a role for developing countries in the liquidity discussions and his political alliance with these countries ensured that, indirectly, their concerns would at least have been presented by him.
19. See 'Speech by the Managing Director to the National Foreign Trade Convention', New York, 16 November 1964 in *International Financial News Survey*, 16, 1964, pp. 441-5.
20. Ibid., p. 444. Evident in this formulation is the drawing of the continuum between procedure and outcome—absence from the decision-making process implying absence from the benefits of the decision.
21. In fact, differentiation among the membership had begun two years earlier with the GAB. It is also important to underline that this differentiation and its consequence, differential treatment, were introduced by the developed countries into the operations of the Fund and breached the principle of uniformity that was the legal core of the institution.
22. Many analyses have tended not to treat in any meaningful way this most important factor of division within the G10. Rather, the G10 is treated as though it was a monolithic entity, with a clearly defined consensus.
23. See Group of Ten, *Report of the Study Group on the Creation of Reserve Assets* (Report of the Deputies of the Group of Ten), 31 May 1965, pp. 57-8, paras. 118 and 119.
24. For a discussion, see Robert Triffin, *Our International Monetary System: Yesterday, Today and Tomorrow*, New York, Random House, 1968, pp. 107-19. It is to be recalled that the United Kingdom was, as yet, not a member of the EEC.
25. This aim was explicitly stated in the Communiqué that followed the April 1967 Meeting of the EEC Finance Ministers: 'In their communiqué, the Finance Ministers indicated that, because of the economic strength of their six countries and, their union in the EEC, they must, in any event, be assured of a proper influence in the Fund, particularly in respect of voting'—see de Vries, *The International Monetary Fund, 1966-71*, Vol. 1, p. 133. This is simply a clear example of the impact of environmental change on the internal processes of an organization.
26. See, for instance, statement of Governor of Egypt, *Summary Proceedings*, 1964, p. 86.
27. IMF, *Annual Report*, 1966, p. 17.
28. Up to this point, the developing countries had no caucusing group within the IMF to present a unified position. This explains in large measure the activist role played by extra-institutional actors—G77, UN system, UNCTAD—in stating their views on

international monetary issues from the mid-1960s to early 1970s. Importantly, also, these countries did not have at their disposal a technical-support infrastructure and thus depended greatly on the technical expertise available within the UNCTAD Secretariat.

29. See 'Final Act, Annex A.IV.19' on international monetary issues, *Proceedings of the United Nations Conference on Trade and Development*, Vol. 1, Geneva, 23 March–16 June 1964, New York, United Nations, 1964, p. 53. This decision called for the convening of a group of experts 'to consider the international monetary issues relating to problems of trade and development with special reference to the objectives and decisions of this Conference, and devoting particular attention to the needs of the developing countries in their trade with one another and with the rest of the world'.

30. Inter-American Committee on the Alliance for Progress (CIAP), *International Monetary Reform and Latin America* (Report to CIAP by the Group of Experts), Pan American Union, General Secretariat, OAS, Washington DC, 1966.

31. Adopted without objection on 17 December 1966.

32. See de Vries, *The International Monetary Fund, 1966–71*, Vol. 1, p. 99.

33. Group of Ten, *Communiqué of Ministers and Governors and Report of Deputies*, July 1966, para. 5.

34. *Summary Proceedings*, 1965, p. 30.

35. Group of Ten, *Communiqué of Ministers and Governors and Report of Deputies*, July 1966, para. 7.

36. As previously indicated, it had another positive impact on the participation of developing countries in Fund decision making. It led to the creation of the first caucusing group—the Group of Nine Executive Directors—among the developing countries as a whole in the Fund.

37. John Williamson, 'The Link' in Jagdish N. Bhagwati, ed., *The New International Economic Order: The North-South Debate*, Cambridge, Mass., The MIT Press, 1977, p. 81. See also Graham Bird. 'Is an SDR link still relevant for developing countries?', *The Banker*, June 1982, p. 63.

38. For a historical account, see Y. S. Park, op. cit.

39. Ibid., p. 1.

40. UNCTAD, *International Monetary Issues and the Developing Countries*, paras. 6 and 12.

41. Ibid., para. 6.

42. See, for instance, statements by Governors of the Philippines and India in *Summary Proceedings*, 1965, pp. 144 and 158 respectively.

43. See de Vries, *The International Monetary Fund, 1966–71*, Vol. 1, pp. 110–11.

44. See Group of Ten, *Report of the Study Group on the Creation of Reserve Assets*, pp. 69–70, para. 138. Another objection raised by the US Executive Director was the possibility that the US Congress, in the event of the activation within the Fund of the link, might respond by reducing foreign aid programmes; in effect, there might be no actual net gain for developing countries from a link arrangement.

45. Group of Ten, *Communiqué of Ministers and Governors*, July 1966, para. 40.

46. Managing Director, 'Developments in the World Monetary System' (address before the Federation of German Industries, Kronberg im Taunas, 25 April 1966), *International Financial News Survey* (Supp.), 29 April 1966, p. 142.

47. See resolution 2626(XXV), 'International Development Strategy for the Second United Nations Development Decade' of 24 October 1970, para. C(52): 'As soon as adequate experience is available on the working of the scheme of Special Drawing Rights, serious consideration will be given to the possibility of the establishment of a link between the allocation of new reserve assets under the scheme and the

provision of additional development finance for the benefit of all developing countries'.

48. De Vries, *The International Monetary Fund, 1966–71*, Vol. 1, p. 108. See also IMF, *Annual Report*, 1966, pp. 16–17. While this consensus was reached by late 1966, shortly after the joint meetings began, the SDR negotiations continued into 1967— clearly implying that developing countries did not press the issue too much.

49. Under the Articles of Agreement, the decision-making process on SDR allocations envisages a decision by the Board of Governors disposing of 85 per cent of the total voting power, on the basis of proposals of the Managing Director, concurred in by the Executive Board—Art. XVIII, Sec. 4(a) and (d).

50. See Triffin, *Our International Monetary System*, pp. 127–8.

51. For an extended description of the SDR scheme, see Richard W. Edwards, jun., *International Monetary Collaboration*, Dobbs Ferry, New York, Transnational Publishers Inc., 1985, Ch. 5, pp. 167–221.

52. The reconstitution provision was analogous to a repayment requirement. Allocations of SDRs are made for basic periods, normally of five years duration, though the Fund may decide to vary the duration of any basic period. So far, in the two allocation periods since the coming into effect of the SDR, allocations were for periods of three years. For the rules regarding reconstitution for the first basic period, see Schedule G of the Articles (first amendment).

53. Anand G. Chandavarkar, *The International Monetary Fund. Its Financial Organization and Activities*, Pamphlet Series, No. 42, Washington DC, IMF, 1984, p. 69.

54. *IMF Survey*, 19 July 1982, p. 213.

55. G. K. Helleiner, 'The Less Developed Countries and the International Monetary System', *The Journal of Development Studies*, **10**, Nos 3 and 4, April/July 1974, p. 351. See also Duncan Cameron, 'Special Drawing Rights', *International Journal*, **36**, No. 4, Autumn 1981, pp. 713–31.

56. UNCTAD, *International Monetary Reform and Cooperation for Development* (Report of the Expert Group on International Monetary Issues), UN, New York, 1969, Chs. 4 and 5.

57. See General Assembly resolution 2626(XXV).

58. See UNCTAD resolution 84(111), 'The international monetary situation', paras 9 and 10.

59. See *Partners in Development* (Report of the Commission on International Development), London, Pall Mall Press, 1969, p. 225.

60. *A Proposal to Link Reserve Creation and Development Assistance: Report of the Sub-Committee on International Exchange and Payments of the Joint Economic Committee*, 91st Congress, 1st Session, Congress of the US, Washington DC, US Government Printing Office, 1969, p. 6.

61. See statement by Governor of Italy, *Summary Proceedings*, 1969, p. 71. See also statement by Governor of France, ibid., 1975, p. 97.

62. Ibid., 1970, p. 159.

63. 'Communiqué: G24', Fifth Ministerial Meeting, 23 September 1973, op. cit., p. 305. See also Williamson, 'The Link', op. cit., p. 94.

64. See 'Communiqué of the Deputies of the G24', 18–19 May 1973, *IMF Survey*, 28 May 1973, p. 156.

65. For an exposition of the many link formulas, see Williamson, 'The Link', op. cit., and Peter Saladin, 'The Link between the Creation of Special Drawing Rights (SDRs) and Development Finance', *Development Dialogue*, 1981, 1, pp. 38–46.

66. See, for instance, the influential UNCTAD Group of Experts' Report of 1969, previously referred to, the Pearson Commission Report and the discussion in the US Congress—the references for which can be found in notes 56, 59 and 60, *supra*.

67. See Asher and Mason, op. cit., p. 401.
68. Ibid., p. 402.
69. This, for instance, is the interpretation of Williamson in his article 'The link', op. cit.—see p. 94. But as we shall shortly see, the position was more complex than this.
70. Committee on Reform of the International Monetary System and Related Issues (Committee of Twenty), *International Monetary Reform: Documents of the Committee of Twenty*, Washington DC, IMF, 1974, p. 95.
71. Ibid., pp. 110–11 for a listing of the membership of the Technical Group.
72. This is for the simple arithmetical reason that their division meant that those EEC countries that were supportive of the link held enough votes within the Group to ensure that the veto could not be activated.
73. Specifically, we are speaking of the fact of the monetary collapse and the renegotiations to reconstruct a credible regime, OPEC's action, the new activism of the developing nations, their NIEO demands and the disunity of the OECD nations.
74. See Sidney Dell, 'International Monetary Issues and the Developing Countries: A Comment', *World Development*, 3, No. 9, September 1975, p. 633. Dell's contention has a great deal of credibility in that he attended meetings of the Technical Group on the link. What is more, his assessment was supported by Fund officials during the interviewing process.
75. Committee of Twenty, op. cit., p. 107.
76. Alexandre Kafka, *The International Monetary Fund: Reform without Reconstruction?* Essays in International Finance, Princeton, No. 118, October 1976, p. 32. Another of Kafka's concerns—and by implication also of the better-off developing countries— can be glimpsed in his observation that: 'There is more awareness today than earlier of, and more disposition to deal with, the problems of the poorest LDCs. But what is lacking is the recognition that even the more fortunate LDCs cannot meet all of their financial needs by borrowing in the markets'—see Alexandre Kafka, 'Comment' in Bhagwati, ed., *The New International Economic Order*, op. cit., p. 102.
77. This was revealed in interviews with two officials who participated in these negotiations. It was intimated that these misgivings were privately expressed to negotiators of developed countries, who were then confirmed in their adamant position.
78. Dell, 'International Monetary Issues and the Developing Countries: A Comment', op. cit., p. 633. See also Havelock Brewster, 'Facing the facts of life in North–South negotiations', *South*, June 1982, p. 33.
79. Committee of Twenty, *International Monetary Reform*, p. 7.
80. Ibid., pp. 47–8. See also Board of Governors' resolution 29-8 of 2 October 1974 establishing the Committee in IMF, *Selected Decisions*, pp. 348–52. An argument could be made that this decision conceivably indicated the probable outcome of the negotiating exercise on the link, had the developing countries remained united and had international economic events not interceded to abort the reform programme. As we shall shortly see, a year later, in 1974, another important decision on resource transfer—the establishment of the Trust Fund—was taken.
81. See schedule D, 2(a) of the Articles of Agreement.
82. Decision No. 5069-(76/72) of 5 May 1976 in *Selected Decisions*, pp. 302–3. Financing of the Trust Fund was to be derived from the profits realized from the sale of one-sixth of the Fund's holdings of gold.
83. Robert Triffin, 'Jamaica: "Major Revision" or Fiasco?' in Edward M. Bernstein, *et al.*, *Reflections on Jamaica*, Essays in International Finance, No. 115, April 1976, p. 47.
84. It is to be noted that the Trust Fund was technically separated from the Fund's regular financial operations. It was a Fund that was administered by the IMF as Trustee and with its own terms and conditions. Eligibility was restricted to an

identified sub-group of developing countries with per capita income in 1973 of less than SDR 300—clearly inconsistent with the fundamental Fund principle of uniformity of treatment of all members. For a description of the Trust Fund, see Ernest Sturc, 'The Trust Fund', *Finance and Development*, 13, No. 4, December 1976, pp. 30-1.

85. *IMF Survey*, 4 September 1978, p. 266.

86. These conditions were concessional in the Fund context, with its normal three-to-five years repayment period, and interest rates that, while normally below market rates, were higher than that for Trust Fund loans. In a sense, the Trust Fund introduced an aid function into the IMF's mandate—see statement of Governor for Brazil, *Summary Proceedings*, 1977, p. 92.

87. Ibid., 1975, p. 210. See also statement by Governors from Panama and Brazil, ibid., p. 106 and ibid., 1977, p. 92, respectively.

88. See 'Communiqué: G24', 11th May 1982, *IMF Survey*, 24 May 1982, p. 151, para. 12. See also *North–South: A Programme for Survival* (Report of the Independent Commission on International Development Issues), London, Pan Books, 1980, p. 210.

89. It is to be remembered that it is constitutionally specified that decisions on allocations should seek, *inter alia*, to avoid 'excess demand and inflation in the world'—Art. XVIII, Sec. 1(a).

90. For a discussion of the Reagan administration view on the multilateral aid agencies, see Robert L. Ayres, 'Breaking the Bank', *Foreign Policy*, No. 43, Summer 1981, pp. 1204-20. See 'Eagle's claws already bloodied', *The Financial Times*, 26 September 1983, on the anti-IMF attitude in Congressional and other public circles in the United States.

91. See IMF, *Annual Report*, 1981, p. 77.

92. For a discussion, see Bird, 'Is an SDR link still relevant for developing countries?' op. cit.

93. See IMF, *Annual Report*, 1981, p. 77. The reconstitution requirement was eliminated, effective from 30 April 1981.

94. This was revealed by several representatives of developing countries during the course of interviews. Publicly, however, the developing countries have continued to make the link a part of their advocacy on international monetary reform—see 'Communiqué: G24', 9 February 1983, *IMF Survey*, 21 February 1983, para. 12. This is an understandable tactic in that these countries cannot be seen to be giving up all their negotiating positions unilaterally.

95. See, for instance, 'Communiqué: G24', 3 September 1982, *IMF Survey*, 20 September 1982, pp. 291-2, para. 11.

96. IMF, *Annual Report*, 1983, pp. 79-80. See also ibid., 1981, p. 81.

97. Ibid., 1983, pp. 77-8. While noting that, since mid-1982, with the curtailment of international bank lending many countries have been unable to maintain or regain an adequate level of reserves, the Executive Director from The Netherlands has written that: 'SDR creation favors the reserve needs of weaker countries; but the fact that the stronger members of the Fund, and in particular the reserve centers, can get by comfortably without this credit mechanism of the Fund is not a good reason not to allow it to perform the useful international function that it can perform ... In a period when the commercial banks are reluctant to expand their overseas credit, there is every reason to use both of the credit mechanisms for which the Fund's Articles provide'—see Polak, 'The Role of the Fund', op. cit., p. 260.

98. Developed countries that have expressed support for a moderate allocation of SDRs include Ireland, Italy, The Netherlands, Belgium, Canada, Finland, Austria,

Luxembourg and France—see *Summary Proceedings*, 1983, pp. 50, 67, 118, 139, 147, 158, 167, 170 and ibid., 1984, p. 46 for the respective positions of these countries.

99. This was indicated by several Fund officials during the interviews. It was also explicitly alluded to by Fund Governors at the 1984 Annual Meeting—see, for instance, statements of Governors from Indonesia and Italy, *Summary Proceedings*, 1984, pp. 60 and 72, respectively.

100. IMF, *Annual Report*, 1981, p. 81.

101. See :'Requiem for the new order', *South*, October 1985, p. 161. The less-than-firm position of the United Kingdom in opposition to an SDR allocation was revealed by all Executive Board participants interviewed. It was also indicated by several of these insiders that, ultimately, the British will go wherever the United States goes on the issue.

102. See, in particular, John Williamson, *A New SDR Allocation?* Policy Analyses in International Economics, No. 7, Institute for International Economics, Washington DC, March 1984.

103. See, for example, *Common Crisis—North–South: Co-operation for World Recovery* (The Brandt Commission), London, Pan Books, 1983, pp. 56–8.

104. See Gold, *Legal and Institutional Aspects of the International Monetary System*, Vol. 1, pp. 469–70.

105. Ibid., p. 485.

106. See, for instance, *Partners in Development*, p. 225 and Bird, 'Is an SDR link still relevant for developing countries?', op. cit., p. 64.

107. For a discussion, see Abdulqawi Yusuf, *Legal Aspects of Trade Preferences for Developing States*, The Hague, Martinus Nijhoff Publishers, 1982.

108. W. D. Verwey, 'The Recognition of the Developing Countries as Special Subjects of International Law beyond the Sphere of United Nations Resolutions' in The Hague Academy of International Law, *The Right to Development at the International Level* (Workshop, The Hague, 16–18 October 1979), The Netherlands, Sijthoff and Noordhoff, 1980, p. 373.

109. Gold has noted that this principle embodies two elements: 'One element is that, with certain exceptions, the Articles of Agreement establish the same rights and obligations for all member countries of the Fund, and the other element is that the policies of the Fund apply equally to all members. The principle can be regarded, therefore, as one that prevents discrimination in favor of, or against, particular members, without regard to their economic strength or weakness or any other characteristic'—Gold, *Legal and Institutional Aspects of the International Monetary System*, op. cit., Vol. 1, p. 469.

110. See A. W. Hooke, 'The Role of the Fund in Developing Countries' in Hooke, ed., op. cit., p. 163.

111. *Summary Proceedings*, 1974, p. 217.

112. 'Summary of Statement by the Managing Director, IMF' in UNCTAD, *Proceedings of the United Nations Conference on Trade and Development*, Vol. 1a, Part 1, Third Session, Santiago de Chile, 13 April–21 May 1972, New York, UN, 1973, p. 332.

113. As Cohen argues, the liquidity problem of the 1960s 'was an aspect of Atlantic-community politics and reflected a resurgent Western Europe demanding a shift in the international monetary balance of power to its favor'—Stephen D. Cohen, *International Monetary Reform, 1964–69: The Political Dimension*, Praeger Publishers, 1970, p. 80.

114. This factor gave to the EEC countries a distinct advantage. They brought to G10 deliberations the weight of a unified position on the issues.

115. As Strange has noted: 'the SDR Agreement appeared to restore to the Fund the authority filched from it by the Group of Ten in the middle 1960s'—Susan Strange,

International Economic Relations of the Western World, 1959–71: International Monetary Relations, Vol. 2, London, Oxford University Press, 1976, p. 261.

116. CIAP, op. cit., p. 20.

117. Dell has written, for instance, in speaking of the SDR negotiations that: 'what won the day was not "the Fund view" but the strong political pressures brought to bear by the developing countries in a variety of international forums, particularly UNCTAD and the United Nations General Assembly'—Dell, 'International Monetary Issues and the Developing Countries: A Comment', op. cit., p. 636.

118. Geoffrey Maynard & Graham Bird, 'International Monetary Issues and the Developing Countries: A Survey', *World Development*, Vol. 3, No. 9, September 1975, p. 615. As Dell has pointed out, it is a mistake to equate the Managing Director with the Fund; the Managing Director did have a view on the issue, but the Fund did not—its view was, in fact, under negotiation: see Dell, 'International Monetary Issues and the Developing Countries: A Comment', op. cit., p. 636.

119. This was revealed by an Executive Board member of a developed country, who was present over most of the years of the SDR and link negotiations.

120. De Vries, *The International Monetary Fund, 1966–71*, Vol. 1, op. cit., p. 121.

Chapter 6

The exchange rate mechanism: the persistence of decision-making marginalization

1. Introduction

A pivotal component feature of the international monetary order constructed at Bretton Woods was the exchange rate mechanism to govern the monetary relations of the Fund's membership. The promotion of exchange rate stability, as well as the maintenance of orderly exchange arrangements, was specified as a principle purpose of the IMF[1] and to this end the Articles of Agreement outlined a code of conduct that members were required to observe in their exchange transactions. The par value system agreed to at Bretton Woods lasted for just over a quarter of a century, but by the late 1960s, into the 1970s, it had become the principal area of controversy and friction among the Fund's members. This period was, in fact, to see the final breakdown of the prevailing arrangements and the initiation of negotiations to reconstruct a new exchange rate regime.

While the controversy related to the technical merits/demerits of the two contending approaches to exchange rates that were the centre of focus at that time—the existing par value mechanism and floating rates—it equally had to do with a struggle over power and participatory rights in international management. What emerged as the fundamental issue of the political contest were continued American privileges and dominance and the demand by major European economic powers for symmetrical rights and obligations—a continuation, to a certain extent, of the struggle begun with the liquidity question. At the beginning of the 1970s the developing countries undertook their own campaign for participatory rights, in opposition to the combined efforts of a narrow group of developed countries to dominate international monetary governance.

2. The Bretton Woods exchange rate mechanism

The experiences with exchange rates in the interwar period were largely influential in determining the perspectives, as well as actual agreement, on the exchange rate mechanism for the Bretton Woods monetary order.[2] The disarray in commercial relations during these years was fed by chaotic monetary relations, manifested in unstable national exchange rates, competitive devaluations and a general absence of consultation in undertaking exchange rate adjustments. In short, the nationalistic imperative guided the approach to exchange rate policy for countries.

An overriding concern, therefore, in the negotiation of a new international monetary system was the assurance of stability and predictability in exchange rates, coupled with a modicum of international cooperation in this area. Thus, the initial proposals formulated by both the Americans and British favoured a system of essentially fixed rates, though there were fundamental differences in the two proposals regarding the question of authority to set and change domestic exchange rates. The American plan originally envisaged an arrangement whereby, firstly, the Fund would have had the authority to set member-countries' rates and, secondly, changes to them would have required the consent of an overwhelming proportion of the Fund's voting power—an 80 per cent majority.[3] Contrastingly, the British plan specified a process under which member-states would agree among themselves regarding their respective rates, with subsequent changes to be sanctioned solely by the Fund's Governing Board, except under clearly defined circumstances.[4]

Anglo–American negotiations resulted in a narrowing of these differences and agreement on the par value mechanism that was subsequently embodied in the Articles of Agreement. At the Bretton Woods Conference, while several countries, including a few developing ones, sought to introduce modifications to the Anglo–American proposal, there were no substantive challenges to the par value mechanism *per se*.[5]

What was agreed was the requirement for member-countries, in consultation with the Fund, to set a par value for the domestic currency either directly in terms of the envisaged numeraire of the system, that is, gold, or indirectly in relation to the US dollar of a fixed weight as of 1 July 1944.[6] Members were further required to maintain the market exchange *vis-à-vis* other currencies within a one per cent margin either side of parity. Except for a transitional provision that allowed members to adjust initial par values as much as 10 per cent, a change in its par value could be proposed by a member, but only when faced with a fundamental disequilibrium in its external payments position. Finally, Fund approval was a *sine qua non* for the implementation of a change in par value.[7]

Interestingly, moreover, the United States was able to have incorporated into the Articles of Agreement a specific provision that gave to that country a special position in respect of the par value arrangement.[8] Under the terms of the provision, the member stood ready to freely buy and sell gold in its exchange transactions and it was indicated that observance of this provision substituted for observance of the obligations of the par value regime.[9] As it turned out in practice, the United States was the only Fund member that signalled its intent to adhere to this provision and, moreover, was the only member to do so over the life-span of the par value mechanism.[10] This central position of the United States in the exchange rate arrangement was a clear indication both of its capacity for leadership and its acceptance of this role in the post-Second World War international monetary order.

In fact, however, the system did not fully operate as intended in the early years of the Fund's existence. Many countries found it difficult, in the face of severe economic dislocations and uncertain circumstances, to observe their international commitments regarding par values and currency convertibility.

Thus, by the end of the first decade of the Fund's operations, less than half the membership had agreed par values for their currencies; in essence, there was a variety of exchange rates in place, including floating and multiple rates. As the Fund's official history observes: 'The first decade of the Fund's existence had proved to be a most difficult environment for the attainment of its exchange rate objectives'.[11]

The situation changed markedly over the following decade, when a gradual process of observance of exchange rate obligations began to occur. By the end of 1965, more than half of the IMF's members—compared with 40 per cent a decade earlier—had par values, including all the major industrialized economies and quite a few developing countries. The overwhelming majority, some 86 per cent, had either fixed exchange rates or relatively stable rates.[12]

3. The collapse of the Bretton Woods exchange rate mechanism: American unilateralism and G10 exclusivism

A review of the last years of the 1960s and the start of the 1970s indicates that exchange rates had become the main preoccupation of the Fund membership. This was an outgrowth of the instabilities that became apparent during the second half of the 1960s with regard to the functioning of the par value arrangement and the consequential tensions introduced into international monetary relations. This situation of growing crisis was to reach a head at the beginning of the 1970s, particularly in the wake of the action taken by the American authorities on 15 August 1971, affecting its exchange transactions.[13]

Exchange rate instability was reflected in the set of crises that several major European countries confronted in the late 1960s and the continuing adjustment difficulties faced by the United States. Faced with a deteriorating external sector in 1966–67, manifested in substantial trade deficits and speculative pressures against its currency, the British devalued the pound in November 1967. The following year, France also confronted a combination of political and economic difficulties that resulted in massive capital flight and the weakening of the franc while, contrastingly, the German economy was strengthening.[14] After much resistance and an emergency G10 Ministerial Meeting in Bonn, West Germany, in November 1968, the French government devalued the franc in August 1969. In September of that same year, the German Deutsche Mark was temporarily floated and then revalued the following month. The persistent American payments deficits were a source of fundamental friction among the world's principal monetary authorities and contributed to destabilizing movements of, and loss of confidence in the American currency.

It was against this backdrop of unsettled exchange markets that the Fund's Executive Directors in January 1969 assumed the task of studying the exchange rate mechanism. While the impetus for the assumption of this task was clearly the exchange rate adjustment problems besetting the major economies, another critical consideration was to abort any effort at decision making on this matter outside the framework of the Fund.[15] The G10 meeting the previous November in Bonn was an unmistakable portent of things to come. At once, then, the issue of decision making assumed a central importance in exchange rate discussions and this early attempt to assert Fund authority in this area could only have resulted from the sensitization process of the liquidity discussions a few years earlier.

Executive Board consideration of this issue indicated the substantial sentiment of the Fund membership against any tampering with existing arrangements. The Report concluded that '[t]he par value system, based on stable, but adjustable par values at realistic levels, remains the most appropriate general regime to govern exchange rates in a world of managed national economies'.[16]

What was immediately instructive, in the context of this incipient debate on the exchange rate system, was the definitive position of the developing countries, in their overwhelming majority, in favour of the existing Fund arrangements. This was most clearly visible at the 1970 Annual Meeting when, in commenting on the Executive Board's report, all developing-country Governors who addressed the issue did so in terms supportive of the par value system.[17] However, while these countries were concerned at this juncture to stake out a clear position on the matter, the significant debate was basically conducted within the G10.

As with the liquidity issue, the divergence among the developed countries was primarily, though not wholly,[18] a Euro–American one, with France in particular at the forefront of the campaign to reduce the privileged position held by the United States in the international adjustment process. Moreover, in terms of the political contest, an interesting element needs to be highlighted. Whereas during the liquidity negotiations, we had witnessed the American efforts to create political alliances with the developing countries to deal with the European challenge, on this occasion it was a European country that did so. Recognizing an identity of interest with the developing countries in safeguarding the par value mechanism, France seized the early initiative in seeking to align with these countries in its defence. It is in this context that we have to place France's argument in 1970, with regard to flexible exchange rates, that:

> ... we should think twice before adding a new factor of uncertainty to the difficulties of the developing countries. These countries are already subject to considerable hazards with respect to the pricing of their principal exports; is it necessary that frequent changes in their exchange rates add a further unknown quantity with regard to the total amount of their resources?[19]

But events in the major exchange markets in 1971 were to prove decisive in the whole debate on the exchange rate situation. In Europe, in the face of substantial dollar inflows, West Germany, along with The Netherlands, took the decision to float their currency.[20] The crucial circumstance, however, was the significant adjustment pressure that confronted the American authorities as a result of its external imbalance and increased pressure on both its currency and gold reserves. The result was the 15 August 1971 announcement.

What was especially noticeable about this announcement, apart from its widespread repercussions throughout the international economy, was its decision-making aspect. Despite the presence of the multilateral framework represented by the IMF, with its explicit objective to promote cooperative solutions, via the consultative process, to international monetary problems, the unilateral American decision was formulated in consultation neither with the Fund nor with member-states. It was a decision that looked solely to the national economic interest of the United States without consideration of its implications for the wider international community.[21]

The American decision carried important consequences on a broad array of areas. At the systemic level, its immediate effect was to weaken, and ultimately to sound the demise of, the Bretton Woods exchange rate system, as well as temporarily to place in abeyance the obligation of dollar convertibility. Many of the main industrial countries moved to floating exchange rates in the aftermath of the American action.[22] At the narrower level of developing countries, it had two major consequences. Firstly, there was the direct impact on their economic welfare.[23] Secondly, it was the single issue—coming so soon after the SDR negotiations—that propelled a broad-based concern among the developing countries about international monetary decision making. This latter concern was most visibly expressed by many Third World Governors at the Fund's 1971 Annual Meeting.[24]

In taking its decision of August 1971, the United States also ignored the international institutional authority in monetary affairs. This marginalization of the Fund clearly recalled the very early stages of the liquidity negotiations and the Managing Director was hard-pressed to remain silent on the matter. Moreover, his response was similar to that at the time of the liquidity controversy. In his barely veiled criticism of the American action, he linked it to a manifest concern for the developing countries. Speaking of real dangers in international monetary relations, he underlined particularly the danger of:

> an abandonment of rules of law providing for orderly and just international economic relations . . . It is in the economic interest of all members and not least of developing members to re-establish the functioning of the international monetary system on the basis of rights and duties.[25]

As with his concern regarding the SDR issue, when an alliance with developing countries was politically important in confronting elitist decision making, a political alliance with these countries was again seen as necessary to confront the unilateral basis of American decision making.

Third World and Fund management concern about decision making was to intensify in the light of the action taken by a limited group of developed countries to deal with the exchange rate crisis stemming from the American measures. In an attempt to reintroduce a semblance of order into exchange rate relations, the G10 countries began a series of negotiations in the final months of 1971; their basic aim was to reestablish the Bretton Woods par value system.[26] The outcome was the Smithsonian agreement of December 1971 regarding the realignment of the currencies of the principal developed countries. The US dollar was devalued relative to gold, the French franc and the British pound, on one hand and the German deutsche mark, Japanese yen and Swiss franc revalued *vis-à-vis* gold.

Once again, developing countries found themselves totally left out of the negotiating process on an issue with evident substantial implications for their economies. In fact, a 1972 UNCTAD study outlined some of the costs that developing countries were required to bear as a consequence of the Smithsonian currency realignments[27] and noted that:

important decisions directly affecting the developing countries—the conditions under which trade barriers would be lifted, the initiation of negotiations on other trade matters, the relative prices of reserve assets, and the margins for permissible exchange rate fluctuations—were taken under conditions in which they had no opportunity to influence the outcome.[28]

It is important to stress that the criticisms by the developing countries of the exclusionary decisional framework on exchange rates were not based on an unreal assessment of their overall importance in the international monetary system. In fact, these countries manifested a keen appreciation of the central role of the industrialized countries in it. These were the countries that dominated international trade and payments relationships; it was to their currencies that the overwhelming majority of the developing countries' currencies were pegged at that time;[29] theirs were the world's main reserve currencies. These considerations unarguably made for a dominant position in international monetary management. As the Governor for Yugoslavia noted at the Fund's 1971 Annual Meeting, 'I concede . . . that the primary responsibility for these events in world exchange relationships rests with the group of industrially developed countries.'[30] But, concession of such a primary responsibility was not the same as concession of a non-role for developing countries:

Acceptance of the primary role of the industrially developed countries in international trade and payments does not imply the acceptance of our [i.e. developing countries] role as a mere spectator of present world events, and especially we do not accept the policy of *fait accompli*. It is at least essential, therefore, that in taking all decisions . . . full attention must be paid to the effects—and not adverse effects—that such decisions may have on further economic development of the developing countries.[31]

What developing countries were arguing basically was the right to participate in international decision making by virtue, at a minimum, of the impact on, and consequences for, their economies of the actions of the major developed countries. Non-participation effectively ensured that their concerns were neither presented nor taken into account during exclusionary decision making. Further, these countries were very supportive of the Fund remaining the appropriate forum for negotiations on monetary issues, particularly since, whatever the limitations of their participatory role in it, they had an opportunity to state their case.[32]

In summation, this period of the late 1960s, beginning of the 1970s, marked a transition to a changed structure of international economic relations. It was the moment of the final manifestation of a past world of unilateral American dominance, counterpoised by the continuing struggle of the new centre of economic power in West Europe, the European Community countries, for a key role in international monetary governance, on the basis of their improved standing in the international economy.

It was also to mark the critical juncture of incipient Third World struggle for recognition of their own right to decision-making participation. The immediate reaction of developing countries to the exchange rate actions of the main developed countries was to significantly transform the political context of international monetary negotiations. As was previously indicated, the developing countries decided in late 1971 to establish their own caucusing group on international monetary affairs, the G24, which began functioning the following year.

4. Reform of the international monetary system

(a) The institutional question

An important outcome of the American action of 15 August 1971 was the inauguration of a series of negotiations aimed at restructuring the exchange rate arrangements, in the first instance, and subsequently, the international monetary system.[33] The first such set of negotiations resulted in the Smithsonian agreement in December 1971 and was basically an affair of the G10 countries. The second series of negotiations was, from the participatory standpoint, more inclusionary and, in a substantive sense, involved overall international monetary reform.

The immediate issue that arose in this context was the negotiation of the institutional framework for the conduct of monetary reform negotiations. Agreement regarding the necessity of monetary reform did not translate automatically into agreement on the locus for such negotiations. In fact, this procedural issue, in itself, was highly controversial as all interested parties argued for a forum that was favourable to their interests. The major actors in this regard were the United States, the EEC countries, the developing countries and the Fund management.

The American discomfort with the G10 during the SDR negotiations in the 1960s has already been noted. Outnumbered at that time by the European Community members, opposed to their perspectives on a SDR facility, and operating in a framework that was informally constituted and thus lacking veto power, the United States had sought to build political alliances with other Fund members, especially the developing nations, to strengthen its bargaining position. In fact, it is important to underscore the fundamental stresses that were besetting the G10 countries, even as they sought to dominate international monetary decision making by operating within an exclusivist context. These internal tensions clearly made for a breach of G10 dominance, once the other interested parties were fully apprised of this reality and took steps to exploit it.[34]

From the American perspective, therefore, the G10 was not seen as the most politically advantageous forum for carrying out the reform negotiations.[35] Rather, the United States was predisposed to a body, delinked from the Fund, but with a larger membership than the G10. Two things are especially important in this regard. Firstly, paralleling its dissatisfaction with the G10, the United States was equally displeased with the Fund *per se*[36] and, thus, was not keen to see either the Fund management and staff or the Executive Board having any significant role in the monetary reform exercise. Secondly, their interest in having a group wider than the G10, with the participation of other industrialized countries outside the G10, as well as the developing countries, was clearly intended to garner support for the American position in the negotiations.[37]

The European Community countries opposed any such approach and instead argued for a committee of the Board of Governors, operating within the ambit of the IMF.[38] Their position was similar to that of the Fund management which proposed a committee, comprising twenty members of the Board of Governors and designated on the basis of the composition of the Executive Board.[39] As for the developing countries, their interest in participation in the decision-making process was best served by such an approach—a position adopted by the Group of 24.[40]

Thus, in terms of the main interests involved—the United States, the European Community, and the developing countries, as well as Fund management—there were simultaneously parallels in views, as well as substantial divergences. Significantly, the major parallel position was the necessity for a larger, more representative body than the G10, with the inclusion of developing countries. It is apparent that all parties recognized the political importance of the participation of the latter group of countries, particularly in the context of their voting support for constitutional amendment to legalize any reform proposals.[41] There was, in addition the jockeying for these countries' support between the principal protagonists in the G10.

The main difference among the various perspectives on the institutional question related to the American preference for a negotiating group, disassociated from the Fund. This position conflicted with the overall interest of the remaining membership in a body linked to the Fund. What is more, even as the United States was constrained to move towards acceptance of the latter approach, it sought to increase its negotiating position with the envisaged committee by arguing that the weighted voting power of the selected representatives should underpin the committee's deliberations.[42] This proposal encountered intense criticism both within the G10 and, interestingly, by senior members of the Fund staff.[43]

These negotiations regarding a forum defined, in the final analysis, the stakes involved in the substantive negotiations—the whole question of international monetary reform. They equally defined the fundamental changes that had taken place in the international economy since the time of Bretton Woods and the heyday of sole American dominance of international economic relations. A quarter of a century after Bretton Woods, a more pluralistic international economic order had appeared, with new centres of power capable of effectively challenging and overcoming American preferences. This was exactly what happened in this initial phase of international monetary reform negotiations with the final agreement in July 1972 to establish the Committee on Reform of the International Monetary System and Related Issues.[44]

(b) Monetary reform negotiations in the Committee of Twenty

With the establishment of the Committee of Twenty to oversee the monetary reform negotiations, developing countries were for the first time to be afforded the opportunity to participate in international monetary decision making from the very outset of the process. The Committee began its work on 28 September 1972 and presented its final report[45] on 14 June 1974.

In addressing themselves to the major areas of monetary reform, developing countries demonstrated an especial concern with the entire question of transfer of resources for development purposes.[46] This was the emphasis of the G24's Second Communiqué—the one immediately preceding the work of the Committee of Twenty.[47] While these countries did have a position on the exchange rate question, it would be no exaggeration to say that negotiations on it were largely dominated by the principal developed countries.

The spectrum of positions on exchange rates extended from the American inclination to move in the direction of floating, European Community advocacy of stability of exchange rates and a par value mechanism—with France in the forefront of the prosecution of their position—and the developing countries' antagonism to floating rates and their predilection for the existing par value arrangement, but modified to include some element of flexibility. As the G24 Ministers noted in their Third Communiqué: 'Ministers reaffirmed their conviction that a system of stable exchange rates based on adjustable par values expressed in SDRs constitutes an essential element of a satisfactory inter-national order'.[48] The essential basis of their antagonism to floating was the addition of greater uncertainty in their domestic economic management and overall economic relations.[49]

But, even as the Committee of Twenty was proceeding with reform negotiations, the exchange markets of the main industrial countries were once again in turmoil in early 1973. Both the American current and trade accounts had shown continuing deterioration throughout 1972, with the deficits of such a magnitude that there was a clear sense that another devaluation of the dollar was imminent, leading to increasing speculative movements against that currency.[50] Against this background, the American monetary authorities began another round of consultations within the G10 to agree on action to curb these destabilizing forces. In other words, while the Committee of Twenty existed as a broad-based forum to address monetary issues, the limited-context, exclusionary G10 was not averse to reactivating closed negotiations on their exchange rate relationships.

The exchange rate measures adopted by several developed countries in early 1973 effectively sounded the death-knell of the par value mechanism. The US dollar was further devalued by 10 per cent in February—a measure that did not stem the flow of speculation against that currency. Further action was necessary and, the following March, after a set of consultations involving a wider set of developed countries than the G10, virtually all the world's major currencies were floated.[51] Significantly, the United States again ignored the Fund, refusing to consult with the institutional authority, as constitutionally required, when changes in par values are being entertained.[52] Nor were the developing countries even remotely brought into the consultative process in this regard, notwithstanding the serious implications of these measures for their economies.[53]

What these countries were rapidly learning was that integration, from a procedural vantage-point, did not automatically or necessarily translate into real participation in decisional processes. They were highly critical of the actions taken by the developed countries, remarking that:

> the manner in which the decisions announced in Paris on March 16 had been taken by a limited number of countries outside the framework of the International Monetary Fund represented a departure from the spirit which had inspired the creation of the Committee of 20 and a setback to the process of international consultation effectively involving the entire member-ship of the Fund.[54]

In the final analysis, a small group of developed countries still continued to determine, whenever they felt it appropriate, the direction that international monetary events should take, to the exclusion of the developing countries.

In the event, negotiations on exchange rate arrangements and overall monetary reform within the ambit of the Committee of Twenty went forward in an environment of widespread floating of major currencies. There was still a strong interest, particularly among the developing countries, the European Community members and Japan, in re-establishing the par value mechanism.[55] Ultimately, however, as already described, events interposed to abort the monetary reform exercise, with the Committee of Twenty agreeing that the time was not propitious to arrive at a consensus on international monetary reform. Nevertheless, the imperative of a reformed world monetary order was emphasized and it was agreed that in any such reformed system, the exchange rate mechanism should be 'based on stable but adjustable par values with floating rates recognized as providing a useful technique in particular situations'.[56]

(c) Exchange rates: negotiations for the second amendment of the Articles of Agreement

The next phase of international negotiations on exchange rates was pursued in the context of negotiation of the second amendment of the Fund's Articles of Agreement. As we have seen, the Committee of Twenty had been unable to arrive at a definitive position regarding a reformed monetary sytem and since a review of the exchange rate system had fallen within the Committee's terms of reference, its inability to fulfil the overall mandate obviously meant that no formal decision was taken in this regard. In the interim, the Fund's provision on exchange rates remained inoperative in view of the unconstitutional floating of their currencies by the majority of developed countries.[57]

Nevertheless, in winding up its work on long-term reform, the Committee of Twenty agreed that a series of immediate measures needed to be taken. Included among these was a request to the Executive Board to prepare draft amendments to the Articles of Agreement, among which was one 'to enable the Fund to legalize the position of countries with floating rates during the interim period'.[58] It was envisaged that, following preparation of the amended articles, they would have then been submitted for consideration of the Interim Committee[59] and, ultimately, formal approval of the Board of Governors. It was against this background that the negotiations of amendments to Article IV on exchange rates began in early 1974, within the framework of the Executive Board and the Interim Committee.

Initial Executive Board consideration of amendments to the exchange rate provisions was based on a preliminary draft prepared by the staff, incorporating formal approval of floating rates, consistent with the above-quoted guidelines provided in the Committee of Twenty's 'Outline of Reform'.[60] Strong objections were expressed by several Executive Directors from both developing countries and developed European nations, as well as Japan, against any movement towards legalizing floating exchange rates.[61] These exchanges once again brought out the two major contending views on the issue—that of the United States, primarily, supportive of the legalization of floating, as against that of the broad majority of the remaining membership, strongly opposed to such a move and with a preference for 'stable but adjustable par values'. These were to represent the principal contending positions over the period of negotiations for a new exchange rate mechanism.

In the face of these irreconcilable positions, the recently-constituted Interim Committee held its second meeting in January 1975 and sought to resolve this situation—an effort that proved unsuccessful owing to the adamant stand of the main protagonists. The Interim Committee referred the issue back to the Executive Board, with the mandate to continue searching for a draft that allowed for 'stable but adjustable par values and the floating of currencies in particular situations, subject to appropriate rules and surveillance of the Fund, in accordance with the "Outline of Reform" '.[62]

By the next stage of the consideration of this issue, three draft amendments were in circulation. There was the French draft, providing for a par value arrangement;[63] there was an American draft that left the freedom of choice to each member-state as to its preferred exchange rate arrangement, in other words, providing members with the freedom to implement floating;[64] and thirdly, the staff proposed an arrangement that included both these options, that is, members were given the choice of observing either par values or floating, subject to clearly defined obligations.[65] Developing countries signalled their preference through the G24 when they 'expressed support for amend-ments envisaging a return at the appropriate time to a system of par values, containing provisions for the establishment of central rates, and empowering the Fund to authorize individual countries to continue the float thereafter in particular circumstances'[66]—a stance that was consistent with the draft prepared by the Fund's staff and that avoided the extremes of the American and French positions. The overwhelming Fund membership, moreover, were supportive of a provision that allowed for both floating and par values. Ultimately, however, further negotiations indicated that the French and American views on the matter appeared to be strongly-held ones.

This stand-off impelled a search for a compromise solution outside the institutional framework of the IMF. In fact, it was on the initiative of an even narrower group than the G10 that this effort at resolving the Franco–American divergence was undertaken. In August 1975 the G5 countries mandated France and the United States to seek a reconciliation of their differences and indicated their willingness to endorse any agreement reached as a result of this bilateral effort.[67] Subsequent Franco–American bilateral negotiations ended in agreement that obtained the imprimatur of the six-nation Western economic summit held at Rambouillet, France in November 1975 and that, in substantive terms, was to serve as the basis for an amended Article IV on exchange rates.[68]

What was agreed between France and the United States, as reflected in amended Article IV, was that members could choose an exchange rate that entailed either:

(i) the maintenance by a member of a value for its currency in terms of the special drawing right or another denominator, other than gold, selected by the member, or

(ii) cooperative arrangements by which members maintain the value of the currency or currencies of other members or

(iii) other exchange arrangements of a member's choice.[69]

The Fund was granted the formal oversight function in regard to exchange rates since it was required to exercise 'firm surveillance' over members' policies in this area.[70] Furthermore, provision was made in amended Article IV for the consideration in the future of a return to the par value mechanism;[71] however, any such decision would have to garner an 85 per cent voting majority, in effect giving to the United States a veto over such a step.

In short, amended Article IV essentially gave to members the freedom of choice as regards their exchange rate arrangements, thus providing *post facto* legalization of floating. This approach clearly met American preferences. At the same time, France was granted the concession of a formal provision that was evidently unattainable in the foreseeable future, given the American veto.

What the second amendment negotiations indicated, as they related to exchange rates, was that, while formal participation had been conceded to developing countries, at least in this area substantive influence still remained basically elusive. The fundamental sense of amended Article IV was negotiated within an even more restricted group than the G10 and outside the institutional context of the IMF. The Fund was subsequently drawn into the process merely to formalize a *fait accompli*.[72] Formal participation of developing countries was evidenced in the virtual parity of representation in the main institutional negotiating forums, the Interim Committee and the Executive Board. But, in so far as exchange rate negotiations both took place outside the Fund and involved a small group of developed nations, it was virtually impossible for developing countries to contribute in a substantive sense to the outcome.

Having said this, however, it is important to underscore that such an assessment, left like that, misses a significant point regarding their participation in the overall amendment negotiations. These negotiations involved a package of amendments, and individual countries, as well as groups of countries, had priority interests. While opposed to floating, developing countries confronted a situation in which the major economies were in fact observing floating for a prolonged period of time. Moreover, although the former held an all-important veto over any proposal to legalize floating, the reality was that the developed countries were already operating outside the constitutional pale of the IMF with their adoption of floating. Ultimately, developing countries were impotent to change this reality and, while manifestly disturbed at the elitist decisional process on exchange rate amendment, it would have been basically futile, from a political standpoint, to stand in the way of the existing reality.[73]

In essence, these countries had other important interests to champion at that time and the amendment negotiations were to a certain extent exploited to obtain some of what they wanted. One of their primary interests in this regard was increased financing within the Fund context. It is no mere accident that the time-period of the negotiations coincided with the establishment of the Trust Fund and the 1975 liberalization of the Compensatory Financing Facility, both of which gave developing countries access to a larger quantum of essentially concessional and low-conditional resources.

Exchange rates in the early 1980s

By the mid-1980s, exchange rates had re-emerged as an area of widespread international preoccupation.[74] The basis for this preoccupation has been the disruptive movements in the currency rates of the world's main developed countries during the first half of the 1980s, affecting their own economic interactions and the economies of the developing countries.

In the post-amendment years, a variety of practices has characterized the exchange rates of the Fund's membership, clearly a reflection, at one level, of the latitude provided by amended Article IV. The developed countries, by and large, have operated floating exchange rates[75]—albeit managed, rather than free-floating. The developing countries, on the other hand, have observed a diversity of arrangements, but with a noticeable shift away from pegged exchange rates, compared to the pre-amendment situation. Thus, by the end of 1985, some 28 per cent of the Fund's developing members were operating under a flexible system of one kind or another; while about 70 per cent of these countries, compared to over 90 per cent at the start of the 1970s, had pegged rates. There was a broad array of pegging arrangements. Some thirty-two developing countries (26 per cent) were still pegged to the US dollar, while fourteen of them were pegged to the French franc and as many as thirty-seven currencies were pegged to either the SDR or a basket of currencies. Ultimately, however, the core exchange rates internationally still remained those of the major currencies, by virtue of the combination of circumstances related to their many-sided role in the international economy.

The single characterization of the exchange relations of the major currencies in the first half of the 1980s has been instability. The manifestation of exchange rate instability at this level has been short-run volatility and misalignment of currencies. As a recent United Nations study has noted: 'Exchange rate volatility has been greater in the period of floating rates (1973–85) than in the past decade of the adjustable-peg par value system (1961–71). The volatility of quarterly nominal exchange rates for seven major currencies was six times as great as under fixed rates'.[76] The major indicator of currency misalignment has been the persistent upward movement in the value of the US dollar in the first half of the 1980s, so that by February 1985 its effective exchange rate was some 50 per cent higher than its average over the years 1974–82.[77]

The effect of the strong US dollar has been reflected in substantial trade and current account imbalances among the main developed countries; on the one hand, the massive, unsustainable trade and current account deficits in the United States, and the counterpart surpluses, on both trade and current accounts, particularly of Japan and West Germany. Developing countries have naturally been seriously affected by these unstable currency relationships,[78] especially in respect of exchange risks in trading relations and the necessity for increased reserves to mitigate unexpected movements in exchange rates.

It was against this background that new efforts at international monetary management became apparent in the mid-1980s. While there have been calls from several sources for urgent international monetary reform,[79] both the G10 and G24 had by 1985 undertaken thoroughgoing examinations of prevailing monetary relations, resulting in the presentation of two reports.[80] Specifically in relation to exchange rates, both Reports stated their concern at exchange rate instability in the 1980s, but at the same time came to different conclusions regarding possible treatment of the problem. Starting off from pointed criticism of the functioning of the present exchange rate system, the G24 argued the need for devising a new exchange rate system that would contribute to greater stability in currency relationships. To this end, the Group's main prescription was the establishment of 'target zones' for the exchange rates of the major currencies. Contrastingly, the G10 Report took the line that, while the floating rate system has shown several deficiencies, there was no need for a fundamental overhaul, but rather improvements within the framework of existing arrangements. Moreover, the G10 rejected the concept of target zones for their exchange rates.

Attention to the exchange rate problem at these levels notwithstanding, it was action at another level that proved quite disconcerting to developing, as well as several developed countries. This was the even more restrictive attempt, involving the G5, to reach agreement at currency stabilization measures. By early 1985, the five largest non-Communist economies had decided that they needed to act together to stop the relentless rise of the US dollar.[81] Their Finance Ministers subsequently met in New York in September 1975 and agreed to coordinate intervention in exchange markets to push the dollar downwards.[82]

Once again, the developing countries found themselves passive observers of an exclusionary process, which was even more restrictive in terms of participation than the G10 process of the 1960s and 1970s. Also finding itself on the sidelines of the action was the Fund, the formal institutional authority, at international level, on exchange rates. In fact, as one analyst has noted, in the period since the introduction of floating in 1973, the Fund has found itself essentially powerless with respect to exchange rate action of the major economies, notwithstanding its formal authority to oversee exchange rate relations.[83] This marginalization of the Fund was in no sense surprising in that the institution had over the years found it increasingly difficult to exert any meaningful influence over the monetary behaviour of the developed countries.

Also significant, however, was the exclusion of the other two members that normally participate in the seven-nation Western economic summits, as well as the non-role of the G10 forum. In fact, both Italy and Canada felt so slighted by their omission that they publicly stated their displeasure at the narrowness of the decision-making group,[84] though it must be stressed that their main concern was not really to open up the process to general participation. Rather, their interest was to ensure its opening-up enough to include them. Other commentators have also started to question the fate of the broader G10 framework, in the face of this activism of the G5.[85]

While the long-term implications of this even more restrictive approach to international monetary management are not immediately discernible, it at once recalls the experiences of the 1960s and much of the 1970s. Even granting that, on the whole, developing countries are cognizant of minimal scope to influence international exchange relations, they have always argued that at the least they should have a role in deliberations on this matter on the basis of the consequences for their economies of exchange-rate policy in the major developed countries. Their exclusion, especially after the gains—however limited—of the 1970s, would seem to signify a disturbing return to elitist decision making. Moreover, a non-role for the Fund merely underscores the increasing marginalization of this institution in international monetary management.

Conclusions

The characterization of the decision-making process that emerges from the presentation indicates distinct phases of international management of exchange rate relations. There was the initial period of American dominance in the first two decades of post-war international monetary relations—a dominance reflected in the role of the dollar as the main reserve and intervention currency, the fact that it was the currency to which the majority of developing-country currencies were pegged and American acceptance of the obligation to buy and sell gold unrestrictedly in its exchange dealings with other countries. The next phase, beginning around the mid-1960s, involved the struggle by the European Community countries, led prominently by France, to minimize the privileged American position and to share in exchange rate decision making. By the early 1970s, this struggle had been rewarded by the recognition of their participatory right under G10 auspices. The beginning of the 1970s, and specifically the American action of 15 August 1971, was to see the initiation of a coherent Third World campaign to assert a right to participate in exchange rate, and broader international monetary management.

These countries did, in fact, achieve a measure of procedural integration into the negotiation process, but procedural participation has not been translated into substantive influence on exchange rate relations. Developing countries still remained at the periphery of the process, a reality that the experiences of the first half of the 1980s have more sharply underlined. For, while there was the pretence of Third World participation in the 1970s in the context of the Committee of Twenty and the amendment negotiations, this pretence has been shed with the reversion to elitist decision making, from both the procedural and substantive perspectives. Moreover, the principal feature of the elitist decision making of the 1980s so far is the even narrower participatory basis of elitist management.

An accurate assessment of the Third World role in decision making on exchange rates over the entire period of the Fund's existence will conclude that these countries have had virtually no influence in determining international exchange rate policy. In fact, not only is their capacity for influence in this area far less than in most other areas of international monetary policy, but these countries have demonstrated a keen appreciation of their limited capacity for influence. The point is that the core exchange rates in international monetary relations are the rates of the major developed countries and these core countries are basically the United States, Japan, West Germany, France and the United Kingdom—the countries comprising the G5.

Particularly in the decade and a half since 1970, there has also been a fundamental marginalization of the IMF—the institutional authority on exchange relations. Confronting the efforts in the late 1960s/beginning of the 1970s at both closed and unilateral exchange rate management, the Fund, *qua* institution, had astutely exploited the divisions among its membership brought on by exclusionary decision making to champion the inclusive Committee of Twenty process. But, apart from this brief triumph, the Fund has found itself on the periphery of the major developments regarding exchange rates, including a brief period of the collapse of the juridical order in this sphere, and notwithstanding the amendment negotiations. For, ultimately it was the Franco-American bilateral negotiations, sanctioned by the six-nation Western economic summit in late 1975, that brought agreement on amended Article IV on exchange rates. And, even with a constitutional mandate in the post-amendment period to exercise firm surveillance over exchange rates, the Fund has been unable in the 1980s, at a time of protracted exchange rate instability, to exert control over the major economies in this regard.

The shift to shared management of exchange rate policy in the early 1970s reflected the underlying shift in the international economic environment, represented by the recovery and growing strength of the EEC economies and their aggressive campaign at international recognition of this fact through the concession of a shared management responsibility. Developing countries likewise, in the early 1970s, sought to exploit their numerical superiority, systemic tensions and the marked and new economic influence of certain of their members to attain a participatory role. In this regard, the environment of negotiations was transformed by the creation of the G24. Integration at the procedural level was accordingly granted these countries in the early 1970s.

Integration at the procedural level, however, involved international monetary relations as a whole; on specific sub-issues, countries and groups of countries either necessarily defined their own priorities or had less capacity for influence. It is in this context that one has to see the absence of a substantive participatory role for the developing nations. The resurgence of elitist decision making in international monetary relations so far in the 1980s parallels at the broader international economic level the retreat of Third World activism in the 1980s and the demise of the NIEO campaign, on the one hand, and a renewed American offensive, supported by a few Western industrialized countries and aimed at imprinting a clear-cut ideological direction to international economic interactions, on the other.

Notes

1. Article 1 (iii), 'Articles of Agreement'.
2. See 'US Commentary: Questions and Answers on the International Monetary Fund', 10 June 1944 in Horsefield, op. cit., Vol. 3, p. 137. See also 'The Role of Exchange Rates in the Adjustment of International Payments' (A Report by the Executive Directors), September 1970 in de Vries, *The International Monetary Fund, 1966–71*, Vol. 2, p. 275.
3. 'The White Plan', in Horsefield, op. cit., p. 43.
4. 'Proposals for an International Currency (or Clearing) Union', ibid., p. 22.
5. For details, see Horsefield, op. cit., Vol. 1, pp. 100–1.
6. Article IV, Sec. 1, 'Articles of Agreement'.
7. Article IV, Sec. 5, 'Articles of Agreement'.
8. See Gold, *Legal and Institutional Aspects of the International Monetary System*, Vol. 2, pp. 82–3.
9. Article 4(b), 'Articles of Agreement'.
10. See Gold, *Legal and Institutional Aspects of the International Monetary System*, Vol. 2, pp. 518–19. See also 'Reform of International Monetary System' (Report of the Executive Directors), 18 August 1972 in de Vries, *The International Monetary Fund, 1972–78*, op. cit., Vol. 3, p. 23.
11. Horsefield, op. cit., Vol. 3, p. 48.
12. See ibid., pp. 48–9.
13. Details of the American measures were briefly outlined in Chapter 2 herein.
14. See Robert Solomon, *The International Monetary System, 1945–76*, Harper & Row, New York, 1977, pp. 151–8.
15. As noted in the Fund's history, the Executive Directors 'were prompted also to undertake such a review because they were concerned that decisions regarding the exchange rates of major currencies, like other key decisions in the Fund's field of interest, were increasingly being taken outside the Fund and that the initiative for any serious consideration of whether, or how, the par value system should be altered might fall to bodies other than themselves'—de Vries, *The International Monetary Fund, 1966–71*, Vol. 1, p. 500.
16. 'The Role of Exchange Rates in the Adjustment of International Payments' (A Report by the Executive Directors, September 1970), ibid., Vol. 2, p. 322.
17. See, for instance, statements by Governors from Burundi, Ceylon (Sri Lanka), Dominican Republic (on behalf of Latin American countries), India, Indonesia, Pakistan, Syria, Trinidad and Tobago, Uganda, UAR, Upper Volta (Bukina Faso, on

behalf of the seven member-states of the West Africa Monetary Union) and Yugoslavia, in *Summary Proceedings*, 1970, p. 184, 179, 102, 43, 77, 197, 133, 144, 182, 202, 169, and 165 respectively.

18. While the United States was in the forefront of the advocacy of greater flexibility for exchange rates, Canada, which had from time to time operated with floating rates, was very supportive of this approach, as was the United Kingdom to some extent.

19. *Summary Proceedings*, 1970, p. 48.

20. See Solomon, op. cit., pp. 176–80.

21. Ironically, it was the United States that took the lead to propose cooperative solutions, through international mechanisms, to international economic problems for the post-war world. It was that country that sought to transcend approaches that looked to narrow, national self-interests. This was the country that now ignored international cooperative approaches in dealing with its adjustment difficulties.

22. At a meeting of European Community Finance Ministers in Brussels on 19 August 1971, the decision was taken that five of the Community's members—Belgium, Luxembourg, Italy, Netherlands and West Germany—would float their currencies. The other member, France, agreed to continue observing a fixed exchange rate. Subsequently, the majority of the remaining developed countries moved to floating exchange rates.

23. As the Fund's Executive Directors noted in a report of 1972: 'The events that followed the actions taken by the United States on 15 August 1971 affected the developing countries in a number of ways. Some of them were affected directly by the 10 percent surcharge on dutiable imports into the United States. For all of them the relative fluctuation in the exchange rates for major currencies posed new problems and uncertainties with respect to their own exchange rate and reserve management policies, the prospects for their terms of trade, and even their development plans. Moreover, the uncertainties in the world economy which followed from the monetary upheaval appear to have reinforced the effects of the slow pace of growth of several industrial economies in depressing the prices of primary products in the last few months of 1971'—see 'Reform of the International Monetary System: Report of the Executive Directors', 18 August 1972 in de Vries, *The International Monetary Fund, 1966–71*, op. cit., Vol. 2, p. 52.

24. See, for instance, statements by Governors from Algeria, India, Nigeria, Tanzania and Yugoslavia in *Summary Proceedings*, 1971, pp. 98, 58, 169–70, 64–5 and 199, respectively.

25. Ibid., pp. 11–12.

26. For a description of these negotiations, see Solomon, op. cit., pp. 188–215.

27. The study noted that the windfall gains accruing to the developed countries as a result of the devaluation of the US dollar in terms of gold were some eight times as much as those obtained by developing countries, while the revaluation of other major currencies relative to the dollar resulted in a reduction of purchasing power in developing countries. Another cost borne by the latter group of countries was increased debt servicing—see UNCTAD, *The International Monetary Situation* (Report by the UNCTAD Secretariat), TD/140/Rev.I, UN, New York, 1972, p. 1.

28. Ibid., p. 40.

29. At the beginning of the 1970s, over 90 per cent of the Fund's developing member-countries had pegged rates to one or other of the currencies of the major industrialized countries, with over 60 per cent of these rates set in relation to the US dollar—various IMF sources.

30. *Summary Proceedings*, 1971, p. 199.

31. Ibid., p. 200.

32. See, for instance, statements by Governors of India, Nigeria, and Mexico at the

Fund's 1971 Annual Meeting in *Summary Proceedings*, 1971, pp. 58, 169–70 and 285 respectively.

33. In the aftermath of the international monetary crisis of 1971, there emerged a broad consensus of the imperative of fundamental reform of the system. As the US Governor observed at the 1971 Annual Meeting: 'For the longer run, the international monetary system required far-reaching reform.' *The Department of State Bulletin*, Vol. 65, No. 1687, 25 October 1971, p. 454. See also statement by the Governor of Tanzania, *Summary Proceedings*, 1971, pp. 64–5.

34. In fact, as the Fund's official history has made clear, the Fund management and staff were quick to exploit these tensions by drawing up a proposal for the constitution of a Committee of the Board of Governors to examine monetary reform—see de Vries, *The International Monetary Fund, 1972–78*, Vol. 1, p. 149.

35. As the then US Treasury Secretary put it: 'The United States wanted a forum in which its inherent economic and financial power could not be offset by procedural conventions'—quoted in ibid.

36. The United States had been especially displeased at the criticism of the then Managing Director who, from the time of negotiations on liquidity creation in the 1960s, had been quite critical of the narrow basis of international monetary decisions. His criticisms of the American actions in August 1971 certainly did not endear him to the American authorities. Thus, from an American perspective, any direct involvement of management and staff was undesirable. And, as the Fund's history points out, the United States also had objections to the Executive Board involvement in the reform negotiation process—see de Vries, *International Monetary Fund, 1972–78*, op. cit., Vol. 1, pp. 151–2.

37. Ibid., p. 152.

38. As explained in the Fund's history, these countries wished to avert American domination of the negotiations and therefore saw a Fund role as one way of ensuring this—see ibid. Moreover, as at the time of the liquidity negotiations in the 1960s, they would have preferred to operate within the exclusive context of the G10. The political realities of the time, however—American discontent with the G10, developing country and Fund management interest in having the negotiations located within the IMF—were not conducive to such an approach.

39. Ibid., p. 151.

40. See Chapter 4 herein.

41. As previously pointed out, amendment of the Fund's Articles of Agreement required a double majority, of both voting power and number of members. From this perspective, the developing countries held a veto over any proposed amendments.

42. See de Vries, *The International Monetary Fund, 1972–78*, op. cit., Vol. 1, p. 154.

43. Ibid.

44. Discussed in Chapter 4 herein.

45. See Committee of Twenty, *International Monetary Reform* (Documents of the Committee of Twenty).

46. See de Vries, *The International Monetary Fund, 1972–78*, op. cit., Vol. 1, p. 165.

47. As the Communiqué put it: 'a reformed international monetary system must have as one of its basic aims the facilitation of a substantial transfer of real resources from the developed to the developing countries.' In fact, the entire Communiqué dealt almost completely with this issue of resource transfers, including a call for a new SDR allocation and the implementation of the link. Just as importantly, no reference was made in it to the exchange rate problem—see 'G24: Communiqué, Second Ministerial Meeting, 24 September 1972, pp. 300–1.

48. 'G24: Communiqué', Third Ministerial Meeting, 24 March 1973, p. 303. It is

interesting to note their advocacy of the SDR, in replacement of gold, as the numeraire of the system.

49. For a discussion, see Graham Bird, *The International Monetary System and the Less Developed Countries*, Macmillan Press, London (2nd edn), 1982, pp. 277–8. See also William R. Cline, *International Monetary Reform and the Developing Countries*, The Brookings Institution, Washington DC, 1976, pp. 6–7.

50. Solomon, op. cit., pp. 228–34.

51. Ibid.

52. De Vries, *The International Monetary Fund, 1972–78*, op. cit., Vol. 1, p. 67.

53. The impact of these exchange rate changes on the developing countries was analysed by the Fund in its 1973 *Annual Report*. Among the negative effects experienced by these countries were a decline of more than 2 per cent in the purchasing power of their reserves and an adverse movement in their terms of trade. The Report also observes that 'exchange rate flexibility in the major industrial countries confronts the developing countries with an assortment of new uncertainties . . . and concludes that the developing countries doubtless suffer a comparative disadvantage in relation to the larger industrial countries'—*IMF Survey*, 10 September 1973, p. 260.

54. 'G24: Communiqué', Third Ministerial Meeting, p. 302.

55. De Vries, *The International Monetary Fund, 1972–78*, op. cit., Vol. 1, pp. 188–90.

56. Committee of Twenty, *International Monetary Reform*, p. 8.

57. It should be remembered that the Fund's constitution provided for the setting of par values and precluded any other type of exchange rate arrangement. For a discussion, see Gold, *Legal and Institutional Aspects of the International Monetary System*, op. cit., Vol. 2, pp. 86–7.

58. Committee of Twenty, *International Monetary Reform*, p. 22, para. 41(b).

59. The formation of the Interim Committee is discussed in Chapter 3 herein.

60. See de Vries, *The International Monetary Fund, 1972–78*, op. cit., Vol. 2, pp. 702–3.

61. Ibid.

62. 'Communiqué: Interim Committee', 15–16 January 1975, para. 6(b), ibid., p. 219.

63. See 'Provisions Regarding Par Values and Exchange Stability under Article IV' by Executive Director for France, Jacques Wahl (9 April 1975) in de Vries, *The International Monetary Fund, 1972–78*, op. cit., Vol. 3, p. 296.

64. See 'Commentary on Alternative Approach to Article IV on Exchange Arrangements' by the Executive Director for the United States, Sam Y. Cross (1 May 1975), ibid., pp. 298–9.

65. Ibid., Vol. 2, pp. 737–8.

66. 'G24: Communiqué', Tenth Ministerial Meeting, 8–9 June 1975, p. 314.

67. For a discussion, see de Vries, *The International Monetary Fund, 1972–78*, Vol. 2, p. 743.

68. Gold, *Legal and Institutional Aspects of the International Monetary System*, Vol. 2, p. 527.

69. Sec. Article IV, Sec. 2(b).

70. Article IV, Sec. 3(b).

71. Article IV, Sec. 4.

72. See de Vries, *The International Monetary Fund, 1972–78*, Vol. 2, pp. 743–9.

73. As Cline has written, 'LDC representatives were probably willing to accept the other major change in the international monetary system—incorporation of floating exchange rates into accepted practice under IMF rules—because it represented little more than *de jure* recognition of a *de facto* reality'—Cline, op. cit., p. 7.

74. See IMF, *Annual Report*, 1985, p. 30.

75. The majority of members within the European Monetary System had a joint float against currencies outside the system, while maintaining the value of individual currencies in relation to the currencies of the other members.

76. United Nations, *World Economic Survey*, 1986, UN, New York, p. 97.
77. IMF, *Annual Report*, 1985, pp. 30–1.
78. G24, 'The Functioning and Improvement of the International Monetary System', *IMF Survey* (supp.), September 1985, p. 7.
79. France argued the imperative of world monetary reform and the convening of an international conference on it—see *New York Times*, 28 March 1985. A Group of Experts set up by the Commonwealth group of countries in late 1982 had argued similarly in their report presented in 1983—see *Towards a New Bretton Woods: Challenges for the World Financial and Trading System*, London, Commonwealth Secretariat, 1983, p. 131.
80. The G10 and G24 reports were published in *IMF Survey* (supp.), July 1985 and September 1985 respectively.
81. See *New York Times*, 3 March 1985.
82. 'Communiqué of the Group of Five', *IMF Survey*, 7 October 1985.
83. Polak has written that, 'since the advent of floating in the early 1970s, the Fund's role with respect to major currencies has shown a persistent decline . . . [t]he Fund has gradually broadened the scope but, at the same time, lowered the depth of its surveillance to a point where its role in connection with the rates for the major currencies has become marginal'—Polak, 'The Role of the Fund', op. cit., p. 246.
84. *The Financial Times*, 16 January 1986.
85. For instance, the President of the European Commission wondered about the fate of the G10, in which smaller industrialized countries participated—*The Financial Times*, 6 May 1986.

Chapter 7

The compensatory financing facility: from procedural participation to substantive success

1. Introduction

The commodity trade problem of developing countries was a central issue at the time of the negotiations in the mid-1940s of the post-war international economic arrangements. The commodity problem was, moreover, a prominent facet of Keynes' vision of an international economic order, forming as it did a component part of his original plans.[1] At Bretton Woods, several participants from developing countries raised the issue and succeeded in having the Conference adopt a resolution on trade relations that pointed to an inter-national concern precisely for commodity trade difficulties.[2]

It was during the negotiations for the ITO that the developing countries embarked—with a measure of relative success—on a systematic campaign to have incorporated into the post-war trade regime provisions that took account of their commodity trade problems. The agreement reached at Havana in 1948 included a section on 'Inter-Governmental Commodity Agreements'.[3] The demise of the ITO ultimately meant that no agreed international instrumentality—however limited the ITO provisions might have been—existed for the regulation of trade in commodities. The search for mechanisms to fill this vacuum in the international trading system has thus been an ongoing theme in the negotiations between developed and developing countries over the entire post-war period.

2. The commodity problem and the developing countries—a summary overview

The point of departure for international preoccupation with the commodity problem has been the perceived instabilities that are associated with both the production and exchange of commodities.[4] In the analytical literature, these problems have both a short-term and a longer-term aspect. Short-term instability has been ascribed to a number of causes, including the low elasticities of both supply and demand in response to price changes for commodities[5] and a tendency for both export prices and earnings of commodities to experience sharp fluctuations, explained in large measure by market conditions, on the demand side, and by domestic supply factors in the commodity-producing countries.[6] More controversially, the longer-term problem is linked to the claim of a secular deterioration in the terms of trade for commodities relative to the manufactured goods that the primary-producing countries needed to import from the industrialized countries.[7]

Though developing countries are neither the sole, nor for that matter, the major producers of many of these commodities, the commodity issue is of particular sensitivity for a host of reasons related to their economic structures. These countries have had—and in many cases continue to have—undiversified economic structures,[8] overwhelmingly dominated by commodity specialization and, in many instances, concentrated in the production and export of one or a few such products.[9] As Rangarajan's study points out, of a list of fifty-nine developing countries examined, twenty-three were dependent in the 1970s on exports of a single commodity for the major share of their export earnings, with six of these countries having a dependence of 80 per cent or more on a single commodity.[10]

Exports of commodities, in short, constitute for many developing countries the preponderant source of their foreign exchange earnings. In this context, price and export revenue instability has a pervasive impact throughout the economy of the typical developing country. A Fund study of 1960 had summed up the harmful consequences of export earnings' instability thus:

> . . . a high degree of instability in a country's export proceeds will give rise to four kinds of burdensome instability: instability in the incomes earned in export industries, relative to those earned in other sectors of the economy; instability in general money incomes and prices; instability in external purchasing power; and, as a consequence of these, instability in real expenditure, particularly real investment.[11]

Short-run commodity instability has been compounded, in the perception of developing nations, by the longer-run factor of the declining purchasing power of their commodity earnings in regard to the manufactured products of the developed countries as a result of the terms of trade argument earlier alluded to.

At the international level, two broad approaches—by no means mutually exclusive—have evolved to deal with the problems linked to commodity trade. There has been the approach that involved price-stabilization measures through the negotiation of international commodity agreements. Such an approach has an effect on the international market mechanisms for trade in commodities and has been beset by innumerable difficulties in the negotiation process between producing and consuming nations.[12]

The second approach has been the system of compensatory financing.[13] Whereas commodity agreements aim at price stabilization, compensatory financing is geared to dealing, in an *ex post* manner, with the balance-of-payments effects of export earnings instability associated with commodity trade.[14] Compensatory financing measures, in contrast to commodity agreements, have had a particular attraction for the developed countries because, from their perspective, 'compensatory financing . . . does not interfere with the normal market forces connected with the sale and distribution of goods and hence does not carry with it side effects which can be harmful.'[15]

The connection between the export earnings instability problem and the IMF relates, firstly, to the balance-of-payments effects of this instability and, secondly, the balance-of-payments financing mandate of the IMF. Compensatory financing is an essentially short-run expedient for dealing with commodity earnings fluctuations and, as such, it was early advocated by the developing countries and their institutional supporters as a proper function of the IMF, concerned as this institution is with temporary balance-of-payments problems.

3. The Fund decision to establish the compensatory financing facility

From the earliest days of its operations, the United Nations system, within its economic mandate, manifested a central interest in the commodity problem, particularly as it affected the developing countries. It was in this context that the General Assembly in 1952 set up an *ad hoc* Committee to prepare a report on practical measures to deal with the commodity trade problems of the developing countries.[16] In its 1953 report, this Committee had as one of its proposals a scheme for compensatory financing under the aegis of the IMF.[17] The Fund, for its part, did not display an interest in the proposal and reacted by merely reiterating that aspect of its mandate that included the extension of temporary financial assistance to members experiencing a decline in export earnings.[18]

The first direct approach from the United Nations organization to the IMF on the question of compensatory financing was made in 1959, when the UN Commission on International Commodity Trade (CICT) requested the Fund to inform it regarding its policies and procedures as they related to international measures designed to compensate for fluctuations in foreign exchange receipts from the export of primary commodities.[19] In response, the Fund presented a report to the CICT in 1960 that endorsed the proposition that the export earnings of primary-producing countries tended to fluctuate more than they did for industrialized countries.[20] The Fund also conceded that balance-of-payments support to assist in the compensation of short-term variations in export earnings constituted a legitimate use of Fund resources. What the Fund was not then prepared to do was either to grant automatic assistance in cases of export shortfalls or to create a special policy pertaining to compensatory financing: in the words of the report, it 'would be neither practicable nor desirable to make the amount of such assistance dependent on any automatic formula, or to provide any separate form of Fund assistance to deal with export fluctuations alone'.[21]

This international institutional concern with the commodity problem was paralleled by the concerted advocacy of the developing members of the Fund, beginning in the late 1950s, of the necessity for international measures to deal with the instabilities in commodity trade. It was the single most consistently expressed theme by these countries at Annual Meetings in the late 1950s/early 1960s.[22] After the appearance of the Fund's report in 1960, the developing nations continued to press the Fund to undertake further studies to see in what ways the institution could help in mitigating the negative balance-of-payments effects of commodity trade instability.

Moreover, the CICT approached the Fund again in 1962 on the issue of compensatory financing.[23] In the interim between the first CICT approach in

1959 and this new request, the problem of commodity trade, in general, and of compensatory financing, in particular, had continued to receive the attention of other international organizations, including the Organization of American States (OAS) and the United Nations,[24] where an evolving consensus on the merits of compensatory finance became increasingly apparent. This time-interval also coincided with a growing aggressiveness of developing countries, now the overwhelming majority in the international system, in regard to the broad issue of trade and the specific problem of commodity trade. This aggressiveness was most forcibly expressed in the campaign for a new institutional structure, under the auspices of the United Nations, to focus on their unique trade difficulties. In addition, it was in 1962 that developing countries manifested the initial inclination to coalesce publicly in defence of their general economic interests. This was the significance of the 'Cairo Conference on the Problems of Economic Development' that was held in July 1962. Among the conclusions reached at this forum was one addressed to the IMF regarding compensatory finance:

> ... the Conference considers the establishment of an international compensatory financing system a matter of great urgency and invites the International Monetary Fund to examine the undertaking of measures for a more effective balancing of payments of developing countries.[25]

This was a call echoed by several developing countries at the 1962 Annual Meeting of the Fund.[26]

These were the contextual circumstances—the United Nations and other extra-institutional structures and the incipient movement towards a group approach to economic issues—against which the Fund staff undertook their second study on compensatory financing, pursuant to the CICT request of 1962. The staff's draft report was submitted to the Executive Board in late 1962 and, in alluding to the plethora of proposals that had emanated from the deliberations of other international bodies, it observed that:

> [t]he proposals advanced, whether for any new compensatory financing institutions or for changes in the policies and practices of the Fund, are evidence that the assistance provided by the Fund under present policies is considered either insufficiently automatic in character or inadequate in amount to deal with the payments problems that arise from fluctuations in exports of primary exporting countries.[27]

The Fund staff proposed and the Executive Board approved the establishment of a new facility to assist countries experiencing temporary shortfalls in export earnings.[28]

It is important to note that, in so far as Fund decision making was concerned, establishment of the Compensatory Financing Facility (CFF) required a majority of the votes cast, since it was not one of the decisions that specifically required a special majority for approval.[29] This meant that, in the time context of which we are speaking, the developed countries, as a whole, and the G10 countries held enough votes to block a decision on the CFF, if they so desired. It also meant, however, that no single country held a veto over its establishment. This decision-making requirement also operates for modifications of the facility. In essence, then, the developed countries saw no problem in the creation of the CFF.

The principal elements of the 1963 CFF could be presented in terms of (i) countries eligible to borrow;[30] (ii) borrowing limits; (iii) product coverage; (iv) repayment period; and (v) conditionality requirements. In regard to beneficiaries or eligible countries, all Fund members could theoretically make purchases under the CFF—see Table 7.1 for a presentation of the major features of the CFF, as it has evolved over the years under the various Fund decisions. The 1963 decision and subsequent decisions further stipulated that the CFF was open to 'particularly primary exporters'.[31] Borrowing limits were set at 25 per cent of the borrowing member's quota and borrowing was intended to cover export earnings shortfalls as they related to merchandise exports alone. The normal repayment provision applicable to borrowing under the regular credit policies of the Fund was also to apply to the CFF; this meant that repayment had to be completed within three to five years after a purchase under the CFF had been effected. The CFF was conceived as an essentially low-conditionality facility, with the basic requirement being simply an undertaking by the borrowing member to 'cooperate with the Fund in an effort to find, where required, appropriate solutions for its balance of payments difficulties'.[32] Borrowing under the CFF, however, was only entertained in the event of a temporary export shortfall occasioned by circumstances beyond the control of the affected country—in other words, a balance-of-payments need had to exist. The overall intent of the Fund decision, in so far as the conditionality requirement that underpins use of Fund resources was concerned, was 'that policies of members drawing under the facility would be subject to less rigorous tests than those applicable in the case of a non-compensatory drawing in the same tranche'.[33]

What needs to be immediately underscored is that the new facility was open to all members of the Fund; from a legal perspective, all Fund members were— and, in fact, remain—eligible to use the CFF. Whereas the discussions within the United Nations and other international forums were explicitly preoccupied with the commodity trade difficulties of the developing countries,[34] the Fund was itself concerned to safeguard the formal principle of the uniform, non-discriminatory treatment of all its members. The 1963 decision, nevertheless, included the previously mentioned qualification that at once strengthened the intent to formally underline the principle of equal treatment, while pointing to the practical significance of the facility, that effectively meant a movement away from the strict application of this principle. The qualification indicated that the intent was to meet the export earnings problem of primary exporting members, in particular. As Gold has noted: 'The Executive Board . . . felt it desirable to introduce language into [the decision] that acknowledged the principle of uniformity'.[35] The stress on uniformity was achieved because the decision, by highlighting that the facility was geared to meet the problems besetting a certain sub-group of members in particular, simultaneously made clear that all members could nevertheless benefit from it.[36]

Yet, the emphasis placed on the problems of a specific sub-set of countries

Table 7.1 Features of the compensatory financing facility under the various Fund decisions pertaining to it

	1963	1966	1975	1979	1981
1. Eligible countries	All Fund members, but particularly primary exporting members				
2. Borrowing limits (as % of quotas)	25%	50%	75%	100%	125%*
3. Product coverage	Merchandise exports only			Merchandise exports and services	Merchandise exports, services and cereal import
4. Repayment requirement			Within 3–5 years after purchase†		
5. Conditionality	Duty to cooperate	(a) for borrowing up to 25% of quota (b) above 25% of quota	(a) for borrowing up to 50% of quota (b) above 50% of quota	(a) for borrowing up to 50% of quota (b) above 50% of quota	duty to cooperate / (a) for borrowing up to 50% of quota (b) above 50% of quota / Fund satisfaction with cooperation of member in situation where appropriate, for balance-of-payments problems

* Joint limit with cereal import facility.

† Effective with the 1966 decision, earlier repayment contingent on improvement of balance of payment.

Source: The various CFF decisions.

for the purpose of the decision was, *de facto*, an admission that these countries were particularly affected by export earnings shortfalls and should be entitled to special treatment by the Fund. The category of primary exporting members was not defined in the decision[37] and while many developed countries are major producers and exporters of primary commodities—and, as we shall see later, several made purchases under the CFF—this was the furthest that the Fund would go, at that time, in isolating the specific balance-of-payments problems of an identified sub-group of its members. Technically, the formulation protected the principle of uniformity, but from a practical standpoint, it implies a less rigorous adherence to the principle. Already, then, the principle of non-discriminatory, uniform treatment had begun to feel the environmental pressure emanating from this new majority group of countries in the international economic system. But, unlike the GATT, which was to succumb to the pressure in 1964,[38] the IMF succeeded in fending off the novel international legal trend towards the granting of preferential treatment to developing countries.

Another important consequence of the 1963 CFF decision, from the point of view of the developing countries, was that, for the first time, the Fund was acquiescing in a breach of its prevailing view of the balance-of-payments problems and causes. The reigning model for balance-of-payments analysis at the time defined the main causative factor for external deficits as the domestic inflationary policies indulged in by member-countries.[39] The CFF was a clear acknowledgement by the IMF that balance-of-payments problems were not all of the same kind or origin and that differential treatment, contingent on the diagnosis of these causes and origins, was a consequential requirement.[40] As the Brazilian Governor noted in 1963:

> Once the point is accepted that underdeveloped countries are inflation-prone, largely as a result of their export structure and the primary product instability, the Fund should take into account the nature of the causes responsible for the disequilibria in balance of payments of those countries which seek Fund assistance. Accordingly, the Fund should establish selective criteria for the use of its resources by nonindustrialized countries, without necessarily relating the assistance with stabilization programs.[41]

Finally, as Bird has observed, the CFF was 'the first formal institutional response to the demands of LDCs'.[42] It was no accident that this first substantive action was taken at the time it was. This was the historical juncture, as already stressed, of definitive environmental changes in the structure, membership and institutional processes of international economic relations. The pressures of these environmental evolutions and the persistent approaches of the United Nations system to have IMF action on the commodity problem all combined to push the Fund towards its 1963 decision. The Fund itself had admitted the efficacy of extra-institutional pressure, when its 1963 *Annual Report* noted that: 'Much thought has lately been given, in international forums and elsewhere, to ways in which useful assistance could be rendered to countries affected by variations in their export earnings. The Fund has closely followed these dicussions, which have contributed to the evolution of its own views on the subject'.[43]

4. The process of revision of the CFF

As is evident from Table 7.1, the Fund's CFF has undergone a process of periodic improvement, embracing several of the important features of the facility. At the same time, there have been modifications of other features which, from the perspective of developing countries, have been considered to be neither improvement nor liberalization. These changes in the CFF were made in 1966, 1975, 1979 and 1981. With regard to the five elements specified in Table 7.1, the only element that has remained untouched has been the country eligibility for borrowing.

(a) The 1966 revision of the CFF

A movement for change in the CFF became discernible in the year immediately following its establishment. Significantly, this movement was led by the newly-created UNCTAD which, at its first Conference in 1964, focused its attention on the trade problems of the developing countries—including those associated with commodities. With specific reference to the CFF, the UNCTAD Conference adopted a resolution,[44] by the terms of which the Fund was invited to consider certain specified improvements in the facility. The major elements of the UNCTAD request to the IMF were:

  (i) to increase the borrowing limit to 50 per cent of quota;
 (ii) to separate the CFF from the regular credit facilities of the Fund and
(iii) to revise the technical aspects relating to the calculation of export shortfalls.

The Fund was also requested to explore ways of refinancing the repurchases of developing countries confronted with persistent export earnings shortfalls.

The UNCTAD request was reflected in the statement of the developing countries at the 1964 and 1965 Annual Meetings of the Fund, when these countries, in the overwhelming majority, referred to the resolution and recorded their support for its content.[45] The Group of Experts set up by UNCTAD in 1965 also endorsed the necessity of a review and improvement of the CFF.[46] UNCTAD's resolution and the supporting position of representatives from developing countries in the Fund spurred another staff study on compensatory financing in 1965. It is important to underline that the 1966 report,[47] in its entirety, addressed itself to the criticisms and suggestions made by UNCTAD of the existing facility. The outcome of this review was a Fund decision to adopt several improvements and other changes in the operations of the CFF.[48]

In keeping with UNCTAD's recommendation, the Fund increased the quota-related limit for borrowing under the CFF to 50 per cent (see Table 7.1).

However, borrowing in any single year could not exceed 25 per cent of quota. Secondly, the Fund decided to make the CFF a floating facility—another UNCTAD recommendation. The significance of the increase in borrowing rights is self-evident; a member could count on a larger quantum of assistance from the Fund in the event of export earnings shortfalls. The new floating status of the facility was also a positive development. Under the original 1963 decision, purchases under the CFF automatically had implications for borrowing under the regular credit facilities by prematurely pushing the purchasing-members into the higher credit tranches, requiring a tougher stand of conditionality:

> ... compensatory drawings were regarded as equivalent to ordinary drawings from the standpoint of their effect on the conditions to be applied to subsequent ordinary drawings. In other words, a compensatory drawing could have the effect of shifting a country's position from the first to the second credit tranche, or from the second to the third, thereby affecting the rigour of the conditions requiring to be satisfied in the event that a further ordinary drawing was needed.[49]

This delinking of the CFF meant that normal credit facilities remained unaffected by CFF purchases.

The Fund took the opportunity of the 1966 CFF review to introduce other modifications that, in certain respects, made the facility more attractive to potential users and, in other respects, represented a measure of restrictiveness. In the former category was the right of reclassification. This meant that a member could make a drawing under the regular credit facilities, but could reclassify this drawing to one under the CFF within a specified time-period— that is, within six months. Such a right, in effect, gave the member an element of flexibility in terms of its use of Fund resources.

Two aspects, in particular, of the 1966 revision signified new limiting factors surrounding the use of the CFF. Firstly, the increased borrowing right of 50 per cent of quota was conceived as a two-tranche system for the purpose of devising CFF conditionality. The initial 25 per cent of CFF credit continued to be effected on the basis of negligible conditionality—the sole requirement being an undertaking to cooperate with the Fund. However, purchases above 25 per cent of quota were to be approved 'only if the Fund is satisfied that the member has been cooperating with the Fund in an effort to find, where required, appropriate solutions for its balance-of-payments difficulties'.[50] As Goreux has indicated, this formulation implies a stricter test of cooperation in that, 'the Fund must ... be satisfied that past cooperation has been adequate. Although the extent of the cooperation required has not been codified, satisfactory performance in the context of a financial program supported by the Fund would be considered as evidence of past cooperation'.[51] The second aspect of the 1966 decision that signified a more restrictive operation of the CFF was the recommendation of an earlier repurchase policy. The expectation is that repayment will be linked to the improvement of the member's balance of payments and reserve situation in that, four years after a CFF purchase was made, the member was expected to expedite repayments if the balance of payments had sufficiently improved.[52] However, this was not an obligatory requirement; rather, it was essentially a recommendation.

This first Fund revision of the CFF was explicitly influenced by the decision on compensatory financing adopted at UNCTAD I[53] and the concerted campaign by the developing countries, on the basis of the UNCTAD decision, within the IMF.[54] This is undoubtedly an example of the measurable impact of environmental circumstances relating to the establishment of UNCTAD and the growth of Third World membership, and their activism, in the international economic system on the Fund's decision making—even if the elements of the substantive claims were not embodied, in their entirety, in the 1966 decision.

(b) The 1975 revision of the CFF

The next phase of Third World criticism of the CFF and the related campaign for changes in its operations became observable almost immediately after the 1966 decision. At Algiers in 1967, the first Ministerial Meeting of the G77 outlined several new elements for an improved CFF, with the objective of making access and borrowing limits to the facility even more favourable.[55] This campaign was taken up at UNCTAD II in 1968 and a decision specifically focused on the CFF was adopted without opposition.[56] Unlike the Fund response after UNCTAD I, the institution on this occasion was more cautious in reacting to UNCTAD's and the G77's recommendations. Speaking before the UNCTAD II Conference, the Fund's representative stated that, 'it was felt that more experience should be acquired before contemplating further changes in the operation of that policy'.[57] He further alluded to a recent Fund initiative requiring the staff to study the problem of stabilizing the prices of primary products.[58]

It was not until 1975, however, that the next important revision of the CFF was undertaken. The background circumstances of the 1975 decision were the fundamental changes in the international economic environment of the mid-1970s. Of particular consequence, as we have already seen, were the general offensive undertaken by the developing countries on the commodity question and the central preoccupation of the international community with this problem—as the US Secretary of State, in his presentation before the seventh Special Session of the UN General Assembly, observed: 'The question of stabilization of income from primary products has become central in the dialogue on international economic concerns'.[59]

Of crucial importance in this context of commodity nationalism—apart from OPEC's action—was the Dakar Conference of Developing Countries on Raw Materials of 3–8 February 1975.[60] This conference manifested a profound radicalization of Third World perspectives in so far as their raw materials were concerned. Starting from the position that, '[t]he inequalities and weaknesses of the present economic system are particularly glaring in the conduct of world trade in commodities',[61] the Dakar Declaration outlined a coherent action programme that developing countries were to undertake to redress their disadvantaged position in the production and exchange of raw materials. Not only did the action programme call for the substantial improvement of the CFF,[62] but it also endorsed the creation of producers' associations and commodity agreements—policies that were anathema to the developed countries because of the implied interference with market forces.

In 1974, moreover, UNCTAD had put out a report that argued a more comprehensive international treatment of the commodity issue and that included the Common Fund proposal.[63] This report also addressed the CFF, pinpointing the major shortcomings of the facility, as seen from an UNCTAD vantage-point. The principal criticisms related to the quota-based limitations on borrowing, the repayment conditions, the formula employed for the calculation of shortfalls, the non-automaticity of loans and the fact that borrowing could only be made if the overall balance of payments was in deficit. These criticisms were reflected in the main proposals on compensatory financing incorporated in the resolution adopted at the 1975 Special Session of the General Assembly. That resolution called for a 'Substantial improvement'[64] in the CFF to widen coverage to include manufactures and services, in addition to commodity exports; to take into account, in determining compensation levels, movements in import prices,[65] to lengthen the repayment period; and to ensure that, as far as possible, compensation for export shortfalls takes place at the same time as they occur.[66]

The major thrust of this radicalized international commodity environment was the achievement of '[a] new structure to govern trade in commodities'[67]—an integral part of the NIEO campaign of the developing countries. It forced the major economic actor, the United States, to admit the centrality of the commodity issue and to attempt to seize the initiative in deflecting the radical tendencies of Third World approaches to the issue. The American answer was a proposal for a development security facility to replace the CFF.[68] Interestingly, this proposed new facility, in the American view, was to be for the exclusive benefit of developing countries, the industrial countries being explicitly excluded from its benefits.[69]

Developing countries were never enamoured by the American proposal, so that, in late 1975, that country conceded the need for a CFF liberalization. Among the changes suggested by the United States was, interestingly, one whereby 'the facility would be used only by developing members and not by the more developed primary producing members, such as Australia, Iceland, New Zealand, South Africa, and others'.[70] In essence, as with the proposed development security facility, the United States was quite prepared to concede the establishment of arrangements within the Fund that catered exclusively to the developing countries.

One can well appreciate the dilemma that confronted the developed countries at this moment—the credible threat posed by the formation of producers' associations and the preference of developing countries for the incipient integrated commodity approach then being canvassed by UNCTAD, in the context of OPEC's actions, and uncertainty as to the outcome of the commodity conflict. In this environment, improved compensatory financing under the aegis of the IMF was clearly an easier option for them.

These were the environmental factors that spurred the 1975 Fund review of the CFF on the basis of what one Fund publication described as the 'broad consensus [that] has formed in support of improvement in the compensatory financing facility'.[71] This review was given high priority on the agenda of the Executive Board after the 1975 Annual Meeting[72] and an Executive Board decision was taken in December 1975 approving further improvements in the facility.[73] The principal features of this new improvement were:

(i) an increase in borrowing limits from 50 to 75 per cent of quota, with a maximum permissible purchase of 50 per cent in any twelve-month period;
(ii) the stricter standard of cooperation, for purposes of conditionality, became operative in respect of borrowing above 50 per cent of quota;
(iii) the time-limit for reclassification of regular tranche purchases to CFF purchases was raised from six months to eighteen months and
(iv) the introduction of an early-purchase procedure. The importance of this feature is that it allows those members with long time-lags in compiling their trade data to use the facility through the practice of estimates of export earnings for up to six months of the year of shortfall.[74]

(c) The 1979 revision of the CFF

The pattern of Third World pressure for further improvements immediately after the achievement of a liberalization of the facility was again evident following the 1975 decision. At its twelfth Meeting in January 1976, the Group of 24 expressed the position that the 1975 liberalization 'fell far short of expectations of the developing countries, and suggested that there should be an early review of the facility.'[75] The 1975 CFF decision was also criticized by the UNCTAD Secretariat in its report on international monetary issues to UNCTAD IV in 1976,[76] by the G77 at its Arusha Ministerial Meeting in 1979, preparatory to UNCTAD V[77] and at UNCTAD V itself.[78] UNCTAD's prescription was a facility under which purchases would be delinked from quotas and balance-of-payments criteria and:

> whose size and conditions for drawings and repurchases *would be designed exclusively to meet the particular needs and capacities of developing countries. These are not characteristics of the IMF facility, which is open to all member countries, both developed and developing, and whose rules are uniformly applicable to all countries*[79] [emphasis added].

Within the UNCTAD framework, moreover, the Common Fund negotiations were being pressed by the developing nations. In essence, the negotiations on international economic relations continued to have, as a central preoccupation, from the mid- to late 1970s, the commodity issue and, as noted by a Fund publication, '[p]roposals for stabilizing export earnings of developing countries proved to be a particularly contentious issue for UNCTAD V'.[80] The upshot of this persistent Third World offensive on the commodity issue, especially as it related to compensatory financing and the IMF, was the adoption at UNCTAD

V of resolution 125(V) on 'Compensatory facility for commodity-related shortfalls in export earnings', against the opposition of the majority of developed countries.[81] By the terms of the resolution, the Secretary-General of UNCTAD was requested:

> [i]n consultation with the International Monetary Fund, to prepare a detailed study for the operation of a complementary facility for shortfalls in earnings of each commodity ... that would provide adequate compensation in real terms to developing countries, paying particular attention to the situation of the least developed countries.[82]

This was the context of the 1979 Fund review of the CFF. Apart from the continuation of a heightened commodity nationalism by developing countries, UNCTAD's resolution 125(V) presaged the coming into being of a rival compensatory financing facility, divorced from Fund management. The specific new operational demands of the developing countries for an improvement of the Fund's facility included:

(i) an increase in borrowing limits from 75 to 100 per cent of quota, with drawings in any twelve-month period increasing from 50 to 100 per cent of quota—in other words, an elimination of annual borrowing limits;

(ii) a lengthening of the repayment period from the existing three-to-five years to one of five-to-seven years;

(iii) countries to be given the choice in the calculation of shortfalls between shortfalls in total receipts from merchandise exports and the combined receipts from merchandise exports and services;

(iv) in the calculation of shortfalls, account to be taken of the increase in import prices;

(v) drawings to be free of any credit tranche conditionality and

(vi) increased import volume resulting from climatic or other factors beyond the control of the affected country to be also taken into account in calculating shortfalls.[83]

In response to this concerted pressure by the developing countries and their institutional supporters, the IMF took a decision, in August 1979, improving further the operation of the CFF.[84] Two of the major demands of developing countries were accepted. Firstly, the 1979 decision approved an increase in borrowing rights from 75 to 100 per cent of quota and an elimination of annual permissible borrowing rights—in effect, countries could borrow in any twelve-month period to the extent of the increased borrowing limit of 100 per cent of quota. Secondly, there was an extension of product coverage to include services. The borrowing member thus had the option of including receipts from tourism and workers' remittances—once adequate data were available—in the calculation of shortfalls.

(d) The 1981 revision of the CFF

The final CFF improvement to date was adopted in 1981, in fulfilment of a direct proposal by the Food and Agricultural Organization (FAO) and World

Food Council (WFC) to the Fund in 1979. In its 1979 report to the General Assembly, the WFC proposed the establishment of a new food import financing facility under the auspices of the IMF. The General Assembly subsequently adopted a resolution that, in its preambular section, underlined the concern of the international community about the strong impact of foodstuff imports on the balance of payments of food-importing developing countries. In its operative section, the resolution invited the IMF, 'to consider providing, within the context of its financing facilities, additional balance-of-payments support for meeting the rise in the food import bills of low-income, food-deficit countries'.[85]

This was by no means a new request. The NIEO resolutions of the mid-1970s had included provisions to facilitate the importation by developing countries of adequate quantities of food without placing undue strain on the foreign exchange resources or unpredictable deterioration in the balance of payments.[86] The NIEO request, however, was a generalized one, directed to the international community as a whole. What was different about the 1979 initiative was the focused direction of the address to the IMF.

Support for the FAO/WFC initiative was garnered from a variety of sources within the Fund. Developing countries naturally associated themselves with it.[87] The Managing Director provided his strong support for the proposal. In his address before the 1980 Annual Meeting of the Fund, he referred to the proposal which was then under study by the Executive Board and observed that the food import facility:

> could alleviate the problems of countries—especially low-income countries—suffering from crop failures or sharp rises in food import costs . . . Because of the present serious situation of the developing countries, I consider that an early and positive decision on this matter would be an important manifestation of our concern for human issues.[88]

Among the developed countries, France also expressed strong public support for the proposal.[89]

Responding to the FAO/WFC approach, the Fund's Executive Board adopted a decision in 1981, by the terms of which it stood prepared to open its financing facilities to cover cereal import excesses of member-states.[90] Once again, in respect of the formulation of the decision, eligibility was theoretically extended to all Fund members. But the practical intent of the decision was clearly specified in the Communiqué of the Interim Committee of 21 May 1981 when it was 'noted that the assistance under the new decision would be of particular benefit to low-income countries'.[91]

The cereal import decision integrated cereal import purchases into the CFF, with potential borrowings for cereal imports and export shortfalls each carrying a quota-based limit of 100 per cent, but with a joint borrowing limit of 125 per cent—see Table 7.1. The main significance of the 1981 improvement was basically twofold: firstly, it increased the potential scope of borrowing under the CFF and, secondly, it broadened product coverage for compensatory financing to cover both export shortfalls and a restricted element of import costs. In the latter respect, the decision can be said to break new ground in acceding, in this limited way, to the import-price indexation claims that developing countries had been advocating throughout the 1970s. Developing countries have, however, been interested in general import-price indexation, rather than the narrower basis of the import financing facility. It is interesting, finally, to emphasize that developing countries recorded 'appreciation to the Managing Director for his efforts in bringing about this facility'.[92]

5. Post-1981 developments—the emergence of regressive trends regarding the CFF

The post-1981 years have seen some clearly regressive developments as regards the Fund's CFF.[93] In the aftermath of the quota increases agreed on for the Fund in 1984, a decision was taken by the Executive Board to reduce borrowing limits under the CFF. Regarding use of either the export shortfall or cereal import component, the borrowing limit was cut back to 83 per cent of quota from the previous 100 per cent and for the joint export shortfall/cereal import borrowing, the new limit was 105 per cent, down from the previous 125 per cent. These new limits were agreed despite the strong opposing claim by the developing nations for an expansion in borrowing rights[94] and their objection to reduced access.[95] It is true that, in terms of the increased quotas agreed under the Eighth General Review of Quotas, borrowing rights, quantitatively, did not decline, compared to the situation prior to the quota increase.[96] But the standard for judging the harshness of this decision is twofold: firstly, the pervasive economic crisis in the developing countries, manifested *inter alia* in further balance-of-payments deterioration, with its implications of higher levels of resource flows and, secondly, the previous practice in the Fund whereby quota increases never before affected borrowing limits under this facility: 'Never in the past has an increase in quotas led to lowering of access limits under the CFF'.[97]

Even more retrogressive was the trend in the Fund towards the application of a harsher standard of conditionality for CFF purchases. As early as 1982, the G24 was lamenting 'the attempt by the Fund to impose a structure of conditionality on the use of this facility, contrary to the original intentions; in their view, this was illogical in view of the exogenous and reversible nature of the problems addressed'.[98] This trend was legitimized in the September 1983 decision regarding guidelines on cooperation as they related to the CFF.[99] The standard of harsher conditionality is at once apparent if one examines the requirements of cooperation flowing from purchases up to 50 per cent of quota under the CFF.

Previous to the 1983 decision, purchases of up to 50 per cent of quota necessitated merely a willingness of the purchasing member to cooperate with the Fund in the search for solutions to its balance-of-payments difficulties. As Goreux has explained it: 'The speed of operations has been a major concern in setting up and administering a compensatory financing facility. A Fund mission does not normally need to visit the country presenting a request.'[100] Consequent upon the 1983 decision, this standard of cooperation was defined to indicate 'a willingness to receive Fund missions and to discuss, in good faith, the appropriateness of the member's policies and whether changes in the member's policies are necessary to deal with its balance of payments difficulties'.[101] Scrutiny of a member's economic policies—unlike the past practice—could thus be undertaken by the Fund before CFF purchases could be made. Moreover, if the Fund found that the:

> existing policies of the member ... are seriously deficient or where the country's record of cooperation in the recent past has been unsatisfactory, the Fund will expect the member to take action that gives, prior to the submission of the request for the purchase, a reasonable assurance that policies corrective of the member's balance of payments problems will be adopted.[102]

What is clear under this decision is that the mere proof of temporary export shortfalls beyond the control of members does not have the effect of activating CFF purchases up to 50 per cent of quota without questioning of economic policies. No longer can it be said that the CFF's 'main attraction to developing countries is the low conditionality on loans. It is one source of International Monetary Fund finance that is almost free from stringent economic criteria and policy prescriptions'.[103] At the same time, it should be pointed out that, in the context of external payments situations of fundamental crisis in the overwhelming majority of developing countries, the reality has been that a growing number of these countries have entered, in recent years, into high conditionality arrangements with the Fund, either under stand-bys or the Extended Fund Facility. Using the 1983 financial year as an indication, of the twenty-seven developing countries that made CFF purchases, twenty were also involved in high conditionality arrangements.[104] In such a context, the practical effect of the harsher standard of conditionality is somewhat mitigated in that these countries would already have had or, conversely, concurrent with the consideration of a CFF purchase would have, a Fund review of their economic situation anyhow.

Developing countries have, nevertheless, reacted strongly against this additional attack on credit sources, especially since it was the only existing one in the Fund that was relatively liberal, with regard to conditionality. The G24 has accused the Fund of emasculating one of its most successful operations—'retrograde steps imposed at a time when developing countries were exceptionally short of liquidity'.[105] This movement towards tougher conditionality under the CFF—as we shall see later—was part of the overall tougher conditionality that became attached to Fund lending post-1981 at the instance of the pressure exerted by a narrow group of developed countries, led by the United States.

6. The principle of uniformity versus differential treatment

The impetus for a compensatory financing scheme came from outside the Fund and the initiative was explicitly concerned with the commodity trade problems of a particular group of countries—the developing countries. In fact, the approach to the Fund was itself couched in language that pinpointed this group of countries. While the Fund's examination of the problem validated concerns articulated by developing countries within the United Nations system, its acquiescence in the search for a solution—in the form of the CFF decision— carefully avoided isolating a particular group of countries for special or differential treatment.

It is interesting once again to examine the sources of this resistance against efforts to introduce explicit preferential treatment for the developing nations in respect of compensatory financing. To this end, the debate at UNCTAD V and VI on the proposed additional compensatory financing facility is instructive for what it says about the perspectives of the developed countries that have opposed a scheme directed solely at the developing countries. In explaining its negative vote against UNCTAD resolution 125(V), the representative of Canada noted that:

> The type of facility proposed, to the extent that it would be accessible to developing producer countries only, would be extremely discriminatory as it would cover products exported in large quantities by developed producer countries.[106]

Pursuant to this resolution, proposals were evolved within UNCTAD for the creation of a complementary financing facility and, at UNCTAD VI, not only did the Conference mandate the Secretary-General to establish an expert group on the issue, but it also invited the IMF 'to consider the establishment of special arrangements for the benefit of the least developed countries'.[107]

This resolution was the subject of heated debate, with many of the developed nations recording reservations about several of its provisions. A principal area of contention was UNCTAD's invitation to the IMF to consider special arrangements for the least developed countries and the basis of their resistance was the discriminatory intent of the proposal. As the United States representative put it, 'Paragraph 1 of the resolution made a proposal to the IMF that it conduct itself in a manner contrary to both its basic articles and its operating procedures.'[108] This position was in clear contradiction to the United States initiative of the mid-1970s to have such an arrangement—pointing to the basic political expediency of the American attitude, at the least.

Yet, formal predilection to the contrary and the strong resistance of several developed Fund members against the introduction of differential treatment, the intent of the framers of the CFF policy was always understood to be directed to the partial solution, at the IMF level, of the commodity instability problem primarily of developing countries.

In so far as the CFF is concerned, the principle of uniform treatment has been *de jure* safeguarded in the Fund. But the test of uniform treatment has to be met at another level—that of practice. The practice of the Fund can most reliably be assessed on the basis of the users or beneficiaries of the facility.

7. The CFF in practice—beneficiaries of the facility

Analysis of the CFF in practice can be made at two levels. Firstly, there is the level of a profile of the principal users of the facility, presented in terms of country-distribution of borrowers (by discrete groups of countries) and the value distribution of borrowings, also in regard to country-groupings. Since the CFF, for most of its existence, has been a low-conditionality facility, then the pattern of its use in relation to the global use of Fund resources represents another level of analysis. This is clearly for the reason that, as a low-conditionality facility, it is a more attractive facility for users.

Table 7.2 presents an evolution of country use, by groups of countries, in respect of each of the major CFF decisions and overall. In value terms, developing countries (IMF categorization) have been by far the major borrowers under the CFF—SDR 10.6 billion of the SDR 12.9 billion or 82 per cent of the total over the 1963–84 years. Developed countries were insignificant users under the 1963, 1966 and 1979 decisions. In Table 7.3, the position is

Table 7.2 Purchases in value terms by groups of countries under the various CFF decisions (SDR millions)

Decision year	Total purchases	Developed countries	Developing countries
1963	87	–	87 (100)*
1966	1135	88 (7)	1047 (93)
1975	3406	1126 (32)	2280 (68)
1979	8305	1064 (13)	7241 (87)
	12933	2278 (18)	10655 (82)

* Percentages in parentheses.
Source: UNCTAD, *Compensatory financing of export earnings shortfalls*, TD/B/1029/Rev. 1, Annex VII, p. 7.

Table 7.3 Number of purchases made by groups of countries

	1963–66	1966–75	1976–79	1979–84
Total purchases	3	54	88	113
Developed countries	–	5 (3)*	11 (8)	4 (4)
Developing countries	3	49 (31)	75 (53)	108 (66)
Others	–	–	2 (1)†	1 (1)‡

* Number of countries making purchases in parentheses.
† Israel.
‡ Hungary.
Source: Various IMF sources.

presented in terms of total number of purchases by groups of countries. For the years 1963–66, only three purchases were made, all by developing countries, while in the years 1966–75, these countries made forty-nine of the fifty-four CFF purchases and, between 1976 and 1984, of the 201 purchases, 183 or 91 per cent were made by developing countries.

A further breakdown of CFF purchases will show that in the period January 1976 to June 1984, of the 120 developing members of the Fund at the end of this period, seventy-six or some 63 per cent made purchases under the CFF.[109] This figure is even more positive—rising to 75 per cent of the developing countries—if we exclude the thirteen OPEC members, which on the whole have hardly used Fund resources over the past decade and a half (in the years 1976–84, only Ecuador and Indonesia used the CFF). Moreover, fifty-one of the seventy-six developing countries made more than one CFF purchase, with many of them making as many as six or eight purchases—for instance, Jamaica, Sudan, Zambia and Sri Lanka made eight purchases each, while Western Samoa and the Dominican Republic made six each, over the life-span of the CFF.

Another interesting feature emerges when we look at the users from the developed countries. Eight such countries (as categorized for the purposes of this analysis) used the CFF between January 1976 and June 1984—Australia, Iceland, New Zealand, South Africa, Greece, Portugal and Turkey. However, none of the major developed countries have used CFF credits.

Turning to the question of CFF drawings in relation to total use of Fund resources, Table 7.4 shows that CFF purchases in the order of 11.71 billion SDRs represented 26 per cent of all Fund credit extended to members in the period 1976–84 and 25 per cent (9.57 billion SDRs of 36.68 billion) to the developing countries. These are favourable proportions when account is taken of the broad range of permanent and temporary facilities—with varying degrees of conditionality—operated by the Fund. If we look at Table 7.5, it indicates that

Table 7.4 CFF drawings in relation to other uses of Fund credit (1976–1984) (billions of SDRs)

	All members	Developed members*	Developing members
Total use of credit	46.23	9.54	36.68
CFF	11.71	2.18	9.53
BSFF	0.53	0.06	0.47
Tranche facilities†	31.86	5.75	26.11
Oil facility	2.14	1.55	0.59

* Developed members' share distorted somewhat by virtue of inclusion of several developing countries—Botṣwana, Lesotho, Swaziland, Malta and Yugoslavia.

† Include credit tranches and Extended Fund Facility.

Source: UNCTAD, *Compensatory financing of export earnings shortfalls*, TD/B/1029/Rev. 1, Annex VII, p. 11.

Table 7.5 Fund purchases under the various facilities by year, 1978–1984
(billions of SDRs)

	1978	1979	1980	1981	1982	1983	1984
Total purchases	1.2	1.7	3.4	6.8	7.4	12.6	7.3
Credit tranches	0.4	0.9	1.8	3.4	2.5	4.9	3.1
Extended Fund facility	0.2	0.2	0.6	2.1	2.1	4.6	3.3
CFF	0.6	0.6	1.0	1.2	2.6	2.8	0.8
	(50)*	(35)	(29)	(18)	(35)	(22)	(11)
BSFF	–†	–	–	–	0.1	0.3	–

* In per cent.
† Less than 50 million.
Source: IMF Survey, 4 February 1985.

CFF purchases represented substantial portions of the purchases by developing countries in 1978, 1979, 1980, 1982 and 1983, while there was a dramatic decline in 1984—probably accounted for by the harsher conditionality associated with CFF credit since the September 1983 decision. In so far as cereal import purchases were concerned, as envisaged, this has been wholly to the benefit of developing countries. Eleven purchases have been made since the coming into effect of the 1981 decision, with seven developing countries being the beneficiaries.[110]

The other important factor to be considered is the impact of the various revisions of the CFF on the inclination of countries to use the facility. A hint of caution is necessary here since clearly it is not solely the fact of liberalization that may induce a country to use the CFF. Developments, particularly in commodity trade, where they are of an adverse nature, would necessarily be a major contributory factor, but improvements should have a positive influence in inducing countries to use CFF credits.

The effect of liberalization can be clearly seen in the comparative positions of the 1966–75, 1976–79 and 1979–84 periods—see Tables 7.2 and 7.3. In Goreux's analysis of the CFF, he identifies the 1975 decision as a 'turning-point'.[111] He points out that in the first thirteen years of its operations, 1963–75, only fifty-seven drawings totalling SDR 1.2 billion were made. Contrastingly, between January 1976 and March 1980, a total of 107 drawings in the amount of SDR 4.0 billion were made, and these latter purchases represented 31 per cent of total Fund credit to all members in this period and 45 per cent if credit extended to the United Kingdom is excluded.[112]

What this analysis of the CFF has shown in practice, is that it has been of overwhelming benefit to the developing members of the IMF, when looked at on the basis of country use and the overall proportion of this low-conditionality facility—at least up to the early 1980s—in total Fund lending. From this perspective, the practical significance of the CFF resides in its concentration on the specific problem of commodity trade instability encountered by developing countries as a whole. Essentially, then, the Fund has at once succeeded in protecting the legal equality of rights in the institution, while in practical terms acquiescing in a large measure of preferential treatment of developing countries.

Conclusions

Between the time of the establishment of the CFF in 1963 and 1981, four series of revisions resulting in improvements in the operations of the facility have been effected by the IMF. These improvements resulted in increased borrowing limits, expressed as a proportion of quotas and wider product coverage for compensatory financing. They also touched other technical features of the CFF's operations, particularly that relating to the calculation of export shortfalls. Because the CFF was, until the early 1980s, a low-conditionality facility, these improvements also represented a significant benefit with regard to the quality of the Fund's credit resources.

One word of caution needs to be introduced in speaking of increased borrowing limits. These have been seen as improvements, based on the fact that developing countries themselves requested these specific quantitative increases on various occasions. A more sophisticated analysis must, however, go beyond quantitative increases and place them within the context of the overall erosion, over time, in the relationship between Fund quotas and indicators pertaining to the growth in world trade and the deterioration in balance-of-payments positions. From this vantage-point:

> IMF quotas ... have grown substantially less than world trade at current prices and far slower than world payments imbalances. Thus ... total IMF quotas which in 1966–68 were equivalent to 16 per cent of deficit developing countries' export earnings and 64 per cent of those countries' current account deficits were *only* equivalent, in 1978–81 to 6 per cent of deficit developing countries' export earnings and *only* 12 per cent of their current account deficits.[113]

Therefore, the increases in CFF borrowing limits have only served to partially offset this broad deterioration of Fund quotas in terms of these crucial indicators.

Each revision of the CFF, as well as the actual decision to set it up has been clearly linked to a process of concerted extra-institutional advocacy, led by the United Nations system and particularly UNCTAD, and intra-mural pressure directed by the developing countries as a group. The process of revision has, in effect, symbolized institutional sensitivity and responsiveness to the balance-of-payments effects of the commodity problem on the economies of developing countries. It is evident from the analysis that these countries have not attained their maximum demands, but, from the beginning, the hypothesis was stated that, in a decision-making context of *de jure* weighted voting and *de facto* consensus—and where the main claimants for a change are in the minority in respect of voting power—maximalist claims will never be achieved.

Not only have the proponents of change had a measurable impact on Fund policy in regard to the CFF, but the changing environmental contexts have, at specific historical moments, been propitious for change. The entire context of the introduction of the CFF pointed to institutional responsiveness in a situation of challenge and uncertainty. The challenge was the prospective new international organization—UNCTAD—and the uncertainty related to the inability of anyone to predict the scope of its influence and effectiveness in international economic relations. Organizations, in a situation of both potential and actual competition, necessarily feel the imperative to adjust in an effort to withstand and, if possible, deflect novel institutional challenges. The bargaining advantage of the developing nations was strengthened by the inclination of the Fund's Managing Director, in the time-period of the early to mid-1960s, to provide support for their demands, to a certain limited extent.

The institution was at the time facing the distinct possibility of a loss of its clientele, and, thereby, influence in international monetary relations. It had already virtually lost regulatory control over the monetary behaviour of the major developed countries, which were tending increasingly to operate outside the ambit of the Fund. A strong and effective UNCTAD, catering to the needs of developing nations, could have dealt the IMF an additional blow by usurping the only clientele left to the institution. Concessions to the developing countries, therefore, became unavoidable for institutional survival and *raison d'être*.

The next period of major responsiveness by the IMF in regard to the CFF— the second half of the 1970s—only strengthens this assessment of the situation. This was a period in which the international economic environment, as we saw, underwent important changes involving developing countries. Moreover, the Third World were again able to present alternatives to what the IMF had to offer—especially the UNCTAD-sponsored Integrated Programme of Commodities. This scheme was philosophically anathema to many developed countries. In an effort to weaken the campaign for its implementation, concessions, in the form of CFF liberalizations in 1975 and 1979, were made to developing countries.

The importance of the environmental explanation is evident when account is taken of the fact that, at the time the CFF was established and since, developed countries have had the voting strength to block it. Apart from those technical aspects of the Third World demands that these countries have continuously opposed, they were, on the whole favourably disposed to improvements in the facility up to the early 1980s.

The retrogressive trends in respect of the CFF in the post-1981 years can also be placed in the context of developments in international economic relations. By the early 1980s, there was the emerging sense of a disunited Third World; there were, also, the new, tougher attitude of the main developed countries in the negotiating process for international economic relations—at the advent of the Reagan administration in the United States—and the counter-threat posed by this government against the entire multilateral economic system. It was an environment of decreased resource flows from all sources and a priority concern with the inflation problem, in the battle against which international deflation was the preferred solution of the leading developed countries. This was not a decision-making context favourable to improvements in the Fund's financing facilities; in fact, it was a decision-making context suitable for the contrary tendency and this is exactly what has occurred with respect to the CFF.

Finally, it is submitted that these retrogressive tendencies as regards the CFF are not necessarily a bad thing for the developing countries. The commodity problem will not be solved by the CFF; this mechanism is merely a temporary expedient that in no way deals with the fundamental causes of commodity instability. It has already been pointed out that the commodity instability problem is caused by factors on both the demand and supply side. While compensatory financing may be appropriate as a counter-cyclical expedient at times of slack demand, its appropriateness is more problematic when the cause has to do with supply factors. As a recent UNCTAD Group of Experts has concluded, it is the supply factors that are important at the level of individual countries.[114] Moreover, while, at a basic level, commodity earnings shortfalls may be said to be temporary, they have in fact been such a recurring phenomenon for many developing countries that are highly dependent on commodities that there is now an element of permanence to the problem.

From this perspective, dependence on a mechanism such as the CFF—and it must be borne in mind that, with the virtual demise of the proposed Integrated Programme of Commodities, compensatory financing remains the only really coherent international instrumentality left to the developing countries—merely intensifies the economic instabilities in these countries. It is in this framework that the most recent UNCTAD initiative on commodity trade instability has to be placed. This is the proposal for a complementary financing facility to address the issue that has been identified as the root cause of the problem—supply instability.[115]

Notes

1. Keynes saw the necessity for international arrangements in the field of money, development assistance, trade and primary products—see 'Proposals for an International Clearing Union', April 1943 in Horsefield, op. cit., Vol. 3, p. 19.
2. See notes 26 and 27 of Chapter 2.
3. See 'Chapter VI' of the ITO Charter signed at Havana on 24 March 1948. For a discussion, see Wilcox, op. cit., Chapter 2, pp. 114-25.
4. The literature on commodity trade instability is extensive, but a standard work is: Alasdair I. Macbean, *Export Instability and Economic Development*, London, George Allen & Unwin Ltd, 1966. For a recent summary review of the issues involved, see UNCTAD, *Consideration of the Substantive Issues Relating to the Question of an Additional Complementary Facility to Compensate for the Export Earnings Shortfalls of Developing Countries* (pursuant to Conference resolution 157(VI), para. 3: Compensatory Financing of Export Earnings Shortfalls), TD/B/AC.37/3, 26 March 1984.
5. Low supply elasticity relates basically to the incapacity of countries to increase production to take advantage of favourable price shifts and, also, the long gestation periods associated with the production of certain commodities. Low demand elasticity has to do, *inter alia*, with the quantitative limits to the use of commodities, and thus the fact that lower prices will not automatically translate into increased demand as well as the tendency to shift to the use of synthetics and substitutes in the face of higher prices.

6. On the demand side, the explanation centres on the business cycle phenomenon in the industrialized countries. On the supply side, a series of circumstances—including variable weather conditions, the occurrence of crop disease, labour problems and governmental production decisions—has an effect on the production capacities of individual countries, in many instances in unpredictable ways and thereby contributing to supply instability.

7. For a discussion, see *Towards a New Trade Policy for Development* (Report by the Secretary-General of UNCTAD), UN, New York, 1964, pp. 11–19.

8. Important shifts in the international division of labour have already been underscored for certain sub-sets of developing countries, but the overwhelming majority have continued to be identified as essentially commodity-producing nations. And, even for many of the countries that have successfully begun the process of economic diversification, through industrialization, the commodity sector still contributes substantially to the national economic welfare.

9. See, for instance, L. N. Rangarajan, *Commodity Conflict: The Political Economy of International Commodity Negotiations*, London, Croom Helm, 1978, Ch. 3, pp. 53–88.

10. For Zambia, copper provided 94 per cent of export earnings, for Mauritius and Cuba, sugar accounted for 90 per cent and 84 per cent respectively, while for Nepal it was rice, with 85 per cent, for the Gambia, groundnuts and groundnut oils, 85 per cent and for Laos, timber, contributing 80 per cent—ibid., p. 82.

11. 'Fund Policies and Procedures in Relation to the Compensatory Financing of Commodity Fluctuations', *IMF Staff Papers*, Vol. 8, November 1960, p. 2.

12. For a discussion, see Rangarajan, op. cit., pp. 34–51.

13. Apart from the IMF's compensatory financing facility, the other major international compensatory mechanism is the STABEX scheme of the EEC/ACP countries under the Lomé Convention. Unlike the IMF's facility, which extends to all Fund members—both developed and developing, as we shall see later—STABEX is restricted to the sixty-four developing countries of the ACP and the ten member-states of the EEC, with access to STABEX credits limited to the former set of countries. For a discussion of the differences between these arrangements, see Louis M. Goreux, *Compensatory Financing Facility*, Pamphlet Series No. 34, Washington DC, IMF, 1980, pp. 80–4 and J. D. A. Cuddy, 'Compensatory Financing in the North–South Dialogue: the IMF and STABEX Schemes', *Journal of World Trade Law*, **13**, No. 1, January/February 1979, pp. 66–76.

14. As Goreux has defined it: 'Compensatory financing may be considered as an insurance scheme allowing members to borrow at low interest rates when their export earnings fall below trend and to repay when their export earnings rise above trend'—see L. M. Goreux, 'Compensatory Financing: the Cyclical Pattern of Export Shortfalls', *IMF Staff Papers*, Vol. 24, No. 3, November 1977, p. 613.

15. Stanley D. Metzger, 'Law and Policy Making for Trade among "Have" and "Have-not" Nations' in John Carey, ed., *Law and Policy Making for Trade among 'Have' and 'Have-Not' Nations* (Background Paper and Proceedings of the Eleventh Hammarskjold Forum), Dobbs Ferry, New York, Oceana Publications, 1968, pp. 22–3.

16. See General Assembly resolution 623(VII) of 21 December 1952.

17. See UN, *Commodity Trade and Economic Development* (report submitted by a Committee appointed by the Secretary-General), Doc. E/2519, 1953, p. 67, para. 225. It is interesting to note that the Committee saw compensatory financing as 'secondary action [which] . . . by its very nature does not attack the root of the disturbances it compensates'—ibid., p. 67, para. 222.

18. See Horsefield, op. cit., Vol. 2, p. 418.

19. Ibid., Vol. 1, p. 532.

20. See 'Fund Policies and Procedures . . . Commodity Fluctuations', op. cit., p. 2.

21. Ibid., p. 4.

22. Thus, of the fourteen Governors from developing countries who addressed the 1961 Annual Meeting, nine alluded to this issue—the Governors of Indonesia, Nigeria, Pakistan, United Arab Republic, Philippines, Ceylon (Sri Lanka), Malaya, Yugoslavia and Mexico in *Summary Proceedings*, 1961, pp. 55–6, 95, 99, 122, 130, 140–1, 150–1, 152 and 167, respectively.

23. Horsefield, op. cit., Vol. 1, p. 534.

24. See *Final Report of the Group of Experts on the Stabilization of Export Receipts*, Washington DC, OAS, doc. 59, Rev. 4, 2 April 1962, and *International Compensation for Fluctuations in Commodity Trade* (report of group of experts appointed by the Secretary-General of the UN), UN, 1961.

25. 'Cairo Declaration of Developing Countries', Cairo, 18 July 1962, in Moss and Winston, comp., op. cit., p. 4, para. 36.

26. See, for instance, statement by Governor from the United Arab Republic, *Summary Proceedings*, 1962, p. 145.

27. 'Compensatory Financing of Export Fluctuations: A Report by the International Monetary Fund on Compensatory Financing of the Fluctuations in Exports of Primary Exporting Countries', February 1963, Horsefield, op. cit., Vol. 3, p. 446.

28. Ibid., pp. 454–6 and Executive Board (hereafter E. B.) Decision No. 1477-(63/8) of 27 February 1963.

29. The original Articles of Agreement made no allowance for special financing policies, which the CFF was. However, as a result of the second amendment, the Fund is empowered to adopt special policies—Art. V, Sec. 3(a)—the decisions for which also necessitate a majority of votes cast.

30. The Fund's financial transactions with its members are cast in the form of 'purchases' of foreign currency in exchange for the domestic currency and 'repurchases' by members of their own currencies. These transactions, in the final analysis, are qualitatively or conceptually no different from loans or borrowing and repayment, in the financial sense. Throughout this study, the terms borrowing or purchasing, on the one hand, and repayment or repurchases, on the other will be used interchangeably.

31. An analysis of the implications of this particular formulation will be made shortly.

32. E.B. Decision No. 1477-(63/8), 5(b).

33. *Progress report on compensatory financing of export fluctuations* (Note by the UNCTAD Secretariat), Doc. TD/7/Supp. 6, 1 November 1967, para. 12. See also Joseph Gold, *Conditionality*, Pamphlet Series No. 31, Washington DC, IMF, 1979, p. 7.

34. It is interesting to note that the IBRD, in a report of 1964 on the primary commodity question, was concerned exclusively with the problem as it affected the developing countries—see IBRD, *Supplementary Financial Measures* (A study requested by UNCTAD, 1964), December 1965. For the IBRD, as already indicated, the issue of differentiation among countries posed no problem from the constitutional standpoint.

35. Gold, *Legal and Institutional Aspects of the International Monetary System*, Vol. 1, p. 490.

36. Ibid., p. 491.

37. But the Fund's practice as regards the categorization of the membership indicated to some extent the concept of primary export-member. In its 1959 *Annual Report*, the Fund noted that: 'Only one of the members purchasing exchange from the Fund during the year is an industrial country, nearly all the Fund's transactions being with countries whose exchange receipts come almost entirely from the export of primary products'—IMF, *Annual Report*, 1959, p. 19. In a word, the category of primary exporting countries is contrasted with that of industrial countries, signifying basically that the reference is to developing countries.

38. As Yusuf observes in regard to the new Part IV on Trade and Development incorporated into GATT in 1965: '[it] introduces for the first time in the GATT

system a clear differentiation between developed and developing countries, and abolishes the play of the reciprocity principle between them'—see Yusuf, op. cit., p. 23.

39. As we shall see in the next chapter, the Latin American countries under the leadership of Prebisch and ECLA, had already challenged and rejected this uni-dimensional model of the inflation problem, arguing that structural economic factors associated with the process of development entailed unavoidable inflation and external disequilibria.

40. Export earnings fluctuations are basically a transitory phenomenon. The analytical literature holds that, whereas permanent balance-of-payments deficits necessitate predominantly adjustment measures, transitory deficits are best treated through the process of temporary financing. This is the context within which the CFF should be placed.

41. *Summary Proceedings*, 1963, p. 165.

42. Graham Bird, *The International Monetary System and the Less Developed Countries*, London, Macmillan Press, 1978, p. 18.

43. IMF, *Annual Report*, 1963, pp. 77–8.

44. See recommendation entitled 'Study of Measures related to the Compensatory Credit System of the IMF' (adopted without dissent), Annex A.IV.17 in *Proceedings of the United Nations Conference on Trade and Development*, Vol. 1, 1964, p. 52.

45. See, for instance, statements at 1964 Annual Meeting by Governors from Guatemala (on behalf of Latin American countries), the Philippines, Sri Lanka (then Ceylon), Nigeria and Yugoslavia in *Summary Proceedings*, 1964, at pp. 50, 59, 97, 114 and 137, respectively.

46. UNCTAD, *International Monetary Issues and the Developing Countries*, p. 15, paras 56–8.

47. See 'Compensatory Financing of Export Fluctuations—Developments in the Fund's Facility' (September 1966) in Horsefield, op. cit., Vol. 3, pp. 469–96.

48. See E.B. Decision No. 2192-66/81 of 20 September 1966.

49. UNCTAD, *Progress report on compensatory financing of export fluctuations*, para. 12.

50. E.B. Decision No. 2192-66/81, B. 5.

51. Goreux, *Compensatory Financing Facility*, op. cit., p. 44.

52. This particular stipulation clearly implied an asymmetrical approach to the repayment problem. It is logical that repayment should be expedited in a situation of improved export earnings, especially in view of the revolving character of Fund resources. It is just as logical that repayment should be delayed or rescheduled in a situation where there has been further deterioration in export earnings of a borrowing member during the period over which repayment is expected. But the Fund has steadfastly refused to follow the logic of its repayment policy by inflexibly insisting on the three-to-five years repayment period for CFF credit, despite repeated claims by the developing countries for a policy of delayed repayment.

53. 'The IMF's compensatory financing facility has been revised in 1966 to take account, *inter alia*, of UNCTAD recommendation A.IV.17'—see 'Summary of Statement by IMF representative', 13 February 1968, *Proceedings of the United Nations Conference on Trade and Development*, Vol. 1, Report and Annexes, Second Session, New Delhi, 1 February–29 March 1968, New York, UN, 1968, p. 209.

54. The 1966 Fund report on the CFF, at its Appendix II, provided excerpts from speeches of Governors at the 1965 Annual Meeting in support of improvement of the facility—see 'Compensatory Financing of Export Fluctuations—Developments in the Fund's Facility', op. cit., pp. 495–6.

55. See 'Charter of Algiers', op. cit., Part Two, C, para. 6.

56. Decision 31(II) on 'Compensatory financing facility', adopted on 28 March 1969. Among the suggestions of this decision were (i) that compensatory financing should also be available for adverse shifts in import prices; (ii) that drawings should be

permitted up to 50 per cent of quotas without either annual ceilings or conditionality; (iii) that repayment obligations should not arise within five years after a CFF drawing; and (iv) that interest charges should be different from those incurred in respect of borrowings under the regular credit facilities of the Fund.

57. 'Summary of Statement of IMF representative', op. cit.

58. Ibid. In fact, out of this study was to emerge a new funding facility in the IMF in 1969—the Buffer Stock Financing Facility (BSFF)—that was closely related to the CFF. Under the BSFF, the Fund extends quota-linked resources to members to assist in financing their contributions to international commodity buffer stock schemes. Under the 1969 decision, a member was eligible to draw to a limit of 50 per cent of quota and combined borrowing limits under the CFF and BSFF were not to exceed 75 per cent of quota. The other elements of the BSFF were basically similar to those of the CFF and, as the Fund's history notes: 'Buffer stock financing was the Fund's answer to the demands of the developing countries in 1967 and 1968 that the Fund and the World Bank pay greater heed to the problem of stabilization of prices of primary products'—see de Vries, *The International Monetary Fund, 1966–71*, op. cit., Vol. 1, p. 269.

59. 'Text of address by US Secretary of State before the 7th Special Session', 1 September 1975, *Department of State Bulletin*, Vol. 73, No. 1891, 22 September 1975, p. 429. See also de Vries, *The International Monetary Fund, 1966–71*, op. cit., Vol. 1, p. 402.

60. The Dakar Conference convened on the initiative of the 1973 Algiers non-aligned Summit Conference and culminated in the adoption of 'The Dakar Declaration'—for the text, see Mutharika comp., op. cit., Vol. 2. The mid-1970s also saw the establishment of a new framework of economic relations between the EEC countries and a group of developing countries in Africa, the Caribbean and the Pacific, under the Lomé Convention. This arrangement included the STABEX scheme.

61. Ibid., p. 1201.

62. Among the improvements requested were (i) the stabilization of export earnings in real terms; (ii) the extension of repayment periods; (iii) the elimination of quota-linked borrowing limits; and (iv) an overall liberalization of the terms of borrowing under the facility—ibid., p. 1212.

63. See UNCTAD, *An Integrated programme for commodities: Compensatory financing of export fluctuations in commodity trade* (report by the Secretary-General of UNCTAD), TD/B/C.1/166, Supp. 4, 13 December 1974. The Common Fund entailed the establishment, through international agreement, of a new financing institution, the resources of which were to be used for the stabilization of prices of a set of core commodities.

64. See resolution 3362(S-VII), I, International Trade, para. 3(d).

65. This claim for compensation in real terms was a variant of the earlier controversial terms of trade argument. The basic proposition of developing nations was that compensation should be aimed at maintaining the purchasing power of export earnings for imports. For a discussion, see Goreux, 'Compensatory Financing: The Cyclical Pattern of Export Shortfalls', op. cit., p. 621 and Marielle Demeocq, 'The Rationale and Modalities for Compensating Export Earnings Instability', *Development and Change*, 15, No. 3, July 1984, pp. 359–80.

66. Resolution 3362(S-VII), II, 'Transfer of Real Resources for Financing the Development of Developing Countries and International Monetary Reform', para. 17.

67. UNCTAD, *New directions and new structures for trade and development* (Report by the Secretary-General of UNCTAD to the Conference), TD/183, 14 April 1976, Nairobi, p. 18, para. 45.

68. 'Text of address by US Secretary of State before the 7th Special Session', op. cit.,

p. 429. The development security facility, as proposed, envisaged credit in the amount of US$2.5 billion or more annually, with a potential total of US$10 billion. The poorest developing countries would have been allowed to convert their loans into grants.

69. Ibid.

70. Margaret Garritsen de Vries, *The International Monetary Fund, 1972–78: Cooperation on Trial*, Vol. 1, Washington DC, IMF, 1985, p. 407.

71. *IMF Survey*, 13 October 1975, p. 306. It was also noted in this report that support for CFF liberalization was stated in the final document adopted at the 7th Special Session and that many Governors of the Fund had supported action along this line at the 1975 Annual Meeting.

72. Ibid.

73. See E.B. Decision No. 4912-(75/207) of 24 December 1975.

74. Goreux, *Compensatory Financing Facility*, op. cit., p. 27.

75. 'Communiqué: G24', 6 January 1976, op. cit., pp. 320–1, para. 16.

76. See *International monetary reform: problems of reform* (report by the UNCTAD Secretariat), Doc. TD/189 of 11 March 1976, para. 59(a).

77. UNCTAD V, *Arusha Programme for Collective Self-Reliance and Framework for Negotiations*, TD/236, 28 February 1979, Manila, Philippines, May 1979, p. 53.

78. See *Action on export earnings stabilization and developmental aspects of commodity policy* (report by the UNCTAD Secretariat), Doc. TD/229, 8 March 1979, paras. 10, 12 and 14.

79. Ibid., para. 14. The significance of the underlined formulation will be discussed in greater detail shortly.

80. IMF Survey, 16 June 1979, p. 188.

81. The voting results on this resolution were seventy-three in favour, twelve against and fourteen abstentions. The twelve countries in opposition and the fourteen abstaining included many of the Group B (developed) countries.

82. Resolution 125(V), 'Compensatory facility for commodity-related shortfalls in export earnings' of 3 June 1979, para. (a).

83. UNCTAD V, *Arusha Programme for Collective Self-Reliance and Framework for Negotiations*, p. 53.

84. See E.B. Decision No. 6224-(79/135) of 2 August 1979.

85. General Assembly resolution 34/110, adopted without vote on 14 December 1979.

86. General Assembly Resolution 3202(S-VI), 2(f).

87. 'Communiqué: G24', 27th September 1980, op. cit., p 355, para. 9.

88. *Summary Proceedings*, 1980, pp. 23–4.

89. Ibid., p. 44.

90. E.B. Decision No. 6860-(81/81) of 13 May 1981.

91. 'Communiqué: Interim Committee', 21 May 1981, *IMF Survey*, 8 June 1981, p. 169, para. 7. This interpretation of the practical intent of this decision is also evident in the Managing Director's comments, quoted above.

92. 'Communiqué: G24', 20 May 1981, *IMF Survey*, 8 June 1981, para. 14.

93. For a discussion, see Sidney Dell, 'The Fifth Credit Tranche', *World Development*, 13, No. 2, February 1985, pp. 245–9.

94. 'Communiqué: G24', 27 April 1983, *IMF Survey*, 9 May 1983, p. 135, para. 19.

95. 'Communiqué: Interim Committee', 25 September 1983, *IMF Survey*, 10 October 1983, p. 296, para. 6(e).

96. As an UNCTAD study has noted, 'in absolute terms there will be an overall increase in resources of about 24 per cent available under this facility'—see UNCTAD, *Consideration of the Substantive Issues relating to the Question of an Additional Complementary Facility to compensate for the Export Earnings Shortfalls of Developing Countries*,

pursuant to Conference Resolution 157(VI), para. 3, TD/B/AC.37/3, of 26 March 1984.

97. *Directions for Reform: The Future of the International Monetary System*, op. cit. p. 27, para. 43.

98. 'Communiqué: G24', 11 May 1982, *IMF Survey*, 24 May 1982, p. 151. See also Polak, 'The Role of the Fund', op. cit., p. 254.

99. See E.B. Decision No. 7528-(83/140) of 14 September 1983.

100. Goreux, *Compensatory Financing Facility*, op. cit., p. 25.

101. E.B. Decision No. 7528-(83/140).

102. Ibid.

103. *South*, November 1982, p. 74. See also Dell, 'The Fifth Credit Tranche', op. cit., p. 247.

104. See Appendix 1, Table 1.5 of IMF, *Annual Report*, 1983, pp. 120–1.

105. *IMF Survey* (Supplement on the Group of 24 Deputies' Report), September, 1985, p. 12, para. 114.

106. UNCTAD, *Proceedings of the United Nations Conference on Trade and Development*, Vol. 1, Report and Annexes, Fifth Session, Manila, 7 May–3 June 1979, New York, UN, 1981, p. 67.

107. UNCTAD resolution 157(VI) on 'Compensatory financing of export earnings shortfalls', adopted 2 July 1983.

108. UNCTAD, *Proceedings of the United Nations Conference on Trade and Development*, Vol. 1, Sixth Session, Belgrade, 6 June–2 July 1983, New York, UN, 1984, p. 52, para. 57. See also statements by representatives of the United States, Australia and Canada— ibid., pp. 52–4, paras 59, 64 and 73.

109. UNCTAD, *Compensatory financing of export earnings shortfalls*, Annex VII, Appendix II, Table 2.

110. In the Fund's 1981/82 fiscal year Korea (South), Malawi and Morocco made cereal import purchases; in 1982/83, Bangladesh, Kenya and Malawi did so and in 1984/ 85, Ghana, Jordan, Bangladesh, Korea and Malawi used cereal imports credits—see IMF, *Annual Report*, 1982, 1983 and 1985.

111. Goreux, *Compensatory Financing Facility*, p. 2. See also UNCTAD, *Compensatory Facility for Commodity-Related Shortfalls in Export Earnings: Review of the Operation of the Compensatory Financing Facility of the International Monetary Fund* (report by the UNCTAD Secretariat), TD/B/C.1/243, 11 January 1983, p. 3, para. 3.

112. Goreux, *Compensatory Financing Facility*, p. 2. As Bird notes: 'The acceleration in drawings under the CFF that occurred in 1976 clearly demonstrates that liberaliza-tion can have a significant effect on drawings. It has been estimated that had the rules governing the CFF remained unchanged in 1976 the amount drawn under it would have fallen by nearly 80 per cent'—Graham Bird, 'Financial flows to develop-ing countries: the role of the International Monetary Fund', *Review of International Studies*, No. 7, 1981, p. 102.

113. UNCTAD, *Compensatory Facility for Commodity-Related Shortfalls in Export Earnings*, p. 5, para. 10.

114. UNCTAD, *Compensatory financing of export earnings shortfalls*, TD/B/1029/Rev.1, 1985, p. 8, para. 22.

115. Ibid., p. 37, para. 130. The proposal envisages the establishment of a new facility, additional to the IMF's CFF, but outside the supervisory authority of that institu-tion, to deal with the longer-term production problem. Proposals for its location include the World Bank and UNCTAD's Common Fund. Membership will be open to all states, though it is proposed that access to loans be restricted to developing countries.

Chapter 8

The conditionality debate: Third World advance and IMF retreat

1. Introduction

By far the most controversial aspect of the Fund's relations with its member-states—from both the historical and contemporary perspectives—has been the conditionality requirement that attaches to the use of its resources under the regular credit and other special facilities.[1] In the words of the Managing Director of the Fund, conditionality 'refers to the economic and financial measures which are needed in a particular country in order to restore a sustainable external position at the end or toward the end of a Fund program.'[2] In fact, conditionality was an important sticking-point in the initial Anglo-American bilateral discussions on post-war international monetary relations and to a certain extent in the pre-Bretton Woods consultative process involving a wider set of countries. It continued to be a source of friction in the very early years of the Fund's operations and has evolved, in contemporary times, into the single most problematic issue confronting the IMF and its membership.[3]

If, also, at the beginning the basic differences on conditionality reflected an Anglo-American—and a wider Euro-American—divergence, contemporary manifestations of the controversy can broadly—though not totally accurately—be presented in terms of a developed versus developing country dissension.[4] If, further, in the earlier period, criticisms were more episodic or derived from narrower groups of the Fund membership, presently the attack is a relatively more generalized phenomenon in that the overwhelming majority of Fund members—the developing countries—are, by and large, involved in expressing their discontent with conditionality.

Conditionality has, in fact, been progressively formulated over the history of the IMF. In terms of its decision-making aspects, one can suggest the following paradigm, closely linked to environmental circumstances: (i) an initial period of unilateral United States dominance over the formulation of conditionality; (ii) followed in the 1960s by a convergence among the developed countries on outlook and definition of the issues involved, in parallel with their expropria-tion, under the aegis of the G10, of international monetary decision making; (iii) the rise of Third World nationalism in the 1970s and a short period of experimentation during the latter half of this decade in response; and (iv) a reversion to the older order, led by a reassertion by the United States and some of its allies at the beginning of the 1980s of their dominant power within the international economic system.

2. The evolution of the conditionality controversy

The Fund's mandate, it will be recalled, embraces the management of the monetary resources contributed by the membership to the capital of the institution. These monetary resources are basically employed to make available temporary financing to members encountering balance-of-payments difficulties. In the pre-Bretton Woods discussions between the Americans and British, the issue of conditional as against automatic availability of IMF credit[5] was a source of profound disagreement between these two countries.[6] As posed at this preliminary stage of the controversy, what was at issue was the principle of conditionality *per se*—the British arguing against, and the Americans in favour.[7]

This Anglo–American divergence was based ultimately on the prospective status of these two countries in the envisaged monetary system. It was essentially a creditor/debtor divergence—a crucial factor in comprehending the conditionality controversy in both its historical and current manifestations. The United States, as the country with the strongest economy in the immediate post-war years, was clearly going to be the principal creditor country in the IMF, while the war-weakened United Kingdom economy placed it in the position of a potential debtor.

The compromise document arrived at by these two countries—'The Joint Statement'—said nothing about this fundamental conflict[8] and one can conclude as to the significance of this silence according to one's preferences. There are those, like Dell, who have interpreted it to mean that opponents of conditionality might have felt that the issue was settled to their advantage[9] while others have inferred a contrary explanation for this silence.[10]

The latter interpretation appears validated by the immediate efforts—once the Fund had begun operations—to integrate understandings on conditionality. This was the import of the initiatives taken by the United States in the Executive Board between 1946 and 1949. In 1946, the United States sought a formal interpretation that Fund credit was to be used for the financing only of temporary balance-of-payments difficulties. The Board adopted a decision whereby it was stipulated that 'authority to use the resources of the Fund is limited to use in accordance with its purposes to give temporary assistance in financing balance of payments deficits on current account for monetary stabilization operations'.[11] This decision established the key time-frame within which the Fund resources are made available—its short-term nature. In 1949, the United States Executive Director formally, 'insisted that drawings from the Fund were required to be temporary, and therefore should be subject to close scrutiny'.[12] In effect, the struggle within the Fund over automatic or conditional credit was joined with the United States clearly using its position of power as the most important creditor nation to force a showdown on the matter.

In a memorandum submitted to the Executive Board in May 1949, the United States Executive Director presented certain definitive proposals to govern use of Fund resources[13] that have been characterized in the Fund's official history as a reassertion 'in unmistakable terms [of] the intention to "police" drawings'.[14] Intensive discussions were carried through in the

Executive Board over the years 1949–52, culminating in the 1952 decision that delineated the guidelines to be followed for obtaining Fund credit.[15] This decision embodied several important elements that were to serve as the basis for the conditionality practice in the IMF: (i) the balance-of-payments problem was to be of a temporary character and stress was placed on the revolving nature of Fund resources—both to be operationalized in the short time-frame for the disbursement of credit and in the requirement of payment within three-to-five years after a borrowing; (ii) the *de facto* automaticity of reserve tranche purchases;[16] and (iii) reference to what was to become a major operational facet of Fund conditionality—the stand-by arrangement (SBA).[17]

Thus, the law of the Fund had evolved by 1952 towards establishing the principle of conditionality. Since the 1952 decision was taken by a competent organ of the Fund, it had the force of law[18]—notwithstanding the silence of the Articles of Agreement in this regard. The 1952 decision was a manifest victory for the American conception of conditional Fund credit:

> It is no secret that the argument was settled under pressure from the US Government, against the solid opposition of the rest of the IMF's membership, for fear that the universal shortage of dollars would cause a run on the IMF's resources unless access to them was made subject to conditions.[19]

The principle of conditional use of Fund credit was thus, in the early 1950s, linked to the governing rule in the Articles of Agreement that specified the quantitative limits to borrowing rights, to set the basic parameters of the lending mandate of the institution. Under the Articles of Agreement, a country had the right to purchase foreign currencies in an amount that did not result in the Fund's holding of the borrowing country's currency rising above 200 per cent of its quota.[20]

The SBA became the principal instrument by which Fund conditional credit was extended to the members.[21] To this end, another Executive Board decision, detailing the features of stand-by credit, was adopted on 1 October 1952.[22] The SBA has been used mainly for purchases in the credit tranches. Under a stand-by, the member was given the assurance that it could use Fund assistance up to the quantitative limit specified in the arrangement, over a defined period, on the basis of the policy understandings agreed to between the borrowing member and the IMF.[23] The practice of the Fund, as regards the duration of disbursement of credits under SBAs, was for one-year arrangements, renewable by decisions of the Executive Board.

A further evolution in the functioning of conditionality was the statement in the *Annual Report* of 1959 on the general standards pertaining to the extension of credit:

> Members were given the overwhelming benefit of the doubt in relation to requests for transactions within the 'gold tranches' . . . The Fund's attitude to requests for transactions within the first credit tranche, that is transactions that bring the Fund's holdings of a member's currency above 100 per cent but not above 125 per cent of quota, is a liberal one, provided that the member itself is also making reasonable efforts to solve its problems.

Requests for transactions beyond these limits require substantial justification.[24]

A minimal level of conditionality was associated with the first credit tranche and progressively higher degrees were expected for the second to fourth credit tranches. In short, conditionality was conceived as a graduated process, linked to the quantitative levels of borrowing desired by a member. However, these decisions, while setting the legal foundation for conditionality and the broad framework for its implementation, did not specify its substantive content.

Other detailed practices of conditionality evolved gradually, in consonance with the experience gained by the fund as it extended credit to members. With regards to SBAs, two operational practices became standard requirements: the phasing of the disbursement of credit and the use of performance criteria to test a member's observance of policy and programmatic understandings.[25] The essence of these operational features of SBAs can be summed up as permitting the Fund a measure of protection against the use of its resources inconsistent with the purposes of the institution.[26]

A review of Fund conditionality practices was undertaken by the Executive Board in 1968. The proximate cause of this review was the SBA agreed for the United Kingdom in 1967. Developing countries were highly critical of certain elements of the arrangement, using as the basis for comparison SBAs entered into between themselves and the Fund.[27] The underlying concern of these countries was evidently to ensure a uniform standard of treatment for all Fund members, in respect of the operational elements of SBAs. This concern was explicitly stated during the review exercise begun by the Executive Board during 1968:

> In effect, the comments of several Executive Directors, especially those of the developing members, suggested that they had serious misgivings about the equality of treatment that members were receiving in respect of the terms of stand-by arrangements, particularly those applying to the higher credit tranches. Were industrial members subject to terms as severe as those being applied to developing members?[28]

The Board's discussions resulted in the 1968 decision on conditionality that, to a large extent, codified the practices as they had evolved over some two decades of Fund operations.[29]

This review coincided with the work relating to the first amendment of the Articles of Agreement. The amended Articles included new provisions that, for the first time, explicitly stated the requirement of conditionality. These were the provisions embodied in Article V, Secs. 3(c) and (d)—first amendment—by the terms of which use of the Fund's resources had to be consistent with its purposes and requiring it to 'adopt policies on the use of its resources that will assist members to solve their balance of payments problems in a manner consistent with the purposes of the Fund and that will establish adequate safeguards for the temporary use of its resources'.[30] Conditionality thereby became clearly specified in the Fund's constitution.

Moreover, the *de facto* automaticity of reserve tranche purchases was transformed into a constitutionally-sanctioned automaticity under the terms of Article V, Sec.3(d). It is obvious that, while from a constitutional perspective, these were new departures, from the overall law of the Fund, they were nothing new.[31] It is important to underline, however, that whereas the legal necessity of conditionality and some of its key operational facets were now underwritten in the principal source of law of the IMF—its Articles of Agreement—its substantive content was not similarly spelled out.[32] In fact, this absence of any clear constitutional guidelines regarding the substance of conditionality meant that there was a degree of latitude given the Executive Board in defining the kinds of economic policies that members were required to implement and to the staff in terms of the determination of the specific details for stabilization programmes.

Another important change in the amended Articles, with fundamental implications for conditional use of resources related to the inclusion of the word 'temporarily' in one of the provisions of the Fund's purposes—that dealing with its financial mandate which was modified to read: '(v) to give confidence to members by making the Fund resources temporarily available to them under adequate safeguards'.[33] The constitutional stipulation of a temporary use of IMF resources set, in effect, the time scale of its lending—the short-term nature of the financing support that the Fund was prepared to extend to members encountering balance-of-payments difficulties.

In essence, then, the boundaries of conditionality have over time evolved in both the law and practice of the IMF. The major elements of this conditionality can be divided, for analytical purposes, into two components: (i) the procedural, operational and legal elements and (ii) the substantive content. With regard to the former, the main features are:

(a) the legal requirement of conditionality;
(b) the temporary use of Fund resources, linked to the revolving concept of these resources and operationalized in the duration period for the disbursement of credit under SBAs—a one-year disbursement period—and in the standard three-to-five year repayment period;
(c) the quantitative, quota-based borrowing limits;
(d) the automaticity of reserve tranche purchases; and
(e) a graduated process of conditionality, related to quantitative levels of borrowing.

Overarching these basic elements of conditionality is the guiding principle of the uniform treatment of members in terms of its application—a principle reaffirmed at the time of the 1968 review.

It is thus possible to test the Fund's responsiveness to the criticisms of developing countries by examining where changes have been made in the major operational and legal facets of conditionality. Because no member is on record as questioning the principle of conditionality itself—once this matter had been resolved in the early years of the Fund's operations—then it is not necessary to focus on this particular aspect. Nor, for that matter, will it be necessary to treat the issues of reserve-tranche automaticity or the norm of a graduated process of conditionality since these elements have also been acquiesced in by the membership as a whole. That leaves us with three means of testing Fund responsiveness:

(i) the issue of temporary use of resources and the related issues of disbursement and repayment periods;
(ii) the principle of uniformity of treatment; and
(iii) the quantitative, quota-based borrowing limits.

As regards economic substance, the analysis will be concerned with assessing—at the broadest level of generality—whether or not there have been changes in the economic orientation of the stabilization programmes normally sanctioned by the Fund.

It is the Executive Board that ultimately determines the broad policy parameters of conditionality, while the management and staff, on the basis of these guidelines, elaborate the detailed contents of particular stabilization programmes. Finally, it should be noted that decisions to use the resources of the Fund are taken by a simple majority of the votes cast in the Board. Moreover, changes in the policies on use of resources and the establishment of any special financing facilities also carry the same requirement. In essence, then, developing countries as a group do not have the voting power to take these decisions, while the developed countries as a whole and the G10 can prevent approval of any of these decisions. Developed countries thus have the dominant say in defining conditionality and approving requests for use of Fund resources.

3. The early experiences of developing countries with Fund conditionality—the bases of the friction

In so far as developing countries, as a whole, are concerned, the issue of conditionality was not the prominent factor in their relations with the Fund for most of the first two and a half decades of its operations. In fact, a perusal of statements of developing countries before Annual Meetings of the Fund in the 1950s and early 1960s attests to this assessment that use of Fund resources was, by and large, bereft of controversy.[34] As it manifested itself in this time-period, the problem with conditionality was essentially restricted to a sub-group of developing countries in Latin America. The dissension revolved around the analysis of the causes of the external deficits experienced by these countries and the policy action required to re-establish equilibrium.

The pattern of use of Fund resources in the 1950s and 1960s can be seen in Table 8.1. What is immediately evident is that, in terms of regional usage among the developing nations, Latin America and Asia were the main users. With regard to Asia, however, it was basically one country—India—that overwhelmingly made use of Fund credit—some 80 per cent of all credit to Asian countries. Essentially, therefore, the Latin American nations were the principal sub-group of developing countries using the Fund's resources. African use was negligible—explainable to some extent by the absence, for most of this period, of substantial African membership in the institution. Another indicator of the preponderant Latin American use of Fund credit is evident in Table 8.2,

Table 8.1 Use of Fund credit, 1952–1981, by groups of countries
(SDRs millions)

	1950s*	1960s	1970s	1980–81
All countries	3,382	21,611	61,795	21,853
Developed countries	1,671	11,500	25,631	1,590
Developing countries	1,651	10,034	36,164	20,269
Latin America	591	3,164	7,685	2,358
Africa	21	797	6,951	5,122
Asia	728	3,373	11,575	7,617
Europe	127	953	6,641	4,684
Oil-exporting	138	610	390	–
Middle-East	44	879	2,923	1,481

* From 1952 to 1959.
Source: *International Financial Statistics* (various issues).

Table 8.2 Stand-by and extended Fund arrangements by groups of countries
(1950s to 1984)

	Stand-by arrangements				EFFs	
	1950s	1960s	1970s	1980–84	1975–79	1980–84
Total	46	222	168	106	11	22
Developed countries	10	28	13	1	–	–
Developing countries	36	194	152	104	11	22
Latin America	32	108	64	25	6	9
Africa	1	44	40	55	3	9
Asia	3	39	43	18	2	4
Europe	–	3	5	6	–	–
Others	–	–	3	1	–	–

Source: *International Financial Statistics* (Suppl.), 1983 and *IMF Survey* (various issues).

which provides a breakdown of the SBAs entered into between members and
the IMF. Latin American countries had thirty-two of the thirty-six SBAs agreed
with developing countries in the 1950s and 108 of the 194 in the 1960s.

Conditionality is, ultimately, more of a problem for Fund debtors. This was
evident in the earliest manifestations of the controversy, when it was the
potential debtors of Europe that confronted the Fund's major creditor, the
United States, on the issue. From this perspective, it is understandable that
Latin America was in the forefront of this initial struggle by developing
countries against the Fund's conditionality practices over this period.

Moreover, the Latin American countries brought to bear a more defined analytical consensus regarding their economic problems. Led by ECLA, under Prebisch, they had not only elaborated, during the 1950s, a coherent analysis of the problematic of development, but also, of the interlinked problem of persistent external deficits and inflation. The Latin American analysis diagnosed the causal factors as inhering in the very structures of their economies and the process of development.[35] Contrastingly, in the IMF view, inflation was not only a domestically generated phenomenon, manifested in excess demand relative to productive and external financing possibilities, but it also smacked of economic mismanagement.[36] The Fund's diagnosis naturally led to prescriptions centring on action to curb excessive credit creation and expansionary public spending policies. The essence of the stabilization model preferred by the IMF was the implementation of action on the demand side of the economy. The range of monetary and fiscal measures that, in varying combinations, appear in Fund-sponsored stabilization programmes include:

 (i) devaluation;
 (ii) tighter credit through an increase in interest rates and a slowing-down in the rate of its expansion;
(iii) the removal of subsidies for basic commodities and services;
(iv) an increase in prices of public utility services;
 (v) a reduction in the size of the public sector; and
(vi) restraints in salary and wage increases.

The Latin American countries found the IMF approach unacceptable, especially as it tended, from their perspective, to affect the process of economic development. Not only was there a fundamental divergence in economic analysis and solutions but Latin American countries emphasized the potential socio-political destabilization inherent in the policy requirements linked to Fund stabilization programmes.[37] The disagreement was thus cast, at this early stage, at both a technical-economic level and a socio-political level—the two inextricably intertwined.

This deep-rooted divergence was not at the time resolved to the benefit of the developing countries. Executive Board discussion of the issue of conditionality in the late 1960s showed a division of outlook between the developing countries, on the one hand, and the developed countries, on the other.[38] With their dominant voting power, the G10 members of the Executive Board were able to ensure that no changes in conditionality were made.

Finally, in respect of this early manifestation of the conditionality controversy, the question of differential treatment was not far below the surface in the advocacy of the Latin American countries. Differential treatment was posed in the sense of the differences in economic structures and development levels between developed and developing countries and the resultant unworkability of a demand management model, based on the experiences of an advanced economy, when applied to a developing economy.[39] It argued the imperative of a different stabilization model, geared to the specific circumstances of developing countries.

4. The 1970s/early 1980s—the current controversy about conditionality

Fund conditionality emerged as a more generalized Third World concern during the 1970s. This widening of concern has to be placed within the context of the severe external deficits that confronted the non-oil developing nations throughout this period and the necessity for financing sources to deal with them. At the same time, the major Latin American nations—for reasons to be presented shortly—were less concerned with the conditionality issue in the 1970s.[40] However, by the early 1980s, there was a sharp re-emergence of their concern so that in the 1980s, so far, conditionality has been an almost global preoccupation of the IMF's Third World membership.

(a) The 1970s—the beginnings of experimentation with conditionality

It is to some extent paradoxical that the extent of this antagonism in the 1970s was reflected, at one level, in the refusal of the developing countries to use Fund conditional resources. The Fund's *Annual Report* for fiscal year 1972/73 has underscored the decline in use—purchases of SDR 1.1 billion were just slightly more than half for the previous year, with over 50 per cent comprising purchases under the reserve tranche. Purchases under SBAs were of the order of SDR 213 million, compared to SDR 220 million the previous year.[41] For most of the 1970s, there was negligible use of Fund credit in the regular tranches that carried substantial conditionality—see Table 8.3. The only year in which high-conditional credit surpassed low-conditional was in 1978 and this was mainly because two developed countries, Italy and the United Kingdom, had entered into substantial SBAs with the Fund. In so far as developing countries were concerned, use was concentrated preponderantly in the low-conditionality CFF and oil facilities—see Table 8.3. This was startlingly expressive of Third World inclination to avoid the IMF, the more so that it coincided with the disruptive shock of historically-large payments deficits for these countries.

It was previously pointed out that, by the mid-1970s, a small sub-group of developing countries was bypassing the Fund in their search for the financing resources to deal with external deficits. Commercial bank credit was a much more attractive proposition to these countries—compared to IMF credit—in that it was readily available to the credit-worthy and in larger amounts than the Fund could have provided in terms of the constraints of quota-based borrowing limits. Moreover, commercial bank credit did not necessitate the implementation of stabilization measures, overseen by an external authority and character-ized by what was seen by the developing countries as harsh conditionality. Thus, the Fund became a negligible source of balance-of-payments financing for several Latin American and Asian middle-income countries in the 1970s.[42] When these countries did use IMF resources for most of the 1970s, it was basically the low-conditionality CFF and oil facility. The African countries, in the main, also continued to ignore the IMF—that is, apart from financing that attracted minimal conditionality—in their efforts to cope with the balance-of-payments dislocations of the 1970s. Of the three major sub-regional groupings

Table 8.3 Low conditional and high conditional purchases, 1976–84 (billions of SDRs)

	1976	1977	1978	1979	1980	1981	1982	1983	1984
I. Low conditional	5.09	2.97	0.41	0.64	1.05	1.56	1.65	4.12	1.28
First credit tranche	0.29	0.78	0.09	0.13	0.16	0.78	0.02	0.03	–
Oil facility	3.97	0.44	–	–	–	–	–	–	–
CFF	0.83	1.75	0.32	0.46	0.86	0.78	1.63	3.74	1.18
BSFF	–	–	–	0.05	0.03	–	–	0.35	0.10
II. High conditional	0.18	1.78	1.96	0.59	1.15	2.82	5.31	6.14	8.88
Credit tranche	0.17	1.59	1.85	0.35	0.93	1.90	2.73	3.68	4.16
EFF	0.01	0.19	0.11	0.24	0.22	0.93	2.58	2.46	4.72
III. Total of I and II	5.27	4.75	2.37	1.24	2.21	4.39	6.96	10.26	10.16

Source: IMF, *Annual Report*, 1983, p. 86 and ibid., 1984, p. 74.

of developing countries, Africa entered into the least number of EFFs and SBAs in the years 1975–79.

In essence, the Fund confronted a crisis of clientele in the 1970s. Developed countries, with one or two exceptions—mainly the United Kingdom and Italy—rarely approached the institution for conditional credit. And the Fund's seemingly natural constituency, the developing countries—in view of the intractibility and persistence of deficits—even in the worst of times during the 1970s stood aloof from the Fund, except when low-conditionality resources were available. One important indicator of this tendency was the dramatic decline in SBAs, the main vehicle for conditional credit, in the 1970s compared to the 1960s—a global total for 168 SBAs were agreed for the 1970s in contrast to 222 in the 1960s, with developing countries agreeing 152, compared to 194 in the 1960s (see Table 8.2).

The problem resided in the refusal of these countries, in so far as they could have avoided it, to undertake the severe adjustment—as they saw it—that had come to be associated with the extension of Fund conditional credit.[43] The reluctance of developing countries to use conditional credit could only have been strengthened by the results of internal Fund analyses of stabilization programmes for the years 1973–75, which pointed to the large number of programme failures.[44]

An internal Fund development that had an impact on use of resources and conditionality in the mid-1970s was the decision, in the wake of the first oil price increase, to emphasize financing over adjustment in regard to its balance-of-payments lending.[45] When linked to the CFF liberalization of 1975 and the Trust Fund of 1976, it can be seen that, in the difficult economic circumstances of the mid-1970s, Fund members had at their disposal the option of using a larger quantum of low-conditionality resources than was previously the case.

In short, the environment for the financing of deficits in the mid-1970s was quite favourable. Outside the Fund, financing sources included commercial bank credit and increased ODA, with the emergence of OPEC as a new source of official development financing at this time. Internally, there were the new, temporary facilities and the improvement of the CFF. In this context, the Fund's regular credit facilities and the new extended fund arrangement were not attractive credit options for developing countries.

This threat to a principal aspect of the IMF's overall *raison d'être*—its financing mandate—reflected in the substantial loss of its clientele among the developing countries was just as evident in the reaction of these countries to the new departure in lending philosophy implied in the establishment of the EFF.[46] This facility was created in 1974, in keeping with a recommendation by the Committee of Twenty for the establishment of a new facility 'under which developing countries would receive longer-term balance of payments financing'.[47] What is immediately apparent is the concern to isolate the problem of the developing countries. This concern was made explicit, from the legal standpoint, in the Executive Board decision on the EFF which specified that: 'The facility, in its formulation and administration, is likely to be beneficial for developing countries in particular'.[48] As the Fund's official history points out, Fund decisions had not previously adverted to a group of members known as 'developing countries'.[49] In effect, the EFF decision signified a sharp departure from past Fund practice and another step in breaching the equality principle of the constitution through the movement towards a differentiation among the membership.

The EFF, in a sense, was a belated response to the earlier divergence between the proponents of the theory of structurally-derived external deficits—with the inference of larger amounts of financing, a longer-term framework for adjustment and a different economic content for adjustment programmes—and the Fund's emphasis on short-term, demand-oriented stabilization. The EFF was pushed by the staff of the institution, supported by the developing and a few developed countries.[50] The decision stipulated that the EFF was conceptualized to deal with 'an economy suffering serious payments imbalance relating to structural maladjustments in production and trade [and] an economy characterized by slow growth and an inherently weak balance of payments position which prevents pursuit of an active development policy'.[51]

A more detailed analysis of the EFF policy, using the indicators earlier suggested for testing Fund responsiveness, brings out the manifest novelty of the facility. Firstly, the time-frame for disbursement of resources under the EFF was lengthened, compared to the one-year SBAs, to three years. Secondly, borrowing limits were set at magnitudes that were larger than those permitted under the regular credit facilities—credit under an EFF was set at a limit of 140 per cent of quota, thereby permitting a member to borrow a maximum of 190 per cent of its quota, without taking into account borrowing under the CFF and BSFF—see Table 8.4. This compares with the 125 per cent borrowing limit

Table 8.4 Possible cumulative purchases under various IMF credit policies pre- and post-supplementary financing facility (SFF)*

	Pre-SFF		Post-SFF	
	Tranche policy	Extended facility	Tranche policy	Extended facility
Reserve tranche	25.0	25.0	25.0	25.0
Credit tranches				
4 × 25	100.0	—	100.0	—
1 × 25	—	25.0	—	25.0
Extended facility	—	140.0	—	140.0
Supplementary financing facility with extended facility	—	—	102.5	140.0
Sub-total	125.0	190.0	227.5	330.0
Compensatory financing	75.0	75.0	75.0	75.0
Buffer stock financing	50.0	50.0	50.0	50.0
Cumulative total	250.0	315.0	352.5	455.0

* The above position as regards possible purchases is expressed as a percentage of quota and represented the situation in the late 1970s and not the current position.
Source: IMF Survey, 18 September 1978, p. 295.

under the regular credit policy. Thirdly, the repayment requirement also indicated the longer-term conception of the EFF—an outside range of four to ten years,[52] in contrast to the three-to-five year period of traditional Fund practice. Finally, in regard to economic orientation, the EFF was concerned with structural and supply-side aspects of the adjustment process, drawing the IMF, theoretically, into the domain of development-oriented adjustment: 'The EFF gives some recognition to the fact that payments difficulties may constitute the monetary manifestation of structural misallocation, and specifically views the balance of payments in the context of development policy'.[53]

From the point of view of developing countries, however, there were serious flaws concerning the EFF. While accepting that it signalled a welcome new departure in Fund thinking,[54] they have criticized two major deficiencies that have operated to circumscribe the attractiveness of the facility. Firstly, conditionality surrounding EFF borrowing was no less severe than that relating to upper credit tranche purchases.[55] Secondly, from the purely economic point of view, many criticisms of the EFF have been heard, especially the fact that, despite its ostensible concern with the structural basis of external imbalances, the adjustment framework, practically, continued to be guided by the traditional tools at the Fund's disposal.[56]

In the initial years of the EFF's existence, developing countries showed a marked disinclination to use the facility. Between 1974 and 1977, only three such arrangements were agreed between developing countries and the Fund and the spokesmen for these countries clearly stated the unattractiveness of using EFF credit—for instance, speaking in 1976, the Governor for Sri Lanka observed:

> The fact that only two countries have so far felt able to draw on this facility testifies to its present emptiness, and the Group of 24 has already gone on record as saying that the facility is likely to remain so, unless conditionalities are considerably diminished. The facility has to take account not only of the time lag between investment in export-oriented industry and the resulting output, but also the complex political realities of developing countries in relation to the timing of corrective actions.[57]

The core issue in the reluctance of developing countries to use a facility set up clearly for their benefit and to address problems peculiarly associated with their economic structures was conditionality.

In fact, in the second half of the 1970s, conditionality re-emerged as the critical issue for most developing countries in their relations with the IMF. An analysis of the content of their criticism, as presented in the various Communiqués of the G24 and statements before Annual Meetings of the Fund by Third World spokesmen, indicated that the principal areas of concern were:

 (i)　the short time duration of Fund arrangements;
 (ii)　the related short maturities of SBA credit;
 (iii)　the limited, quota-linked credit availabilities;
 (iv)　the over-emphasis on demand management in the stabilization programmes;

(v) the absence of any effort to set conditionality with due regard to the cause of balance-of-payments deficits; and

(vi) the inordinate share of the adjustment costs that fell on developing nations.

What was demanded, *inter alia*, were an overall review of Fund conditionality, longer-term financing arrangements in terms of quantitative credit availabilities, duration of disbursement and repayment periods, the setting of conditionality taking into consideration the ‚cause of deficits and a re-orientation of the economic content of adjustment to promote investment and production.[58]

The second half of the 1970s, therefore, witnessed a conjuncture of circumstances that propelled the Fund to undertake a review of its conditionality practices. Rising Third World criticism, both within and outside the IMF, took place in the context of the economic nationalism of the times and the overall North–South negotiations.[59] It was buttressed by the favourable factor of alternative sources of external financing, especially commercial bank lending and increased ODA, but also low-conditionality IMF credit. The refusal of the developing nations to use high-conditionality resources was the most dramatic threat to the Fund.

The implications of this combination of environmental realities and internal trends were lost on neither the Fund management nor its major shareholders, the developed countries. A more amenable attitude towards the re-examination of conditionality became apparent. As the Governor from the United Kingdom observed in 1977:

> I know that some of my colleagues are concerned about the conditions attached to Fund drawings. There might be an advantage in further discussion of this question. My view is that conditionality must be flexible and realistically related to the problems of our member countries and that, in present world circumstances, it is very important that the time scale of adjustment should be realistic. It is no good increasing the Fund's resources if those who need them most are unable to accept the conditions for their use.[60]

It was in this context that in 1978 the Fund began its review of conditionality that culminated in the 1979 Executive Board decision on new guidelines.[61]

The 1979 decision was by no means a radical new departure as regards conditionality.[62] Among the new features that met some of the concerns of the developing countries were: (i) the possibility of SBAs of a longer-term framework and (ii) the acceptance by the Fund of the need, in devising adjustment programmes, to ‘pay due regard to the domestic social and political objectives, the economic priorities, and the circumstances of members, including the causes of their balance of payments problems’.[63] The harshness of conditionality has been assessed, *inter alia*, by the time-period within which adjustment is expected to take place, so that one-year SBAs have always been seen as necessitating a swift and, thereby, harsh period of adjustment. This decision envisioned a longer time-frame for SBAs, thereby sanctioning a more gradual approach to the adjustment process. One of the principal charges against Fund conditionality is that it is so designed as to have a pervasive impact on the socio-economic priorities and objectives of members, the more so as the Fund is philosophically committed to a liberal, market-oriented economic order. From this perspective, its policy preferences have clashed fundamentally with those of its members, for instance, that are committed to a socialist organization of the economy.[64] The first part of the provision referred to at (ii) above was seen as a protective device by developing countries for a policy of Fund non-interference in economic policy matters. Another significant achievement was the second part of this provision requiring the Fund to take account of the cause of balance-of-payments deficits in the designing of stabilization measures.[65]

These new facets of conditionality have to be seen against the background of other developments that had become manifest in the Fund throughout the late 1970s. Particularly important in this regard were, firstly, a movement towards the provision of larger amounts of credit to members, and secondly, an effort to strike a balance between the conventional demand-management approach to the balance-of-payments difficulties of developing countries and a supply-side approach, geared to dealing with structural economic problems.

Using the various tests of responsiveness suggested earlier, several conclusions regarding conditionality may be drawn. To begin with, there was a shift, in principle from purely short-term to medium-term stabilization measures, as required by the particular case. This was the effect of the EFF, the longer time-context of SBAs, which could be for as long as three years, and the temporary SFF and its successor, the enlarged access policy (EAP). Not only was there a lengthening of disbursement periods under these various financing policies, but longer repayment periods were also envisaged.

In so far as borrowing limits are concerned, the Fund moved in the 1970s to increase the amounts of financing that a member could potentially get. At one level, this was achieved as a result of action taken to raise quota resources in the Fund. Two major quota increases were approved in the second half of the 1970s—in 1975 and 1978—under the 6th and 7th General Review of Quotas.[66] At another level, increased borrowing was attained mainly as a result of the establishment of the new permanent and temporary facilities, but also through the expansion of borrowing limits under the CFF and BSFF. Possible cumulative access limits with the EFF and SFF can be seen in Table 8.4, while for the EAP, the maximum combined limit at the beginning of 1985 was between 558 and 600 per cent of quota. What the Fund was endeavouring to do by substantially increasing credit availabilities was to give members an incentive to approach it, especially in respect of higher-conditionality borrowing. The thinking was that countries would be less hesitant to utilize conditional resources demanding tough adjustment measures if they were assured of a substantial mass of resources.[67]

Moreover, the import of the EFF, SFF and EAP was a subtle change in the Fund's outlook on the balance-of-payments problem, essentially of the developing countries. Longer-term financing, longer repayment periods and larger credit availabilities together implied a modified view of the problem—

stressing an approach to adjustment that was more gradualist than had previously been the case. This subtle change was also mirrored in important changes in the economic orientation of stabilization that became increasingly apparent in the latter half of the 1970s. In fact, the novel Fund approach was unmistakably stated by the Managing Director at the 1980 Annual Meeting;

> As regards the nature of the *adjustment* to be undertaken, I would like to describe the new thrust of our policy ... [O]ur programs must endeavour to create conditions conducive to the improvement of supply. This will require, of course, supportive measures on the demand side so as to keep the claims on resources in a sustainable relationship with their availability ... The adjustment programs we support will thus be an integral part of a longer-term strategy for fostering investment and growth.[68]

In the Managing Director's statement, there was a clear sense that adjustment policies stressing growth and structural factors would take precedence over policies stressing deflation and economic retrenchment.[69]

It is incontestable that the criticisms by the developing countries of conditionality in the second half of the 1970s, combined with their reluctance to use high-conditionality credit, had forced the membership to fundamentally reassess the appropriateness of Fund financing.[70] The practical consequences of the new departure in the framing of stabilization programmes, as well as the larger credit resources available to borrowing countries, were evident in the quick step-up in use of Fund resources under the various facilities, of low and high conditionality, in the last year of the 1970s and the beginning of the 1980s. Williamson's study has shown that there was 'a surge in Fund lending under high-conditionality arrangements between mid-1979 and mid-1981',[71] attributable to an easing in Fund conditionality from mid-1979. This increased borrowing from the Fund is clearly discernible for the two-year period, 1980–81, when over one-third the amount of total credit drawn in the 1970s was granted—see Table 8.1. The developing countries used some SDR 20 billion of these resources, compared with 36 billion over the entire 1970s. While eleven EFFs had been concluded with developing countries in 1975–79, sixteen were entered into in 1980–81 alone.

(b) The 1980s—Fund retreat on conditionality

The disposition towards experimentation with conditionality did not last long in the IMF. Already, in 1980, there were a few developed countries that had expressed apprehensions at the new directions taken by the Fund in its lending functions. The Governor for West Germany cautioned at the 1980 Annual Meeting that, 'it should be made clear that its [the Fund's] monetary character must be preserved. The Fund was created as the guardian of internal and external monetary stability. It should resist all attempts that might call this mandate into question. The conditionality of its lending must be maintained'.[72] It was during the following year, however, that a concerted attack by a few developed countries was launched against what they perceived as a laxer attitude in the application of conditionality.

The critical factor in this regard was the new United States government that assumed office in January 1981. On taking office, the new administration, with its crusading commitment to the free market system, advocated a curtailment of the lending functions of the multilateral financial institutions. As regards the IMF, this reappraisal of position was clearly stated at the 1981 Annual Meeting when the US Governor argued that: 'In our judgment, it is critically important— to the IMF as an institution, to individual borrowing countries, and to the world economy in general—that Fund financing be used only in support of sound and effectively implemented economic adjustment programs'.[73] For various reasons, these countries were in a strong position in the time-context of the early 1980s to have their way in forcing a retreat on the new experiment with conditionality.

To begin with, the external environment had seen a sharp deterioration. Reference has already been made to the decline in the North–South negotiations and the waning of the commodity nationalism of developing nations. There was, also, a shrinking of financing options for these nations.[74] 1982 saw the explosion of the debt crisis, and the growing unwillingness of the commercial banks to lend to Third World nations. A significant, spontaneous source of alternative balance-of-payments financing for the creditworthy among them was therefore lost. Moreover, ODA from both the developed and OPEC countries, was on the decline in the recessionary circumstances of the early 1980s. A source of concessional financing for the poorer developing countries was thus also affected.

With reference to internal Fund developments, a decision was taken to discontinue SDR allocations, which had recommenced on 1 January 1979—another action that circumscribed the financing choices for developing countries. The IMF itself confronted its own funding difficulties,[75] while, as the largest contributor, historically, to Fund quotas, the United States held a trump card in respect of new financing for the Fund under the 8th General Review of Quotas, which was then being negotiated. Finally, the beginning of the 1980s witnessed one of the most powerful changes in the IMF's operations as it related to its financing mandate. In contrast to the 1970s, a growing number of developing countries had no alternative but to borrow from the Fund in the environment of limited financing options. The Fund, in short, had virtually become an institution catering almost exclusively to developing countries, with all the implications for lending conditions.[76]

Whereas in the 1950s, 1960s and 1970s, developed countries utilized Fund resources in substantial proportions—see Table 8.1—in the early 1980s, the only such countries that found it necessary to draw upon IMF credit were Greece, Portugal, Turkey and South Africa. Over the years 1980–84, developing countries were beneficiaries of the various Fund facilities in the proportion of nearly 90 per cent of all credit extended. As an example, in 1983, of the SDR 12.6 billion in drawings, all were made by developing countries.[77] While the African countries had, until the late 1970s, largely succeeded in avoiding the use of high-conditionality credit, the 1980s have so far shown a different pattern.[78] In the 1970s, the African region, with the largest numerical membership of developing countries in the IMF, had entered into the fewest numbers of SBAs—thirty-nine of 153 (or 25 per cent of the total) for developing countries. In comparison, Latin American had sixty-four or 42 per cent and Asia forty-four or 28 per cent—see Table 8.2. In the period 1980–84, by contrast, the African countries had surpassed the other two major regional subgroupings in SBAs-a total of fifty-five of 104 or 52 per cent, compared with twenty-five or 24 per cent for Latin America and eighteen or 17 per cent for Asia. A similar picture emerges if we look at EFFs concluded—see Table 8.2. Africa, along with Latin America, had the most EFFs in the years 1980–84—nine EFFs— compared to three for the years 1975–79.[79]

Even more important for the advocates of increased conditionality was the reappearance in the early 1980s of the major Latin American countries as borrowers from the Fund. Faced with serious debt servicing difficulties of the massive debts they had contracted from the commercial banks during the 1970s and the beginning of the 1980s, the middle-income countries of Latin America—in the context of the pervasive recession besetting the international economy, protectionism in the industrialized countries, low commodity prices and the cutback in commercial bank lending—had no viable option but to approach the Fund. Major financing arrangements were agreed between the Fund and Argentina, Brazil and Mexico in 1983: Argentina concluded an SBA in the amount of SDR 1.5 billion and Mexico entered into an EFF in the amount of SDR 3.4 billion, in January 1983, while Brazil agreed an EFF of SDR 4.2 billion in March of that same year.[80]

What was interesting in the Fund's response to the debt crisis were, firstly, the immediacy of its reaction and, secondly, the pivotal role it played at this initial stage. A joint strategy, involving the Fund, major industrialized countries, the relevant debtor countries and the commercial banks, was evolved to deal with the problem. At a time when the banks were increasingly reluctant to lend, the Fund was able to draw them into its cooperative strategy for debt management.[81] Clearly, the explanation relates to the immense sums of money involved, the potential destabilization of the international financial system that could flow from debt repudiation and the fact that the Western, and particularly the American, banking system was involved.

However, there has been increasing criticism by debtor countries of the Fund's role in the management of the debt crisis, particularly the type of stabilization programmes that borrowing countries were required to enter into. In fact, the debt crisis took place at the very moment that the Fund was turning its back on the conditionality experiment and reverting to purely demand-based adjustment. The debtor countries, particularly from Latin America, were increasingly unwilling to expose themselves to a process that they had rejected two decades ago and, while they did undertake Fund-sponsored programmes at the beginning, the negotiations were often accompanied by tremendous acrimonious debate.

Many indicators of the Fund's retreat on the conditionality experiment can be presented. Already, in respect of the CFF, reference has been made to the attachment, for the first time, of high-conditionality requirements for borrowing under the facility in the early 1980s. EFFs, which had proved increasingly attractive to developing countries in the initial years of the 1980s, have recently been on the decline. Whereas sixteen EFFs were agreed over the years 1980–81, only six were agreed in 1982 and 1983, and no new EFFs were concluded during 1984 and up to 30 April 1985. There has been a substantial reduction in permissible borrowing limits: consequent upon the quota increase approved after the 8th General Review of Quotas in 1983, 'normal access limits were reduced in stages from 150 percent to 95–102 percent of quota, 450 percent to 280–395 percent, over three-year periods and from 600 percent to 408 percent cumulatively'.[82] This curtailment in access to Fund credit has been the result of an initiative by the United States for a reduction in borrowing rights, including a disbandment altogether of the policy of enlarged access.[83] As regards the orientation of stabilization programmes, there has been a re-emphasis on the adjustment of demand[84] and a downplaying of the structural adjustment experiment of the late 1970s/early 1980s.

This reassertion of demand-based adjustment was a clear indication that the Third World claim that adjustment should take account of the external causes of deficits[85] was being discounted. The Fund management, in recent years, has consistently avoided taking these causal factors into consideration in the type of stabilization programmes it sanctioned, insisting that, in the search for a solution to the balance-of-payments problem, it is not so much the cause, as the time-scale—whether it is short-term or long-term—that is important.[86]

This position clashes with the spirit, if not the intent, of the provision in the 1979 decision on conditionality—previously indicated—that due regard should be paid to the causes of balance-of-payments problems in the formulation of adjustment programmes. It is true, as Gold argues, that:

> the language in which the Fund expresses its intention is that it will 'pay due regard' to the considerations listed in the paragraph. As used in the Articles of Agreement and in the practice of the Fund ... the phase connotes something less than a direction to give decisive effect to the considerations to which the Fund must pay due regard.[87]

It is just as true, however, that the incorporation of such a provision—expressly at the instance of the overwhelming majority of its membership, the developing countries—in a decision of a major organ of the IMF was not meant to be devoid of meaning in terms of practical consequences. It clearly created expectations in so far as its advocates were concerned. In fact, a former senior Fund official, who was also at the Bretton Woods Conference as part of the American delegation, has made clear that a key Bretton Woods principle is 'that adjustment of the balance of payments should be related to the cause of the problem'.[88]

The refusal of the Fund in recent years to grant commensurate weight to the causes of the external deficits of the developing countries in the formulation of stabilization programmes has meant that, 'developing countries were faced with a burden of adjustment out of all proportion to their degree of responsibility for the imbalances arising in the international payments system'.[89] As many economic analysts have argued, the taking into account of the causes of deficits does not imply that adjustment is not needed; rather, it lessens the full impact of the austerity measures that countries may need to undertake.[90]

What is incontestable is that this reversal of policy regarding conditionality has attracted some of the bluntest criticisms of the Fund in its history. In fact, it is extremely instructive to listen to the harsh criticism of the Jamaica Prime Minister before the Fund's 1985 Annual Meeting—Jamaica, under its present government, has been one of the developing countries that had enthusiastically accepted the conditions of the IMF funding initially;

> The prevailing wisdom . . . emphasizes the adjustment programmes through tight demand management. The result is severe austerity which, in the final analysis, cuts services and reduces growth. This austere path carries social and political costs which are often counterproductive to the final objective of achieving adjustment without sacrificing stability.[91]

What was also castigated by the Jamaican Prime Minister was the drastic pace of change implied in the demand management model of adjustment. Brazil, in the latter part of 1985, indicated its unwillingness to continue the path of IMF stabilization that imposed 'an unnecessary recession on the country'[92] and preferred to move to a positively directed adjustment, founded on economic growth and restructuring.

Increasingly, in the 1980s, there has been widespread criticism by developing countries of a Fund conditionality practice that is embedded in purely technical terms and divorced from the other crucial realities of borrowing countries—a refusal to construct and implement stabilization programmes linked to what is also socially and politically prudent and feasible.[93] The paradox of this criticism is that the Fund's own evaluation of the causes for the breakdown of SBAs and EFFs in recent years point to the fact that 'political constraints' and 'weak administrative sytems'[94] accounted for 60 per cent of the failures. Moreover, it is not as though there were a consensus within the economic profession on the issues involved in the adjustment process generally and, more so, as it impinges on developing economies.[95]

It is not that the Fund management is oblivious to these considerations.[96] The management's position, however, is that these are issues of a highly sensitive nature from the perspective of national sovereignty and are best left to domestic governmental authorities.[97] Accordingly, its functions have to be kept narrowly technical 'if it is to be effective in the exercise of its role as a promoter of the adjustment process'.[98] The adjustment process is not nor can it be purely technical in the circumstances of developing economies; it is inextricably bound up with social and political considerations. Its ultimate success is undeniably predicated on the level of political support it can garner from the populace and governmental authorities.[99] The latter would hardly be fully committed to programmes that entail pervasive hardships, threatening to their political survival. As one analyst put it:

> This argument is both illogical and impractical . . . In the case of stabilization programs . . . serious outside attempts to anticipate political and administrative obstacles and to design programs to cope with them are more likely to be constructive and practical than interventionist. Failure to identify and lessen such obstacles is in fact both irresponsible toward the governments and peoples concerned and wasteful of the external agency's resources.[100]

5. Conditionality—the tension between change and retrogression

It is apparent from the analysis that the IMF found itself compelled, in the second half of the 1970s, to sanction change in various indices of its conditionality requirements—particularly in respect of borrowing limits, repayment schedules, the economic orientation of adjustment and the breach of the equality principle. It is further evident that the pressure for change in the contours of conditionality emanated from developing countries. The combination of their harsh public criticism of the institution and refusal to use high-conditionality resources were important factors conducing to change. The Fund's own analysis of the outcome of stabilization programmes, agreed with developing countries in the mid-1970s, pointed to a less confident view of the efficacy of its preferred stabilization framework.

There were other factors at work, however, propelling the process of experimentation. It is to be remembered that a new Managing Director was appointed in 1978.[101] There is every indication that the new Managing Director played a pivotal role in ushering in the brief period of experimentation with conditionality.[102] As one Executive Board participant revealed to the author:

> The new Managing Director wanted to reassert the central role of the Fund in balance-of-payments financing and to be thought of as an activist Managing Director. When he took over, the existing situation—negligible use of resources and, in fact, high levels of repayment—was far from suitable for the realization of these aims. His directive to the staff was to get some programmes going, even if it meant a slackening of conditionality.[103]

The Managing Director has steadfastly refused to concede that there was a change in conditionality,[104] much less to endorse this interpretation. Any such endorsement would betray not merely the inconsistency, but would also call into question the technical credibility of the Fund's reigning stabilization model—in that the changes evident at the end of the 1970s were based, in part, on an effort to attract back a clientele, rather than a scientific analysis of the issue.

It was also intimated that the Managing Director's hand was strengthened by an apparent division among his staff on the issue of conditionality. This division was alluded to repeatedly in interviews with both Executive Board and staff officials. The view was that the Fund is no monolith when it comes to balance-of-payments analysis and solutions, with the manifest implication that there is a degree of sympathy for a less inflexible outlook on conditionality.[105]

Both the Managing Director and the staff that supported him, however, could only go as far as the success of their experiment or the acquiescence of the major creditor-countries would allow them. Once the Reagan administration embarked on the campaign to reaffirm conditionality in all its rigour, then the experiment was effectively disavowed by some of its major supporters—including the Managing Director.[106] The hand of the opponents of a relaxation of conditionality was strengthened by several factors, especially the fact that negotiations for the replenishment of the capital base of the Fund were then being pursued. A Fund, strapped for resources and faced with the potential call on its credit of unprecedented proportions by developing countries, found it difficult to resist the demands of the important creditor-countries for a reassertion of the conventional framework of conditionality.

The developing countries themselves should not escape a measure of blame for this state of affairs. As the actual debtors to the institution, they were the ones most prominently concerned to ensure the continuation and evolution of the experiment. Yet, there were elements of disunity in the Third World position that made it easier to obtain the reversal of policy. This was most tangibly apparent in the two conferences, held by subgroups of developing countries, on the international monetary situation in June/July 1980.[107] Both conferences were critical of the operations of the Fund. The criticisms differed substantially, however, in both degree and kind, with the 'Arusha Initiative' signifying a radical, ideological attack on the institution, while the Abu Dhabi statement was more moderate in the scope of change advocated. This divergence in perspectives among the developing countries was alluded to in the course of interviews as a factor facilitating the reversal of the conditionality experiment of the late 1970s.

Intra-Third World division has been manifested at another level. In the post-1973 years, an important means of replenishing Fund resources has been through borrowing from members in strong economic positions. The developing, oil-exporting countries were significant sources of financing for the Fund. The new creditor status of many of these countries, and especially of Saudi Arabia and to a lesser extent Kuwait, has meant that theirs became the concerns of the typical creditor, rather than of debtors.

In fact, it was repeatedly pointed out to the author that the interests of a Saudi Arabia are hardly different from those of other major creditors from developed countries and that this has been lately evidenced in its behaviour on the issue of conditionality. A single, current example provided by representatives from developing countries was the debate among Third World Executive Directors of a proposal canvassed by the African membership, in particular, for the activation of the 'hardship' clause in the Fund's Articles of Agreement-Article V, Sec. 7(g)—that was not previously used. Under the terms of this provision, the Fund, 'on the request of a member, may postpone the date of discharge of a repurchase obligation . . . [on the basis] that a longer period for repurchase . . . is justified because discharge on the due date would result in exceptional hardship for the member'. The context of this initiative was the tremendous foreign exchange constraints facing many of the poorer developing nations in Africa and elsewhere, their burgeoning debt service obligations and the deceleration in economic growth. A decision to activate this provision necessitates a 70 per cent majority of the total voting power so that no single state held a veto over this decision. Agreement among developing countries was a first important step towards a serious consideration of the proposal. Agreement has, however, been relatively hard to achieve because the Saudi Arabian Executive Director has insisted on repayments on time to the Fund.

Resistance to change, therefore—while led by a small group of developed countries—is as much a creditor phenomenon. Especially for the creditor from developing countries, whose surplus is the result of a depletable resource such as oil, the concern is to ensure that its investible surplus is secure and readily available, if needed. Another facet of this preoccupation with repayment has to do with the fact that, in so far as its financial activities are concerned, the IMF now caters overwhelmingly to developing countries. This factor has only served to magnify the concern of creditors with the issue of repayment: their worry is about the continuing integrity of resources tied up in loans to some of the poorest developing countries.[108]

Conclusion

It is evident from the presentation that conditionality has not remained unchanged over the history of the Fund. Significant, though not radical, changes were implemented, particularly in the second half of the 1970s. Change was most visibly evident in the opening of a host of new borrowing windows, continuing the breach of the original one-window approach of the Fund that was begun with the creation of the CFF. Change was embodied in the important modifications at the constitutional level and in the decisions and practices of the Fund.

This period of experimentation was the result of the campaign led by the Fund's developing membership for an overhaul of conditionality and was facilitated by the existence of favourable external circumstances. Alternative sources for balance-of-payments financing and the economic nationalism of the developing countries to use high-conditionality credit and their doctrinal behaviour of the Fund in this regard. Faced with a loss of clientele—and, thereby, of its central role in balance-of-payments financing—the institution was amenable to the consideration of change. Internally, the refusal of developing countries to borrow high-conditionality credit and their doctrinal challenge of the adjustment process favoured by the Fund brought into question the overall legitimacy of the financing mandate of the institution.

The reversal of the conditionality experiment in the early 1980s was similarly facilitated by the conjuncture of favourable external and internal circumstances. Externally, in the difficult international economic environment of the time, alternative balance-of-payments financing sources were no longer available to developing countries; secondly, with the collapse of the NIEO negotiations, there was a muting of the economic nationalism that was so prevalent in the 1970s. These external factors, when combined with the assumption of office of the ideologically-inclined government in the United States in 1981, strengthened the forces interested in aborting the conditionality experiment. A coherent counter-campaign led by the United States and involving such major developed countries as West Germany, the United Kingdom, and Japan, successfully turned back the novel departures of the 1970s before they could have solidified into routine, everyday practice.

Notes

1. The Fund's official history has used such epithets as 'mounting and intense' and 'vitriolic' to describe the criticisms of Fund conditionality—see de Vries, *The International Monetary Fund, 1972–78,* Vol. 1, pp. 481 and 489, respectively. See also, Bahram Nowzad, 'The IMF and Its Critics', *Essays in International Finance*, No. 146, December 1981, p. 9.
2. 'A conversation with Mr de Larosiere', *Finance and Development*, June 1982, p. 4.
3. The depth of the current controversy is attested by the broad-based attack that has been vented against Fund conditionality by, among others, government leaders, intergovernmental institutions, academic economists and non-governmental groups. See, for example, *Development Dialogue*, No. 2, 1980, pp. 5–6 and 7–9 for the harsh criticisms of Prime Minister Manley of Jamaica and President Nyerere of Tanzania. An early critical work is Cheryl Payer, *The Debt Trap: The International Monetary Fund and the Third World*, New York, Monthly Review Press, 1974. Aspects of the Fund's conditionality practices were not immune from criticism by its sister institution, the World Bank which, in its 1983 *Annual Report*, argued that: 'Austerity programs and attempts to achieve trade surpluses are exacting a heavy toll. Just as seriously, in some countries, reductions in public expenditures have particularly affected investment projects, which could have adverse consequences for future living standards. Private investment has also declined sharply, in response to reduced demand, uncertain prospects, and high interest rates'—IBRD, *Annual Report*, 1983, p. 34.
4. This will become evident as the analysis progresses.
5. While this divergence is here posed in stark terms of conditional versus automatic credit, in fact the British position did concede a measure of conditionality to govern use of Fund resources—for a discussion, see Sidney Dell, 'On Being Grandmotherly: The Evolution of IMF Conditionality', *Essays in International Finance*, No. 144, October 1981, p. 15.
6. For a review, see ibid., Horsefield, op. cit., Vol. 1, pp. 67–77 and Gardner, *Sterling-Dollar Diplomacy in Current Perspective*, op. cit., pp. 88–95 and 114–17.
7. See Horsefield, op. cit., Vol. 3, p. 19 and p. 86.
8. Adolfo C. Diz, 'The Conditions Attached to Adjustment Financing: Evolution of the IMF Practice' in *The International Monetary System: Forty Years after Bretton Woods*, op. cit., p. 218.
9. Dell, 'On Being Grandmotherly', pp. 177–8. See also Ariel Buira, 'IMF Financial Programs and Conditionality', *Journal of Development Economics*, Vol. 12, Nos. 1/2, February/April 1983, pp. 111–12.
10. Eduardo Weisner, 'Discussion' in *The International Monetary System: Forty Years after Bretton Woods*, p. 237. See also Southard, op. cit., p. 16 and E. Walter Robichek, 'The IMF's Conditionality Re-examined' in Joaquin Muns, ed., *Adjustment, Conditionality and International Financing* (Papers presented at the seminar on 'The Role of the International Monetary Fund in the Adjustment Process', held in Vina del Mar, Chile), 5–8 April 1983, IMF, 1984, pp. 67–8.
11. E.B. Decision No. 71–2, of 26 September 1946.
12. Horsefield, op. cit., Vol. 1, p. 244.
13. The American proposals specified that purchases from the Fund should be evaluated against 4 criteria: (i) that the par value of the member was an appropriate one; (ii) that the deficit was temporary; (iii) that the purchase was not needed for purposes of rehabilitation or development and (iv) that the member was taking steps to assume the full obligations of the Articles—ibid., pp. 244–5.

14. Ibid., p. 245.
15. E.B. Decision No. 102-(52/11) of 13 February 1952.
16. At this time of the Fund's history, it was known as the gold tranche, but was changed to the reserve tranche after the second amendment of the Articles of Agreement.
17. See E.B. Decision No. 102-(52/11), op. cit. It should be noted that the original conception of the SBA was that of an assured line of credit in case of need. As time went on, however, it became the mechanism under which regular Fund credit was actually extended to members.
18. Basically, the *corpus juris* of the IMF is embodied in the provisions of (i) the Articles of Agreement; (ii) the By-Laws, Rules and Regulations and (iii) the decisions of its competent decision-making organs.
19. Robichek, 'The IMF's Conditionality Re-examined', op. cit., p. 68.
20. When a member needs to use Fund credit, it purchases the required amount of foreign exchange with an equivalent amount of its domestic currency. In effect, since a member contributed 75 per cent of its quota in its own currency, then the maximum permissible borrowing right was 125 per cent of quota, which was divided into five tranches—the reserve tranche and four credit tranches.
21. For a discussion of SBAs, see Omotunde E. G. Johnson, 'Use of Fund resources and stand-by arrangements', *Finance and Development*, **14**, No. 1, March 1977, pp. 19–21 and p. 35.
22. E.B Decision No. 155-(52/57) of 1 October 1952.
23. The Articles (second amendment) define the SBA to mean 'a decision of the Fund by which a member is assured that it will be able to make purchases from the General Resources Account in accordance with the terms of the decision during a specified period and up to a specified amount—Art. XXX(b).
24. IMF, *Annual Report*, 1959, p. 22.
25. As Guitian put it: 'phasing of the drawings on Fund resources at specified intervals during the period of the stand-by arrangement was established. In turn, the program of policy action agreed with the members was formulated in explicit quantified form so that its implementation could be verified. The verification of policy performance ... was synchronized suitably with the phasing of resource disbursements ... so the latter would be dependent on the former'—see Manuel Guitian, 'Adjustment and Interdependence: The Challenge to Conditionality', unpublished paper prepared for a seminar on 'Adjustment and Growth in the Current World Economic Environment', Estoril, Portugal, 16–19 January 1985, p. 4.
26. Joseph Gold, *Conditionality*, Pamphlet Series No. 31, Washington DC, IMF, 1979, p. 27.
27. The Brazilian Director—supported by virtually all the Directors from developing countries—'drew particular attention to the fact that it contained no provisions for phasing, no performance clauses, and relatively few ceilings on variables, such as credit expansion, that were often subject to ceilings under the terms of stand-by arrangements (i.e., performance criteria). In other words, although this stand-by arrangement was in the highest credit tranches, it lacked both a quantitatively defined program and the usual clauses contained in stand-by arrangements'—de Vries, *The International Monetary Fund, 1966–71*, Vol. 1, p. 342.
28. Ibid., p. 343.
29. E.B. Decision No. 1345-(62/23) of 23 May 1962, as amended by Decision No. 2620-(68/41) of 1 November 1968. The major features of this decision were (i) the inclusion of consultation clauses in all SBAs; (ii) the omission of phasing and performance clauses for SBAs that do not go beyond the first credit tranche; (iii) the inclusion of phasing and performance clauses in all other SBAs and (iv)

performance clauses covering performance criteria necessary to evaluate implementation of the programme, though there was no specification of a general rule as to the number and content of performance criteria.

30. Art. V, Sec. 3(c) (first amendment).
31. Gold, *Conditionality*, op. cit., p. 9.
32. So far, this component has not been addressed in this analysis. In fact, the treatment of this aspect of the issue will be done at a high level of generality since it goes to the core of both economic theory and practice—a concern that is not central to the object of this study. What is more, there is an extensive literature on the substantive aspects of conditionality, spanning the different approaches that have become evident over the years. Major recent works are John Williamson, ed., *IMF Conditionality*, Washington DC, Institute for International Economics, 1983 and Tony Killick, ed., *The Quest for Economic Stabilization: The IMF and the Third World*, New York, St. Martin's Press, 1984.
33. Art 1(v) (first amendment).
34. Thus it is that the Governor for the then United Arab Republic could in 1960 laud the 'constructive role played by the Fund' in the international monetary system and the Governor from India in 1961 could approvingly allude to 'the flexibility and understanding with which the Fund has approached its growing tasks'—see *Summary Proceedings*, 1960, p. 68 and ibid., 1961, p. 76, respectively.
35. See Raul Prebisch, 'Economic Development or Monetary Stability: The False Dilemma', *Economic Bulletin for Latin America*, 6, No. 1, March 1961, pp. 1–25.
36. De Vries, *The International Monetary Fund, 1966–71*, Vol. 1, p. 363. For a review of the IMF/Latin American conflict, see David Felix, 'An Alternative View of the "Monetarist"–"Structuralist" Controversy' in Albert O. Hirschman, ed., *Latin American Issues: Essays and Comments*, New York, The Twentieth Century Fund Inc., 1961, pp. 81–93 and Stephen D. Krasner, 'The IMF and the Third World', *International Organization*, 22, No. 3, Summer 1968, pp. 679–83.
37. See, for instance, statement by the Brazilian Governor at the 1959 Annual Meeting—*Summary Proceedings*, 1959, p. 65.
38. De Vries, *The International Monetary Fund, 1966–71*, Vol. 1, p. 345.
39. Krasner, 'The IMF and the Third World', op. cit., p. 675.
40. This should not be read to mean that these countries neither had nor expressed continuing interest in the issue. Rather, compared to their vanguard role in the earlier confrontation with the Fund, circumstances had changed to such an extent that it was not an issue that touched the main Latin American countries in an immediate sense.
41. *IMF Survey*, 10 September 1973, p. 263.
42. As Polak noted, for these countries, 'the banks dislodged the Fund'—see Polak, 'The Role of the Fund', op. cit., p. 252. See also Graham Bird, *World Finance and Adjustment: An Agenda for Reform*, New York, St Martin's Press, 1985, p. 61.
43. In the words of the G24: 'The conditionalities attached to the various credit facilities of the Fund need to be reviewed, bearing in mind that members have been discouraged from making use of some of the Fund's resources available to them on account of severe conditionalities'—'Communiqué: G24', 14th Ministerial Meeting, 26 April 1977, op. cit., p. 325, para 4(iv).
44. See T. M. Reichman, 'The Fund's conditional assistance and the problems of adjustment, 1973–75', *Finance and Development*, December 1978, pp. 38–41. Reichman's study focused on twenty-one SBAs in the years 1973–74 and concluded that 'only one third of the programs . . . can be deemed to have been successful—in the sense that (i) policies were broadly implemented; (ii) the balance of payments and the general economic situation at the end of the program period were better

than at the beginning, and (iii) this improvement proved to be sustainable, either with a continuation or with an adaptation in policies'. This high level of programme failure could only have served to raise questions about the efficacy of the policy preferences of the Fund.

45. Manuel Guitian, 'Fund conditionality and the adjustment process: the changing environment of the 1970s', *Finance and Development*, March 1981, p. 8.
46. The background circumstances of the EFF may be found in de Vries, *The International Monetary Fund, 1972–78*, op. cit., Vol. 1, pp. 361–83.
47. Committee of Twenty, *International Monetary Reform: Documents of the Committee of Twenty*, p. 18.
48. E.B. Decision No. 4377-(74/114) of 13 September 1974, as amended by Decisions Nos. 6339-(79/179) of 3 December 1979 and 6830-(81/65) of 22 April 1981, para. I(i).
49. De Vries, *The International Monetary Fund, 1972–78*, op. cit., Vol. 1, p. 368.
50. Ibid., pp. 362–8. Among the developed countries in support of the facility were Italy and The Netherlands, while West Germany, Japan and Canada were opposed to it.
51. E.B. Decision No. 4377-(74/114), para. I(ii)(a).
52. In the original EFF decision, the repayment requirement was five to eight years after EFF disbursements—see E.B. Decision No. 4377-(74/114), para. 5—but this was lengthened to four to ten years in the follow-up decision of 1979—see E.B. Decision No. 6339-(79/179), para. 5.
53. Killick, ed., *The Quest for Economic Stabilization*, op. cit., p. 149.
54. See, for instance, statement by the Governor of Mauritania on behalf of Africa in *Summary Proceedings*, 1974, p. 35.
55. See Manuel Guitian, *Fund Conditionality: Evolution and Principles and Practices*, Pamphlet Series, No. 38, IMF, Washington DC, 1981, p. 20.
56. As Girvan notes: 'the conditionality attached to the Extended Facility was still the same combination of monetary-cum-fiscal contraction and relative price adjustment that applied to drawings from the upper credit tranches, the corresponding implication being that the payments deficits to be treated with the new facility were still assumed to have their origins in imbalances amenable to such treatment'— Norman Girvan, 'Swallowing the IMF Medicine in the "Seventies"', *Development Dialogue*, No. 2, 1980, p. 57. See also Williamson, *The Lending Policies of the International Monetary Fund*, p. 17 and Stephen Haggard, 'The Politics of Adjustment', *International Organization*, 39, No. 3, Summer 1985, p. 506.
57. *Summary Proceedings*, 1976, p. 202. See also statement by Governor for Central African Republic (on behalf of Africa), ibid., p. 125.
58. See, in particular, 'Communiqué: G24', 13th Meeting, 1–2 October 1976, op. cit., p. 324, para. 6 and 19th Meeting, 'b. Outline for a Programme of Action on International Monetary Reform', 28 September 1979, op. cit., p. 340, para. IV.10.
59. De Vries, *The International Monetary Fund, 1972–78*, op. cit., Vol. 1, pp. 489 and 495.
60. *Summary Proceedings*, op. cit., 1977, p. 62.
61. E.B. Decision No. 6056-(79/38) of 2 March 1979.
62. Gold, *Conditionality*, op. cit., p. 15.
63. E.B. Decision No. 6056-(79/38), para. 4.
64. As President Nyerere of Tanzania states: 'I do not know whether there are now people who honestly believe that the IMF is politically or ideologically neutral. It has an ideology of economic and social development which it is trying to impose on poor countries irrespective of their own clearly stated policies'—'No to IMF Meddling . . .', op. cit., p. 8.
65. This aspect of the decision will be discussed at greater length shortly.
66. Quotas were increased overall by 33.6 per cent in 1975 and 50.9 per cent in 1978. Of

the seven General Quota Reviews since the Fund started operations and the 1978 decision, increases were approved on four occasions—three of which occurred in the 1970s alone—in 1970, 1975 and 1978.

67. See 'A conversation with Mr de Larosiere', op. cit., p. 5.

68. *Summary Proceedings*, 1980, p. 22. It is to be noted that the Managing Director himself speaks about the 'new thrust of our policy'. As we shall see later, he will not accept that there was any change in Fund policy.

69. As Killick has written: 'adjustment policies were still regarded as essential, but the nature of the required economic changes was now perceived differently; as structural and, therefore, as taking longer to achieve. By contrast with the situation prior to 1974, the existence of a large, unviable BoP deficit could not be taken as even *prima facie* evidence of domestic mismanagement'—Killick, *The Quest for Economic Stabilization*, op. cit., p. 206.

70. For a discussion, see John Gerard Ruggie, 'Political Structure and Change in the International Economic Order: The North–South Dimension' in John Gerard Ruggie, ed., *The Antinomies of Interdependence: National Welfare and the International Division of Labor*, New York, Columbia University Press, 1983, pp. 463–4.

71. Williamson, *The Lending Policies of the International Monetary Fund*, op. cit., p . 47. It is true that this step-up in borrowing from the Fund coincided with another series of oil price increases and the re-emergence of recessionary conditions in the developed economies. While there is a linkage in these factors in terms of need for large financing resources, the behaviour of the developing nations in avoiding high-conditionality credit in the mid-1970s, when they confronted a similar external environment, lessens the explanatory weight of these factors.

72. *Summary Proceedings*, 1980, p. 73.

73. Ibid., 1981, p. 109. The US Treasury Under-Secretary was even blunter when he noted: 'We want to push the IMF's conditionality back to where it was'—*The Wall Street Journal*, 21 September 1981. For a general discussion, see Robin Pringle, 'Reaganomics enters the Fund', *The Banker*, September 1981, pp. 89–91.

74. See Killick, *The Quest for Economic Stabilization*, op. cit., pp. 2–3.

75. See 'Address of Managing Director: before the 1982 Annual Meeting', *Summary Proceedings*, op. cit., 1982, pp. 25–6.

76. As we shall shortly see, this development had the consequence of an intensified concern within the institution about the integrity of its financial resources.

77. *IMF Survey*, 6 February 1984, p. 40.

78. For extended discussions, see G. K. Helleiner, 'The IMF and Africa in the 1980s', *Essays in International Finance*, No. 152, July 1983 and S. Kanesa-Thasan, 'The Fund and adjustment policies in Africa', *Finance and Development*, September 1981, pp. 20–4.

79. See Kanesa-Thasan, op. cit., p. 20.

80. IMF, *Annual Report*, 1984, pp. 109 and 115.

81. When we omit the principal borrowers from the Fund from the mid-1970s onwards—whose creditworthiness was certification enough for the commercial banks—the Fund has historically played a crucial role of conferring its seal of approval on the domestic economic policies of members wishing to borrow from both private and official external sources. A Fund-sponsored programme was often a prerequisite in this regard. There was a fundamental change in this 'certification' role of the Fund to one of a 'catalyst' in the context of the debt crisis—for a discussion, see 'Historian Traces Origins and Development of Fund Involvement in the World Debt Problem', op. cit., pp. 4–5.

82. 'Report of the G24 Deputies on the Functioning and Improvement of the International Monetary System', *IMF Survey*, Supp., September 1985, p. 129, para. 121.

83. See, for instance, *The South*, November 1983, p. 66, *The Financial Times*, 27 September 1983 and *Far Eastern Economic Review*, 10 October 1985, p. 87.

84. Bird, *World Finance and Adjustment*, op. cit., p. 44.

85. The Managing Director, in his report to the 1981 Annual Meeting, pointed to the intensity of the external shocks to which the non-oil developing countries had been exposed over the two preceding years—see *Summary Proceedings*, op. cit., 1981, p. 19.

86. Nowzad, *The IMF and its Critics*, op. cit., pp. 15–16.

87. Gold, *Conditionality*, op. cit., p. 22.

88. 'Principles of Bretton Woods Conference seen as Relevant to Current Problems', *IMF Survey*, 29 October 1984, p. 331.

89. Sidney Dell, 'The World Monetary Order', *Third World Quarterly*, October 1980, 2, No. 4, p. 711.

90. As Jeker notes: 'to make a distinction between the causes and the origin of balance of payments disturbances is still a relevant one as it should be a guiding principle in determining not the conditionality but the *amounts* and *terms* of balance of payments support accorded to a country, i.e. the means as well as terms of the drawing (interest rate, maturity, grace period) should be a function of a country's adjustment cost it would have to incur. By granting more generous terms to countries whose balance of payments suffered from externally caused disturbances . . . the countries will be allowed to lengthen their adjustment period and maintain a certain development process'—Jeker, 'Conditionality and Stand-by Credits . . .' op. cit., p. 42.

91. *The Sunday Gleaner* (Jamaica), 13 October 1985. The Jamaican example is instructive from another point of view. Over the past decade, two governments with diametrically opposed ideological perspectives—the socialist government of Prime Minister Manley of 1972–80, and the capitalist government of present Prime Minister Seaga, in power since the end of 1980—have had recourse to Fund financing. The former entered these arrangements reluctantly, while the latter had enthusiastically courted and accepted Fund demand-oriented stabilization. Yet, in the end, both governments have ended up by castigating the Fund's adjustment process.

92. *The New York Times*, 12 August 1985.

93. See, for instance, Joan Nelson, 'The Politics of Stabilization' in Richard E. Feinberg and Valeriana Kallab, eds, *Adjustment Crisis in the Third World*, New Brunswick, Transaction Books, pp. 99–118 and Stephen Haggard, 'The Politics of Adjustment', *International Organization*, 39, No. 3, Summer 1985, pp. 505–34.

94. Killick, *The Quest for Economic Stabilization*, op. cit., p. 261.

95. As Helleiner notes: 'On the issue of the precise nature of IMF conditionality when it is required, one must tread cautiously. The appropriate pace and phasing of policy and adjustment, the distribution of the burdens, the precise mix of policy instruments, are all matters of political as well as technical judgment. Even capacities, which they often (especially in missions to smaller and poorer countries) are not, these issues are tricky and not ones on which there is a professional consensus'—see G. K. Helleiner, 'Lender of Early Resort: The IMF and the Poorest', *The American Economic Review*, 73, No. 2, May 1983, p. 353.

96. Criticisms along these lines have also emanated from certain quarters of the OECD: 'A pervasive deficiency of many stabilization plans was the neglect of measures to protect essential social services from further damage by budgetary retrenchment and price adjustments or to raise the efficiency of these services'—OECD, *Development Cooperation*, Paris, OECD, November 1984, p. 38.

97. Recent examples include the riots in the Dominican Republic in April 1984 after the imposition of sharp increases in the prices of food, medicines and other goods,

following a Fund SBA and the protests in Jamaica in January 1985 after fuel price increases—see *New York Times*, 30 April 1984 and 19 January 1985, respectively.

98. See, for instance, 'Address of the Managing Director', *Summary Proceedings*, 1980, p. 22 and C. David Finch, 'Adjustment Policies and Conditionality' in Williamson, ed., *Conditionality*, op. cit., pp. 76–8.

99. This was repeatedly indicated to the author by representatives of developing countries during the interviewing process. See also, Haggard, 'The Politics of Adjustment', op. cit., p. 505.

100. Nelson, 'The Politics of Stabilization', op. cit., p. 100.

101. This was the French national, Jacques de Larosiere.

102. The Managing Director and staff play a crucial role in regard to the implementation of conditionality. While the Executive Board provides the broad guidance and oversight of conditionality, the administration has a wide discretionary latitude in its implementation—see Crockett, 'Issues in the use of Fund resources', op. cit.

103. This was in fact stated by an Alternate Executive Director from a European country. See also Pirzio-Biroli, 'Making sense of the IMF conditionality debate', op. cit., p. 123.

104. See 'A conversation with Mr de Larosiere', op. cit., pp. 4–5. See also Killick, *The Quest for Economic Stabilization*, op. cit., p. 207.

105. As Pirzio-Biroli notes: 'There remain a number of "old timers" in the Fund who cannot quite cope with this more pragmatic approach. These are heartened by the most recent tendency of the Fund to somewhat tighten its conditions again'—see Pirzio-Biroli, 'Making sense of the IMF conditionality debate', op. cit., p. 142.

106. An important consideration underpinning the easy retreat of the Managing Director had to be the fact that his term of office was due to expire in 1983 and reappointment was premised on the absence of opposition from the United States.

107. The Arusha Conference was sponsored by the governments of Jamaica and Tanzania, which in the late 1970s had some of the most difficult negotiations with the IMF. It was held in Arusha, Tanzania and resulted in the 'Arusha Initiative'—see General Assembly Doc. A/S-11/AC.1/2 of 28 August 1980. The Abu Dhabi meeting was Arab-sponsored, though other developing countries attended—see 'Report—Meeting of Experts of Developing Countries on the Reform of the International Monetary System', Abu Dhabi, 25–28 June 1980, TD/B/AC.32/L1 of 7 July 1980.

108. Interestingly, the Fund found it necessary for the first time in 1985 to declare two of its developing members—Guyana and Vietnam—ineligible to use its resources because of a default in repayment of past loans.

Chapter 9
Conclusion

The central focus of this study has been the participatory role of the Third World countries in IMF decision making. The analysis of this issue of participation hinged around the fulfilment of three tasks. These were (i) an elucidation of the content of the demands by developing countries for full and effective participation, on the basis of equality, in the decision-making process; (ii) a portrayal and evaluation of the bargaining capabilities they bring to bear and the constraints they face in the political process of the Fund and (iii) an assessment of the institution's responsiveness to their demands. Analytically, therefore, participation was conceptualized as a twofold process: firstly, procedural participation which entailed an examination of the formal and informal decision-making process and the place of these countries within it and, secondly, substantive participation whereby a participatory role was seen as a function of both an involvement in defining the content of institutional policies and programmes and the achievement of direct benefits as a result of this involvement. While it is not the intent to summarize the major trends that have emerged during the course of the analysis, certain dominant elements need to be stressed.

With regard to the content of participation, the initial concern of the developing countries in the 1960s/early 1970s was to obtain a recognition of their right, as a matter of principle, to participate in international monetary decision making. They were at the time interested in an international process that permitted them a role in defining the issues to be negotiated, and in actual participation in the process, once negotiations had begun. The principle of participation was conceded during the SDR negotiations of the 1960s and reaffirmed at the start of the 1970s when these countries were integrated into the monetary reform negotiation process. But, concession of the principle of participation was by no means synonymous with actual or substantive participation, in the sense of either capacity to influence or real influence in the process. In fact, once the principle of participation was conceded, the preoccupation thereafter has been to ensure that the formal decision-making infrastructure of the Fund provided the mechanisms that allowed them to participate, and also that informal processes of participation—whether at the level specifically of the developing countries or at the broader level of international groupings—facilitated the presentation of their views.

The overarching interest, however, has been to redefine the principle of participatory equality that has traditionally served as the basis for the conduct of international relations, and to obtain international approval of their novel redefinition. Developing countries, in the context of the IMF, have never based their argument on an elusive abstract equality. Rather, they have demonstrated a clear-sighted appreciation of the limits of abstract equality, divorced from the realities of the international economic situation.

In their new conceptualization, the aim was to obtain recognition of an equality of standing for discrete groups of countries—in the case of the IMF, the developed and developing groups—rather than for countries, individually. It has represented the acute appreciation of these countries that different ordering principles are required for international financial institutions, with operational mandates, if they are to perform the tasks set them. It has derived from the recognition that the main contributors—until the mid-1970s, exclusively the developed countries—have been firmly resistant to any attempt at transposing to these institutions the traditional meaning of equality.

Group equality has both procedural and substantive implications. Procedurally, it signifies that decision-making mechanisms should be so structured as to give to identifiably coherent groups of countries equality of participation, practically speaking. Thus, voting strength, distribution of seats in limited-membership bodies, the power of veto and the majority rule should all ensure that these groups stand in a relationship of equality to each other. Substantively, it means that in the distribution of the benefits of international economic cooperation, a first-order reference point should be the group so that there is an equitable distribution between groups. Moreover, such an approach permits the application of differential treatment in respect of the requirements and the rights of cooperative endeavours. By formally recognizing differences among discrete groups of countries, an institution at once signals its sensitivity to differences in capacities, needs and, ideally, obligations.

One offshoot of the group approach is that it leads to the identification of groups. This has created problems within the context of the IMF which, from the constitutional point of view, originally made no differentiation among the membership and which, in fact, in its original doctrinal approach acted on the basis of the principle of uniformity in the treatment of members. Initial doctrinal inflexibility has gradually—as with most things in the Fund, after a certain time-lag—felt the sway of the international environmental realities that made a distinct separation of the developed from the developing countries. The IMF responded by grudgingly conceding this reality in terms of its practical behaviour, while keeping the fiction of legal uniformity. But even the latter has slowly evolved in that the Fund's constitution, consequent on the second amendment in 1978, has recognized a separate category of developing countries.

This achievement should not be played down. Enough has been said and written about the insignificance of most of the developing countries, when acting individually, in the overall scheme of things. Formal recognition of the group identity in the Fund consolidates the preferred operating approach of these countries and confers on them, in a relative sense, an increased influence within the policy-formation process of the institution.

While the developing countries have clearly achieved certain gains in their struggle for effective participation in Fund decision making, and while these gains have by no means been negligible, they are still limited in the context of their overall demands—a major yardstick against which they are to be judged. The achievements in regard to voting power, standards of representation and veto power, and in the growing recognition of a separate category of developing members which has facilitated the formulation of special policies to deal with their unique problems, have not, when all is said and done, fundamentally changed the structure of power in the IMF.

Developed countries still exert an inordinate control over the activities of the Fund when we set it in the proper context of numerical membership, the users of the resources of the institution, and those who are most affected by and least capable of protecting themselves against the negative effects of international monetary developments. Unarguably, decision-making structures have to grant a large recognition to those who bear major responsibility for the functioning of an arrangement. Developed countries provide the overwhelming bulk of the financial resources—particularly the usable resources—of the Fund; the exchange rate policies, and overall monetary and economic policies, of the major developed countries have a pervasive and substantial impact throughout the international economy. It is therefore understandable that they should have a large say in determining the direction of policy in the Fund.

What is particularly unacceptable to developing countries, however, is the inequity of a system where a few major contributing-countries, which basically do not use the Fund's resources and are thus unaffected by its policies, are the ones that seek to impose, by way of their control of the policy-making process, their view of economic organization and management. Similarly, these countries have confronted a system wherein, even granting the centrality of a few developed countries in exchange rate arrangements, decisions in this regard are exclusively taken by a narrow set of these countries—this, despite the clear effect of such decisions on the economies of the developing countries. This brings us to the other fundamental aspect of decision-making participation—what is achieved in terms of substantive policies, by way of participation. In this regard, the analysis has focused overwhelmingly on the Fund's financial mandate with three of the four issues examined having to do with an aspect of the Fund's financial activities, and the other dealing with exchange rate arrangements.

The analysis has shown that, in evaluating the participatory influence of Third World countries in defining the substantive Fund policies examined in the study, a clear distinction has to be drawn between exchange rate and financial matters. As regards the former, these countries have been unable to exert any meaningful influence. Contrastingly, in each of the areas of the Fund's financial responsibility looked at—the SDR, CFF and conditionality-based lending—there was a modest measure of achievement, particularly in the decade of the 1970s.

While conceding these achievements up to the end of the 1970s, however, the process of reversal of the 1980s, so far, has served to dilute the full effect of these gains. While two sets of SDR allocations were made in the 1970s, we are already into the second half of the 1980s, and no further allocation is in sight, owing to the firm resistance of four developed countries. The SDR facility is ultimately meaningless in the absence of decisions on allocations and the more so when the technical analysis and economic conditions argue in their favour, as they presently do. The most satisfying of the special facilities to the Third World, the CFF, which was originally envisaged as a low-conditionality facility, was also the target of the general hardening of conditions in the IMF in the 1980s. Borrowing limits have been curtailed and the conditionality surrounding CFF borrowings now approximates that which is applied to financing under the regular facilities.

Conditionality, as we have seen, has been the touchstone of the state of relations between the Fund and its Third World membership. The fact is that, as things presently stand, the Fund's financial mandate essentially only caters to the needs of developing nations. They are the ones that are placed in the position of having to implement the policies that go along with conditionality if they wish to obtain the Fund's financial support, to start with, and its imprimatur of their economic policies—increasingly a *sine qua non* for borrowing from other international sources, both private and public.

Thus, we have the anomalous situation of the users having only minimal influence in formulating the types of policies that they will have to implement once they approach the Fund. In other words, the people directly involved and affected face the basic paternalism—interestingly, the very apprehension that one of the institution's founding fathers, Keynes, had—of being told how best to organize their monetary affairs. This is one of the most crucial areas in which the Fund's decision-making process has proved grossly inappropriate and it will remain an area of controversy until it is rectified.

There has been change in the Fund after hard-fought battles waged by developing countries, with the support of certain external institutions. The central proposition of the study was that institutional decision making is profoundly affected by environmental developments. This proposition was clearly established during the course of the analysis, where it was seen that decision making signifies a continuum that embraces the special formal decision-making infrastructure, the informal processes and the external environment of the institution.

Paradigmatically, the Fund's decision-making process, as influenced by environmental circumstances, has so far been a four-stage process. The initial post-war phase saw virtually unchallenged American dominance. The second phase, basically the 1960s, involved a sharing of decision-making control with the major West European countries and Japan, following the economic reassertion of these countries. For the Third World countries, the third phase, that lasted for most of the 1970s, was the most fruitful and influential, except in the area of exchange rates, since they were able to make a substantive breach of the elitist control of Fund decision making by obtaining a not insignificant share in the governance task. As we saw, these achievements were set within a specific external context of an intense Third World economic nationalism and an aggressive championing of their claims, based on their unity, their elaboration of a competing vision of international economic organization and, to a certain extent, the acknowledged economic influence of a small sub-group of their members. Finally, the contemporary phase has actually witnessed, at best, a standstill in the process of Third World integration into Fund decision making, and at worst, a reversal of some of the gains of the 1970s. These regressive trends have occurred in step with the changed environment of the counter-challenge of the major developed countries under the leadership of the

United States, concerned to reaffirm the Bretton Woods order of international economic relations.

Interestingly, change in the Fund has always been a delayed action. We saw this in both the 1960s and 1970s, regarding the CFF and conditionality experiment. Such is the case presently with the problem of debt.

The onset of the debt crisis in the second half of 1982 provided the Fund with the ideal opportunity to recoup its central position—lost in the 1970s—in balance-of-payments adjustment with regard to the developing countries. In the radically changed international economic environment of the early 1980s, and facing severe debt servicing and balance-of-payments difficulties, developing countries found themselves operating in a context of seriously restricted financing options. This was the setting for Fund reassertion, through the assumption of the leadership role in managing the debt crisis.

The Fund took the initiative in arranging financing packages, linked to the implementation of stabilization measures, for debtor countries—an approach characterized by a process of debt restructuring, commercial bank agreement to provide financing and Fund supervision of debtor-country performance by means of an adjustment programme and a modest amount of Fund financing. The changed nature of Third World/commercial bank relations is reflected in the fact that, unlike in the 1970s when bank financing enabled these countries to altogether avoid the IMF, in the new situation, bank credit was tied to Fund supervision and conditionality.[1] Most serious for debtor-countries was the fact that these developments took place at the very moment that the Fund was disavowing its conditionality experiment and reverting to its traditional stabilization framework, entailing substantial domestic deflation.

Developing countries have been warning since the start of the 1980s that the debt problem cannot be resolved on the basis of the traditional stabilization process re-introduced by the Fund after the briefest of experiments with conditionality in the late 1970s. They have argued for a process that stresses growth-oriented adjustment. These pleas fell on the deaf ears of the major Fund members. Then, in late 1985, with the plan sponsored by the United States,[2] an evident shift in outlook, consistent, to some extent, with the position advocated by developing countries, was made. In its emphasis on growth-oriented adjustment, the American proposal was conceding the impracticality of the wholly deflationist approach of the IMF. The intervening environmental circumstances are once again critical in terms of explaining this apparent shift.

At one level, domestic politics in several debtor-countries were coming under increasing stress during 1984–85 as these countries followed the debt strategy of this initial phase that called for the implementation of stabilization programmes agreed with the IMF, involving a high degree of austerity and sacrifice. The year 1984 was to see the outbreak of serious riots in some Latin American countries, including Brazil, the Dominican Republic, Peru and Jamaica.[3] If riots were the most visible manifestation of domestic difficulties, then the whole negotiating process with the IMF was another crucial indication of debtor-country dissatisfaction with the strategy that gave a central role to the IMF. The negotiating process increasingly became characterized by public acrimony, while stabilization programmes repeatedly met with failure and had to be renegotiated.[4] In short, the Fund and its strictly demand management approach to the programmatic content of stabilization became the focal target of debtor-country criticism.

Relatedly, and at another level, it was in 1984 that the Latin American debtors began to come together to discuss common approaches to the debt problem. There was, firstly, the important conference in Quito, Ecuador in January 1984, sponsored by the Economic Commission for Latin America and the Caribbean (ECLAC) and the Latin American Economic System (SELA), two major regional economic institutions.[5] This conference resulted in the elaboration of the 'Quito Declaration and Plan of Action'. Latin American countries reconvened in June 1984 in Cartagena, Colombia to consult on, and to seek to coordinate their approach to the debt problem.[6]

It was in 1985 that two rather extreme solutions were advocated by individual Latin American countries. Peru courted a break with the IMF-led debt strategy by making clear that only a specified proportion of its foreign exchange earnings would be used to service its debt[7] and Cuba—not a member of the Fund—hosted an international conference on debt, at which strong sentiments were expressed for debt repudiation altogether.[8] Also in 1985, Brazil, the major debtor-nation, stated its clear refusal to undertake any more Fund-recommended adjustment in dealing with its external debt. The demonstration effect of the Latin American action became palpable among another important set of regional debtors—the African countries. At the 1985 OAU summit, growing calls were made for a Third World approach to the problem. Nigeria took the decision not only to have nothing to do with the Fund, but, like Peru, indicated that only a specified proportion of its foreign exchange earnings would go to debt servicing.[9] In such a context, there emerged a growing sense of a loss of Fund authority in dealing with debtor-countries.

In short, there was a change—to some extent, even radicalization—of the environment within which the debt problem had to be dealt, in contrast to the period of the emergence of the problem in 1982-83. There was a sense of a shifting balance of forces in this radicalized context as countries individually adopted rejectionist positions vis-à-vis the Fund and as there emerged the potential of a joint debtor-country strategy.[10] The Third World countries were once again seeking to lead this process. The push of this environmental reality has served to force major developed countries to rethink their own approach, and ushered in a new strategy in the debt crisis with the announcement of the Baker Plan in late 1985. While it is too early to assess the efficacy of this new approach, it is clear that it occurred in response to unmistakable restlessness among debtor-countries and their frontal challenges to an IMF-led process. This was clearly the import of the refined approach that emphasized growth-oriented, rather than demand-management adjustment and the effort to bring the World Bank into the picture. There is a sense in this regard of a reduced IMF role, and possibly even institutional marginalization.

Nevertheless, developing countries do have limited capabilities to bring about change in the IMF. The range of instruments at their disposal is severely restricted: their political unity, extra-institutional support, ability from time to time to ignore the institution and, importantly, their capacity to disrupt the international monetary system. Each of these instruments, however, requires favourable contextual circumstances to be in any way efficacious. For instance, the debtor-countries have the clear potential to disrupt, in a major way, international financial arrangements. But such a process is only conceivable in the context of a group approach.

One of the most interesting features of the 1960s and 1970s was the measurable impact that UNCTAD had on certain areas of Fund operations, especially its CFF. Extra-institutional support was a key element of the bargaining strength that developing countries used to obtain changes in the CFF. Particularly in the context of the 1960s, there was a measure of apprehension within the Fund concerning UNCTAD. But there has been, in recent years, a noticeable dilution of the influence that UNCTAD has had on the Fund.

There has been increasing disillusionment among the major developed countries regarding UNCTAD. It has come to be seen as too inextricably bound up with Third World concerns and advocacy. There is some merit in this particular accusation. UNCTAD's identification with Third World interests— and in defining solutions for their international economic difficulties—was understandable at the beginning. The developed countries not only dominated the Bretton Woods institutions, but the latter reflected in large measure either their preoccupations or their preferred solutions. UNCTAD, therefore, was merely providing to the weaker members of the international economic system a counterbalance to this dominant control by the stronger members of a crucial part of international institutional arrangements. Moreover, the developed countries also had their own formal and informal coordinating groups in monetary affairs—the OECD's Working Party 3 and the G10. The developing countries had no comparable frameworks at the time. UNCTAD, in essence, filled this vacuum for them at a particular historical moment.

However, this should have been a transitional measure. In so far as UNCTAD is part of the United Nations system, with a universal vocation, it could not very well identify, more or less permanently, with a particular group of members. This was a charge that developing countries had directed at the IMF, in partial justification of their earlier difficulty with that institution. They should have expected no less from developed countries, over time.

The fact is that developing countries have been loath to establish, on a formal basis, technical-support structures—a key shortcoming in their negotiations with developed countries.[11] The latter have shown a keen awareness of the value of formally constituted institutional mechanisms in major areas of international relations—e.g. economic, OECD; military, NATO.[12] There has also been a formalizing of annual summit meetings among the seven major industrialized countries since the mid-1970s, permitting them to review and define—if possible—common positions on a broad range of international issues. When allied with their informal processes, the G5 and G10, it is evident that these countries are capable of bringing to bear commonly elaborated outlooks, underpinned by technical backing, on the issues.

Apart from the G77 and the non-aligned movement—and not all developing countries are members of the latter—both of which are basically informally constituted, developing countries do not have a parallel process of well-defined institutions that bring not only coherence, but technical support to their advocacy. There is a large dependence on outside institutions, particularly UNCTAD, and its role is now too controversial to be of any major influence. There is nothing wrong with UNCTAD having a preoccupation with these problems of special interest to developing nations—its work on the commodity problem has been generally applauded, even within the IMF. But the developing countries need to create their own formal mechanisms, in support of the increasingly technical issues with which they are confronted.

Developing countries have also been constrained in using, as some developed countries have done, threats of withdrawal from organizations or the actual withholding of budgetary contributions.[13] With regard to the latter, such a threat will be patently incongruous in the light of the negligible proportions of the budgets that they individually provide. When the developed countries, above all the United States, withhold contributions—as currently seen in the case with the United Nations—the effects are substantial. Specifically in relation to the IMF, budgets are not contributed by governments. They derive essentially from the charges that members are required to pay for financial transactions within the Fund, as well as investment earnings. So, there is no question of withholding budgetary contributions. This is the principal reason why the two Bretton Woods institutions have not faced a recurrent budgetary problem, as has the United Nations system.

For the IMF, the central problem is its operational, rather than administrative, funding. These come from the quota contributions of members and, as was previously stressed, apart from the fact that developed countries provide the major portion, it is their currencies, by and large, that are critical to the Fund's financial function. Finally, since the Fund has become in recent years an important source of balance-of-payments financing, almost exclusively for developing countries, threats to its operational resources—even were they feasible—would mainly affect these countries.

Another significant tactic that some developed countries have employed when they are displeased about the functioning of an organization and wish to force change, is either the threat of, or actual, withdrawal. The United States, in particular, has used this expedient—in the ILO in the 1970s and currently, together with the United Kingdom, in UNESCO. Once again, the United States is in a strong position to do so because it provides a substantial portion of budgetary resources. Withdrawal, therefore, has a visible impact on the organization's operations. Withdrawal of an individual Third World country has no such comparable impact—Indonesia withdrew temporarily from the IMF in the 1960s, but managed to change nothing. Withdrawal would only have an effect if all or an overwhelming majority of Third World nations were to leave.

Where developing countries have had an effect, as we saw, is when they have refused to use Fund resources. But, for such a step to be either feasible or fruitful, environmental circumstances have to be particularly favourable—for example, in the second half of the 1970s, when alternative sources of balance-of-payments financing were available.

Looking ahead a little, the regressive tendencies of the first half of the 1980s would seem to have serious implications for the participatory role of developing countries in international economic relations. The post-war multilateral process is clearly under threat; even more so is the United Nations component of that process, including UNCTAD. One of the disturbing aspects of the process of reversal in the IMF is the threat it poses to an appropriate role for the developing countries in future international monetary reform negotiations.

The fact is that, increasingly, calls are being made at this time for a new phase of negotiations for monetary reform purposes. The last such series, albeit aborted, did mark the start of full participation of developing countries in international monetary negotiations. The present danger that they face is the reversion to exclusivist arrangements that ignore them altogether. Over the past year, in the context of worrisome exchange rate instabilities among the world's major currencies and uneven economic performances among these countries, there has been a noticeable intensification in the periodicity of G5 meetings, so much so that other developed countries have expressed serious misgivings about the narrow participatory basis of the discussions (recently, the decision was taken to integrate Italy and Canada into the G5 forum). These developments hark back to an earlier period, when the G10 acted exclusively on international monetary issues, ignoring both the developing countries and the central institution, the IMF, until the time for ratification of their agreements.

However, it would not be as easy now to ignore the developing countries. They are far more organized than at the beginning of the 1960s. They are far more conscious of the stakes involved, on the basis of those earlier experiences. They know that, because of their deeper integration into the world financial and trading systems, ultimately the workability of international monetary solutions also depends on their acceptance. Finally, they have a blocking power over any such agreements. In fact, developing countries have already started to prepare for the eventuality of a new set of international monetary negotiations, as witnessed by the coherent document they prepared in late 1985, covering all the major monetary issues.[14] Therefore, while the tendencies of the G5 remain disturbing, the environment of the 1980s is sufficiently different from that of the 1960s to circumscribe the scope of exclusivist arrangements.

In so far as Fund decision making is concerned, voting power still remains of fundamental importance to developing countries, notwithstanding the actual practice of consensus decision making. This has been the area of least success for them. It has to be accepted, anyhow, that restructuring of voting power to obtain a position of relative equality with developed countries—the 50 per cent target—while desirable, is unrealistic in the near term. Ruling elites have not been historically known to voluntarily give up positions of dominance, on behalf of an enlightened sharing of governance with new claimants, the more so when the latter do not have the material wherewithal to enforce their claims. More realistically, developing countries will have to aim for the less ambitious process of small, incrementally significant additions to their voting power over a period of time.

In any process of readjustment of voting power several things need to be stressed. Firstly, developing countries will have to continue to press for a change in the allocation of basic votes, especially if it is decided to undertake monetary reform negotiations. The argument for an increase in basic votes is twofold: the re-establishment of its position in overall voting power, and ensuring that it truly serves the purpose for which it was established—the sense of participation it gives to smaller members. Its proportional dilution in global voting power is inconsistent with its primary objective. Secondly, while financial contributions and responsibility for the functioning of the system have to remain core elements in structuring voting power, overwhelming dependence on these criteria are unacceptable in today's context. Other supplemental criteria, in keeping with the changes in the international economic context, can be envisaged: numerical membership, and importantly, the issue of dependence on the institution, measured in terms of use of its resources.

Those depending on the institution should have an equal say, at least, together with the major contributors, in defining the policies relating to use of the Fund's resources. They are the ones that will have to implement these policies, with far-reaching effects on their economies. Prescriptions—whether real or imagined—only serve to weaken commitment to adjustment efforts. Countries wish to both seem and to actually be in control of issues that touch vital national interests. This was one of the major issues determining Nigeria's decision, in early 1986, to ignore the Fund, even though its stabilization effort will probably entail as much hardship as that which the Fund normally recommends.

One of the interesting developments, in so far as readjustment of voting power is concerned, has to do with the growing interest in, and accession to, membership of the socialist countries. From one perspective, allocations of voting power to these countries can have a negative effect on that of developing countries. From another, while these countries will not necessarily be automatic supporters of developing countries, their position as minority and new members may force them to align, as a matter of convenience, if nothing else, with the older group of minority members. If developing countries can define common interests with them, especially since—judging from the experiences of those socialist nations that have already joined the Fund—they will be potential borrowers, the possibility exists of a strengthened Third World in the Fund decision-making process.

Another priority for developing countries will have to be appointment of a Deputy Managing Director who is a national of one of these countries. Their case is strong in this regard. Both the Managing Director and his Deputy have traditionally come from a Western European country and the United States, respectively. A similar pattern exists in the World Bank—the President is by tradition an American and the Vice-President a West European. There is nothing sacrosanct about this tradition, particularly in view of the changes in the international economy since the time of Bretton Woods. The fact is that the Fund's management, as we have seen, can play a crucial role in the policy-making process.

Notes

1. Robert E. Wood, *From Marshall Plan to Debt Crisis*, Berkeley, University of California Press, 1986, pp. 287–8. See also David T. Llewellyn, 'The Role of International Banking' in Loukas Tsoukalis, ed., *The Political Economy of International Money: In search of a new order*, London, Royal Institute of International Affairs, 1985, p. 211.
2. This is a plan announced by the US Secretary of the Treasury at the 1985 Annual Meeting of the Fund. As regards the plan's financial aspects, the basic elements are (i) the proposal that commercial banks lend $20 billion to the fifteen largest debtor-countries over a three-year period; (ii) a matching $9 billion credit line from the World Bank and the IADB over the same period and for the same countries; and (iii) that the $2.7 billion in repayments due to the Fund for Trust Fund loans be channelled back to the poorest developing countries. The proposal envisaged a growth-oriented approach to adjustment, founded on the strengthening of free-market policies within domestic economies.
3. See *New York Times*, 9 October 1983, 27 April 1984 and 2 May 1984.
4. See *Financial Times*, 12 June 1984 and *New York Times*, 12 August 1985. See also Christine A. Bogdanowicz-Bindert, 'World Debt: The United States Reconsiders', *Foreign Affairs*, Winter 1985/86, **64**, No. 2, p. 266.
5. The Quito Conference was the result of an initiative of the President of Ecuador in 1983, appealing to the regional economic institutions to formulate a Latin American response to the debt crisis.
6. This became known as the Cartagena group. Eleven Latin American countries participated, including the major debtors—Mexico, Brazil, Argentina, Venezuela, Chile and Peru.
7. The new Peruvian President announced during his inaugural address that Peru would devote no more than 10 per cent of export earnings to debt servicing—see *Time*, 12 August 1985.
8. See Fidel Castro, 'To pay tribute to the empire or to pay tribute to the homeland' (Dialogue with the Delégates to the Trade Union Conference of Latin American and Caribbean Workers on the Foreign Debt), 18 July 1985, La Habana, Editora Politica, 1985. See also *New York Times*, 25 August 1985.
9. *Financial Times*, 3 January 1986.
10. See 'Debt Crisis: Kissinger warns U.S. must act now to prevent Latin catastrophe', *New York Post*, 25 June 1984.
11. For a discussion, see Shridath S. Ramphal, 'Not by Unity Alone: The Case for Third World Organisation', *Third World Quarterly*, 1, No. 3, July 1979, pp. 43–52. See also Julius Nyerere, 'Third World Negotiating Strategy', *Third World Quarterly*, 1, No. 2, April 1979, pp. 20–3.
12. The socialist countries also have formal organizations in economic matters, COMECON, and military, the Warsaw Pact.
13. For a discussion, see Victor-Yves Ghebali, 'La politisation des institutions specialisés des Nations Unies', in Nicholas Jequier, ed., *Les Organisations Internationales: Entre l' Innovation et la Stagnation*, Lausanne, Switzerland, Presses Polytechniques Romandes, 1985, pp. 81–97.
14. See 'Report of the G24 Deputies on the Functioning and Improvement of the International Monetary System', op. cit.

Appendix 1

Financing facility of the fund

Buffer Stock Financing Facility (BSFF): created by the Fund in 1969, it is intended to assist members to meet their contributions to international commodity buffer stock schemes. Under the 1969 decision, a member was eligible to draw to a limit of 50 per cent of quota (currently 45 per cent), though, unlike the CFF, there is no annual borrowing limit. In so far as conditionality is concerned, the borrowing member is required to cooperate with the Fund to find solutions to its balance-of-payments problem. Repayment is to be completed in three-to-five years after a drawing.

The Oil Facility (OF): established by the Fund on a temporary basis in 1974, following the oil price increases the previous year. The first OF came into effect in June 1974 for a period of approximately one year, while the second came into effect in April 1975, for a similar period. Open to all members of the Fund, it was basically a low-conditionality facility—the requirement of cooperation being the essential condition. Repayment was to be completed seven years after an OF purchase.

The Supplementary Financing Facility (SFF): established in 1979, on a temporary basis. It was intended to address the balance-of-payments problems of those members whose imbalances were large relative to their quotas. SFF credit was made available through either an upper credit tranche stand-by arrangement or an Extended Fund Facility Arrangement, thus making it subject to substantial conditionality. Disbursement periods were normally longer than the traditional one-year programmes—three years. Larger credit was also available and repayment was expected from 3.5 to 7.5 years after a drawing. The SFF was discontinued in March 1981.

The Enlarged Access Policy (EAP): the SFF replacement, it was set up in 1981. Also envisaged to cope with members' balance-of-payments needs that were large in relation to their quotas. Like the SFF, credit under the EAP was extended either through high-conditionality stand-by or extended arrangements. Disbursement periods could be for as long as three years and repayment was expected from 3.5 to 7 years after an EAP drawing.

Appendix 2

The programme of interviews

This will be a brief explanation of the approach that was followed in the programme of interviews with Fund officials. Firstly, there was no standardized set of questions that was posed to the officials interviewed. There were many reasons for this. Interviews were conducted with a diverse set of officials—management, staff and governmental-representative (the latter from both developed and developing countries)—at various hierarchical levels and with different specializations. Some had served for long periods of time, while others were relatively new to the Fund. In short, the interviews were formulated in such a way as to take advantage of each individual's strong point.

Secondly, the linking theme of the study—and thus of the interviews—was Fund decision making, and a set of substantive issues was used as a filter for its examination. Particular individuals dealt with or were exposed to particular issues; some, because of their longer service in the institution, had a more extensive memory of these issues, while others were better placed to give a partisan view of the issues. This factor also argued for the avoidance of standardized questions.

It was often the case that interviews took their own momentum. The author always had a set of aims and a series of basic questions for each interview. But, once the process started, it usually took unexpected directions, leading into new areas that were not initially suspected. In this regard, it should be pointed out that the Fund, because of the intense controversy it has stirred up, is not only more amenable to opening up to the public, relatively speaking, but is urged on by the need to explain its side of the story. This made more for a dialogue than an interview.

In a word, the author is not in a position to provide a sample of questions posed. But, as references are made throughout the study to these interviews, a good idea could be had of the types of issues raised.

Bibliography

1. Sources

A. *International Monetary Fund:*
Proceedings and Documents of the United Nations Monetary and Financial Conference, Bretton Woods, New Hampshire, 1–22 July 1944, Department of State, US Government Printing Office, Washington, 1948.

International Monetary Fund, *Summary Proceedings of the — Annual Meeting of the Board of Governors, 19—*, Washington DC (various issues).

——, *Annual Report of the Executive Directors for the Fiscal Year ended April 30, 19—*, Washington DC, 19— (various issues).

Finance and Development (various issues).

IMF Survey (various issues).

'Fund Policies and Procedures in Relation to the Compensatory Financing of Commodity Fluctuations', *IMF Staff Papers*, 8, November 1960, pp. 1–29.

Managing Director, IMF, 'Summary of Statement to UNCTAD I', *Proceedings of the United Nations Conference on Trade and Development*, First Session, Geneva, 23 March–16 June 1964, Vol. 2, UN, New York, 1964.

'Speech by the Managing Director to the National Foreign Trade Convention', New York, 16 November 1964, *International Financial News Service*, Vol. 16, 1964, pp. 441–5.

Managing Director, IMF, 'Developments in the World Monetary System' (address before the Federation of German Industries, Kronberg im Taunas, 25 April 1966), *International Financial News Survey* (Supp.), 29 April 1966, pp. 141–4.

——, 'The Role of the Fund in the International Monetary System', *IMF Survey*, 23 October 1972, pp. 88–91.

Reform of the International Monetary System: A Report by the Executive Directors to the Board of Governors, Washington DC, IMF, 1972.

Managing Director, IMF, 'Summary of Statement to Third Session of UNCTAD', *Proceedings of the United Nations Conference on Trade and Development*, Santiago de Chile, 13 April–21 May, 1972, Vol. 1a, Pt. 1, UN, New York, 1973.

Managing Director, IMF, 'Excerpts from an address on "National Sovereignty and International Monetary Cooperation"' (to the American Philosophical Society, Philadelphia, Pennsylvania, 19 April 1973), *IMF Survey*, 23 April 1973, pp. 114–16.

Committee on Reform of the International Monetary System and Related Issues, International Monetary Reform: Documents of the Committee of Twenty, IMF, Washington DC, 1974.

Proposed Second Amendment to the Articles of Agreement: A Report by the Executive Directors to the Board of Governors, Washington DC, IMF, March 1976.

Deputy Managing Director, IMF, 'Address on Monetary Reform and the Developing Countries', *IMF Survey*, 1 March 1976, pp. 66–7.

——, 'Summary of Statement to Fourth Session of UNCTAD', *Proceedings of the United Nations Conference on Trade and Development*, Nairobi, 5–31 May 1976, Vol. 2, UN, New York, 1977.

Managing Director, IMF, 'Address before the 1978 Euromarket Conference on "Financing the LDCs: the Role of Public and Private Institutions"', London 8 May 1978, *IMF Survey*, 22 May 1978, pp. 145–50.

——, 'Address before ECOSOC', Geneva, 3 July 1981, *IMF Survey*, 20 July 1981, pp. 222–5.

——, Address on 'The Role of the International Monetary Fund in Today's World Economy', Council on Foreign Relations, Washington DC, 8 June 1982, *IMF Survey*, 21 June 1982, pp. 177–86.

'A conversation with Mr de Larosiere', *Finance and Development*, June 1982, pp. 4–7.

By-Laws, Rules and Regulations, Washington DC, IMF, 39th Issue, 1 July 1982.

Managing Director, IMF, 'Address before ECOSOC', Geneva, 13 July 1982, *IMF Survey*, 19 July 1982, pp. 209–13.

——, 'Remarks on "The IMF and the Developing Countries"', University of Neuchâtel, Switzerland, 3 March 1983, *IMF Survey*, 7 March 1983, pp. 73–5.

International Monetary Fund, *Selected Decisions of the International Monetary Fund and Selected Documents*, Tenth Issue, IMF, Washington DC, 30 April 1983.

Managing Director, IMF, 'Speech delivered at the Annual Meeting of the Association of Reserve City Bankers on the Indebtedness of Developing Countries', *IMF Survey*, 8 May 1983, pp. 139–44.

——, IMF, 'Text of Address delivered before the Sixth Session of UNCTAD', *IMF Survey*, 13 June 1983, pp. 161–6.

——, 'Address on "Current Policies of the IMF: Fact and Fiction"', *IMF Survey*, 9 January 1984, pp. 2–6.

——, 'Remarks on "Adjustment programs supported by the Fund: Their logic, objectives, and results in the light of recent experience"', Centre d'études financières, Brussels, 9 February 1984, *IMF Survey*, 6 February 1984, pp. 33–47.

International Monetary Fund, *Selected Decisions of the International Monetary Fund and Selected Documents*, Supplement to Tenth Issue, IMF, Washington DC, 31 March 1984.

B. *United Nations and UNCTAD:*

General Assembly resolutions (various).

UN, *Commodity Trade and Economic Development* (report submitted by a committee appointed by the Secretary-General), Doc. E/2519, 1953.

——, *International Compensation for Fluctuations in Commodity Trade* (report of group of experts as appointed by the Secretary-General of the UN), 1961.

'Commodity and trade problems of developing countries: institutional arrangements' (report of the Group of Experts appointed under Economic and Social Council Resolution 919 (xxxiv)), *Official Records, Ecosoc*, 36th Session, Geneva, 1963.

UN, *Towards a Dynamic Development Policy for Latin America*, New York, UN, 1963.

Towards a New Trade Policy for Development (report of the Secretary-General of UNCTAD), UN, New York, 1984.

UNCTAD, *International Monetary Issues and the Developing Countries*, TD/B/32 and TD/B/C. 3/6, 1965.

Progress report on compensatory financing of export fluctuations (Note by the UNCTAD Secretariat), Doc. TD/7/Supp. 6, 1 November 1967.

UNCTAD, *International Monetary Issues: Progress Report on International Monetary Reform* (Note by the Secretariat of UNCTAD), TD/7/Supp. 7, 2 November 1967.

UNCTAD, *International Monetary Reform and Cooperation for Development* (report of the Expert Group on International Monetary Issues), UN, New York, 1969.

Trade and Development Board, *International Monetary Issues* (Note on consultation between the Managing Director of the IMF and the Secretary-General of UNCTAD), TD/B/C.3/98 and TD/B/C.3/98/Add. 1, 8 December 1971.

UNCTAD, *The International Monetary Situation* (report by the Secretariat of UNCTAD), Doc. TD/140/Rev. 1, 1972.

'Address by President Houari Boumedienne of Algeria before the Sixth Special Session of the General Assembly', *General Assembly Official Records*, A/PV 2208, 10 April 1974.

UNCTAD, *An integrated programme for commodities: compensatory financing of export fluctuations in commodity trade* (report by the Secretary-General of UNCTAD), TD/B/C.1/166, Supp.4, 13 December 1974.

——, *Trade and Development Board, 1973–74: Documents*, TD/B/AC.12/1–4.

United Nations, *A New United Nations Structure for Global Economic Cooperation* (report of the Group of Experts on the Structure of the United Nations System) Doc. E/AC.62/9, 28 May 1975.

'Statement by the Permanent Representative of the United States of America to the Seventh Special Session of the General Assembly', *General Assembly Official Records*, A/PV/ 2327, 1 September 1975.

UNCTAD, *International Monetary Issues: Problems of Reform* (report by the UNCTAD Secretariat), Doc. TD/185, 11 May 1976.

The Balance of Payments Adjustment Process in Developing Countries (Report to the Group of Twenty-Four), UNDP/UNCTAD Project INT/75/015, New York, 1979.

UNCTAD V, *Arusha Programme for Collective Self-Reliance and Framework for Negotiations*, Manila, May 1979, Doc. TD/236.

UNCTAD, 'Action on export earnings stabilization and developmental aspects of commodity policy: report by the UNCTAD Secretariat' (Doc. TD/229), *Proceedings of the United Nations Conference on Trade and Development*, Fifth Session, Manila, 7 May–3 June 1979, Vol. 3, UN, New York, 1979.

——, *Assessment of the progress made towards the establishment of the new International economic order*, Doc. TD/B/757, 25 September 1979.

——, *International Monetary Issues*, Doc. TD/B/C.3, 26 June 1980.

Trade and Development Board, *Report of the Ad Hoc Intergovernmental High-Level*

Group of Experts on the Evolution of the International Monetary System, Doc. TD/B/AC.32/L.4, 4 August 1980.

UNDP/UNCTAD, *Studies on International Monetary and Financial Issues for the Developing Countries: Determination of Quotas and the Relative Position of Developing Countries in the International Monetary Fund* (Report to the Group of Twenty-Four), UNCTAD/MFD/TA/14, 15 May 1981.

UNCTAD, *Compensatory Facility for Commodity-Related Shortfalls in Export Earnings: Review of the Operation of the Compensatory Financing Facility of the International Monetary Fund* (Report by the UNCTAD Secretariat), TD/B/C.1/243, 11 January 1983.

UNCTAD VI, *Commodity issues: a review and proposal for further action*, TD/273, 11 January 1983.

UNCTAD, *International Financial and Monetary Issues* (report by the UNCTAD Secretariat), TD/275, 26 January 1983.

——, *Consideration of the Substantive Issues Relating to the Question of an Additional Complementary Facility to Compensate for the Export Earnings Shortfalls of Developing Countries* (pursuant to Conference Resolution 157(VI), para. 3; Compensatory Financing of Export Earnings Shortfalls), TD/B/AC. 37/3, 26 March 1984.

UNCTAD, *Compensatory financing of export earnings shortfalls*, TD/B/1029/Rev. 1, 1985.

Committee for Development Planning, 'Report on the Twenty-first session and Resumed Twenty-first session' (Geneva, 19–21 November and New York, 20–23 April, 1985), *Official Records, Economic and Social Council*, 1985, Supp. No. 9, NY, United Nations, 1985.

United Nations, *World Economic Survey*, 1986, UN, New York, 1986.

C. *Other Official Documents:*

US Treasury Department, *The Bretton Woods Proposals: Questions and Answers on the Fund and Bank*, Washington DC, US Government Printing Office, 15 March 1945.

'Inaugural Address of the President, January 20, 1949', *Department of State Bulletin*, Vol. 20, No. 500, 30 January 1949.

'Aid to Underdeveloped Areas as Measures of National Security: Statement by Secretary Acheson' (before the Senate Committee on Foreign Relations on the Point 4 legislation, 30 March 1950), *Department of State Bulletin*, Vol. 22, No. 562, 10 April 1950.

Final Report of the Group of Experts on the Stabilization of Export Receipts, Washington DC, OAS, Doc. 59, Rev. 4, 2 April 1962.

Group of Ten, *Report of the Study Group on the Creation of Reserve Assets* (Report to the Deputies of the Group of Ten), 31 May 1965.

IBRD, *Supplementary Financial Measures* (a study requested by UNCTAD), 1964, IBRD, December 1965.

Inter-American Committee on the Alliance for Progress, *International Monetary Reform and Latin America* (report to CIAP by the Group of Experts), Pan American Union, General Secretariat, OAS, Washington DC, 1966.

Group of Ten, *Communiqué of Ministers and Governors and Report of Deputies*, July 1966.

A Proposal to Link Reserve Creation and Development Assistance (Report of the Sub-Committee on International Exchange and Payments of the Joint Economic Committee), 91st Congress, 1st Session, Congress of the US, Washington DC, US Government Printing Office, 1969.

Partners in Development (Report of the Commission on International Development), London, Pall Mall Press, 1969.

Hearings before the Sub-Committee on Europe and the Near East and South Asia of the Committee on Foreign Affairs, 93rd Congress (1st and 2nd Sessions), 1 November and 19 February 1974, Washington DC, US Government Printing Office, 1974.

'Declaration of the OPEC Summit Conference, 1975' as reproduced in Alfred George Moss and Harry Winston, comp., *A New International Economic Order: Selected Documents, 1945–75*, Vol. 1, UNITAR.

Towards a New International Economic Order: A Final Report by a Commonwealth Experts Group, London, Commonwealth Secretariat, 1977.

Jankowitsch, Odette & Karl P. Sauvant, comp., *The Third World without Superpowers: The Collected Documents of the Non-Aligned Countries*, Vols. 1–4, New York, Oceana Publications, 1978.

OECD, *The Impact of the Newly Industrializing Countries on Production and Trade in Manufactures* (report by the Secretary-General), Paris, 1979.

'Outline for a Program of Action on Monetary Reform Endorsed by the Group of 77 in September 1979', *IMF Survey*, 15 October 1979.

Report of the Meeting of Experts of Developing Countries on the Reform of the International Monetary System, Abu Dhabi, 25–28 June 1980, UN Doc. TD/B/AC.32/L.1, 7 July 1980.

The Arusha Initiative: A Call for a United Nations Conference on International Money and Finance, General Assembly Doc. A/S-11/AC.1/2, 28 August 1980.

The North–South Dialogue: Making it Work (Report by a Commonwealth Group of Experts), London, Commonwealth Secretariat, 1980.

Sauvant, Karl P., comp., *The Collected Documents of the Group of 77*, Vols. 1–4, New York, Oceana Publications, 1981.

The Brandt Commission Papers (Selected Background Papers prepared for the Independent Commission on International Development Issues, 1978–79), Geneva–The Hague, IBIDI, 1981.

Towards a New Bretton Woods: Challenge for the World Financial and Trading System, London, Commonwealth Secretariat, 1986.

Directions for Reform: The future of the International Monetary and Financial System (Report by a Group of Experts), India, Vikas Publishing House, 1984.

2. Books

Abi-Saab, Georges, ed., *The Concept of International Organization*, Paris, UNESCO, 1981.

Acheson, Keith A. L. *et al.*, *Bretton Woods Revisited*, London, Macmillan Press, 1972.

Akins, Michael Ernest, *United States Control over World Bank Group Decision-Making*, Ann Arbor, Michigan, University Microfilms International, 1981.

Asher, Robert E. *et al.*, *The United Nations and Economic and Social Cooperation*, Washington DC, The Brookings Institution, 1957.

Bedjaoui, Mohammed, *Towards a New International Economic Order*, Paris, UNESCO, 1979.

Bergsten, Fred C., *The Dilemma of the Dollar: The Economics and Politics of United States International Monetary Policy*, New York, New York University Press, 1975.

——, *et al.*, *The Reform of International Institutions* (A Report of the Trilateral Task Force on International Institutions), The Trilateral Commission, 1976.

——, *Managing International Economic Independence: Selected Papers of C. Fred Bergsten, 1975–76*, Lexington, Mass., Lexington Books, 1977.

Bhagwati, J. N. ed., *The New International Economic Order: The North–South Debate*, Mass., Cambridge University Press, 1977.

——, & John Gerard Ruggie, eds, *Power, Passion and Purpose: Prospects for North–South Negotiations*, Cambridge, Mass., The MIT Press, 1984.

Bird, Graham, *The International Monetary System and the Less Developed Countries*, London, Macmillan Press, 1978.

Blau, Peter M. & Richard W. Scott, *Formal Organizations: A Comparative Approach*, San Francisco, Chandler Publishing Co., 1962.

Camps, Miriam, *The Management of Interdependence: A Preliminary View*, New York, Council of Foreign Relations, 1974.

Claude, Inis L. jun., *Swords into Plowshares: The Problems and Progress of International Organization* (3rd edn), New York, Random House, 1964.

Cline, William, *International Monetary Reform and the Developing Countries*, Washington DC, Brookings Institution, 1976.

Cohen, Stephen D., *International Monetary Reform, 1964–69: The Political Dimension*, New York, Praeger Publishers, 1970.

Cox, Robert, ed., *International Organization: World Politics, Studies in Economic and Social Agencies*, London, Macmillan Press, 1969.

——, & Harold K. Jacobson, eds, *The Anatomy of Influence: Decision Making in International Organization*, New Haven, Yale University Press, 1974.

de Vries, Margaret Garritsen, *The International Monetary Fund, 1966–71: The System under Stress*, Vols 1–3, Washington DC, IMF, 1976.

——, *The International Monetary Fund, 1972–1978: Cooperation on Trial*, Vols 1–3, Washington DC, IMF, 1985.

Edwards, Richard W., jun., *International Monetary Collaboration*, Dobbs Ferry, New York, Transnational Publishers, Inc., 1985.

Fishlow, Albert *et al.*, *Trade in Manufactured Products with Developing Countries: Reinforcing North–South Partnership*, New York, The Trilateral Commission, 1981.

Gardner, Richard N. & Max F. Millikan, eds., *The Global Partnership: International Agencies and Economic Development*, New York, Praeger, 1968.

Gardner, Richard N., *Sterling-Dollar Diplomacy in Current Perspective: The Origins and the Prospects of our International Economic Order* (new expanded edn), New York, Columbia University Press, 1980.

Gold, Joseph, *Voting and Decisions in the International Monetary Fund*, Washington DC, IMF, 1972.

—, *Legal and Institutional Aspects of the International Monetary System: Selected Essays*, Washington DC, IMF, 1979.

— , *Legal and Institutional Aspects of the International Monetary System: Selected Essays*, Vol. 2, Washington DC, IMF, 1984.

Gosovic, Branislav, *UNCTAD: Conflict and Compromise—The Third World's Quest for an Equitable World Economic Order through the UN*, Leiden, A. W. Sijthoff, 1972.

Haas, Ernest, *Beyond the Nation State*, Stanford, Cal., Stanford University Press, 1964.

Hadwen, John G. & Johan Kaufman, *How United Nations Decisions are Made* (2nd edn), Leiden, A. W. Sijthoff, 1961.

Hallwood, Paul and Stuart Sinclair, *Oil, Debt and Development: OPEC in the Third World*, London, George Allen & Unwin, 1981.

Hansen, Roger D., *Beyond the North–South Stalemate*, New York, McGraw-Hill, 1979.

— , ed., *'The Global Negotiations' and Beyond: Toward North–South Accommodation in the 1980s*, Austin, Texas, University of Texas, 1981.

Helleiner, G. K., *A World Divided: The LDCs in the International Economy*, Cambridge, Mass., Cambridge University Press, 1976.

— , *International Economic Disorder: Essays in North–South Relations*, London, Macmillan Press, 1980.

Horsefield, Keith J., *The International Monetary Fund, 1945–65: Twenty Years of Monetary Cooperation*, Vols 1–3, Washington DC, IMF, 1969.

Independent Commission on International Development Issues, *North–South: A Programme for Survival*, London, Pan Books, 1980.

— , *Common Crisis: North–South Cooperation for World Recovery*, London, Pan Books, 1983.

Jacobson, Harold K., *Networks of Interdependence: International Organizations and the Global Political System*, New York, Alfred A. Knopf, 1979.

Jha, L. K., *North–South Debate*, Delhi, Chanakya Publications, 1982.

Killick, Tony, ed., *Adjustment and Financing in the Developing World: The Role of the International Monetary Fund* (IMF in association with the Overseas Development Institute), Washington DC, IMF, 1982.

— , ed., *The Quest for Economic Stabilization: the IMF and the Third World*, New York, St Martin's Press, 1984.

Laszlo, E. & Joel Kurtzman, eds, *Political and Institutional Aspects of the New International Economic Order*, New York, Pergamon Press, 1981.

Lewis, Arthur, *The Evolution of the International Economic Order*, Princeton, Princeton University Press, 1977.

Luard, Evan, ed., *The Evolution of International Organization*, London, Thames & Hudson, 1966.

MacBean, Alasdair I., *Export Instability and Economic Development*, London, George Allen & Unwin, 1966.

Mason, Edward S. and Robert E. Asher, *The World Bank since Bretton Woods*, Washington DC, The Brookings Institution, 1973.

Meagher, Robert F., *An International Redistribution of Wealth and Power: A Study of the Charter of Economic Rights and Duties of States*, New York, Pergamon Press, 1979.

Nincic, Djura, *The Problem of Sovereignty in the Charter and in the Practice of the United Nations*, The Hague, Martinus Nijhoff, 1970.

Olson, Mancur, jun., *The Logic of Collective Action*, New York, Schocken Books, 1968.

Oppenheim, L. (H. Lauterpacht, ed.), *International Law: A Treatise*, Vol. 1, 8th edn, London, Longmans, Green & Co., 1955.

Payer, Cheryl, *The Debt Trap: The International Monetary Fund and the Third World*, New York, Monthly Review Press, 1974.

Pfeffer, Jeffrey & Gerald R. Salancik, *The External Control of Organizations*, New York, Harper & Row, 1975.

Pfeffer, Jeffrey, *Power in Organizations*, Marshfield, Mass., Pitman Publishing Inc., 1981.

Polanyi, Karl, *The Great Transformation*, Boston, Beacon Press, 1944.

Rangarajan, L. N., *Commodity Conflict: The Political Economy of International Commodity Negotiations*, London, Croom Helm, 1978.

Roll, Eric, *The World after Keynes: An Examination of the Economic Order*, London, Pall Mall Press, 1968.

Sauvant, Karl P. & Hago Hasenpflug, eds, *The New International Economic Order: Confrontation or Cooperation between North and South?*, London, Wilton House Publications, 1977.

Sauvant, Karl P., *The Group of 77: Evolution, Structure, Organization*, New York, Oceana Publications, 1981.

Scammell, M. W., *The International Economy since 1945*, New York, St Martin's Press, 1980.

Schermers, Henry G., *International Institutional Law*, Vol. 2, Leiden, A. W. Sijthoff, 1972.

Scott, Richard W., *Organizations: Rational, Natural and Open Systems*, Englewood-Cliffs, New Jersey, Prentice-Hall Inc., 1981.

Solomon, Robert, *The International Monetary System: 1945-76*, New York, Harper & Row, 1977.

Spero, Joan Edelman, *The Politics of International Economic Relations*, London, George Allen & Unwin, 1977.

Strange, Susan, *International Economic Relations of the Western World, 1959-71: International Monetary Relations*, Vol. 2, London, Oxford University Press, 1976.

Streeten, Paul, *Development Perspectives*, New York, St Martin's Press, 1981.

Syz, John, *International Development Banks*, Dobbs Ferry, New York, Oceana Publications Inc., 1974.

Taylor, Paul & A. J. R. Groom, eds, *International Organisation: A Conceptual Approach*, London, Pinter, 1978.

Tew, Brian, *The Evolution of the International Monetary System: 1945-77*, London, Hutchinson & Co., 1977.

Thompson, James D., *Organizations in action*, New York, McGraw-Hill Book Co., 1967.

Triffin, Robert, *Gold and the Dollar Crisis*, New Haven, Yale University Press, 1960.

—, Robert, *Our International Monetary System: Yesterday, Today and Tomorrow*, New York, Random House, 1968.

Tucker, Robert, *The Inequality of States*, New York, Basic Books, 1977.

ul Haq, Mahbub, *The Poverty Curtain: Choices for the Third World*, New York, Columbia University Press, 1976.

van Dormael, Armand, *Bretton Woods: Birth of a Monetary System*, London, Macmillan Press, 1978.

Wilcox, Clair, *A Charter for World Trade*, New York, The Macmillan Co., 1949.

Williamson, John, *The failure of world monetary reform: 1971–74*, New York, New York University Press, 1977.

—, *IMF Conditionality*, Washington DC, Institute of International Economics, 1982.

Wood, Robert E., *From Marshall Plan to Debt Crisis*, Berkeley, University of California Press, 1986.

Yusuf, Abdulqawi, *Legal Aspects of Trade Preferences for Developing States*, The Hague, Martinus Nijhoff Publishers, 1982.

3. *Articles*

Abbott, George C., 'Effects of Recent Changes in the International Monetary System on the Developing Countries', *Aussenwirtschaft*, March 1979, pp. 59–76.

Abdalla, Ismail-Sabry, 'Bringing democracy into the world monetary system', *Euromoney*, April 1977, pp. 49–55.

—, 'The Inadequacy and Loss of Legitimacy of the International Monetary Fund', *Development Dialogue*, No. 2, 1980, pp. 25–53.

Abi-Saab, Georges, 'The Third World and the Future of the International Legal Order', *Revue Egyptienne de Droit International*, **29**, 1973, pp. 26–66.

Alexsson, Runo *et al.*, 'Organization Power in Organizational Decision-Making' in Malcolm Warner, ed., *Organizational Choice and Constraint: Approaches to the Sociology of Enterprise Behaviour*, London, Saxon House, 1977, pp. 41–63.

Allott, Phillip, 'Power Sharing in the Law of the Sea', *American Journal of International Law*, **77**, No. 1, January 1983, pp. 1–30.

Amin, Samir, 'Self-Reliance and the New International Economic Order', *Monthly Review*, **29**, No. 3, July/August 1977, pp. 1–21.

Amoussou-Adeble, Moise, 'Le Tiers-Monde et le Fond Monetaire International', *Genève-Afrique*, No. 2, 1970, pp. 85–97.

Amuzegar, J., 'The North–South Dialogue: From Conflict to Compromise', *Foreign Affairs*, April 1976, pp. 547–62.

—, 'A Requiem for the North–South Conference', *Foreign Affairs*, October 1977, pp. 136–59.

—— , *Oil Exporters' Economic Development in an Interdependent World*, Occasional Paper No. 18, Washington DC, IMF, 1983.

Avramovic, Dragoslav, 'The Debt Problem of Developing Countries at end-1982', *Aussenwirtschaft*, 38, 1983, pp. 65–86.

Ayres, Robert L., 'Breaking the Bank', *Foreign Policy*, No. 43, Summer 1981, pp. 104–20.

Bachrach, Peter & Morton S. Baratz, 'Decisions and Non-Decisions: An Analytical Framework', *The American Political Science Review*, 57, 1963, pp. 632–42.

Bedjaoui, Mohammed, 'Non-Alignment et Droit International', *Recueil des Cours*, 1976 (III), pp. 337–42.

Behrman, Jack N., 'Towards a New International Economic Order', *The Atlantic Papers*, 3/1974, pp. 5–80.

Bergsten, Fred C., 'The Threat from the Third World', *Foreign Policy*, No. 11, Summer 1973, pp. 102–24.

—— , 'The Response to the Third World', *Foreign Policy*, No. 11, Winter 1975, pp. 3–34.

—— , 'Interdependence and the Reform of International Institutions', *International Organization*, 30, Spring 1976, pp. 361–72.

Robert O. Keohane & Joseph S. Nye, jun., 'International Economics and International Politics: A Framework for Analysis', *International Organization*, 29, No. 1, Winter 1975, pp. 3–36.

Bernstein, Edward M., 'The International Monetary Fund', *International Organization*, 22, No. 1, Winter 1968, pp. 131–51.

—— , *et al.*, 'Reflections on Jamaica', *Essays in International Finance*, No. 115, April 1976, p. 63.

Besteliu, Raluca M., 'The procedure of consensus in the adoption of decisions by the International Monetary Fund and the International Bank for Reconstruction and Development', *Revue Roumaine d'études internationales*, 4(38), 1977, pp. 517–26.

Bhagwati, Jagdish N., 'Why there is no mileage left in Global Negotiations', *The World Economy*, 6, No. 2, June 1983, pp. 137–45.

Bird, Graham, 'Financial flows to developing countries: the role of the International Monetary Fund', *Review of International Studies*, No. 7, 1981, pp. 98–107.

—— , 'Conditionality and the Needs of Developing Countries', *Intereconomics*, 1, January/February 1982, pp. 32–6.

—— , 'Is an SDR link still relevant for developing countries?' *The Banker*, June 1982, pp. 63–7.

Bogdanovicz-Bindert, Christine A., 'World Debt: The United States Reconsiders', *Foreign Affairs*, Winter 1985/86, 64, No. 2.

Brewster, Havelock, 'Facing the facts of life in North–South negotiations', *South*, June 1982, pp. 33–4.

Buira, Ariel, 'IMF Financial Programs and Conditionality', *Journal of Development Economics*, 12, 1983, pp. 111–36.

Cameron, Duncan, 'Special Drawing Rights', *International Journal*, 36, No. 4, Autumn 1981, pp. 713–31.

Campolongo, Alberto, 'Voting Power in the International Monetary Fund', *IL Politico*, No. 4, December 1971, pp. 640–5.

Chandavarkar, Anand G., *The International Monetary Fund: Its Financial Organization and Activities*, Pamphlet Series No. 42, Washington DC, IMF, 1984.

Clausen, Alden W., 'Third World Debt and Global Recovery', *Aussenwirtschaft*, September 1983, pp. 246–59.

Cohen, Benjamin, 'Balance-of-payments financing: evolution of a regime', *International Organization*, **36**, No. 2, Spring 1982, pp. 457–78.

Cox, Robert, W., 'Ideologies and the New International Economic Order: reflections on some recent literature', *International Organization*, **33**, No. 2, Spring 1979, pp. 257–302.

—— , 'The crisis of world order and the problem of international organization in the 1980s', *International Journal*, **35**, No. 2, Spring 1980, pp. 370–95.

Crockett, Andrew D., 'Stabilization Policies in Developing Countries: Some Policy Considerations', *Staff Papers*, **28**, No. 1, March 1981, pp. 54–79.

—— , 'Issues in the use of Fund resources', *Finance and Development*, June 1982, pp. 10–15.

Cuddy, J. D. A., 'Compensatory Financing in the North–South Dialogue: The IMF and Stabex Schemes', *Journal of World Trade Law*, **13**, No. 1, January/February 1979, pp. 66–76.

D'Amato, Anthony, 'On Consensus', *Canadian Yearbook of International Law*, Vol. 8, 1980, pp. 104–22.

Dell, Sidney, 'International Monetary Issues and the Developing Countries: A comment', *World Development*, **3**, No. 9, September 1975, pp. 633–7.

—— , 'The World Monetary Order', *Third World Quarterly*, **2**, No. 4, October 1980, pp. 706–20.

—— , *On being Grandmotherly: the Evolution of IMF Conditionality*, Essays in International Finance, No. 144, October 1981.

—— , 'The Fifth Credit Tranche', *World Development*, **13**, No. 2, February 1985, pp. 245–9.

Demeocq, Marielle, 'The Rationale and Modalities for Compensating Export Earnings Instability', *Development and Change*, **15**, No. 3, July 1984, pp. 359–80.

Desai, R. R., 'World Monetary Reform?' *Yearbook of World Affairs*, 1966, pp. 186–200.

Diaz-Alejandro, Carlos, 'Less Developed Countries and the Post-1971 International Financial System', *Essays in International Finance*, No. 108, April, 1975.

de Vries, Margaret Garritsen, 'Economic Shocks of 1970s Viewed as Signs of Profound Change in World Relationships', *IMF Survey*, 7 January 1980, pp. 1–5.

de Vries, Tom, 'Jamaica, or the non-reform of the international monetary system', *Foreign Affairs*, April 1976, pp. 577–605.

—— , 'Remarks on International Monetary Relations and a New International Economic Order', *Netherlands International Law Review*, **24**, 1977/3, pp. 538–41.

Feis, Herbert, 'The Geneva Proposals for an International Trade Charter', *International Organization*, **2**, No. 1, February 1948, pp. 39–52.

Felix, David, 'An Alternative View of the "Monetarist"–"Structuralist" Controversy' in Albert O. Hirschman, ed., *Latin American Issues; Essays and Comments*, New York, The Twentieth Century Fund Inc., 1961, pp. 81–93.

Finkelstein, Lawrence S., 'International Organizations and Change', *International Studies Quarterly*, **18**, No. 4, December 1974, pp. 485–520.

Finlayson, Jock A. & Mark W. Zacher, 'International trade institutions and the North/South dialogue', *International Journal*, **36**, No. 4, Autumn 1981, pp. 732–65.

Fisher, Allan, 'Relative Voting Strength in the IMF', *The Banker*, April 1968, pp. 334–40.

Fleming, J. M. & G. Lovasy, 'Fund Policies and Procedures in relation to the Compensatory Financing of Commodity Fluctuations', *Staff Papers*, November 1960, pp. 1–29.

Frank, Isaiah, 'Toward a new framework for international commodity policy', *Finance and Development*, **13**, No. 2, June 1976, pp. 17–20.

Friedman, Wolfgang, 'The Relevance of International Law to the Process of Economic and Social Development', in Richard A. Falk and Cyril E. Black, eds, *The Future of the International Legal Order: Wealth and Resources*, Vol. 2, Princeton, Princeton University Press, 1970, pp. 3–35.

Geiser, Hans, 'A New International Economic Order: Its Impact on the Evolution of International Law', *Annales d'Etudes Internationales*, **9**, 1978, pp. 89–106.

Ghebali, Victor-Yves, 'La politisation des institutions specialisés des Nations Unies' in Nicolas Jequier, ed., *Les Organisations Internationales: Entre L'Innovation et la Stagnation*, Lausanne, Switzerland, Presses Polytechniques Romandes, 1985, pp. 81–97.

Gilpin, Robert, 'The Politics of Transnational Economic Relations' in Robert O. Keohane & Joseph S. Nye, jun., eds, *Transnational Relations and World Politics*, Cambridge, Mass., Harvard University Press, 1972, pp. 48–70.

Girvan, Norman, 'Swallowing the IMF Medicine in the Seventies', *Development Dialogue*, No. 2, 1980, pp. 55–74.

Gold, Joseph, '. . . To contribute thereby to . . . development . . .' aspects of the relations of the International Monetary Fund with its developing members', *Columbia Journal of Transnational Law*, Fall 1971, pp. 267–302.

——, 'Weighted Voting Power: Some limits and Some Problems', *American Journal of International Law*, **68**, No. 4, October 1974, pp. 687–708.

——, *Voting Majorities in the Fund: Effect of Second Amendment of the Articles*, Pamphlet Series No. 20, IMF, 1977.

——, 'The Structure of the Fund', *Finance and Development*, **16**, No. 2, June 1979, pp. 11–15.

——, *Conditionality*, Pamphlet Series No. 31, IMF, 1979.

——, 'The Fund's Interim Committee—an Assessment', *Finance and Development*, **16**, No. 3, September 1979, pp. 32–5.

——, 'The origins of weighted voting power in the Fund', *Finance and Development*, **18**, No. 1, March 1981, pp. 25–8.

——, 'Professor Verwey, the International Monetary Fund and Developing

Countries', *Indian Journal of International Law*, **21**, No. 4, October–December 1981, pp. 497–512.

Goreux, Louis M., 'The use of compensatory financing', *Finance and Development*, **14**, No. 3, September 1977, pp. 20–4.

——, *Compensatory Financing Facility*, Pamphlet Series No. 34, 1980.

Gosovic, Branislav and John Gerard Ruggie, 'On the creation of a new international economic order: issue linkage and the Seventh Special Session of the UN General Assembly', *International Organization*, **30**, No. 2, Spring 1976, pp. 309–45.

Guitian, Manuel, 'Fund conditionality and the adjustment process: the changing environment of the 1970s', *Finance and Development*, March 1981, pp. 8–10.

——, *Fund Conditionality: Evolution of Principles and Practices, International Monetary Fund*, Pamphlet Series No. 38, IMF, 1981.

——, 'Adjustment and Interdependence: The Challenge to Conditionality' (unpublished paper prepared for a seminar on 'Adjustment and Growth in the Current World Economic Environment'), Estoril, Portugal, 16–19 January 1985.

Haggard, Stephen, 'The Politics of Adjustment', *International Organization*, **39**, No. 3, Summer 1985, pp. 505–34.

Helleiner G. K., 'The Less Developed Countries and the International Monetary System', *The Journal of Development Studies*, **10**, Nos 3 and 4, April/July 1974, pp. 347–73.

——, 'Lender of Early Resort: The IMF and the Poorest', *The American Economic Review*, **73**, No. 2, May 1983, pp. 349–53.

——, 'The IMF and Africa in the 1980s', *Essays in International Finance*, No. 152, July 1983.

Hexner, E., 'The Executive Board of the International Monetary Fund: A Decision-Making Instrument', *International Organization*, **18**, No. 1, Winter 1964, pp. 79–96.

'How Peru's President views the IMF and the banks', *Euromoney*, March 1978, pp. 28–9.

'International Monetary Fund', *The Economist*, 27 September 1980, pp. 111–17.

Jacquemot, Pierre, 'Le F.M.I. et l'Afrique Subsaharienne', *Le Mois en Afrique*, Aoûte-Septembre 1983, pp. 107–20.

Jeker, Rolf, 'Voting Rights of Less Developed Countries in the IMF', *Journal of World Trade Law*, **2**, No. 3, May–June 1978, pp. 218–27.

——, 'Conditionality and Stand-by Credits of the International Monetary Fund and the Less Developed Countries', *Aussenwirtschaft*, March 1980, pp. 34–52.

Jenks, C. W., 'Unanimity, the Veto, Weighted Voting, Special and Simple Majorities and Consensus as Modes of Decision in International Organization' in R. Y. Jennings, ed., *Cambridge Essays in Honour of Lord McNair*, 1965, pp. 48–63.

Jessup, Philip C., 'The Equality of States as Dogma and Reality: Introduction', *Political Science Quarterly*, **60**, No. 4, December 1954, pp. 527–31.

Johnson, Omotunde E. G., 'Use of Fund resources and standby arrangements', *Finance and Development*, **14**, No. 1, March 1977, pp. 19–21 and 35.

Jones, Edgar, 'The Fund and UNCTAD', *Finance and Development*, September 1971, pp. 29–32.

Kafka, Alexandre, 'The IMF: The Second Coming?' *Essays in International Finance*, No. 94, Princeton, July 1972.

— , 'The International Monetary Fund: Reform without Reconstruction?' *Essays in International Finance*, No. 118, October 1976.

Kanesa-Thasan, S., 'The Fund and adjustment policies in Africa', *Finance and Development*, September 1981, pp. 20–4.

Khan, Mohsin S. and Malcolm Knight, 'Sources of payments problems in LDCs', *Finance and Development*, December 1983, pp. 2–5.

Kincaid, Russell, 'Conditionality and the use of Fund resources—Jamaica', *Finance and Development*, 18, No. 2, June 1981, pp. 18–21.

Knorr, Klaus, 'The Bretton Woods institutions in Transition', *International Organization*, 2, No. 1, 1948.

Krasner, Stephen D., 'The IMF and the Third World', *International Organization*, 22, No. 3, Summer 1968, pp. 670–88.

— , 'Transforming International Regimes—What the Third World Wants and Why', *International Studies Quarterly*, 25, No. 1, March 1981, pp. 119–48.

— , 'Power Structures and Regional Development Banks', *International Organization*, 35, No. 2, Spring 1981, pp. 303–28.

Krause, L. B. & J. S. Nye, jun, 'Reflections on the Economics and Politics of International Economic Organizations', *International Organization*, 29, Winter 1975, pp. 323–42.

Laidlaw, Ken & Roy Lashley, *Fund for the Future—UNCTAD: Common Fund for Commodities*, London, Development Press Services, 1980.

Levi, Warner, 'Are Developing Countries More Equal Than Others?', *The Yearbook of World Affairs*, 1978, pp. 286–302.

Lister, Frederick K., *Decision-Making Strategies for International Organizations: The IMF Model*, Monograph Series in World Affairs, University of Denver, Vol. 20, No. 4, 1984, p. 142.

Llewellyn, David T., 'The Role of International Banking' in Loukas Tsoukalis, ed., *The Political Economy of International Money: In search of a new order*, London, Royal Institute of International Affairs, 1985.

Marquez, Javier, 'Developing Countries and the International Monetary System: Selected Issues', in Hans W. J. Bosman & Frans A. M. Alting von Geusau, eds, *The Future of the International Monetary System*, Leiden, A. J. Sijthoff, 1970, pp. 119–35.

— , 'Developing Countries and the International Monetary System: The Distribution of Power and its Effects', in *Money in a Village World* (Papers from a Colloquium on the Interests of the Developing Countries and International Monetary Reform), Geneva, Committee on Society, Development and Peace, 1970.

Maynard, Geoffrey & Graham Bird, 'International Monetary Issues and the Developing Countries: A Survey', *World Development*, 3, No. 9, September 1975, pp. 609–31.

McIntyre, E., 'Weighted Voting in International Organizations', *International Organization*, Vol. 3, No. 4, 1954, pp. 484–97.

Metzger, Stanley D., 'Law and Policy Making for Trade among "Have" and "Have-Not" Nations' in John Carey, ed., *Law and Policy Making for Trade among "Have" and "Have-not" Nations* (Background Paper and Proceedings of the Eleventh Hammarskjold Forum), Dobbs Ferry, New York, Oceana Publications Inc., 1968, pp. 5–45.

Mohammed, Azizali F., 'The Decision-Making Process in the International Monetary Fund' (unpublished paper presented at the 'Fifth International Seminar of Economic Journalists'), New Delhi, 11–13 February 1985, p. 8.

Murphy, Craig N., 'What the Third World Wants: An Interpretation of the Development and Meaning of the New International Economic Ideology', *International Studies Quarterly*, **27**, No. 1, March 1983, pp. 55–76.

Nelson, Joan M., 'The Politics of Stabilization', in Richard E. Feinberg and Valeriana Kallab, eds, *Adjustment Crisis in the Third World*, New Brunswick, Transaction Books, 1984, pp. 99–118.

Nowzad, Bahram, 'Managing external debt in developing countries', *Finance and Development*, **17**, No. 3, September 1980, pp. 24–7.

— , 'The IMF and its Critics', *Essays in International Finance*, No. 146, 1981.

— , *The Extent of IMF Involvement in Economic Policy-Making*, The AMEX Bank Review Special Papers, No. 7, 1983.

Nyerere, Julius, 'Third World Negotiating Strategy', *Third World Quarterly*, **1**, No. 2, April 1979, pp. 20–3.

Park, Y. S., *The Link between Special Drawing Rights and Development Finance*, Princeton Essays in International Finance, Princeton, No. 100, 1973.

Paszyunski, Marian, 'The Concept of the New International Economic Order and the Socialist Countries', *Development and Peace*, **1**, Autumn 1980, pp. 26–41.

Payer, Cheryl, 'The Perpetuation of Dependence: IMF and the Third World', *Monthly Review*, **23**, No. 4, September 1971, pp. 37–49.

Pirzio-Biroli, Corrado, 'Making Sense of the IMF Conditionality Debate', *Journal of World Trade Law*, **17**, No. 2, March/April 1983, pp. 115–53.

Polak, Jacques J., 'The Role of the Fund' in *The International Monetary System Forty Years after Bretton Woods* (Proceedings of a Conference held at Bretton Woods), New Hampshire, May 1984, pp. 245–71.

Prebisch, Raul, 'Economic Development or Monetary Stability: The False Dilemma', *Economic Bulletin for Latin America*, **7**, No. 1, March 1961, pp. 1–25.

Pringle, Robin, 'Reaganomics enters the Fund', *The Banker*, September 1981, pp. 89–91.

Ramcharan, B. G., 'Equality and Discrimination in International Economic Law (X): Development and International Economic Cooperation', *The Yearbook of World Affairs*, 1981, pp. 207–24.

Ramphal, S. S., 'Not by Unity Alone: The Case for Third World Organization', *Third World Quarterly*, **1**, No. 3, July 1979, pp. 43–52.

Rao, V. K., 'Monetary Reform and the Developing Countries', *Euromoney*, August 1972, pp. 7–9.

Ravenhill, John, 'What is to be done for Third World commodity exporters? An evaluation of the STABEX Scheme', *International Organization*, **38**, No. 3, Summer 1984, pp. 537–74.

Reichmann, T. M., 'The Fund's conditional assistance and the problems of adjustment, 1973–75', *Finance and Development*, December 1978, pp. 38–41.

——, & Richard Stillson, 'How successful are programs supported by stand-by arrangements?' *Finance and Development*, March 1977, pp. 22–5.

Renniger, John P. & James Zech, *The 11th Special Session and the Future of Global Negotiations*, New York, UNITAR, September 1981.

Riad, Fouad Abdel-Moneim, 'Formal Equality and Substantive Equality' in Gray Dorsey, ed., *Equality and Freedom: International and Comparative Jurisprudence*, 3, New York, Oceana Publications, pp. 1041–8.

Robichek, Walter, 'The IMF's Conditionality Re-examined' in Joaquin Muns, ed., *Adjustment, Conditionality and International Financing* (Papers presented at the seminar on 'The Role of the International Monetary Fund in the Adjustment Process', held in Vina del Mar, Chile, 5–8 April 1983), IMF, 1984, pp. 67–75.

Rweyemamu, Justinian, 'Restructuring the International Monetary System', *Development Dialogue*, No. 2, 1980, pp. 75–91.

Russell, R. W., 'Transgovernmental Interaction in the International Monetary System, 1960–72', *International Organization*, 27, No. 4, Autumn 1973, pp. 431–64.

Saladin, Peter, 'The Link between the Creation of Special Drawing Rights (SDRs) and Development Finance', *Development Dialogue*, 1, 1981, pp. 38–45.

Schweitzer, Pierre-Paul, 'Political Aspects of Managing the International Monetary System', *International Affairs*, 52, No. 2, April 1976, pp. 208–18.

Smole, Janko, 'Protecting the Interests of Developing Countries in Monetary Reform', *Euromoney*, October 1972, pp. 37–9.

Sohn, Louis B., 'Weighting of Votes in an International Assembly', *The American Political Science Review*, Vol 38, No. 6, December 1944, pp. 1192–1203.

Southard, Frank A. jun., 'The Evolution of the International Monetary Fund', *Essays in International Finance*, No. 135, December 1979.

Strange, Susan, 'What is economic power and who has it?' *International Journal*, 30, No. 2, Spring 1975, pp. 207–24.

Stodgill, Ralph M., 'Dimensions of Organization Theory', in James D. Thompson, ed., *Approaches to Organizational Design*, University of Pittsburg Press, 1966, pp. 1–50.

Stone, Carl, 'Jamaica in crisis: from socialist to capitalist management', *International Journal*, 40, Spring 1985, pp. 282–312.

Sturc, Earnest, 'The Trust Fund', *Finance and Development*, 13, No. 4, December 1976, pp. 30–1.

Tornudd, Klaus, 'From Unanimity to Voting and Consensus: Trends and Phenomena in Joint Decision-Making by Governments', *Conflicts and Cooperation*, 17, No. 3, 1982, pp. 163–77.

Tunkin, Gregory, 'International Law in the International System', *Recueil des Cours*, 4, 1975, pp. 9–218.

van Houten, Leo, 'The Framework for Policy Making in the Fund' in A. W. Hooke, ed., *The Fund and China in the International Monetary System*, Washington DC, IMF, 1984, pp. 24–52.

Verwey, W. D., 'The Recognition of Developing Countries as Special Subjects of

International Law beyond the Sphere of United Nations Resolutions' in the Hague Academy of International Law, *The Right to Development at the International Level* (Workshop, The Hague, 16–18 October 1979, The Netherlands, Sijthoff & Noordhoff, 1979, pp. 372–96.

——, 'The New International Economic Order and the Realization of the Right to Development and Welfare—a Legal Survey', *Indian Journal of International Law*, 21, No. 1, January–March 1981, pp. 1–78.

Weinschel, Herbert, 'The Doctrine of the Equality of States and its Recent Modifications', *American Journal of International Law*, 45, No. 3, July 1951, pp. 417–42.

Weintraub, Sidney, 'What life is left in the North–South Dialogue?' *The World Economy*, 2, No. 4, February 1980, pp. 453–65.

Williamson, John, *A New SDR Allocation?* Policy Analyses in International Economics, No. 7, Institute for International Economics, Washington DC, March 1984.

Wittebort, Suzanne, 'Saudi Arabia's new clout at the IMF', *Institutional Investor* (inter. ed.,) September 1981, pp. 141–50.

Young, Oran R., 'Regime Dynamics: the rise and fall of international regimes', *International Organization*, 36, No. 2, Spring 1982, pp. 277–97.

Zamora, Stephen, 'Voting in International Economic Organizations', *American Journal of International Law*, 72, 1980, pp. 566–608.

4. Newspapers

Financial Times (various issues).
New York Times (various issues).
Wall Street Journal (various issues).
Washington Post (various issues).

Index